Contents

D1806315

BRITISH POLITICS AND PEOPLE
1760 - 1980

Peter Lane

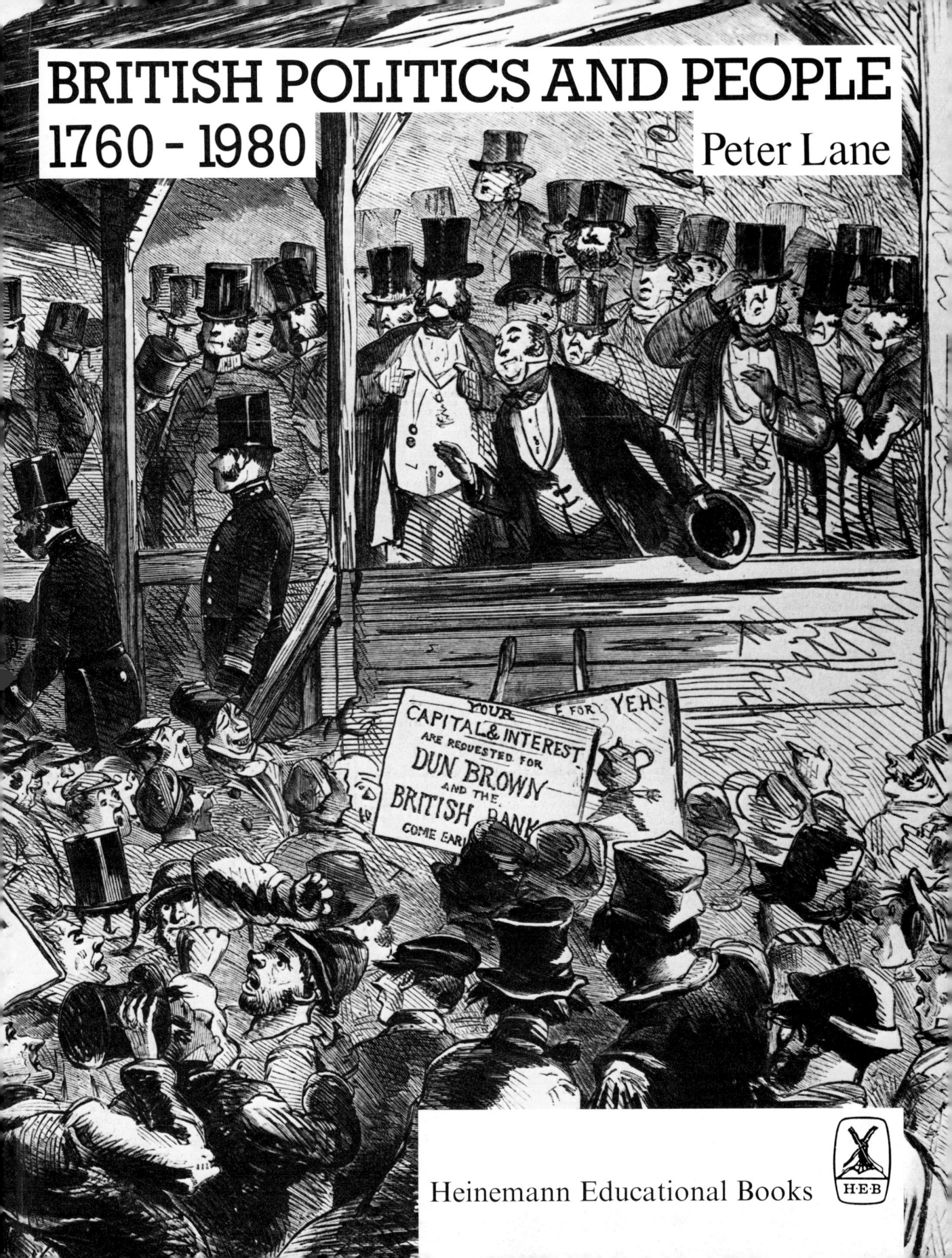

Heinemann Educational Books

Heinemann Educational Books Ltd

22 Bedford Square,
London WC1B 3HH

LONDON   EDINBURGH   MELBOURNE
AUCKLAND   HONG KONG   SINGAPORE
KUALA LUMPUR   NEW DELHI   IBADAN
NAIROBI   JOHANNESBURG   EXETER (NH)
KINGSTON   PORT OF SPAIN

© Peter Lane 1981
First published 1981

British Library Cataloguing in Publication Data

Lane, Peter
British politics and people, 1760–1980.
1. Great Britain – Social conditions
I. Title
941.07   HN385
ISBN 0-435-31550-1

Filmset and printed in Great Britain by
BAS Printers Limited, Over Wallop, Hampshire

Acknowledgements

The author and publishers wish to thank the following for permission to reproduce illustrations:

Australian Information Service: Fig. 18.3.
B. T. Batsford Ltd.: Fig. 3.1.
BBC Hulton Picture Library: Figs. 1.1, 3.2, 5.1, 6.1, 9.2, 10.1, 11.2, 13.2, 13.3, 14.1, 15.2, 16.3, 18.2, 23.2, 26.3, 29.2, 30.1, 30.3, 31.1, 31.3, 32.2, 34.1, 34.3, 35.2, 36.1, 36.2, 36.3, 37.2, 38.1, 38.2, 38.3, 39.1, 39.2, 40.1, 40.2, 40.3, 41.3 and 42.2.
Camera Press: Figs. 44.1 and 44.3.
Courtauld Institute of Art: Fig. 19.2.
Mary Evans Picture Library: Figs. 1.2, 4.3, 5.2, 5.3, 6.3, 6.4, 9.1, 14.2, 16.2, 17.2, 20.1, 20.2, 20.3, 21.1, 22.1, 24.1, 24.2, 24.3, 28.3, 32.3, 32.4 and 34.2.
Giles and the *Sunday Express*: Fig. 42.1.
Greater London Council: Figs. 29.1 and 31.2.
Illingworth and Associated Newspapers Group Ltd.: Fig. 44.2.
Illustrated London News: Fig. 14.3.
Keystone: Figs. 41.2, 45.3, 46.1, 46.2 and 46.3.
Lancashire Record Office: Fig. 19.1.
Mansell Collection: Figs. 10.3, 13.1, 23.1 and 30.2.
Morning Star: Fig. 37.3.
National Maritime Museum: Fig. 4.2.
National Portrait Gallery: Fig. 12.2.
Papas and the *Guardian*: Fig. 45.2.
Popperfoto: Fig. 42.3.
Punch: Figs. 15.3, 21.2, 22.3, 25.1, 26.1, 26.2, 27.1, 27.3, 28.1, 28.2, 29.3, 32.1, 33.1, 36.4 and 37.1.
Science Museum: Figs. 1.3 and 9.3.
Trustees of the Sir John Soane's Museum: Fig. 2.3.
Vicky and the *Evening Standard*: Figs. 43.2 and 43.3.
Victoria and Albert Museum: Fig. 10.2.

Maps and diagrams by Malcolm Booker.

Preface

In writing this book I have tried to present information to the pupils who study this period of history for their examinations and to show why and how the British political system developed and evolved to the point where they themselves can look forward to voting at the next or next-but-one election.

I have also aimed to give pupils an insight into how historians work by including evidence in the form of documents and contemporary illustrations. The illustrations have been carefully integrated into the text and some of them have been used as the basis for the sorts of questions which examiners like to ask. The documents appear at the end of each chapter and, again, have been used as a means of preparing for examinations, as well as illustrating what has been covered in the main text.

In addition, I have endeavoured to help pupils to acquire and practise a number of skills – by asking them to write, research, compare, criticize, draw and paint. There are a wide variety of questions and I hope that pupils of different interests and at different stages of development will find enough to interest and challenge them. The questions in the worksheets are divided into sections: those in (A) require a short answer which can be found in the text; those in (B) involve imaginative or reconstructive work – writing a letter, diary or headline, sometimes a conversation; and those in (C) are less demanding.

I hope that this book may be a starting point from which students will continue with a study of topics and subjects which interest them.

Peter Lane

Cover illustrations:
The Peterloo Massacre, Manchester, 1819 (*Mansell Collection*). Armistice Day, 11 November 1918 (*BBC Hulton Picture Library*). Scottish Hunger Marchers, 1932 (*BBC Hulton Picture Library*). Winston Churchill, 1939 (*Keystone*).

Title-page illustration:
The Election drawn by Phiz in 1857. This shows the hustings with the candidates and their friends. Few of the crowd had the right to vote. They enjoyed the bribes they received from the candidates. The patriotic cry for 'Pam' (Lord Palmerston) appealed to the crowd (*Mansell Collection*).

1 The Economic Background, 1760 - 1830

Britain in 1760

It is very difficult for us to imagine the sort of country in which George III became King in 1760. There were only about 6 million people in England and Wales – less than the population of present-day London. Most of these people lived in small villages; their main work was farming. Apart from London there were some towns – although we would think them very small. Norwich and Bristol were the two biggest. They had populations of about 30,000. Exeter, Liverpool, Newcastle, Leicester, and other towns had only about 20,000 people – about 4,000 families.

Self-sufficiency

Today, with our motor cars, lorries, trains, and aeroplanes, we are used to travel. We are also used to buying goods in our shops – goods brought by one or other of the methods of transport. But in 1760 few people ever left the village in which they were born. There was very little that people needed to buy from outside the village – maybe a pot for the kitchen, and salt for cooking and preserving. But most things people made for themselves, or bought from someone else in the village.

The poet Wordsworth lived in the Lake District. Writing in 1810 he said:

> From the time of the erection of these houses until sixty years ago [i.e. 1750] society underwent no change. Enough corn was grown in these vales [through which no road had yet been made] to provide bread for each family, and no more. Every family spun, from its own flock, the wool with which it was clothed.

Industry

Although farming was the main occupation of three-quarters of the people, there was some industry. Britain had for a long time been famous for its woollen cloth. This was made from the wool of the millions of sheep that roamed over the fields of the open countryside. But even this world-famous industry was simple and not at all like a modern

Fig. 1.1 Spinning was a cottage industry. The thread was spun and reeled on this simple machine. It was then boiled in a pot over the fire.

industry. Most of the work was carried out in the simple houses in which villagers lived (Fig. 1.1).

In the Lake District the people spun and wove only enough wool to make their own clothes. But in East Anglia, the South-West, and around Gloucester there was a thriving cloth-making industry. Wool merchants or clothiers went around the farms to buy up raw wool. They took this to the villagers and paid them to make it up into cloth. When it was finished the merchant sold it either in a market town or to an exporter.

Foreign Trade

There were other industries in Britain in 1760. Iron was made in small furnaces in the Weald of Kent and around the Forest of Dean. Ships were built in yards

1

in Liverpool, Dartmouth, and Newcastle. There were potters, brewers, and furniture-makers, and some of what they made was sold abroad. The British had a growing trade with India and America where Englishmen were founding the British Empire (see Chapter 18). From Bristol and Liverpool, slavers went out to West Africa carrying brandy, cloth, guns, and iron. They exchanged these goods for slaves who were then taken to the West Indies and bought by the owners of sugar plantations. On the voyage from the West Indies the British ships carried sugar, cotton, coffee, spices and other commodities which could be sold in England or in Europe.

This growth in trade led to the growth of some towns. Liverpool, Bristol, Hull, Whitehaven, Newcastle and, above all, London, expanded as trade grew. This foreign trade also made many people very wealthy – the owners of ships, the merchants who handled the exporting and importing, and the bankers who helped finance the trade. These were the men who had the money to build fine houses in the expanding towns and to buy up landed estates in the countryside. They also had enough money to spare for lending to other people – those who wanted to build a road, a canal, or a factory. Britain's foreign trade provided much of the money that was needed for her Industrial Revolution.

Agriculture

Britain's main industry in the eighteenth century was agriculture. It is not surprising, therefore, that the first signs of modernization took place in that industry. For most of the century British farmers produced so much food that a great deal of it was exported – which thus brought in extra income to the farmers. For the first half of the century this glut of food led to a fall in food prices – which was good for the people living in towns who had to buy the food. As they were paying less for their food they had money to spare. They spent this on other things such as clothes, houses, furniture, and so on. This created a further demand for these goods. Therefore, there were more clothes-makers, furniture-makers and so on. They, in their turn, wanted other goods. So the demand for goods grew rapidly and this helped spur the movement for industrial change.

The Agricultural Revolution

Because corn prices were falling from 1700 to about 1740, British corn farmers had to find some way of making their farms more efficient. As the population was expanding Britain's dairy farmers had to try to produce more milk, meat, and other commodities.

Therefore, there was a twofold spur driving farmers to become more efficient. There was a third factor, though, which was perhaps the most important. Most of the land was owned by large landowners who rented out parts of their estates to tenant farmers. These in turn employed labourers to work their farms. Some of these landowners sold out to the rich merchants who had made their money out of industry or trade. These new owners brought to their estates the habits of profit-making which had made them rich in the first place. They were the owners who led the movement which has become known as the Agricultural Revolution. They forced their tenants to agree to enclose what had been open fields into separate farms, each surrounded by its hedge or wall. They persuaded Parliament to pass Acts which allowed them to enclose the vast commons which surrounded every village – and on which the villagers had been allowed certain rights (Extract 1.1). They spent vast sums of money on draining waste land, bringing this into cultivation so that greater quantities of food were produced, more cheaply.

They also brought in new crops. Perhaps the most famous was the turnip which could be grown on the lighter soils of East Anglia. This root crop was left in the ground to be eaten by sheep and other animals in the winter time – and their manure improved the quality of the soil so that it could be used the next year to grow wheat or some other crop. It is not surprising that farmers talked of the 'golden hooves of the sheep' (Extract 1.2).

Also, turnips and other root crops acted as winter food for animals which previously had to be slaughtered in a massive killing in the autumn of each year. This meant that there was more fresh meat and milk available, with the result that people's diet improved. This in turn led to a healthier population. Fewer died – and so there were more people to be fed, clothed, housed, and so on. This meant that there had to be other changes in British industry to provide for this growing population.

The First Industrial Revolution – in Textiles

The population of Britain increased during the eighteenth century. This led to an increase in the demand for British goods – clothes, houses, and so on. At the same time the British acquired an Empire – in India, Canada, and the West Indies. This again led to an increased demand for goods to export to these countries (see Chapter 4). The existing system of production (Fig. 1.1) could not meet the demand. Therefore, it had to change.

From 1730 onwards men tried to make machines

that would enable workmen to produce more. Since the textile industry was the major industry, most of the improvements took place within it. In 1733 John Kay invented the *flying shuttle* which speeded up the weaving process and allowed a weaver to produce more and wider pieces of cloth. But weavers could already use as much yarn as six or more spinners could produce. There was a need for better spinning-machines. In 1767 James Hargreaves, a Blackburn weaver, patented the *spinning-jenny*. Although it was operated by hand, it allowed the spinner to operate eight spindles at the same time – instead of one as in Fig. 1.1. Later jennies worked 120 spindles. But Hargreaves's machine produced a weak thread which was only good enough for the horizontal or *woof* thread in a weave. In 1769 Richard Arkwright produced a *water frame* which spun threads strong enough to be used for the vertical or *warp* thread of the weave.

The shuttle and the jenny were worked by hand and were small enough to fit into the cottage (Fig. 1.1). But Arkwright's frame, as its name suggested, was driven by water-power. It was also very big and could not fit into the cottage. So factories had to be built near flowing streams – which drove the water-wheel that powered the frames. This was the start of the factory system. In 1779 Samuel Crompton, a Bolton weaver, produced a *mule*, so called because it was a mixture of Hargreaves's jenny and Arkwright's frame. This produced high-quality thread.

The weavers were now trying to cope with the output of these many new spinning-machines – and still using the hand-looms. Even with Kay's shuttle they were unable to cope. In 1786 the Reverend Edmund Cartwright produced a *power-operated loom*. This meant that the two main processes of the textile industry were now fully mechanized. Spinners and weavers now worked in factories where vast machines were handled by a few people to produce huge quantities of material (Fig. 1.2).

Iron and Coal

The first simple machines were made of wood, but the later and larger machines were made of iron. The increase in the demand for these machines led to a growth in the demand for iron. Britain was fortunate in that during the eighteenth century the Darby family discovered how to produce iron in furnaces heated with coke. Until this discovery all iron had been produced in charcoal-fired furnaces. By the middle of the eighteenth century supplies of charcoal were running out and prices had soared. The Darby discovery meant that ironworks could now be opened on or near the coalfields of South Wales, the Clyde region, and the North-East.

Steam-engines

The first steam-engines had been invented in the seventeenth century to pump water out of Cornish tin-mines. Thomas Newcomen, a blacksmith from Dartmouth in Devon, had made some improvements in Captain Savery's original engine. But even the Newcomen engine was cumbersome and expensive to run, and it had only a simple pumping action.

James Watt, a Glasgow University instrument-maker, made a number of improvements in Newcomen's engine. Between 1765 and 1769 he made this engine more efficient so that it used less coal. He also showed how it could be used by ironmasters to drive the bellows used in their larger furnaces. This was much more efficient than the water-wheels previously used.

But it was the development of Watt's sun-and-planet system of cogs and wheels that transformed not only the steam-engine but the whole of British industry. This new engine, patented in 1781, transferred the simple to-and-fro pumping action of the older engines into a rotary motion. The engine could now be used to drive machinery – and the old water-frame was replaced by the steam-driven machines. The modern factory system had been born.

Towns and Transport

As industry and trade grew so did towns. Old ones expanded – Liverpool, London, Bristol, and so on. New ones grew up on coalfields where factory owners sited their steam-driven machinery. Towns grew up in South Wales and Scotland where men produced the coal and iron to make the new machines.

Fig. 1.2 Mule spinning in Manchester in 1835. Look at the boy cleaning inside the machine. Children did much of this dangerous work.

Fig. 1.3 The Stockton to Darlington railway line was opened on 27 September 1825.

But none of this would have been possible without a revolutionary change in the method of transport. There had been little, if any, improvement in the road system since the Romans left Britain in the fifth century, but in the eighteenth century Britain found a new generation of road-builders. Macadam, Metcalf, Rennie, Telford and others built fine roads and bridges which allowed the increased volume of traffic to flow more freely. But more importantly, Britain learned to use its waterways. Men made rivers navigable where they could build canals. Along these man-made waterways barges carried the iron, coal, limestone, food, and other materials to and from the industrial towns and ports. Without these changes the Industrial Revolution would have quickly ground to a halt.

As a sign that change was continuous came the development of the railway system. The opening of the Stockton–Darlington line in 1825 was a major stage in Britain's industrial progress (Fig. 1.3). Goods could now be carried quickly and cheaply over long distances. It is significant that we end this period, 1760–1830, in the year in which the Liverpool–Manchester line was opened. This was a longer line than the one at Stockton and showed that British engineers could build huge tracks of line. During the next forty years, 1830–70, Britain became covered with a network of railway lines and British engineers built similar networks in foreign countries. This led to a vast expansion in the demand for British iron, coal, and engineering equipment – and so to a continuation in the industrial progress started around 1760.

Rip Van Winkle

If a man had fallen asleep in the year 1500 and woken up in 1700 he would have noticed very little change. But if a man had fallen asleep in 1700 and woken up in 1830 he would have been amazed at the changes that had taken place. In 1830 there were huge towns in which thousands of people worked in factories where steam-driven machinery produced vast quantities of goods. There were canals along which these goods were moved. There were also the new railway lines along which engines rushed at speeds of up to 40 miles (64 kilometres) per hour. Britain had indeed changed.

The Effects of these Changes

This is not a study of the industrial, economic, or social history of the last 200 years. Instead, we will be looking at the political developments that have taken place in this period. But it has to be emphasized that few, if any, of these changes would have taken place if there had not been those industrial changes. Chapters 2–5 show how even the first Industrial Revolution led to a demand for political reform. In Chapters 6 and 7 the ways in which war affected the development of industry and the demand for political change are discussed. These demands increased after the wars, as seen in Chapters 8–10 – although they did not come to fruition until 1832 as we shall see in Chapter 12. But the seeds of these changes – and for later changes that affect the ways in which we live – were sown by that first Industrial Revolution of the eighteenth century.

4

Questions

Extract 1.1

Cottagers

The Cottagers have little parcels of land on the field, with a right of common for a sow and three or four sheep, by the help of which and with the profits of their daily labours they make a comfortable living. Their land gives them wheat and barley for bread and, in many places, beans to feed a hog for meat. With the straw they thatch their cottage, and winter their cow, which gives them a breakfast and supper of milk for nine or ten months of the year. They also have the right to cut turf, roots and furze which is a great advantage to those who have not money for fuel.
(Addington, *Reasons for and against Enclosing*.)

1. Cottagers were those people who had no land of their own. They lived on the edges of the common land. What benefits did they get from this common land?
2. Why did they suffer when the commons were enclosed? What, do you think, might they have done after enclosure?
3. Why did they get no milk for two months a year? (See also Extract 1.2.)
4. Do you agree that they made a comfortable living? (See also Fig. 1.1.) Give reasons for your answer.

Extract 1.2

Turnips

Before the introduction of turnips it was not possible to cultivate light soils. It was also difficult to support livestock throughout the winter. Feeding and preparing sheep and cattle for market during this season was hardly thought of unless there was plenty of hay which only happened in a few instances.
(Robert Brown, *Treatise on Rural Affairs, 1811*.)

1. The animals ate the turnips in the fields. Why was this good for the soil?
2. Why was the introduction of the turnip good for animal breeding?
3. Why did this lead to a more plentiful supply of fresh meat and milk?
4. Why were people healthier in 1800 than they had been in 1700?

Fig. 1.1

1. How many spindles were worked by the wheel?
2. Why was this spinner less productive than the machine spinner (see Fig. 1.2)?
3. Why did the increase in the size of machines lead to the building of factories?

Worksheet

(A)
1. Use the following words as guides to answer the question: 'Why did the population grow during the eighteenth century?'
Animal food; wheat prices; death rate; birth rate.

2. Make a list in which you link together the following dates, names, and machines:
1733; 1765; 1769; 1779; 1782.
James Watt; Richard Arkwright; James Hargreaves; John Kay; Samuel Crompton.
The flying shuttle; the mule; the rotary steam engine; the spinning-jenny; the water frame.

3. Explain in two sentences why Arkwright has been called 'the father of the factory system'. Why do some people think that James Watt has a right to that title?

(B)
1. Imagine that someone has been brought on a time machine from 1760 to a modern town. Make a list of the things which they would find strange about (i) our towns (ii) our standard of living.

2. Write the letter that might have been sent by the former worker in the cottage (Fig. 1.1) who had gone to work in a factory (Fig. 1.2). He might have written about the machines, noise, size of output, fellow-workers, hours of work, his house in the factory town, and so on.

(C)
1. Make a time chart for the years 1760–1830, marking on it:
(a) the inventions in the textile industry;
(b) the improvements in the steam-engine.

2. Make a poster that might have been used to advertise EITHER the opening of the local canal OR the arrival of the Enclosure Commissioners.

3. Draw and illustrate the triangle of trade that linked Liverpool with (i) the coast of Africa, and (ii) the West Indies or the American colonies.

2 The Political Background, 1760-1830

Our main aim is to study the political developments that have taken place since 1760. But we will not be able to understand these changes until we have a clear idea of what in fact was changed. So we have to understand the political system of which George III became head on his accession to the throne in 1760.

The Power of the King

During the seventeenth century there had been an almost continual struggle between King and Parliament. In the 1640s this struggle led to a civil war, the execution of King Charles I, and the setting up of a republican form of government. In 1660 the republicans invited King Charles II to become King. When he died in 1685 his brother, James II, became King. The dictatorial policies of James II frightened most of the politicians, and in 1688 they invited James's daughter, Mary, and her husband, William of Orange, to come to England to take the throne.

The politicians wanted to make sure that no future King would try to run the country as the Stuarts had done. They passed a number of Acts of Parliament which the new monarchs had to accept. This 'Glorious Revolution' which put William and Mary on the throne tried to settle the question of how Britain was to be governed. Briefly, it said:

1. The King had the right to choose his own ministers and to decide what policies he wanted these ministers to follow.
2. But he had to get Parliament's approval for those policies. In particular, he had to come to Parliament each year to ask for any money he needed. This meant that Parliament would have to meet at least once each year.

This arrangement was a compromise – no one got all that he wanted. The King had to depend on Parliament's approval of his policies while Parliament had to allow the King the power to choose his own Cabinet and to decide his government's policies.

Parliament

But what would happen if the King wanted to follow a certain policy and Parliament voted against this? Which of the two would be the stronger – the King or Parliament? One part of our story is the examination of the way in which the power of Parliament increased.

We have to remember that Parliament consists of two Houses. There is the House of Lords in which sit the members of the nobility, bishops, and judges. In addition, there is the House of Commons in which sit the elected representatives of the voters. In the eighteenth century the House of Lords was much more important than the House of Commons. Part of our study will be to see when, why, and how this changed, so that today the House of Commons is the more important of the two Houses.

Political Parties

Today we expect members of the House of Commons and many members of the House of Lords to belong to one or other of the major political parties.

This is a very recent development. Throughout most of our period M.P.s had little loyalty to a political party. Indeed, in 1760 the majority of M.P.s took very little interest in politics. They wanted to be elected because this gave them a chance to make money or to get some other reward for themselves or a relative. But many M.P.s did not come to Parliament often. It was, after all, a long way from Newcastle to London when the only way of travel was in a slow, uncomfortable, and expensive coach.

Whigs and Tories

There were some politicians who had strong views about important political matters. Some thought that the power of the King ought to be increased; they thought that the Glorious Revolution had dangerously weakened it. Politicians with these views were nicknamed *Tories*. This was an English version of an Irish word meaning a plundering outlaw. Another group of politicians wanted to increase the power of Parliament, and to lessen the power of the King. The Tories nicknamed these politicians the *Whigs* – a Scottish word to describe the rebels who had attacked Edinburgh in 1648.

But we have to remember that the majority of M.P.s and Lords did not support either of these two groups. The Whigs and the Tories were only small groups of politicians.

The Whigs in Power 1714–60

The Glorious Revolution allowed the King the right to choose his own ministers. This was the way in which William and Mary ruled; it was the way in which Queen Anne ruled from 1702 to 1714.

But when Queen Anne died in 1714 there was a problem as to who should succeed to the throne. The Tories thought that James II's son ought to be asked to become King. However, he was a Catholic and under the terms of the Act of Settlement (1701) was not allowed to become Monarch. The Tories were prepared to set this Act to one side in their determination to have an English-born king. The Whigs, on the other hand, argued that the Act of Settlement had to be followed. This meant that the rightful heir to the throne was George, the Elector of Hanover. In 1714 George came to England and ascended the throne as George I, the first of the Hanoverians.

It is hardly surprising that when he came to choose his ministers he should choose them from among the Whigs, and when he died in 1727 his son, George II, did exactly the same. So from 1714 to 1760 there was a long period during which the Cabinet consisted entirely of Whig politicians.

Parliament and the people did not object to this. The policies followed by a succession of Whig governments were popular. Under Sir Robert Walpole's government, 1721–40, the country prospered, trade increased, costs of living fell and taxes were lowered. So Walpole had little trouble in getting approval for his policies.

No one noticed that an important change had taken place in the way in which the country was governed. Until 1714 the Monarch chaired meetings of ministers. However, King George I knew little English, and did not attend such meetings. Therefore, one of the ministers had to act as chairman. This led to the use of the term Prime (or first) Minister to describe the one who acted as chairman (Fig. 2.1).

The House of Lords

We have seen that in 1760 Britain was still an

Fig. 2.1 This cartoon of Walpole was produced in 1840. The caption was: 'The Statue of a Great Man or the English Colossus.' Walpole's opponents resented the power he had as Prime Minister.

agricultural country. It is not surprising, then, that the most important politicians were the owners of the land.

The more important landowners were the dukes, earls, viscounts, and lords. They sat in the House of Lords which had about 200 members as well as twenty-six Bishops representing the Church of England.

The House of Commons

The House of Commons was a much larger House. Here there were 548 M.P.s; forty-five of these sat for Scottish seats. There were two M.P.s from each of the forty-six counties, giving a total of ninety-two county M.P.s. But the largest group were the 417 M.P.s who represented the boroughs or towns.

From about the year 1200 onwards towns had grown as centres for industry and trade. One sign of a town's growth was the *Charter* which its citizens obtained from the owner of the land on which the town was built. This Charter allowed the town to choose its own council, fix its own rates – and to choose two M.P.s.

The largest part of the population lived in the southern half of the country. It is not surprising, then, that most of the chartered boroughs were in this half also. In 1762 there were forty-two M.P.s for Cornish

Fig. 2.2 Parliamentary representation before 1832.

1. *Burgage boroughs* were those where the right to vote belonged to people who owned certain buildings or plots of land. Rich noblemen often bought up these buildings or plots and so controlled the election in the borough. William Pitt the Elder described these as 'pocket boroughs' because they were in the pockets of the landowner.

2. *Scot and lot boroughs* were those in which the franchise was given to everyone paying some local taxes or rates. This often gave the vote to every householder – as was the case in Penrhyn in Cornwall.

3. *Corporation boroughs* were those in which the franchise was limited to members of the local council or corporation. In Chapter 13 we will see that local councils were very corrupt, and that they kept down the numbers of council members. This meant that only 110 people had the right to vote in Bath although there was a population of about 25,000.

4. *Potwalloper boroughs* were those in which the franchise was given to everyone who owned a fireplace on which a pot could be boiled. This meant that there was a wide franchise – as in Honiton in Devon.

5. *Freemen boroughs* were those in which all freemen of the town – usually the members of the craft guilds – had the right to vote. But in some places, as in Grampound (Fig. 2.2) the council named their own freemen – and so ensured control of the election.

Elections

In over half of the boroughs there was never an election to choose the M.P.s. The local landowner who had the borough in his pocket simply named the borough's representatives. The East India Company, the government, and other groups also bought boroughs (Fig. 2.2).

In other boroughs there would only be a handful of electors and their votes could be bought by the highest bidder. These were called *rotten boroughs*. It is not surprising that the government of the day could ensure the election of its candidates in some of these boroughs – the government, after all, had more money than most landowners. The promise of a contract, a job, or a title, would be enough to get the support of the voters.

Buying a Seat

Some landowners used their 'ownership' of a borough's franchise to make money. Wilkes paid

boroughs plus the two county M.P.s. On the other hand, there were only twelve M.P.s representing the six boroughs in Lancashire which also, of course, had two county M.P.s. We might find it difficult to imagine the situation in which Cornwall was three times more important than Lancashire (Fig. 2.2). But this helps to remind us that our study begins at a time when agriculture was the main industry.

The Right to Vote

Today we are given the *franchise* (or the right to vote) on reaching the age of 18. In 1760 there was no such simple, uniform qualification for the franchise. In the county election the vote was given to people who owned land which the rating authorities estimated to be worth 40 shillings (£2) a year. The men who rented their farms, or *leaseholders*, did not have the franchise even if they rented farms worth more than 40 shillings a year for rating purposes. In some counties the large landowners bought up all the freeholds and so made sure that they controlled the elections.

But at least in the counties there was some uniformity of qualification. In the boroughs the right to vote varied according to ancient customs:

Fig. 2.3 This is one of a series of paintings about elections by the artist William Hogarth. The candidates and their friends sat beneath their different flags. The voters climbed the stairs to the Returning Officer. His polling book (on the right) contained the list of voters.

£7,000 for the borough of Aylesbury, Romilly, the great legal reformer (Chapter 9), paid £10,000 for one of the seats at Westbury, 'the property of Lord Abingdon'.

Where elections took place there was a great deal of corruption. The election went on for a week or more – until all the voters had cast their votes. They did so at the hustings (Fig. 2.3). The agents of the various candidates spent a good deal of money to win support among the mob – which did not have the vote but which could frighten voters into doing what the agents wanted. Here again the richest men usually won.

The Elected Member

Why did people pay vast sums of money to become M.P.s? Some did so because they saw it as a way of getting on in their own jobs. Thus many M.P.s were serving officers in the Army or Navy. By using their vote in the Commons in the right way they could expect to win promotion. Admiral Rodney (Chapter 4) was one such man.

Other M.P.s hoped to get a government job. There were about 200 M.P.s in the Parliament of 1763 who were called *placemen*. They sold their votes in the Commons to support the government in return for a government job – often worth £7,000 for which the M.P. had to do little if anything. These jobs were called *sinecures*.

No Demand for Change

For many years few people thought that there was anything wrong with this corrupt, muddled and inefficient system.

But the steam-engine was to lead to a demand for political change. We saw in Chapter 1 that it was because of the steam-engine that industrialists built their factories on or near coalfields. In time it became obvious that it was unfair that East Looe and West Looe should each have two M.P.s while Manchester with its huge population had none.

The steam-engine also led to the creation of a small group of very wealthy industrialists, the owners of factories, railways, canals, and banks. In time, some of these became as rich as the landowners. They paid their taxes, but had no share in the political system. It was this *middle class* in the new industrial towns that led the demand for political reform, as we shall see in Chapter 12.

Questions

Extract 2.1 (See also Fig. 2.3.)

Sometimes, when there is an opposition candidate, bloody heads have been seen. But here the election is already as good as settled.

The vote was to be taken at Covent Garden – a big, open-air market place. A scaffold [or platform] had been erected for the voters who sat on benches erected one above another on an inclined slope.

The President, or Returning Officer, sat on a chair. The whole of it was however only knocked together with wooden posts and planks.

In front of this scaffold where the benches ended were laid mats from which the candidates were to address the people. In the area in front of this had gathered a crowd of people mainly of the lowest class. The orators bowed low to this rabble and always addressed them as gentlemen. As soon as the candidate began to speak the whole crowd was as still as the raging sea becomes after a storm and all shouted, 'Hear him'. And as soon as he had ended his address a great 'Hurrah!' rose up from every throat, and everyone – even the dirtiest coalheaver – waved his hat.

(C.P. Moritz, *Journeys of a German in England in 1782*, 1798.)

Extract 2.2

During these times of election, the candidates have to keep an open table. Some times they have to treat three hundred people in a day. He who makes the most people drunk may depend on the greatest number of votes. Good strong beer will achieve all you want with the drinking countrymen; but they that are sober must be won over with money. The influential man who can bring in the support of others, will have twenty, and sometimes thirty guineas for his vote. He that will give the price may have all the votes he wants.

(Le Blanc, *Letters on the English and French Nations*, 1747.)

1. What evidence is there in Extract 2.1 that elections were not always held?
2. Why might a candidate decide to withdraw from the contest before election day?
3. Why did the candidates pay attention to the 'lowest class'? How might these be used to influence the decisions of the few voters?
4. What was meant by 'have to treat three hundred people a day'? Why did some people enjoy elections?
5. Why was an election an expensive business for the candidates? Why were they willing to spend money to get returned to Parliament?

Fig. 2.1

1. How does the artist give the impression of (i) Walpole's power, and (ii) the weakness of his opponents?
2. Who, in theory, ought to have been the most important person in the system of government? Why did Walpole become so important?

Fig. 2.2

1. Why was it right that the majority of M.P.s should come from southern England in 1700? Why was it not right in 1800?
2. Find and name examples of seats that were (i) controlled by the government (ii) controlled by merchant companies (iii) 'rotten', and (iv) particularly noted for their corruption.
3. Find examples of constituencies that might be described as (i) potwalloper (ii) freemen, and (iii) scot and lot.

Worksheet

(A)
1. Explain briefly why George I chose Whigs as his ministers in 1714. Why did he not choose any Tories?

2. Give three reasons why the Whig governments were popular between 1720 and 1742.

3. Which county had the larger number of M.P.s in 1760 – Cornwall or Lancashire? What does that tell you about the size of the population of these counties in 1760? How do you account for the importance of Cornwall and other southern counties?

4. Write two sentences on the elections in each of the following boroughs: Penrhyn; Bath; Honiton; Grampound. (Take care, because each of them was a different sort of borough from the others.)

5. Explain in your own words what was meant by (i) placemen (ii) sinecure.

6. Explain why the Industrial Revolution led to a demand for (i) a new distribution of seats in the House of Commons, and (ii) a change in the laws on the franchise (the right to vote.)

(B)
1. Imagine that someone has come from the eighteenth century to a modern election. What are the main things that would surprise him about (i) the election (ii) the sorts of people who become M.P.s (iii) the importance of modern political parties?

(C)
1. Draw a poster used to announce the calling of an election in the 1760s.

2. Draw a coat of arms that a town might have designed and the title page of its first Charter.

3 George III's Governments, 1760-83

'Be a King'

George III became King when his grandfather died in 1760. The first of the Hanoverians born in England, he had been educated by the Marquess of Bute. Some people thought that he tried to set himself up as a dictator. In fact all that he tried to do was to use the powers that had been given to the Crown by the Settlement of 1688–9. He thought, rightly, that his grandfather and George I had allowed the Whigs to grow too powerful.

The Government and War in 1760

In 1760 England was involved in a war with France. Britain's ally was Frederick of Prussia; France's ally was Maria Theresa of Austria. For Prussia and Austria this was a European war. For England and France the war was part of the struggle for colonial possessions in India, Canada, and the West Indies.

This war began in 1756, and at first England did very badly. But a change of government saw William Pitt in charge of the war; by 1759 England was victorious. In Canada the defeat of the French was assured by the capture of Quebec. Victories by Clive and Admiral Watson ensured that large parts of India came under the control of the English East India Company.

To Extend the War?

Spain had not been involved in the war, but by 1761 it was clear that she intended to come in on the side of France. Pitt wanted to declare war on Spain, before she could declare war on Britain, in order to attack Spanish colonial possessions in America and the Caribbean, and so enlarge the British Empire – and trade.

But King George III wanted to bring the war to an end. He wanted to give all his attention to domestic affairs – and to restore the power of the Crown. He was also anxious to limit the power of Pitt; there was a danger that he might become the new Colossus (Fig. 2.1 on p. 7).

George's First Prime Minister

In 1762 Pitt resigned rather than agree with the King's ideas on peacemaking, and George III now had his former tutor, the Marquess of Bute, as Prime Minister. This pleased Bute's mistress, George III's mother. But the appointment annoyed a large number of influential people, some of whom had been Bute's friends in the Hell–Fire Club. Members of the club included the Earl of Sandwich, John Wilkes, and William Hogarth, the artist.

Bute's Government

Bute honoured some of his high-living friends. Sir Francis Dashwood, founder of the Hell–Fire Club, became Chancellor of the Exchequer, but John Wilkes did not become Governor of Canada as he had expected. Wilkes never forgave Bute for this.

However, Dashwood was not very successful. The government increased taxes to pay for the war, and Dashwood put a tax on cider. A popular song written at the time had a last line, 'No Bute, no cider, King, Sir'. (Fig. 3.1.) It was the opposition to this tax that forced Bute to resign from office in April 1763.

Fig. 3.1 A cartoon, drawn in February 1763, attacking Dashwood and the cider tax.

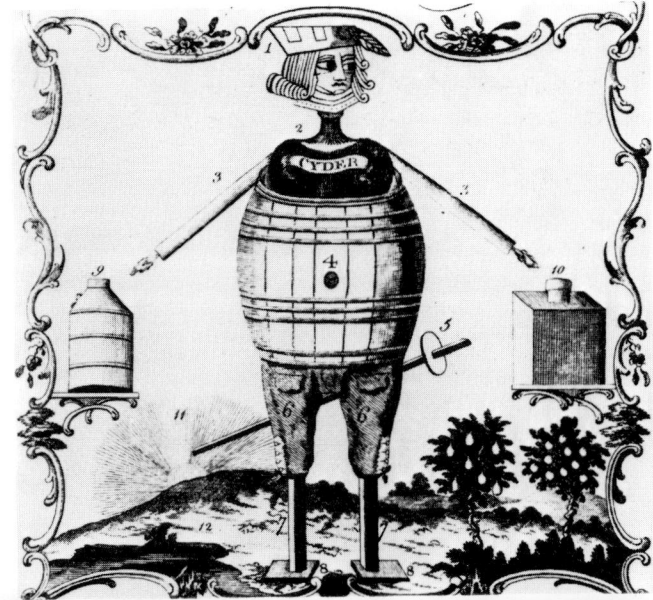

George III did not want to accept the resignation but was forced to do so when Bute was unable to get a majority in the House of Commons.

Bute, Wilkes, and the Peace of Paris, 1763

Wilkes and his friend, Charles Churchill, founded a newspaper called the *North Briton* – a sly reference to the Scottish Marquess of Bute. In issue Number 5 of their paper they told the story of Bute's affair with the King's mother. This made popular reading, but angered the King and Bute.

But it was issue Number 45 of the paper that really gave Wilkes a place in the history books. This appeared after the government, still under Bute, decided to make peace with France and to abandon the King of Prussia. Prussia had to continue the war on its own.

In his attack on Bute and the King (Extract 3.2) Wilkes as good as called the King and Bute liars. He appealed to the voters not to let the government of the country remain in the hands of those friends of the King who would destroy all liberal institutions. Public reaction was violent; people burned jackboots in the streets as well as petticoats, a reference to the King's mother.

The King and Wilkes's Arrest

There was no real proof that Wilkes had written the article, because it was unsigned. So the King forced the government to issue a *General Warrant* ordering the arrest of everyone connected with the *North Briton* – the publishers, printers, editors, and work-people. This was a dangerous weapon since it allowed the King to arrest anyone thought to be linked with any criminal act without having any evidence against him.

Wilkes was arrested and thrown into the Tower of London to await his trial. The London mob rioted in favour of 'Wilkes and Liberty'; noblemen were dragged from their carriages and sedan chairs, rolled in the gutter and had '45' chalked on the soles of their shoes.

Fig. 3.2 A contemporary cartoon of the signing of the Treaty of Paris. The King sits with Britain's gains in front of him while Bute (centre) explains the cost of the war and of getting the Treaty through Parliament. Henry Fox, the King's party manager, is on the right with the 'devil Wilkes' behind.

The Lord Chief Justice heard the case against Wilkes. The judge agreed that as an M.P. he had the right to comment on the government's activities, so Wilkes was released, and became even more of a hero to the mob. Bute was almost killed as he entered Parliament while when the King went riding in his royal coach the mob smashed the windows. The King decided to get his revenge on Wilkes.

On 15 November 1763 Wilkes's former friend, the Earl of Sandwich – now a member of the government and a friend of the King – read out in Parliament the *Essay on Women*, a pornographic parody of Pope's *Essay on Man*. Wilkes had composed this poem for the amusement of his friends at the Hell–Fire Club. But now it was produced as evidence that Wilkes was guilty of blasphemy and of circulating indecent literature. The Commons voted by a majority of forty-four that Wilkes was guilty. He was declared to be an outlaw, and thus liable to arrest. However, he had guessed what the verdict would be and had fled to France.

The Peace of Paris

Meantime the King and Bute managed to get the Commons to approve the Peace of Paris which ended the war with France. Henry Fox, father of the more famous Charles James Fox, acted as the King's agent in bribing various M.P.s to support the King's proposals (Fig. 3.2 and Extract 3.1). The King, it seemed, had won the day over the powerful Pitt and the popular Wilkes.

The Weakened Whigs

If the Whigs had been a united political party the King would not have been able to get his own way so easily. In fact, the Whigs were not a single party; there were groups of M.P.s and Lords who supported different prominent Whig leaders. There were Rockingham Whigs, Grafton Whigs, Townshend Whigs, and so on. These leaders and their supporters were jealous and suspicious of the power of the rest. So while the King was unable to force the Commons to accept Bute after April 1763, he was able to choose between one or other of the many Whig leaders until he found one that would do exactly as he wanted.

The King's Friends

As we shall see in Chapter 4, the main problem facing governments after 1763 was the question, what was to be done about the American colonies? No government managed to produce an answer. So after 1763 there was a rapid succession of weak governments.

So, it seemed, the King was unable to find a government which could deal with the main problem of the time. One reason for this was that each government faced the opposition of the other Whig leaders' supporters.

In the spring of 1766 a group of M.P.s, anxious to find some way of helping the King, argued, 'His Majesty should have the free choice of ministers and he should not put the management of affairs into the hands of the leaders of any party.' These M.P.s thought that most M.P.s 'have always acted on the principle of support for the Crown'. This earned them the nickname of the *King's Friends*.

Wilkes and the Middlesex Election 1768

While the King and his successive governments tried to grapple with the American problem, John Wilkes came back to stand as a candidate for Middlesex in the general election. He hoped that the mob would help get him elected.

To make sure of the mob's support, Wilkes forced the Warden of the King's Bench prison to take him into gaol as the publisher of a pornographic poem. The mob, thinking that he had been arrested by the King, rioted. On 10 May 1768 troops were called out to defend the prison, and were stoned by the mob. One man, William Allen, was shot by the soldiers – who happened to be Scottish (Fig. 3.3). The affair

Fig. 3.3 During the riots outside the King's Bench prison where Wilkes was under arrest the troops were stoned and mobbed. William Allen was chased by three soldiers and shot. The soldiers were Scottish and the affair was treated as an attack on English liberties by Bute, the King and the Scottish soldiers.

was portrayed in cartoons and poems as an attempt by George III, under the influence of the Scottish Marquess of Bute, to attack the liberties of Englishmen. The magistrate who gave permission for the soldiers to fire was tried for murder.

Wilkes was elected for Middlesex. However, the King persuaded Parliament not to allow him to take his seat, since he was a traitor, an outlaw, a blasphemer, and a pornographer. The elections had to be held again. On this and a third occasion Wilkes won, but still Parliament decided to give the seat to his opponent, Lutrell, even though Wilkes had gained 1,143 votes to Lutrell's 296.

This led to an agitation about the rights of electors to decide who was to be their M.P. Wilkes was finally allowed to take his seat in 1774. The issue had been decided against the King.

The Commons and the Press

Wilkes had been released from prison in 1770. He became an alderman of the City of London and a magistrate.

In 1771 the House of Commons sent a messenger to arrest two London printers who had published reports of parliamentary debates. Wilkes, as a magistrate, ordered that the messenger be arrested for violating the privileges of the City of London. The Commons decided to leave Wilkes alone but ordered that the other magistrates who had sat with him should be sent to the Tower for the rest of the parliamentary session. There was public outcry at the Commons' wish for secrecy, and the result was that while the Commons claimed that it was illegal to publish reports of its proceedings, it never again tried to enforce this claim. This was an important step in the relations between Parliament, the Press, and the people.

Lord North

By 1770 the King had tried most of the leading Whigs as Prime Minister; they all came to grief over the American problem (Chapter 4). In 1770 the King appointed Lord North, who had been Chancellor of the Exchequer since 1767. The 200 or so placemen plus those M.P.s who were the King's Friends, enabled North to get a majority of forty in a debate in January 1770. He seemed to have a better idea of how to deal with the American question which won him more support from the divided opposition. In March 1770 he had a majority of 163. At last it seemed the King could rely on a minister staying in power.

Some M.P.s thought that the King ought to govern without regard to party. Edmund Burke, a Whig supporter of Lord Rockingham, thought otherwise. In 1770 he wrote *Thoughts on the Cause of the Present Discontent* in which he examined the conflict between the Commons and the electors of Middlesex. He thought that the main reason for the unrest was George III's influence on political affairs. George I and George II had not tried to exercise such influence – and there had been no problems. Burke claimed that the King ought to allow the Whigs to govern without any interference.

North and America

North's government, however, did not find a solution to the American problem. Indeed, it did worse. It drove the Americans into revolution. Then it lost the war.

Many people in England supported the claims of the Americans. Burke, Pitt, Charles Fox, and Wilkes led the attack on North's policies.

The obvious failure of the government during the war led to a growth in demand for political change. Pamphlets were produced, and societies were formed to promote the idea of reform. Burke demanded the abolition of the system of placemen as a means of lessening the influence of the Crown, and in 1780 the Commons passed a resolution proposed by John Dunning, 'that the influence of the Crown has increased, is increasing, and ought to be diminished'.

The Gordon Riots

The continued defeats of English troops in America and the fall in the level of trade and employment owing to the war had made the London mob restless.

In 1778 Parliament passed a Roman Catholic Relief Act which did away with most of the penalties inflicted on Roman Catholics. The Protestants of Scotland formed the Protestant Association and the half-mad Lord George Gordon, an M.P. who hated Lord North, became President of the London Protestant Association. On 3 June 1780 Gordon led a mob to Parliament to petition for the repeal of the Relief Act. From 4 June to 8 June the mob terrorized London, burning chapels and houses, freeing prisoners from Newgate (Fig. 5.2 on p. 27) and other gaols and attacking the Bank of England. Magistrates were slow to order troops out because they remembered the Allen affair on (p. 13). But on 9 June troops were finally called in and order restored.

North out of Office

By October 1781 the American war was sliding to its disastrous end, and many M.P.s began to desert North. In March 1782, while peace negotiations were taking place, Lord North told George III that he could no longer command a majority in the Commons. George III allowed North to resign.

Rockingham's Government

George III was now forced to ask Lord Rockingham to form a government again. He had been Prime Minister in 1765–6 and was leader of one of the more important groups of Whigs.

Rockingham died in July 1782 and was succeeded by Shelbourne. However, many of Rockingham's supporters refused to stand by him. In February 1783 the Shelbourne government made peace with the Americans – and angered the Tories, North's supporters, and many of the other Whig groups.

Fox and North

Charles James Fox had been a leading opponent of North's government. But in February 1783 these two former enemies made common cause against Shelbourne. George III was very angry but he had little choice; he had to agree to a government that was led by the Duke of Portland but in which Fox and North were the leading members.

The new government had a large majority in the Commons. Outside Parliament many of Fox's former supporters were amazed that he had chosen to make an alliance with North whom he had always denounced as the King's mouthpiece. In addition this new government accepted the Treaty of Versailles, which confirmed the peace treaty with the Americans; people therefore wondered what the dismissal of Shelbourne had been about. If it had been about the terms of the peace treaty, why had Fox and North now accepted those same terms? Many people began to think that Fox and North were more concerned with getting power than with the real interests of Britain.

The India Bill 1783

In December 1783 Fox brought in a Bill to deal with the problems of governing large parts of India (p. 11). He proposed that the political work of the East India Company should be controlled by seven commissioners to be appointed by the government.

This would give Fox and North a new chance to increase the influence of the government – which M.P.s would sell their votes in return for being one of the commissioners?

The Commons passed the Bill but the King used his influence with the Lords to make sure that the Bill was rejected. The King then called for the resignation of the Coalition government. In the week before Christmas 1783 he appointed William Pitt, then only 24, First Lord of the Treasury and Prime Minister.

Questions

Extract 3.1

George III and the vote for the Peace of Paris 1763

Fox set himself to work. He directly attacked the members of the Commons. A shop was publicly opened at the Pay Office where the members flocked and received their bribes in bank bills. Twenty-five thousand pounds was issued in one morning; and in a single fortnight a vast majority was bought which approved the peace. 'The King', it was announced, '*would* be King, would not be dictated to by his ministers as his grandfather had been.'

The Bill was passed by 223 votes to 63. Nothing can paint the importance of this victory so strongly as what the Princess of Wales said on hearing the news. 'Now', said she, 'my son is King of England.' Fox, having used rewards, thought that the time had come to use punishments. Whoever held a place and had voted against the Treaty was instantly dismissed.

(Horace Walpole, *Memoirs of the Reign of King George III*, 1847.)

1. What two methods did Fox use to ensure the passage of the proposed Peace?
2. Who was the King's 'grandfather' (line 9)? Which minister above all others had dictated to him? Which minister wished to dictate to George III about the proposal to end the war in 1763?
3. How far does this extract support the view that 'George III intended to rule as well as reign'?
4. What was meant by holding 'a place'? Why could the King 'instantly' dismiss people holding a place?

Extract 3.2

Wilkes and the Peace of Paris, 1763

The King's speech has always been considered by the legislature and by the public to be the Speech of the Minister. This week has given the public the most outrageous instance of ministerial effrontery [cheek] ever imposed on mankind. The Minister's speech last Tuesday is not equalled in the history of this country.

I am sure that all foreigners, especially the King of Prussia, will hold the Minister in contempt. He has made our King say: 'My hopes have been fully answered by the happy results which the allies of our Crown has gained from this treaty. The powers at war with my good brother, the King of Prussia, have agreed to terms which that great Prince has approved!' The infamous lie of this whole sentence is apparent to all mankind. No advantage has been gained by that Prince from our negotiations, but he was basely deserted by the Scottish Prime Minister of England.

(John Wilkes writing on 23 April 1763.)

1. What was the name of the newspaper in which this article appeared in 1763?
2. Why did Wilkes choose that particular name for his newspaper?
3. Who was 'the Minister' referred to in line 5?
4. Why did Wilkes write about an 'infamous lie'?
5. Which other leading politician agreed that Britain ought to have continued the war against France? Why?

Worksheet

(A)

1. Explain how the Whigs had become 'too powerful' (p. 11) by 1760.

2. Why did Bute have to resign in 1763? What does this tell you about the relationship between the King and Parliament? How did the King usually get his own way?

3. Write two sentences on each of the following: General Warrrants; King's Friends; Gordon Riots.

4. Why did Wilkes (i) go to France in 1763 (ii) return from France in 1768?

5. What enabled Lord North to govern after 1770? Why did he have to resign in 1782?

(B)

1. Write the letter which might have been sent by:
(a) Wilkes explaining why he was angry when he did not get a government job in 1761;
(b) one of Wilkes's opponents after the riots at his trial in 1763;

(c) Henry Fox to explain why and how the Peace of Paris had been approved by Parliament in 1763;
(d) an M.P. who had voted for Dunning's resolution (p.14);
(e) one of Fox's opponents, December 1783.

(C)

1. Write the headlines that might have appeared above reports on:
(a) George III in 1761 – in papers controlled by Bute, Bolingbroke, and a Whig M.P.;
(b) Britain's victories on land and sea, 1759;
(c) Bute's appointment as Prime Minister – in papers controlled by the King, the Whigs, and Wilkes;
(d) the formation of the Fox–North Coalition, 1783 – in papers controlled by the King, Fox, and Fox's opponents;
(e) the debate over the India Bill, 1783 – in papers controlled by the King, Fox, and the East India Company;
(f) the appointment of the younger Pitt, December 1783 – in papers controlled by the King, Fox, Pitt himself, and someone who remembered 1759.

4 The American Revolution, 1775-83

British Colonies

Today, the United States of America is one of the world's great powers, but in 1760 there was no such country. There were thirteen separate states along the eastern seaboard of North America (Fig. 4.1). By 1760 about 2½ million people lived there. Each colony had its own government; every man and woman was allowed to vote in elections. They choose their own State Parliament (or legislative assembly). But these Parliaments had little real power. In each state there was a governor appointed by the British government. He had the power to set aside any decisions made by the State Parliament.

The Colonies and British Industry

Look at the figures in the following table:

Table 4.1 Markets for British exports in the eighteenth century

	Percentages			
	1700	*1750*	*1772*	*1797*
Europe	85	77	49	38
North America	6	11	25	32
West Indies	3	3	12	25
East Indies and Africa	4	7	14	13

The American colonies took a great deal of British exports – tools, weapons, nails, steel, clothes, and dishes. So Birmingham gunkeepers, Dudley nail-makers and Staffordshire potters did a large trade with the colonies. As the *London Magazine* boasted, 'The American is clothed from head to foot in our manufactures.'

This export trade was important for the British. The manufacturers made their profits; many workmen were employed to produce the goods, and thus had money to spend. The goods had to be exported – and there was a growth in the size and wealth of British ports, such as Bristol and Liverpool.

① Massachusetts ⑤ New York ⑨ Maryland
② New Hampshire ⑥ New Jersey ⑩ Virginia
③ Connecticut ⑦ Pennsylvania ⑪ North Carolina
④ Rhode Island ⑧ Delaware ⑫ South Carolina
⑬ Georgia

Fig. 4.1 The American Revolution, 1775–83.

Mercantilism

The American colonies were founded during the seventeenth century, at a time when the British believed that colonies existed for the benefit of the Mother Country. The colonies were supposed to produce things for the Mother Country. So America was valuable as a source of timber, iron, hemp, furs, fish, and tobacco.

In addition to this, colonies were supposed to buy whatever the Mother Country produced. The *Boston Gazette* complained that 'a colonist cannot make a button without some button-maker of Britain bawling and complaining'. So while the Americans were allowed to produce iron from their ironfields, they were not allowed to make iron goods – they had to buy these from Britain.

Trade with foreign countries had to be carried in ships made in the colonies or in Britain. Britain did not want to help the merchant navies of France, Holland, or Spain. This was the law as set out in the Navigation Acts of 1650 and 1661.

The Benefits to the Colonies

This colonial system was obviously of great value to the British, although they argued that the colonists also gained. The colonies, Britain claimed, had a safe market for whatever goods they produced.

Britain provided the army needed to protect the colonists from the French and the Indians. In Fig. 4.1 you can see that in 1760 the French had a colony in Canada as well as a settlement in New Orleans. The French had made friends with the Indian tribes living along the Ohio Valley which linked Canada and New Orleans. The French only wanted to buy furs from the Indian fur-trappers; this made the Indians richer. But the British came to settle; they wanted to take lands away from the Indian people by driving them beyond the limits of the frontiers of the British colonies. The French, on the other hand, wanted the Indians to hold on to their tribal lands and then make them part of whatever colony France might set up. Therefore, the French and Indians were allies against the British colonists.

The British government kept an army of about 30,000 men in America to defend the colonies from attack from the Indians and French, and during the Seven Years' War (1756–63) the British had sent much larger armies as well as squadrons of ships to attack French Canada.

Colonial Grumblings

The colonies had started with a handful of settlers, but as time went on their populations grew in size. They also grew in confidence. By 1760 few of the colonists thought that they owed much loyalty to a far-away country which most of them had never seen. They began to complain about the system that forced them to produce some things and prevented them from producing others.

Walpole (Fig. 2.1 on p. 7) and other ministers had the sense to see that the colonists might be right, so their governments did not apply the law too

rigorously. They turned a blind eye to the growth of colonial trade with foreign countries.

Until 1763 the colonists were afraid to do much more than grumble. If they had tried to throw the British governors and army out of their states they might have been attacked by the French in Canada. But in the Peace of Paris (1763) Canada became a British colony. There was now no danger of a French attack from the north.

Indian Lands

In Fig. 4.1 you can see that the colonies lay along the seaboard, and the Allegheny Mountains lay between them and the interior. With the removal of the French menace, many colonists thought of 'going west' to find more land. But this might have meant a war against the Indians – and more expense for the British government which would have to send more armies.

So the British government first decided to allow only a slow movement into the Indian lands. This angered the colonists. But even that slow expansion frightened the Indians. In 1763 a chief called Pontiac united many of the Indian tribes in an attack on British-held forts in the Ohio Valley, and many soldiers were killed. For fourteen months there was a savage war in which many settlers were massacred. But the colonists made no attempt to raise armies for their own defence; this, they argued, was the job of the British government. In 1766 the Indians were defeated. A treaty was signed by which the British government promised that the Indians would be left alone.

To make sure that this treaty was obeyed the British government sent more soldiers to America. This cost about £350,000 a year. We have seen that one of the main problems facing the Bute government in 1763 was the question of taxation (p. 11). But now, either the British taxpayer had to pay even more taxes – to provide the £350,000, or the Americans could be made to pay.

The Grenville Government, 1763–5

From 1764 each of George III's governments tried to find some way of finding this money, but all their attempts failed. Indeed, each of them only increased colonists' anger with Britain:

The Sugar Act 1764 put a tax on all the sugar imported into the colonies from the West Indies. This provided about £45,000 a year. But some colonists were angered by the power of the British government to tax the colonists.

The Mutiny Act 1765 compelled the colonists to pay for the every-day needs of British troops stationed in America. The colonists resented this.

The Stamp Act 1765 led to even more of an outcry in the colonies. This Act said that a government stamp would have to be fixed to newspapers, advertisements, and various legal documents (Extract 4.1). The British themselves had been paying such a stamp tax since 1694, so they saw nothing wrong in asking the colonists to pay it. They hoped to get £100,000 from this tax.

Colonial Opposition 1765

The Sugar Act was hated by the merchants – but there were few of them. It was the Stamp Act which raised opposition throughout the colonies. They had been unwilling to unite to provide armies to fight the Indians, but the tax united them. Delegates from many colonies met in New York in 1765 to discuss the measure. They took as their slogan, 'No taxation without representation', arguing that it was illegal for a British Parliament to put a tax on the colonists.

There were protest meetings throughout the colonies. Stamp collectors were attacked, offices raided, and stamps burned. Merchants agreed to boycott British goods. There was a drop in the sale of such goods – which led to unemployment in Britain and a drop in manufacturers' profits.

Fig. 4.2 Two Bostonians tarring and feathering an English customs officer in 1774. The cockade on the man's hat shows that he was one of the Sons of Liberty. What does the '45' on the other man's hat mean?

1766–70

When Grenville's government was defeated in the House of Commons, Rockingham, another Whig, became Prime Minister. He cancelled the Stamp Act – which pleased the colonists. But he then passed the Declaratory Act which claimed that the British had the right to impose taxes if they wanted to. This only angered the colonists.

In 1767 Townshend tried to raise £40,000 by putting import taxes on various goods exported from Britain to America, e.g. glass, paper, lead, and tea.

Once again the Americans raised the cry of 'no taxation without representation' and boycotted British goods. More importantly, the State Parliament of Massachusetts sent a letter to all the other Parliaments asking them to unite with one another to help to make the boycott really work.

Lord North 1770

In 1770 Lord North became Prime Minister. He repealed all the Townshend duties except the one on tea: he kept this one to show that the British had the right to impose such taxes. This angered the Americans, and there was serious rioting in Boston (Fig. 4.2). British soldiers were sent to stop the rioters; three people were killed in what became known as the Boston Massacre of 1770.

1772–4

The British government sent ships to patrol the American coast to make sure that smuggling was stopped. One of these ships, the *Gaspée*, ran aground off Providence in Rhode Island (see Fig. 4.1). The colonists rowed out and burnt the ship.

But the British government did not understand American feelings. In 1773, the North government passed the Tea Act. Before this, Indian tea had been taken to Britain where it paid an import duty of 5p per pound; it was then re-exported to America. The Act of 1773 changed this, and tea could be taken straight to the colonies from India. Instead of paying a British tax of 5p, the colonists would pay only a little over 1p per pound.

The colonists resented the British tax even though it meant they could have cheaper tea. On 16 December 1773, 150 men disguised as Red Indians boarded three teaships in Boston harbour. They tipped £18,000 worth of tea overboard in what became known as the Boston Tea Party (Fig. 4.3).

Support in Britain

A number of British people supported the colonists. In 1770, Edmund Burke, a Whig M.P., wrote *Thoughts on the Present Discontent*, which attacked George III's system of government. He spoke in the Commons in defence of the Americans' argument against unfair taxation. He was supported by Charles James Fox, then only 25, but already an outstanding speaker. Wilkes, not surprisingly, supported the colonists, but perhaps the most important defender of the Americans' claims was the former Prime Minister, William Pitt, now the Earl of Chatham (Extract 4.2).

North and George III

But the King and his Prime Minister thought that they could defeat the colonists by showing firmness. In 1774, Parliament passed the *Intolerable Acts* which closed the port of Boston, dismissed the State Parliament of Massachusetts, put a force of soldiers in that colony, and allowed its British governor to send criminals to Britain for trial. This policy was intended to frighten the people of Massachusetts and to warn the people of the other colonies.

Fig. 4.3 The Boston Tea Party, 1775.

The Quebec Act 1774

At the same time Parliament passed the Quebec Act. This allowed the French people living in Canada to keep their Catholic religion, their French language, and their existing system of government. We will learn more about this Act in Chapter 18, but here we should notice that the American colonists saw in this an attempt to prevent their expansion to the north.

1775

In 1774 fifty-five men from twelve colonies met at Philadelphia to discuss the 'present unhappy state' of affairs between Britain and the colonies. One result of this meeting (or Congress) was a decision to form local association committees throughout the various colonies. These collected military supplies, raised local armies, and led the resistance against the Intolerable Acts.

In April 1775 the first shots were fired. General Gage, a British General married to an American woman, had been sent to take charge of the government of Massachusetts. The local committee had collected arms at Concord, but Gage sent a force to destroy these supplies. On the way there was a fight at Lexington; the British lost 244 men because the Americans were very capable riflemen, used to hunting wild animals.

Three weeks later, on 10 May 1775, the Second Continental Congress met in Philadelphia – with representatives from all thirteen colonies. This set up the Continental Army and appointed George Washington as Commander.

Bunker Hill, June 1775

The colonists tried to get control of Boston, and in doing so, their army clashed with the British forces at Bunker Hill. The British won this battle but suffered such heavy losses that the Americans were encouraged to continue their struggle.

At the same time there was a reluctance to go the whole way and separate themselves from the Mother Country. Congress sent an Olive Branch Petition to George III to ask him to agree to settle the colonists' complaints peacefully, but the King refused.

1776

In April 1776 the colonists opened their ports to world trade in defiance of the Navigation Acts. They also set up their own local governments to take the place of the British governors, most of whom had fled. In May 1776, North Carolina, Rhode Island, and Virginia announced their independence, and on 4 July 1776, the Continental Congress approved their Declaration of Independence (Extract 4.3). There was now no going back.

The War, 1776–8

In the autumn of 1776, a British army under Lord Howe captured New York, driving out a smaller army led by Washington. Howe wasted the chance of chasing and maybe capturing Washington, because he preferred to stay in New York. In September 1777, Howe defeated Washington at Brandywine, but instead of chasing him, Howe allowed Washington to spend the winter in Valley Forge, only 22 miles (35 kilometres) away.

British forces were sent out to reinforce the existing armies. One, under General Burgoyne, was sent to advance from Canada to link up with Howe who was supposed to march north from New York.

But messages did not always get through from Britain. Once again, Howe did not march and Burgoyne's army was defeated by the colonial army at Saratoga in October 1777.

This defeat was very important. It persuaded the French, Spanish, Dutch, and others to support the rebellious colonists. The French declared war early in 1778 and Spain followed in June 1779. In 1780 Britain had to face the League of Armed Neutrality in which the Baltic countries refused to accept British claims of the right to search shipping going to and from America.

The War, 1778–83

Having failed to win the struggle in the north, the British switched to the southern colonies. General Cornwallis defeated small armies in Georgia and in both the Carolinas, and then marched into Virginia. Here the colonial army was much stronger. Cornwallis decided to march to Yorktown to await reinforcements expected from Britain.

But tax-cutting governments had allowed the Navy to run down after 1763, and the Navy was unable to defeat the combined French and Spanish fleets. When Cornwallis got to Yorktown he found that the French had defeated the British Navy in Chesapeake Bay and had landed a French army which besieged him in Yorktown. In October 1781, he was forced to surrender, and this was the end of real fighting in America.

The War Elsewhere

America's allies tried to destroy British power in other parts of the world. Gibraltar was besieged by the French and the Dutch. General Elliott managed to hold them off until Admiral Howe's ships raised the siege. The French Admiral, de Grasse, led a combined Franco-Spanish fleet in attacks on the West Indies. These valuable islands were saved by the victory gained by Admiral Rodney in the Battle of the Saints (April 1782). In India, Warren Hastings and Admiral Hughes managed to keep the French at bay and to defeat native risings in support of the French; this is also discussed in Chapter 18. Nearer home, there was the threat of an uprising in Ireland (see Chapter 10).

All in all, the British government was glad to arrive at a truce with its many enemies and to negotiate the settlement which was signed at Versailles in 1783. This recognized the independence of the thirteen colonies (November 1782) and agreed that they had the right to settle the land between the Ohio and the Mississippi which the Quebec Act had claimed for Canada. Britain had to give France the islands of St Lucia and Tobago in the West Indies as well as Senegal in Africa; Minorca and Florida went to Spain.

Table 4.1 (on p. 17) shows that the Americans still traded with Britain. Indeed the level of trade went up once the war was over. Britain's industrial power may have suffered little because of the loss of her former colonies, but not so the King's power. George III was never again as confident and ambitious as he had been. On the other hand, the ordinary people of the country began, for the first time, to take a more active interest in politics. The Americans had claimed the right not to pay taxes to a Parliament in which they had no representatives, but the majority of British people had no say in the election of their Parliament. Some of them began to demand that right, and so began the demand for parliamentary reform (Chapters 5 and 12).

ing the expenses of defending the British colonies in America and whereas it is just and necessary to make further provision of raising further revenue towards the said expenses be it enacted that there shall be raised throughout the Colonies in America. . . .

For every parchment or piece of paper on which shall be written any plea in any Court of Law within the Colonies, a Stamp Duty of three pence. . . .

For any copy of any will . . . a Stamp Duty of six pence. . . .

For any certificate of any decree taken at any University or College . . . a Stamp Duty of two pounds. . . .

For any licence for selling spirits or strong liquor . . . a Stamp Duty of twenty shillings. . . .

For every pack of playing cards, the sum of one shilling. . . .

And for every pair of dice, the sum of ten shillings. . . .

For every newspaper . . . a Stamp Duty of one penny for every copy. . . .

1. What duties had been granted in 'the last session of Parliament'?
2. Why did the British government think the Stamp Act was 'necessary'?
3. What did the first three taxable items have in common?
4. What did the next three have in common?
5. What effect would the tax on newspapers have on their price? British newspapers paid such a tax in the nineteenth century; the Stamp Office was at Somerset House in the Strand, London. How did this affect the location of London's printing presses?
6. How would tax officers recognize playing-cards or newspapers on which duty had not been paid?

Extract 4.2

The Earl of Chatham (William Pitt) on the American War, 1777

As to conquest, my lords, I repeat it is impossible. If I were an American, as I am an Englishman, while a foreign troop was landed in my country, I would never lay down my arms-never-never-never.

Questions

Extract 4.3

The Declaration of Independence, 4 July 1776

We, the representatives of the United States of America, in Congress assembled, appealing to the Supreme Judge of the world for the rightness of our intentions, solemnly publish and declare that these United Colonies are, and of right ought to be, Free and Independent States.

Extract 4.1

The Stamp Act 1765

Whereas by an Act made in the last session of Parliament several duties were granted towards defray-

We hold these truths to be self-evident, that all men are created equal, that they are endowed by their Creator with certain unalienable rights, that among these are Life, Liberty, and the pursuit of Happiness. That to secure these rights, Governments are instituted among men, deriving their just powers from the consent of the governed. That whenever any form of government becomes destructive of these ends, it is the right of the people to abolish it . . .

1. Why, according to the British government, had colonies been set up?
2. What 'liberty' did Americans not enjoy in (i) foreign trade, and (ii) manufacturing, because of the doctrine of mercantilism?
3. What, according to this Declaration, was the purpose of setting up a government?
4. Why had they not been prepared to rebel against Britain before 1763?
5. What issues led them to unite in 1775–6?
6. Which people in the colonies were excluded from 'Life, Liberty and the pursuit of Happiness' – at least until 1863?

Fig. 4.1

1. Find out when each of these thirteen colonies was set up.
2. Make a note of the religious beliefs of the founders of (i) Massachusetts (ii) Pennsylvania, and (iii) Maryland. Why did these religious differences make the question of uniting more difficult?
3. Why, do you think, were the first colonies set up along the coast?
4. Find out the name of the General who died in the capture of Quebec.
5. When did Britain take possession of the territory marked Canada?
6. Why had the British set up military forts at Ticonderoga, Oswego, and Fort Dusquesne? Why were these and other forts a burden to the British taxpayer?
7. Why did the colonists wish to move inland about 1770? Why were the British government unwilling to agree to this expansion.
8. Which generals were supposed to have marched from (i) Canada, and (ii) New York in 1777? Which valley would they have used for their journeys?
9. Why was Saratoga so important in American history?
10. Write a paragraph on the importance of (i) Lexington, and (ii) Philadelphia in the history of America 1775–6.
11. Explain the reasons for the surrender at Yorktown in 1781. Why was it so important?
12. How far was it right to talk about 'The Boston revolution' rather than the American Revolution?

Worksheet

(A)
1. What were the benefits to Britain of her American colonies?

2. Explain why the colonies cost the British government a great deal of money (i) from 1740 to 1763 (ii) after 1763.

3. Write two sentences on each of the following: Indian lands; Pontiac's rebellion; the Boston Massacre; the *Gaspée*; the Intolerable Acts.

4. Make a summary of the steps by which the colonists went from protesting to rebellion between 1765 and 1775.

5. Make a summary of the course of the war (i) in America (ii) elsewhere between 1776 and 1782.

6. Why did the British lose the war in America?

(B)
1. Write the letters that might have been written by:
(a) a British manufacturer explaining the importance of the American market;
(b) an American after the French had been driven from Canada, 1763;
(c) an American protesting about the Stamp Act;
(d) one of the men who took part in the burning of the *Gaspée*;
(e) one of the men who signed the Olive Branch Petition;
(f) a Frenchman on the war after 1780;
(g) a British soldier who had been at Yorktown in 1780.

(C)
1. Write the headlines that might have appeared above reports on:
(a) the French withdrawal from Canada;
(b) the Boston Tea Party;
(c) Lexington;
(d) Bunker Hill;
(e) the Declaration of Independence;
(f) Saratoga.

2. Make a time chart and mark on it the main dates and events mentioned in the text. Write a brief note to explain each date and event you have chosen.

3. Draw a diagram to show the way in which the colonies were governed in 1760.

4. Paint or draw a poster which might have been used to attract people to take part in the Boston Tea Party.

5 William Pitt the Younger Part 1: 1783-93

William Pitt the Younger was the son of a former Prime Minister, also called William Pitt (later the Earl of Chatham), who had led the country to victory in the Seven Years' War. Because of this war Britain had won a larger Empire in India, Canada, and the West Indies.

In 1780 the younger Pitt became M.P. for Appleby, which was one of those rotten boroughs discussed in Chapter 2. Because of his name and the training he had received from his father, he was soon asked to become a minister. Rockingham wanted him in his government in 1782, but Pitt refused, because Rockingham had never supported his father. But when Shelbourne became Prime Minister in 1782 Pitt agreed to join the government: Shelbourne had supported the older Pitt. So, in 1782, when he was only 23, Pitt became Chancellor of the Exchequer.

Becoming Prime Minister

In Chapter 3 we saw that Shelbourne's government was a short one and that its successor, the Fox–North government, was defeated over the question of the India Bill (p. 15). To everyone's surprise the King asked Pitt to become Prime Minister in December 1783.

Fox called Pitt's government the 'mincepie government', claiming that he would have Pitt out of power as soon as Christmas 1783 was over.

The General Election 1784

Many people agreed with Fox – they thought that no King's man could hold power in a Commons that was angry about the result of the American War. Pitt's government was often defeated in votes in the Commons, but he slowly impressed many people with his ability and his honesty – at a time when most M.P.s thought only of making money out of their positions. Many M.P.s were bribed to support Pitt and keep him in power.

Among the voters in the country the name of Pitt gained him a great deal of popularity: most people remembered his father. They hoped that the son would also make the country greater and richer. So, in the country, there was growing support for the young man in the winter of 1783–4. When he thought that he had gained enough support, the young Pitt asked the King to dismiss Parliament and call a general election in April 1784.

Fox protested. There had been an election in 1780 and normally there would not have been another one until 1787. Fox argued that what the country needed and demanded was a new government – led by him – and not an election.

In stressing this, Fox forgot the arguments he made in 1782. It was at that time that the Lord North government was very unpopular – because of the defeats in America. Fox and his supporters were very popular in the country and among the voters, and Fox had argued that the King ought to dismiss the Parliament elected in 1780 and have fresh elections. These would have given him a great victory – and power.

Now, in 1784, Fox claimed that the King had no right to call an election. But he did. Fox himself managed to hold his seat in the Westminster constituency (Fig. 5.1), but about eighty of his supporters lost their seats, defeated by candidates supporting Pitt, who now had a majority in the Commons.

What Had to Be Done?

The American War had interrupted Britain's industrial progress and there was a reduction in the volume of goods imported and exported. Because of the American War there was a drop in the amount of tobacco coming from Virginia (p. 17), so Bristol, Liverpool, and other ports suffered, and the nailmakers, potters, and others who used to sell their goods in America found that their trade dropped off. Industrialists were asked to produce munitions and other war materials. This meant that they spent less money on other things; there were, for example, fewer roads and canals built during the period of the war.

A reduction in trade led to a *trade depression*. Unemployment rose, food was scarce, and feeling against the government was growing.

After the election in 1784 Pitt set about restoring the country's trade and industry.

Import Taxes

For many centuries the British government had put a tax on all goods coming into or leaving the country. These taxes are called *customs dues, excise duties*, or *tariffs*. There was, for example, a tax of 119 per cent on all the sugar coming into the country. This meant that a load of sugar which should have cost £100 actually cost £219 after the tax had been paid. This tax, then, doubled the price of sugar, so less was bought. And because the sugar sellers of the West Indies sold less to Britain they had less money to buy goods from the Mother Country. Therefore, the potters and other exporters had less trade.

It can be seen then that Britain suffered from high prices (of sugar) and low exports – and less chance of work for the workers in various industries.

Fig. 5.1 The Duchess of Devonshire and one of her friends using their charms to persuade voters to support Fox in the Westminster constituency in 1784.

Free Trade

In 1776 a Scottish writer, Adam Smith, in his famous book *The Wealth of Nations*, wrote that if every country did away with all import and export taxes there would be a rise in the volume of goods bought. For example, if sugar taxes were cut, the price would drop by half; more people would buy sugar, and this would lead to higher employment in the West Indies. This would give the people there more money. They would then buy more goods – including goods made in Britain – and this would lead to more work for people in Britain. They would then have more money, which they would spend on things made in this country; there would therefore be even more work for people in factories, shops, offices, shipping, and so on.

Pitt and Free Trade

Pitt had read Smith's book. He saw sense in the argument for taking off the various taxes and making trade free. He cut the tax on sugar from 119 per cent to 20 per cent; he also cut the tax on tea from 100 per cent to only $12\frac{1}{2}$ per cent. One result of this was that smuggling was no longer profitable. Another was to bring down the cost of living in Britain.

We will see later why he did not abolish the taxes completely, but he did lower them. He also produced a very much simpler and clear *Book of Rates* which explained what taxes had to be paid on various goods coming into or leaving the country.

Bonded Warehouses

There was a slow growth in the volume of British trade. More ships sailed to India and other countries, taking away British produce and bringing home foreign goods.

A considerable number of the imports came into Bristol and other ports, but were not for sale in Britain itself. Spices from India, tobacco from America, furs from Canada and other goods were brought here only to be re-exported again to another country in Europe.

Until Pitt's time, import taxes had to be paid on these goods as they landed. This pushed up their price when they were sold in Europe. Pitt set up a system of *bonded warehouses* where these goods were stored, free of tax, under government guard, until the time came to export them. These goods paid no import taxes – so that they were cheaper than they would have been. More were sold at the lower price, which increased the volume of trade.

Luxury Taxes

By cutting the various import taxes Pitt helped to increase the volume of trade and the level of employment, wages, and profits. However, the government itself had a smaller income, and Pitt had to get money from another source. He put taxes on a number of things which only the better-off bought. There were taxes on racehorses, carriages, clocks, hair-powder for wigs, and servants. He also put a tax on windows so that people with a lot of windows in their homes paid a high tax while people with only one or two paid none.

Some of these taxes led to changes in fashion; wig-making almost died out as men and women learned to do without the more expensive powders and wigs. Architects built houses that had spaces where they would have put windows if it had not been for the extra tax.

Trade Treaty with France, 1786

In 1786 Pitt sent a minister, Eden, to make a treaty with France. In his *Eden Treaty*, the French agreed to cut their taxes on wine, silk, and other produce coming from France. This led to a drop in the price of such goods – which pleased the English. It also led to a rise in the volume of British sales in France – which pleased British manufacturers, workers, and shippers.

Taxation

Pitt was not only Prime Minister, he was also his own Chancellor of the Exchequer. He had to deal with the taxes paid by the British people. We have seen that one of the things he did was to tidy up the *Book of Rates* of taxes paid on imports and exports. Instead of separate taxes for each different type of goods, there was now a single tax which applied to all commodities.

He did a similar thing with taxes in general. Until 1786 each different tax – on, for example, cider or sugar – was put into a separate account. Each time the government spent money – on ships, soldiers' pay, etc. – each piece of spending was put against a particular tax. This was very complicated.

In 1786 Pitt set up the Consolidated Fund: all taxes were paid into a single account, and all spending was taken out of that account. This cut down on the amount of work done at the Treasury. It also made it more difficult for dishonest clerks and politicians to cheat.

Efficiency

This was another part of Pitt's policy. He set about making the government more efficient so that fewer people had to be employed. This led to a drop in the money paid out by the government – and so to a lower rate of taxation. Pitt set up a system whereby every department's accounts were examined by accountants. This *audit* led to more efficiency, less dishonesty, and thus lower spending.

The Sinking Fund

To help pay for various wars the British government had borrowed a lot of money from rich people, and each year the government had to pay interest on that loan. By 1786 the total borrowed (or the National Debt) was £240 million, and the interest on that came from the taxes paid by the British people.

Walpole (Fig. 2.1 on p. 7) had set up a fund to try to reduce the size of this debt; Pitt carried this a stage further (Extract 5.1). The government set up a Board to take charge of special taxes. Each year the Board had to use this money to repay part of the National Debt. In the following years the Board would collect the interest which was paid on that part of the Debt – and use that to repay even more. Pitt hoped that in time he would be able to wipe out the debt altogether. This would have led to a great reduction in taxation. Unfortunately, the wars against France and, later, Napoleon, meant that he had to borrow more money and the Debt increased again.

A Reformer

Pitt was younger than most other Prime Ministers had been; he was also more honest than most politicians. So it is not surprising that he was prepared to listen to proposals for reforming some of the evils that existed.

Slavery

Since the time of Elizabeth I British traders had sailed the coast of Africa, bought slaves, and sold them in the West Indies. Indeed many had been sold in Britain itself. Slavery was abolished here in 1772, but the slave trade continued to flourish after that date.

Pitt became aware of the evils of that trade through his friend, William Wilberforce. In 1791, he, Granville Sharp, and Thomas Clarkson organized a campaign to get the slave trade stopped, and Pitt set up a Committee of M.P.s to examine the trade. One Act was passed to improve conditions in the slave-ships, but two other Bills, which would have ended the trade completely, were defeated in the Commons. Pitt voted for these Bills, but too many M.P.s were under the control of merchants or companies which were against the ending of the slave trade. Pitt might have continued with the campaign but once war started against France in 1793 he gave up his interest in any reform.

Parliamentary Reform

There was a growing interest in politics after the American War. One sign of this was the founding of various Reform Associations throughout the country. In 1782 Pitt had introduced a Reform Bill, but this had been defeated. As Prime Minister he introduced another Bill. This proposed that thirty-six rotten boroughs should lose their M.P.s so that some of the growing towns could have the right to be represented in the Commons. But even this modest proposal was defeated. Too many M.P.s were frightened that they might lose their seats if reform started. And, because of the French War, Pitt did not pursue this reform after 1793.

Ireland

We will study this part of Pitt's policy in some detail in Chapter 10. Here we ought to note that Pitt tried to help the Catholics who were the majority in Ireland but who had very few rights. This was very brave in view of the anti-Catholic feeling in the country (Fig. 5.2). The King refused to allow Catholics to have a vote in elections. Pitt had promised them this, so he resigned as Prime Minister in 1801 (Fig. 5.3).

Fig. 5.2 The burning of Newgate during the Gordon 'no-popery' riots of 1780.

Fig. 5.3 The resignation of Pitt in 1801.

The Regency

Pitt normally got on very well with George III. But he was afraid to try to force the King to give way over the question of Emancipation, because he knew that the King could easily be driven insane. Indeed, in 1788, long before the Emancipation question, George III had been declared insane. This meant that there was no one to take charge of the country. Some people proposed that the King's eldest son should be appointed Prince Regent to reign in place of his father until he recovered. But this Prince was a great friend of Fox, and Pitt feared that, if he became Regent, he would use his power to push Pitt from office and appoint Fox as Prime Minister. So there was much political wrangling over this question in 1788, with Fox and the King's son doing their best to force Parliament to pass a Regency Act and Pitt and his supporters preventing them from succeeding.

Fortunately for Pitt the King recovered in 1789. The Prince did not become Regent until 1810 when his father was declared insane again.

Foreign Policy, 1783–93

In 1783 when Pitt came to power, Britain was faced by a number of hostile countries. Holland, France and Spain had helped the colonists to defeat Britain, and Denmark, Russia, Sweden and other countries had formed the Armed Neutrality Alliance (p. 21) against Britain.

Pitt wanted to win the friendship of some if not all of the European powers. He also wanted a period of peace during which British industry and trade would have a chance to recover from the effects of the American war. This meant that he did not want to be forced to go to war in Europe or anywhere else but he did want to have an active foreign policy.

His chance came over the question of relations between Holland and the neighbouring Austrian Netherlands (now called Belgium). The Austrian Emperor, Joseph II, was anxious to make his Netherlands Empire into a great trading centre. In order to do this he had to force the Dutch to open the River Scheldt to trade so that his people could trade directly with India. This would enable him to develop Antwerp as a major port. But the British did not want this to happen; they wanted no threat to the port of London. Neither did the Dutch want any threat to the prosperity of their major port, Rotterdam. In 1784 Joseph's troops attacked along the Dutch frontier. The Dutch fought back and France announced that she would help Holland.

Pitt was in an awkward position. He did not want to see Austria develop Antwerp but neither did he want to see France have too much influence over Holland. He sent Sir James Harris as ambassador to Holland to try to persuade the ruler, William V, not to give too much attention to French offers of help. But he had little success. Fortunately Joseph II's chief minister, Kaunitz, did not want to risk a war against France. In November 1785 Austria signed a treaty agreeing that the Scheldt would not be open to trade. Immediately afterwards Holland signed a commercial and military alliance with France.

Pitt saw that his best chance was to try for an alliance with Prussia which was opposed to Austria and to the increased influence of France. In August 1786 Frederick the Great, the King of Prussia, died. He was succeeded by his nephew, Frederick William II, whose sister was the wife of William V of Holland. Frederick William was in favour of the idea of an alliance with England and he also wanted to help his sister and her husband in Holland, where Parliament was now controlled by the anti-English and pro-French party called the Patriots. In June 1787 his sister was arrested on the orders of the Patriot party; she appealed to her brother and he demanded that the authorities should punish the people responsible for this insult. They turned to France for help and refused to agree with Frederick's demands. So Frederick made an alliance with Britain. In September 1787 Prussian troops supported by a smaller British army entered Holland. There was a danger that France might come to Holland's side and so start a major war, but Louis XVI agreed to remain neutral. The Prussian and British armies restored William V to the powers he had lost to the Patriots and in 1788 Britain, Prussia and Holland signed a Triple Alliance for mutual defence against France, or any other power which threatened to upset the balance of power in Europe.

The Triple Alliance was brought into action in 1790 when Russia tried to conquer Sweden. If Russia had succeeded she would have made the Baltic into a Russian lake and threatened the source of the iron ore, timber, and other goods which Britain bought from that region. Pitt used the Triple Alliance to force Russia to make a peace that left Sweden independent.

Empire

In Chapter 18 we will see how Pitt dealt with the development of the Empire in Canada, India, and Australia.

Recovery

By 1792 Pitt's government had succeeded in making Britain richer and more prosperous than she had been before the American War. The Americans were once again buying 90 per cent of their manufactured goods from Britain and the Industrial Revolution was going ahead at an increasingly rapid rate. Coal, iron and other industries flourished. Canal building began again and the years 1790–1 were nicknamed the years of 'canal mania'. British exports in 1792 were nearly three times as valuable as they had been in 1775.

Pitt succeeded in restoring confidence to the traders and industrialists; there was more work, better wages, and more food in industrialized Britain. Pitt looked forward to a long period of peace during which this progress would be maintained. Unfortunately the country became involved in a long war with France.

Questions

Extract 5.1

The Sinking Fund 1786

> Several previous Acts of Parliament have said that all the money which at the end of any quarter is surplus from the various public funds should be used as a Sinking Fund for the repayment of the National Debt. Owing to the great increase of that Debt, it has now become necessary to set up a new plan for its reduction. Be it enacted that at the end of each quarter of a year there shall be set aside out of the Sinking Fund a sum of two hundred and fifty thousand pounds to be paid to the Bank of England and applied by the Board of Commissioners to the reduction of the National Debt.
> (Public General Acts, 26 George III, c. 31.)

1.   The National Debt had grown from £20 million in 1697 to £50 million in 1713; £78 million in 1748; £138 million in 1763; and £249 million in 1784. Draw a set of bar graphs to show these increases. Find out the names we give to the wars that ended in 1713, 1748, 1763, and 1783.
2.   How much did Pitt intend to set aside for a Sinking Fund each year?
3.   Explain how the Sinking Fund would lead to a reduction in the Debt.
4.   Why, in time, would this have led to a reduction in the level of taxation?
5.   Why did the wars against France (1793–1815) lead to an increase in the size of the National Debt?

Extract 5.2

An expanding economy 1806

The rapid increase in recent years in the manufactures and trade of this country is well known. The immediate cause of that increase is the spirit of enterprise and industry among a free people, left to the exercise of their talents. They employ a vast capital, much labour and mechanical ingenuity. They use the benefits of visiting foreign countries to form new and to confirm old trading connections. They find out the wants, tastes, habits and discoveries of other countries. They bring these home and help our own manufacturers. At the same time they open up new markets for our industries. Our commerce and manufactures have increased in such a degree as to pass the most optimistic hopes of the ablest political writers who had written about the future age . . .
(Report from the Committee on the State of the Woollen Manufactures of England, 1806.)

1. What evidence is there in this extract that the Industrial Revolution was well under way by 1806?
2. Who in particular had written about trade in the 'future age'?
3. How does the writer explain the successes of Britain in trade with foreign countries?
4. Why was an expansion of British trade good for (i) employers (ii) shippers, and (iii) workers in Britain?

Fig. 5.1

1. Lady Devonshire (on the left) and the other wives of Whig Lords handed out kisses and cuddles to voters promising to vote for Fox. Write a report which might have appeared in a newspaper under the heading 'The Westminster Election, 1784'. You might want to re-read pp. 8–9 for other examples of corrupt practices in elections.

Worksheet

(A)
1. Write two sentences on each of the following: The 'mincepie' administration: the *Wealth of Nations*.

2. How did the American War affect Britain's industrial development? (Were there some industries which lost trade? Were there others which got larger orders?)

3. Show how and why a reduction in tariffs leads to (i) more exports, and (ii) a fall in the cost of living.

4. Write two sentences on each of the following: Bonded warehouses; luxury taxes; the Eden Treaty.

5. Explain in your own words how the Sinking Fund worked. Why did the Fund not prevent a rise in the National Debt after 1793?

6. What was the importance of the Regency question in 1788? (You might show how the question was seen by (i) Fox (ii) Pitt (iii) the Regent (iv) George III.)

(B)
1. Write the letters that might have been sent by:
(a) a friend of Pitt's father when the younger Pitt became Prime Minister in 1783;
(b) a former smuggler after Pitt's cuts in tariffs;
(c) a friend of Wilberforce on the subject of slavery.

6 William Pitt the Younger Part 2: 1793-1806

The French Revolution 1789–92

In 1788–9 the British celebrated the anniversary of their Glorious Revolution which increased the power of Parliament and lessened that of the King (pp. 6–7).

By 1789 the French King had spent a lot of money on wars against Britain (p. 26), but he had nothing to show for it. Britain, at least, had an Empire and a growing foreign trade.

The French King had no idea of where to find the money to run his country, so he called a meeting of the French States General – or Parliament – which had not met for 175 years. The representatives of the common people forced their King to give it more powers than he had meant it to have. The Paris mob, encouraged by this success, rioted as the London mob had done in support of Wilkes (Fig. 3.3 on p. 13) and Gordon (Fig. 5.2 on p. 27).

Within a few weeks of the first meeting of the French Parliament it was obvious that there had been a political revolution in that country. The King's power had been lessened. To many people in Britain it seemed as if history was repeating itself.

British Opinion of the French Revolution 1789–92

Many people in Britain welcomed the news from France. Fox, the leading Whig, saw it as a victory for the common man (Fig. 6.1). Tom Paine, who had fought with the American colonists against Britain, wrote *The Rights of Man*, a book which supported the ideas of the French Revolution. Wordsworth, the poet, wrote, 'Bliss was it in that dawn to be alive . . .'

Pitt was less sure. He feared that these changes inside France would lead to changes in other countries in Europe. Edmund Burke was another who was frightened. He wrote *Reflections on the Revolution in France* in which he said that in time there would be bloodshed, war, and a dictatorship.

Fig. 6.1 Fox is shown bringing Pitt's head to the French Revolutionary leader, Dumourier, who dined at St James's on 15 May 1793.

France at War, April 1792

Many French nobles fled from France to live in Austria or Prussia. These governments decided to put an end to the revolution in France, so in April 1792 Austria and Prussia invaded France.

At first they were victorious: they marched towards Paris. The French government, frightened at the thought of defeat, turned on anyone who appeared to welcome the news of the Austrian–Prussian victories. In September 1792 there began the terrible massacres in which thousands of people were executed. The news of these events shocked people in Britain.

In November 1792 the French government issued the *Edict of Fraternity*. This called on the lower classes in every country to rise up against their Kings and nobility. It offered other people the support of a French army once the Austrians and Prussians had been defeated.

Surprisingly, they were defeated by armies raised from untrained peasants, led by men quickly promoted from the ranks and led by a government which forced the people to give every assistance to their armies.

In January 1793 the French government realized that the King could not really support the revolutionary movement in a war against fellow Kings. He was, in their terms, a traitor. They executed him. But the news of his execution and, later, that of his Queen, Marie Antoinette, and her children, made people realize that the French Revolution was a violent one. Did people want such a change in their own country?

The Invasion of Belgium 1793

The French armies defeated the invaders. They drove them out of France and into the area now called Belgium. In 1793 this was known as the Austrian Netherlands. Here they promised to free the people from Austrian rule. They also promised to open the River Scheldt to world trade and to make Antwerp once again a great port.

We have seen how the British acted in 1788 when Joseph II threatened to do just that. So in 1793 Britain joined Austria and Prussia in their war against France. Paine and other supporters of the revolution were opposed to this declaration of war; Fox (Fig. 6.1) argued that Britain ought instead to support the French.

Pitt and the War

Pitt was a very successful Prime Minister between 1783 and 1793. Many people at the time thought that he would be equally successful in war; after all, his father had been a great war leader.

But Pitt was unlike his father, and thought that France could never hold out in a long war. She was, he knew, a bankrupt country, so he planned for only a short war.

After 1783 he had cut government spending – to help him in his work of lowering the level of taxes. Therefore, in 1793 the Army and the Navy had both run down and were quite unprepared for a war.

Pitt decided that all he had to do was to send a small army to Holland to help the Austrians and Prussians while he sent a naval force to the West Indies to win back the French-occupied islands there.

But the Army in Holland was led by the Duke of York who 'marched them up to the top of the hill and marched them down again' without ever winning any battles. The expedition to the West Indies was a total disaster. Over 10,000 men died from yellow fever or dysentry – and Britain gained none of the French islands.

The Navy

Pitt hoped to use the Navy as his father had used it in the Seven Years' War: fleets blockaded French ports to cut France off from world trade; ships carried British troops to Europe and to attacks on the French colonies; and other ships led raids on the French coast to help people inside France who were resisting the revolution.

But the Navy was too small to do what Pitt wanted. Most sailors had been forced to join the service and they were badly treated by their officers, who were often not really qualified to do their jobs properly. In 1793 a naval force was sent to Toulon in the south of France. Here there was resistance to the revolution. The British landed an army and helped the resistance, but it was a disaster. The French troops were led by a young Corsican, Napoleon Bonaparte. They drove off the British without difficulty and the Navy returned home in despair.

There were, however, some successes. Admiral Howe was in charge of a naval force patrolling the northern coast of France. On 1 June 1794 he came across a French fleet guarding corn ships making their way to France; he won the battle against the French fleet (Fig. 6.2) but the corn ships escaped – so even this was a partial defeat.

But the Navy did capture the Cape of Good Hope which had once been part of the Dutch Empire. This was a useful staging post on the trade route to India.

The First Coalition 1793–7

When Pitt took Britain into the war in February 1793 he formed a coalition with other countries outside France. Spain, Holland, Austria, Prussia, England, and Sardinia (with the initials SHAPES) were joined by Russia, but there was little unity among such allies. Britain was concerned with trade, colonies, and a naval war; Russia, Austria, and Prussia were almost at war with each other over the division of Poland.

A series of French victories led to the break-up of the alliance. In 1795 Prussia, anxious to keep an eye on Polish affairs, made a separate peace with France;

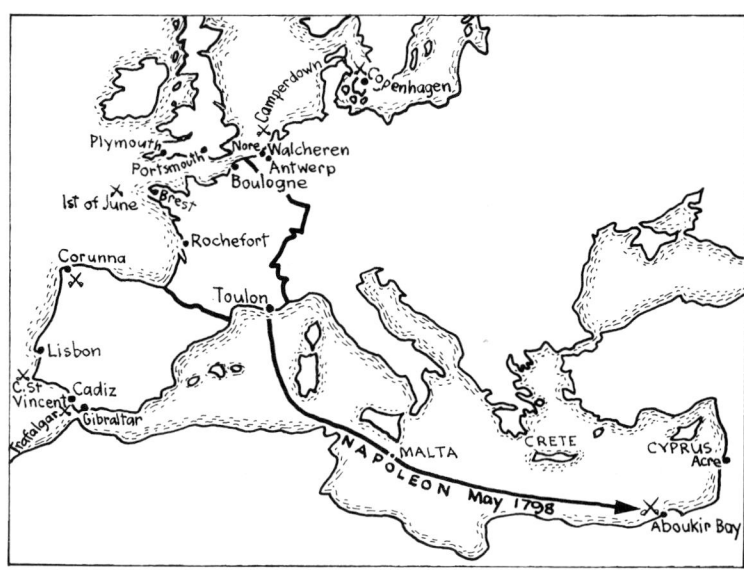

Fig. 6.2 The Naval Wars, 1793–1815.

in 1796 Sardinia also did so. In 1797 France defeated Austria at the Battle of Rivoli and then made peace.

In 1796 Spain and Holland declared war on Britain. They hoped the French War would give them an opportunity to seize some of the British Empire for themselves.

1797: A Year of Crisis: the Navy

In April 1797 there was a mutiny among the sailors at Spithead. This was a protest against the work of the press-gangs which kidnapped men to serve in the Navy. The pressed sailors also objected to the fact that they were often not paid for months at a time and that they lived in terrible conditions – badly fed, poorly housed below deck, and subject to the cruelty of many officers. This mutiny was brought to an end when Lord Howe, the Commander of the Fleet, agreed to improve the men's conditions of service.

In May, news of this mutiny reached the ships based at the Nore. Here the mutiny was led by men who preached revolution. The ringleader was Richard Parker. He succeeded in gaining the support of many sailors, and for a few days he had full control of all the ships in the fleet. He even blockaded London. However, this rising was put down and Parker and twenty-eight of his leading supporters were hanged.

1797 in Ireland

Tone formed the United Irishmen in 1790 (p. 55). In 1796 the French tried to send an invading force to Ireland, but this failed, and by 1797 Tone was preaching revolution throughout Ireland. Although the rising did not take place until 1798 there was the fear, in 1797, that the country might flare up at any moment.

1797 – Spain and Holland

Both these countries had large navies. They might have been a threat to Britain's trade and to her various colonies, but the British Navy was successful in two major battles. In February 1797 Admiral Jervis with the help of a young officer, Horatio Nelson, defeated the Franco–Spanish fleet at Cape St Vincent, and in October Admiral Duncan defeated the Dutch fleet at the Battle of Camperdown (Fig. 6.2).

1798 – Napoleon in Egypt

In 1797 Napoleon led the French army which defeated the Austrians at Rivoli, and in 1798 he took his army to Egypt. He hoped to get to India, the source of a great deal of Britain's wealth. He defeated the Turks (who ruled Egypt at that time) at the Battle of the Pyramids and prepared to march to India.

Nelson, Commander of the British Mediterranean Fleet, sailed after Napoleon. He destroyed the French fleet at Aboukir Bay (Fig. 6.2). This left Napoleon stranded. His army was then defeated at the Battle of Acre by a British army supported by a fleet led by Sir Sidney Smith. Napoleon had to make his way back to France – and India was saved.

The Second Coalition 1798

Britain, Austria, Russia, and Turkey (BART from their initials) formed the Second Coalition. Pitt hoped to use British money to help the allies to provide the armies needed to defeat the French; Austrian and Russian armies succeeded in driving the French from Italy, but a Russian and British force failed against the French in the Netherlands (Belgium and Holland). The Duke of York signed a truce with the French. This angered the Russians who left the Coalition.

Then the French defeated the Austrians at the Battle of Marengo (June 1800) and Hohenlinden (December 1800). The Austrians then signed a treaty with France. They too left the Coalition. Once again Britain was on her own.

Armed Neutrality 1800

Russia joined Sweden and Denmark in an alliance. They resented Britain's claims to the right to search ships going to France, and intended to stop Britain getting the timber she needed from the Baltic region. Napoleon hoped to use the navies of these countries to help him defeat Britain.

Once again the Navy saved Britain. Admiral Sir Hyde Parker commanded a fleet sent to deal with this threat. He was a cautious commander, but his second-in-command was Horatio Nelson. Nelson destroyed the Danish fleet in the harbour of Copenhagen (Extract 6.1).

The Treaty of Amiens 1802

Pitt resigned in 1801 over the question of Catholic Emancipation (p. 27). The new Prime Minister, Addington, made peace with France. A treaty was signed at Amiens in March 1802. Britain handed back all the colonial territories she had captured – except Trinidad (from Spain) and Ceylon (from Holland). The French agreed to withdraw their forces from Rome, Naples, and Egypt, and the British agreed to withdraw from Malta which they had taken from the Knights of St John.

War again – May 1803

But few thought that the peace would last. The French were building an invasion fleet at Boulogne, and Britain on her side could not leave Europe under the control of Napoleon, now the ruler of France.

Pitt came back to power in April 1804. He formed a Third Coalition with Austria and Russia, but this had little success. Napoleon defeated the Austrians at the Battle of Ulm (October 1805) and then defeated the combined armies of Austria and Russia at Austerlitz (December 1805). On 26 December Austria made peace with France and this Third Coalition broke up.

Trafalgar – October 1805

By March 1805 Napoleon had his fleet ready for the invasion of Britain. One fleet was to sail from Brest (Fig. 6.2), cross the Atlantic, and go on to the West Indies. Another fleet led by Admiral Villeneuve was to sail from Toulon (Fig. 6.2) to meet French and Spanish fleets stationed at Cadiz, then it too was to sail to the West Indies. It was planned that all the combined fleets were to sail back across the Atlantic, defeat the British fleets in the English Channel and get to Boulogne in June 1805. The fleets would guard the French army as it sailed in invasion barges to Britain.

Nelson chased after Villeneuve's fleet to the West Indies but never caught up with him. By August 1805 Villeneuve was back in France. Nelson realized that Napoleon's main aim was the invasion of England, and came back to Portsmouth in August 1805. In late September he was back at Cadiz where Villeneuve had taken his fleet for a refit. On 19 October the French and Spanish fleets came out of port and on 21

Fig. 6.3 In this cartoon, drawn by Gillray in 1798, Pitt straddles Parliament like a colossus. His pockets are stuffed with 'resources for supporting the war', and he dangles the world on a string. Pitt's supporters kiss his right foot while his opponents are trampled with the left.

October met Nelson's fleet at Trafalgar. British victory there meant that there was no danger of a French invasion.

Pitt's Domestic Policies, 1793–1806

The Lord Mayor had entertained Pitt after the victory at Trafalgar. He praised Pitt as 'the saviour of Europe' (Fig. 6.3). Pitt replied that 'Europe is not to be saved by any single man. England has saved herself by her exertions and will, I hope, save Europe by her example.' Pitt died in January 1806.

Until 1793 Pitt had been a reformer – trying to do something about the slave trade, corrupt elections, and other evils (p. 26). But once the country went to war he changed, and he persuaded Parliament to pass a series of repressive Acts. These made life difficult for anyone suspected of not supporting the government.

1793: The *Aliens Act* was meant to stop foreigners entering the country.
1794: *Habeas Corpus* was abolished. People could now be arrested, put into jail without trial and kept there as long as the government wanted. Thomas Hardy, Horne Tooke, and other members of *Cor-responding Societies* were, as the name suggests, writing letters to people in France. They were arrested. Tom Paine fled to France and some of the leaders of the Societies were sent to Botany Bay in Australia (p. 103).

1795: The *Seditious Practices Act* forbade any criticism of the King (Fig. 6.4) or the government. The *Seditious Practices Act* said that any meeting of more than fifty people was illegal.
1799: The *Combination Acts* made it illegal for men to form or join trade unions.

Napoleon, the Master of Europe

We have already seen that Pitt died in January 1806. By then Austria had left the Coalition; Prussia joined it in August 1806. But by the end of the year Napoleon's armies had defeated the Prussians in Battles at Jena and Auerstadt, so Prussia made peace with France. Russia stayed in the Coalition until July 1807. Then Napoleon met the Russian Tsar Alexander I at Tilsit, and they made peace with each other; Russia became France's ally. Britain was now more than ever on her own.

Fig. 6.4 The mob attack the King's coach in October 1795.

Questions

Extract 6.1

The Battle of Copenhagen, 1801

The action began at five minutes past ten. The contest had certainly, at one p.m. not gone in favour of either side. Lord Nelson was at that time walking the starboard side of the quarterdeck. A shot through the mainmast knocked a few splinters about us. He said, 'It is warm work and the day may be the last to any of us at a moment. But mark you I would not be anywhere else for thousands.' He now walked quickly, as could be seen from the stump of his right arm. After a turn or two he said to me, 'Do you know what's shown on board the Commander-in-Chief? No. 39.' I asked him what this meant. He answered, 'Why, to leave off action. Now damn me if I do.' He then said to Captain Foley, 'You know, Foley, I have only one eye . . .' and then putting the glass to his blind eye, he said, 'I really do not see the signal.'

(*Colonel Stewart's Narrative.*)

1.   Who was 'the Commander-in-Chief' at Copenhagen?
2.   What did the writer mean by 'No. 39'? Why did ships use coded signals. How were these sent from ship to ship?
3.   What does this extract tell you about Nelson's character?
4.   How did he pretend that he was not disobeying his Commander?
5.   What does the extract tell you about Nelson's previous injuries?
6.   Why was this battle an important one for the British people?

Fig. 6.2

1.   Why is Camperdown marked on this map? What is the importance of the battle there?
2.   Who commanded the British fleet at the Battle of St Vincent? Why was this an important battle?
3.   Why was there a battle at Copenhagen in 1801?
4.   Why were the British concerned about the possible growth of Antwerp?
5.   What was the aim of Napoleon's invasion of Egypt? Why did it fail?

Worksheet

(A)
1.   Write two sentences on the way in which each of the following thought about the French Revolution: Tom Paine; Edmund Burke; Pitt; Fox.

2.   Explain the importance of each of the following: The Edict of Fraternity; the opening of the River Scheldt.

3.   Make a list of the mistakes that Pitt made as a war leader.

4.   Make a list of the ways in which the Royal Navy was used during the war against France.

5.   Explain why people thought of 1797 as 'a year of crisis for Britain'.

6.   Why did some countries form the Armed Neutrality? Why was it a danger to Britain? How was this danger defeated?

7.   Pitt's government after 1793 has been described as 'harsh'. Do you agree? Why? What defence would Pitt have made of his policies at home?

(B)
1.   Write the letters that might have been sent by:
(a) a soldier sent to the West Indies;
(b) a sailor in the Nore in 1797;
(c) a sailor in Nelson's fleet in 1798;
(d) an Englishman living in France during the September Massacres, 1792.

(C)
1.   Write the headlines that might have appeared above reports on:
(a) the calling of the States General, 1789 – in papers controlled by Fox, Pitt, Tom Paine, and the French King;
(b) the execution of the French King, 1792 – in papers controlled by Fox, Pitt, Paine, and refugees from France;
(c) the Glorious First of June – in papers controlled by Pitt, Fox, and the French government;
(d) the formation of the First Coalition, 1793 – in papers controlled by Pitt, Fox, French refugees, and the French government;
(e) the naval mutinies – in papers controlled by Fox, Pitt, and the French government;
(f) the signing of the Peace of Amiens, 1802 – in British and French papers;
(g) the news of Trafalgar – in British and French papers;
(h) Nelson's death.

2.   Draw a poster calling for volunteers to join a regiment to fight against the French.

7 Politics after Pitt's Death, 1806-15

After Pitt died Lord Grenville became Prime Minister, and appointed Fox as Foreign Secretary. He tried to make peace with Napoleon but failed. He died in September 1806. But his supporters in the government managed to persuade Parliament to pass an Act abolishing the slave trade (March 1807). Grenville's government fell in April 1807 because the King again refused to agree to Catholic Emancipation.

The Duke of Portland was Prime Minister until 1809. His successor, Spencer Perceval, was murdered by a madman in the lobby of the House of Commons in 1812, and the Earl of Liverpool replaced him as Prime Minister. He stayed in power until his death in 1827.

The War after Pitt's death

By 1806 the war had come to a stalemate. Napoleon, with his massive army, controlled most of Europe, but was unable to invade Britain. Britain controlled the seas, but her army was much too small to launch an attack on Europe.

The Continental System

Napoleon knew that he could not invade Britain after 1805, so he decided to attack the country's trade. He said that the British were 'a nation of shopkeepers', because they bought raw materials from abroad and

Fig. 7.1 Napoleon's empire, 1810.

sold manufactured goods in exchange. By attacking her foreign trade he hoped to force Britain to make a peace.

While he was in Berlin in 1806 Napoleon issued the *Berlin Decree* which stated that British goods were not to be allowed into European ports (Fig. 7.1). After the Treaty of Tilsit in 1807 (p. 35) Russia accepted this arrangement, and after 1807 it was also extended to include Spain and Portugal (Extract 7.1).

This was known as the Continental System. In 1807 Napoleon issued the *Milan Decree* which stated that neutral ships which went to British ports would be seized by the French when they came out. Napoleon knew that if British trade could be cut down, Britain would not have the money she needed to pay her allies. Napoleon might then manage to force Britain to submit to him.

Conditions in Britain

During the war, which started in 1793, Britain's Industrial Revolution went on at an increasing rate. There was a huge demand for cannon and other guns, and the result was a vast expansion in the iron industry, with new and larger furnaces and ironworks being opened. This led to an increased demand for coal. By 1800 over 16 million tons a year were being dug out. This was the first product to measure its yearly output in millions of tons.

More industrialists used Watt's new steam-engine in their factories, ironworks, potteries, and coal-mines. The mill owners of Lancashire and Yorkshire enlarged their mills to produce the millions of uniforms needed by the Army and Navy. But better machinery meant that there was unemployment among the hand-workers (Extract 7.2).

In the Midlands and the North workmen attacked factories where new machines were installed. They were led by a mythical character called Ned Ludd; his followers were known as Luddites.

The Continental System interfered with British trade (Extract 7.1), and this led to more unemployment. But some manufacturers managed to find new markets in South America – which was to prove important in the 1820s (pp. 48 and 62).

Farmers and the War

There was a fall in the amount of grain imported into Britain once the war started. This led to a rise in the price for home-grown corn, which resulted in a rise in the price of bread.

Some farmers took advantage of the high prices for corn, and ploughed up less fertile land. It had not been worth while using this land when prices were lower.

Wages, Food and Riots

There were years when the harvests were poor – owing to bad weather; in such years (1809 and 1810) prices rose very sharply. But because of industrialization and the Continental System many workers got low wages or, worse again, were unemployed. It is not surprising that there were many cases of violent food riots (1810) and outbreaks of machine-wrecking (1810–12), even the murder of the Prime Minister (1812).

The Orders in Council

As an answer to Napoleon's Berlin and Milan Decrees the British government issued Orders in Council. These declared that all countries that agreed to the Continental System would be blockaded. The British Navy was able to make sure that these Orders were kept, and life became hard inside Napoleon's Europe. Goods became scarce, manufacturers were not able to sell their goods abroad, and unemployment spread across Europe. Napoleon had to allow goods to be smuggled in (Extract 7.1).

Portugal, 1807

If the Continental System was going to work, Napoleon had to control the coast of Portugal (Fig. 7.1). He invaded Spain, made his brother, Joseph, King of Spain and then invaded Portugal. The British sent an army to help the Portuguese.

The Spaniards were angry at the dismissal of their King and the way in which Napoleon had put his brother on their throne, and they rose against Napoleon. Even though their armies were defeated, they played a large part in the final downfall of Napoleon. If you look at a map of Spain you will see that it is a very mountainous country. There were very few and very poor roads across these mountains. This meant that the French armies in Portugal and Spain found it very difficult to keep in touch with France.

Spain was also a very poor country. The French army was used to getting its supplies from the country in which it found itself, but this was not possible in Spain. Napoleon realized that Spain was a country where large armies starve and small armies get beaten.

The hilly country also provided the Spanish people with ideal country in which to organize themselves into small groups which attacked the French armies as they struggled across the mountains. These irregular troops were known as *guerrillas* – a word which we now use in our own language.

The War, 1807–9

In June 1808 a British army was sent to help the Portuguese fight the French invaders. The army commander was Sir Arthur Wellesley, who was to become better known as the Duke of Wellington.

In August 1808 he defeated the French at Rolica and Vimiero (Fig. 7.2). The French then signed the Convention (or agreement) of Cintra, and agreed to leave Portugal. The British allowed the French army to take away all its arms and equipment. This angered people in Britain. Wellesley was recalled in disgrace – although he was not to blame for the agreement.

In his place, Sir John Moore was sent out to command the British forces, and Napoleon himself went to Spain to take charge of his French armies. The Spaniards had managed to drive Napoleon's brother from Madrid but in August 1808 Napoleon captured Madrid and put Joseph back on the Spanish throne.

Moore had been leading the British army from Portugal to help the Spaniards. When he heard about the fall of Madrid he turned to the north. He hoped to cut Napoleon's army off from its way back into France, but this failed. In January 1809 Moore led his army to Corunna where he was attacked by the French. He died in defence of the city, but he managed to get 24,000 of his army of 30,000 on to British ships and safety. This was one example of the benefit of Britain's control of the sea.

The Peninsular War after 1809

After Moore's death Napoleon left Spain to deal with Austria, and appointed Marshall Soult as commander of the French forces in Spain.

In April 1809 Wellesley returned to Portugal to lead the British forces. He had already commanded successful armies in India and had a reputation for being a very strict – but fair and good – commander.

In May 1809 he defeated Soult at Oporto. In July 1809 he won the Battle of Talavera (Fig. 7.2). After this battle he was given the title of Viscount Wellington of Talavera.

Napoleon replaced Soult with Marshall Masséna. He brought new armies from France. This forced Wellington to retreat to the lines at Torres Vedras. Here he had three strong lines of defence which Masséna was unable to break down. Behind these lines Wellington and his forces were well supplied by the British fleet. The French army, though, ran out of food and found life very hard.

Wellington and the Army

We have seen that men were kidnapped (or pressed) to provide sailors for the Royal Navy (p. 33). Soldiers were recruited in a different way. A rich man would raise his own regiment – of cavalry or of footmen. This is why, for many years, most regiments

Fig. 7.2 The Peninsular War, 1808–14.

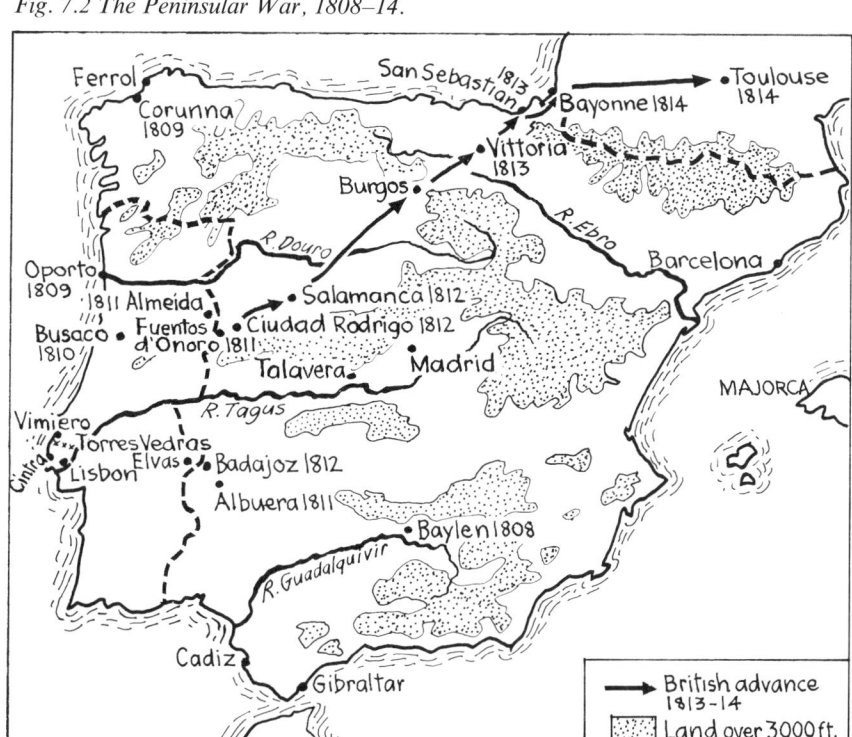

were known by the name of their 'owner', for example, Paget's Horse and Cornish's Dragoons.

The Treasury paid the 'owner' a sum of money to feed and pay the men who joined this regiment. Young men also paid him large sums of money to become officers. This buying of commissions was abolished in the 1870s.

And the ordinary soldier? He joined to get away from home, often because of unemployment. But he had a hard life. Wellington described the British Army as 'the scum of the earth'. He and other commanders felt it necessary to treat these recruits very harshly. They wanted to make sure that the men would do whatever they were told without any questioning. This helps to explain the cruelty with which they treated their men.

During their campaigns in Portugal and Spain the British troops suffered some of the shortages from which the French had already suffered. This helps to explain why, after a victory, many soldiers behaved very cruelly to the people of a captured town.

The War, 1809–13

Masséna spent the winter of 1809–10 besieging the lines of Torres Vedras. When he was forced to give up the siege because his army ran out of supplies, he retreated, and Wellington led his army out to chase Masséna. He wanted to capture Badejoz and Ciudad Rodrigo which commanded the two routes from Lisbon to Madrid. Wellington defeated Masséna at Fuentes d'Onoro (1811) and Almeida (1811) and another General, Beresford, defeated the French at Albuera (1811). In 1812 the two major fortresses were captured. The looting at Badejoz was very severe.

In August 1812 Wellington captured Madrid. He then withdrew to the frontier of Portugal to wait for the next year's campaign. There was little fighting during the winter months because of the difficulty of marching in wet, muddy conditions.

In June 1813 Wellington had a string of victories at Burgos, Vittoria, San Sebastian, and Pamplona (Fig. 7.2). The French had at last been driven out of Spain. There then followed the crossing of the Pyrenees and the pursuit of the French on their own soil.

The American War, 1812–14

As part of its campaign against the Continental System the British government insisted on the right to search merchant ships of any country. This was meant to cut down the volume of goods going to or from France.

This angered the Americans. They insisted on their right to trade with anyone they liked, and declared war on the British. But they had another, very important, reason for going to war. They hoped to use this chance to invade and capture Canada.

In 1813 the Americans invaded Toronto and set fire to the city. In 1814 the British Army attacked and burnt Washington, including the President's house. To hide the marks of the fire the Americans used whitewash. This is why this house became known as the White House.

There were several naval encounters in which the Americans showed that they were better sailors than the British. But they did not have enough ships to do any harm to the over-all British effort. Also, people on both sides did not really have their hearts in the war. Everyone preferred to trade rather than to fight. In 1814 peace was restored between the two countries by the signing of the Peace of Ghent.

Napoleon and Russia, 1812–15

Napoleon described the Peninsular War as 'the Spanish ulcer' which drained away men and supplies. Even more disastrous, however, was his Russian campaign. In 1812 the Russian Tsar, Alexander I, decided that he had to trade with Britain. He could no longer accept the Continental System.

Napoleon took 250,000 men into Russia in June 1812. He won a costly victory at Borodino and fought his way to Moscow which he entered in September 1812. Much to his surprise, however, he found the city deserted – the Russians had gone. So in October, as the snow started to fall, Napoleon led his men back towards France. During their retreat his men were attacked by Russian guerrillas, suffered because of the hard winter, and died in large numbers.

A Fourth Coalition

In 1813 the British Foreign Secretary, Lord Castlereagh, arranged a Coalition between Russia, Austria, Prussia, and Britain. Britain would supply the money to arm her allies. Wellington's army won a victory at Toulouse (Fig. 7.2). The European Allies defeated the French at the Battle of the Nations at Leipzig in October 1813 and both the British and her Allies marched towards Paris.

Paris fell to the Allies on 31 March 1814. In April Napoleon gave up the French throne and went into exile on the island of Elba. The Allies then sat down to arrange a peace treaty. In January 1815 the various diplomats and peacemakers went to Vienna to continue their discussions so that the peace treaty is generally described as one made by the *Congress of Vienna*.

But in March 1815 Napoleon escaped from Elba and returned in triumph to France. He reached Paris in March. The Allies had to give up their peacemaking and turn again to the fighting.

In June Napoleon left Paris to advance into the Netherlands. Here he was outnumbered by allied troops led by the Prussian, Blücher, and the Duke of Wellington. On 18 June the armies met at Waterloo. After a hard fight Napoleon's army was defeated. He returned to Paris. Once more he gave up his throne, but this time the Allies sentenced him to exile on the lonely island of St Helena where he died on 5 May 1821.

The Congress of Vienna

We have to understand something of this Congress if we are going to understand British foreign policy after 1815. The Allies wanted to make sure that France would not rise again to make war on Europe. It was for this reason that the son of the last King was put on the throne. They also put back on their thrones all those older rulers who had lost their thrones to Napoleon. This, it was hoped, would prevent the growth of liberalism or revolution in those countries.

The Allies also strengthened the countries that had boundaries with France. Austria gave up her territory in the Netherlands; this was joined to Holland to form a larger, stronger country. Prussia, another ally, was given large territories on the River Rhine. Austria was given Lombardy and Venetia in the north-east of Italy – to make sure that France would not be able to invade that country.

The British pretended that they wanted no territorial rewards for their part in the wars. In fact, as we have seen, they had already made their gains. They had the former French West Indian islands of St Lucia, Tobago, and Trinidad. They had also taken from Holland the Cape of Good Hope, Mauritius, and Ceylon. In the Mediterranean they held on to Malta and in the North Sea they kept Heligoland (Fig. 7.1). Britain had done well out of the war – at least in territory. The next chapter discusses how the war and the peace affected life in Britain.

Questions

Extract 7.1

The Continental System; Report of a Select Committee, 1812

Can you tell the Committee what was the state of trade between 1808 and 1811? – In 1807 we felt the effect of the Berlin Decree; we were excluded from the Continent. In 1807 we had trade with the South of Europe, particularly Portugal which was ended by the French invasion of that year. In 1808 trade revived; many goods were taken in through Heligoland; many exports were made to the Baltic and trade increased in the Mediterranean. A very large trade opened up when the Portuguese Royal Family fled to Brazil. In 1809 trade through Heligoland was very great. Napoleon had his hands full and had no time to attend to the coast; during that year trade was uninterrupted. And trade to South America was very great. What has been the state of trade for the last eighteen months? – Very depressed; for the last year it has been recovering but for the previous six months it was very depressed.

What do you blame for that depression? – We think it was due to the effect of the Berlin and Milan Decrees.

1. What was the Berlin Decree? Who issued it and what did he intend it to do?
2. How did Britain reply to this Decree?
3. Where was Heligoland (Fig. 7.1)? Why was it important? Which other islands were used in this way by the British?
4. Why did the Portuguese royal family leave their country in 1808? Why did they go to Brazil?
5. How did this affect British trade with South America?
6. From this extract can you say whether Napoleon's Continental System worked as he meant it to?

Extract 7.2

A Select Committee on the Woollen Trade, 1802–3

(John Collins called in and examined.)
Where do you live?
At King's Stanley in Gloucestershire.
Which Parish Office do you serve?
The Office of the Overseer.
Do you know if any weavers have been out of work?
They have.
Has their number been considerable?
Sometimes they have not had work for a month or two, they then ask for Parish Relief.

When is work more slack than normal?
Generally, the autumn time of the year is more slack than the spring. They cannot work when it is a severe frost.
How high have the Poor Rates been?
They are double what they were twelve years ago.
You say that since the spinning-machines were introduced there have been more weavers. Former spinners became weavers. Are they not better off?
There is an overflow of hands. There were 170 looms not working in January.
Is not cloth for the Army made in that district?
Yes.
I suppose that many looms went out as soon as the Peace was signed?
That might be the case.

1. Why was there normally more unemployment among weavers in the autumn than the spring?
2. How did the invention of spinning-machines affect employment among weavers in Gloucestershire?
3. How might the rise in food prices have affected the level of the Poor Rates? What other reason can you give for the rise in these Rates?
4. Which Peace is referred to in this extract? How did it affect the weavers?
5. Why was there a drop in overseas orders for British cloth after 1793? How did this affect the employment of weavers in Gloucestershire?
6. Why was Gloucestershire a centre of cloth-making? How was employment there affected by the growth of the woollen industry in Yorkshire?

Fig. 7.1

1. Make a list of the countries that were affected by the Continental System.
2. Why were the British anxious to smuggle goods into Europe?
3. Why did Napoleon agree to allow this smuggling?
4. Why could Britain enforce a blockade of Europe? How did this affect (i) supplies, and (ii) prices in Europe?
5. Which countries broke with the Continental System in 1807 and 1812?
6. Explain the importance of the attack on the Danish navy in 1807.

Worksheet

1. Make a list of the ways in which the Royal Navy was used in the wars against Napoleon.

2. Write two sentences on each of the following: Berlin Decree; Orders in Council; Luddites.

3. Show how and why the long period of war affected Britain's industrial development. (Were there some industries that lost trade? Were there others that got more orders than they might otherwise have done?)

4. Explain why there was a rise in unemployment after 1805. Why was unemployment particularly high during 1812–14?

5. Why was there an increase in food production during the war? How did this benefit (i) the farmers, and (ii) the landowners?

6. Explain why (i) Russia, and (ii) Portugal disobeyed Napoleon's decisions which are known as the Continental System. How did Napoleon try to deal with each of these countries?

7. Why did Britain go to war against the United States of America in 1812? Write two sentences on (i) the war on land, and (ii) the war at sea.

8. Make a list of the territories gained by Britain as a result of the wars.

(B)
1. Write the letters that might have been sent by:
(a) a soldier who had watched the burial of Sir John Moore in Portugal;
(b) a French soldier during the Peninsular War;
(c) a British soldier after the capture of Badajoz;
(d) from Vienna after Napoleon's return in 1815.

2. Make a time chart for the years 1804–15, using the dates and events mentioned in the text. Write a line to explain why each date or event was important.

(C)
1. Write the headlines that might have appeared above reports on:
(a) the Continental System – in French, British, Russian and Portuguese papers;
(b) the food riots, 1810 – in papers controlled by the government, the Whigs, and the Radicals;
(c) the murder of the Prime Minister, Perceval – in papers controlled by the government, the Whigs, the Radicals, the French;
(d) Napoleon's return from Elba – in British and French papers.

2. Draw a poster that might have been sent out by a group of Luddites.

8 Government and People, 1815-22

Paying for the War

When the war started the National Debt was about £280 million. We saw on p. 26 how Pitt tried to bring that figure down through the work of the Sinking Fund. But in 1815 the government's borrowing (or the National Debt) had risen to £834 million. In 1789 the government had to pay about £9 million in interest on the money it had borrowed. In 1815 this yearly interest was £31 million. The government had to collect a large amount in taxation each year to pay this interest.

The End of the War and Unemployment

As soon as the war ended the government cancelled all its orders for guns, cannon, clothing, ships, and other supplies. Employers in the iron, engineering, textile and other industries employed large numbers of people. The cancelling of orders led to a great increase in the number of these workers being sacked. So there was a rise in the level of unemployment.

The people who worked in these war-based industries were well-paid. When they were working they spent their wages on food, clothing, housing, and other necessities. After being sacked they had no income because there was no social security system such as we have today. They could not buy clothes and other goods. This meant that employers in the clothing and other industries could not sell as much of their output. So they too had to sack many people.

Ex-soldiers, Ex-sailors and the Irish

As soon as the war ended the government dismissed about 500,000 soldiers and sailors from the forces. They joined the many thousands of unemployed who once worked in gun-making and other war-based industries.

In addition, there was another large group of people looking for work. These were the thousands of Irishmen and women who came from Ireland in the hope that they would find work in one of Britain's booming industries.

Industrialization and Unemployment

Britain's industries, however, were unable to provide work for all these unemployed people. The efficient rotary steam-engine worked new and better machines. Children were able to work the factory-based machines. So thousands of former hand-workers found that they could not get work. This had been happening ever since the first machine was invented and it continued after the war. Obviously, this meant a rise in the number of people out of work.

Agriculture, Machinery and Unrest

As already seen (p. 38) British farmers did well during the long war; they received high prices for their produce. Many of them ploughed up less fertile land so that they could increase their output as much as possible.

But once the war ended there was a drop in the demand for food. The government no longer bought large supplies for the Army and Navy; the unemployed workers could no longer afford as much as they had done. So there was a drop in demand – and this led to a fall in prices. Farmers therefore received a much smaller income after the war than during it.

This led them to cut the wages paid to their labourers. Many farmers also sacked their men and employed Irish workers who were willing to take much lower wages. Other farmers bought threshing-machines so that they did not need to employ labourers to thresh the corn during the winter months.

There was a good deal of unemployment, therefore, in agricultural counties after 1815. The angry agricultural workers had their own form of Luddite movement (p. 38). They burned stacks, attacked threshing-machines and maimed animals in their fury. This unrest came to a head in 1830 when a mythical Captain Swing led the labourers of the farming counties in the South and South-East. Many labourers were sent to gaol; others were sentenced to prison in Australia (p. 103).

Wages and Living Conditions

Therefore, in both town and country there was a high level of unemployment. Even for those who had work the level of wages was very low. This meant that the majority of people were unable to afford to pay rent for a whole house – so they rented only a room or two, living in overcrowded houses which quickly became slums. Nor could they afford decent clothes, shoes, or food. It is not surprising that the people living in such terrible conditions were willing to listen to those who promised to make life better for them (p. 45).

Wages and Prices

The fall in the demand for iron, coal, clothing, and other products led to a fall in their prices. This meant that many manufacturers closed their works, mines, or mills. The drop in prices meant that businessmen who might have been thinking of building a new factory or mill decided not to do so. Thus there was a check to Britain's industrial progress.

There was a sharp drop in the price of corn – partly because of the end of the government's demand for supplies for the Army and Navy, but mainly because of the very good harvests of 1815 and 1816. This led to a drop in the price of bread – which, it might be thought, would have been good news for the people (Fig. 8.1). But it was not so. In 1815 a loaf of bread

weighing 4 lb cost one shilling and four pence (about 8p). If you weigh a loaf at home you will find that it weighs about $1\frac{3}{4}$ lbs, so we can say that about $2\frac{1}{4}$ modern loaves cost about 8p. But the farm-workers only earned about 55p a week and the mill-hands about 75p a week. If you compare this with the price of bread you will see that a farm-worker was paid about 14 loaves a week and the town worker about 21 loaves.

Taxation and Living Standards

In 1798 Pitt had brought in a 'temporary tax' on incomes from land, trade, professions, pensions, or employment. This tax had to be paid by anyone earning more than £60 a year. Therefore, anyone earning £70 a year had to pay tax on £10 and anyone earning £100 paid tax on £30. People earning higher incomes paid about 10 per cent of their taxable income to the government.

This tax was therefore paid by the well-to-do: rich farmers, landowners, owners of mines, mills, and other factories. As soon as the war ended Parliament decided that the tax had been a wartime necessity, and that now the war was over there was no need for the tax to continue.

But, as we have seen, the government still had to find a lot of money to pay for the increased interest on the larger National Debt. Since the government was not going to take it directly from the better-off, it had

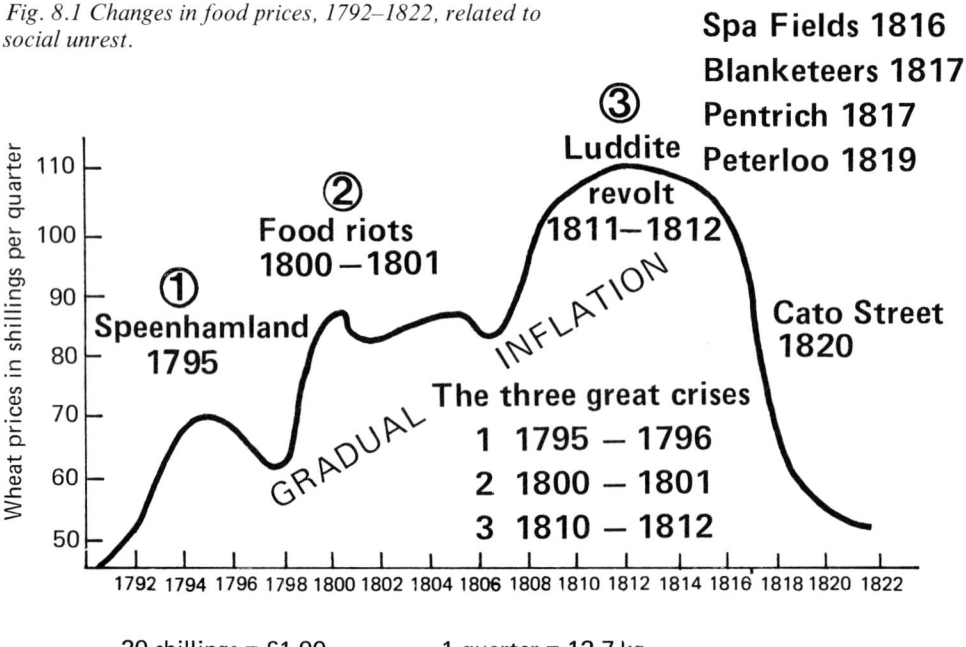

Fig. 8.1 Changes in food prices, 1792–1822, related to social unrest.

20 shillings = £1.00   1 quarter = 12.7 kg

to get it indirectly by putting taxes on all sorts of goods. Salt, sugar, candles, tea and other goods were taxed. The poor bought these goods if they could. Therefore it was the poor who paid the taxes which were needed to pay interest to the better-off who had loaned their money to the government.

These taxes put up the cost of living – and pushed down the standards of living of the ordinary people.

Corn Laws

Parliament was controlled by the landowners – which helps to explain why it decided to abolish income tax. It also helps to explain why it passed the Corn Laws.

In 1812 farmers had been able to get £6.35 for each 28 lb sack of corn they took to market. This was a very high price (Fig. 8.1). Good harvests in 1815 and 1816 led to a large amount of corn being brought to market, but there was also a lower demand for corn in the hard years of 1815 and 1816. This led to a drop in the prices which farmers could get for their produce. In 1815 they only got £2.37 for each 28lb sack of wheat.

Many farmers had agreed to pay high rents to landowners – lower prices meant that they could not afford those rents. So landowners were also facing a drop in income. They used their power in Parliament to pass the Corn Laws. These stated that no foreign corn should be allowed into Britain until the price of home-grown corn had reached £4 for 28 lbs. This meant that bread prices were kept higher than they would have been if there had been a free importation of corn. Because people had to spend more on bread they therefore had less money to spend on other things. This meant that there was a drop in the demand for clothes, furniture, and other products. This resulted in a slow-down in the process of industrialization.

The People Demonstrate in 1815–22

We have seen that there was a Luddite movement in industry in 1811 and 1813 (p. 38), and that there was a Captain Swing movement in the agricultural counties in 1830 (p. 43). These were the angry people's answer to the conditions of pay, work, and living. But there were many other examples of the people's anger at their conditions in post-war Britain.

In 1816 there were riots in London while the Corn Bill was being discussed in Parliament, and food riots in many towns throughout the country. Luddites destroyed machinery; miners in Wales rioted against a cut in wages; and the unemployed rioted in Birmingham and other towns. There was also a riot

after a meeting at Spa Fields in London.

In 1817 unemployed workers marched from Manchester hoping to make their way to London where they wanted to ask the government for help. They carried blankets in which they were going to sleep at night. However, these *Blanketeers* only reached Derby before returning home – empty-handed.

In Derby itself there was a Luddite rising by the unemployed workers, but this was put down by the Army. Three of the leaders were hanged and eleven more were sent to prison in Australia – for life.

When the Prince Regent was on his way to open Parliament the mob attacked him – as they had his father in 1795 (Fig. 6.4 on p. 35). This greatly alarmed the government and it announced that it was suspending the *Habeas Corpus Act*. This meant that suspected trouble-makers could now be arrested and kept in prison without trial.

In 1819 there was wide-scale unrest (Fig. 8.2). The most famous event took place in St Peter's Field in

Fig. 8.2 Postwar Britain, 1815–22.

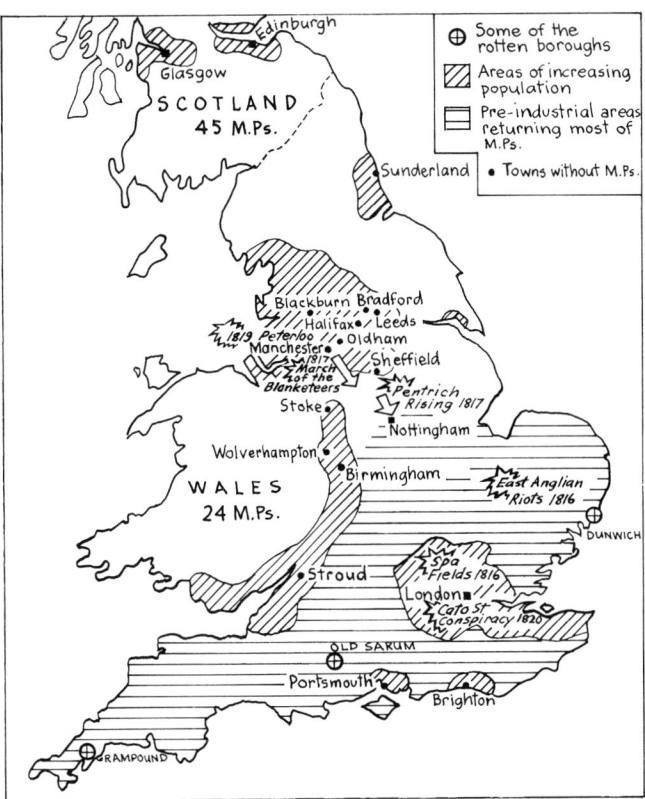

Manchester. Henry Hunt, one of the leaders of the popular movement, went there to speak to the workers from the cotton towns of Lancashire. He and others like him thought that life would be better if working-class people were elected to Parliament. Many thousands came to hear Hunt, and the size of the crowd frightened the Manchester magistrates. They ordered the local Yeomanry to disperse the crowd. Eleven people were killed, and hundreds were injured. In mockery of the name Waterloo this became known as the Peterloo massacre (see illustration on the front cover).

The Government and the Unrest

The government seemed to have no idea of the way in which the majority of people lived. Most of the ministers in government were landowners who knew nothing about conditions in industrial towns. Nor did they think that the government ought to do anything about the poor living standards, the harsh working conditions, the low wages, and the high level of unemployment. Indeed they seemed to go out of their way to make things even worse for the ordinary people. The Corn Laws kept the price of bread higher than it might have been. The indirect taxes pushed up prices of goods. There were severe Game Laws passed in 1816 which were aimed against poachers. Anyone caught with a net for catching rabbits or a fishing-net was to be sentenced to seven years' gaol in Australia – even if he had not actually done any poaching.

The suspension of Habeas Corpus and the use of the Army against the demonstrations of the workers and unemployed showed that the government hoped to crush the people's anger by violent methods.

The Six Acts, 1819

After Peterloo the government passed a series of Acts which are sometimes called the Gag Acts. One of these made it illegal for anyone to try to train a private army or give military training to people. Another made it illegal to hold meetings, such as the one in St Peter's Field. A third allowed magistrates and judges to punish very severely anyone who wrote an article or a pamphlet critical of the government. A fourth imposed a stamp tax (p. 19) of 2p on every newspaper or pamphlet. This would put up the prices of such papers, and it was hoped that fewer would be sold. A fifth Act allowed magistrates to order a search of any house where they thought there might be weapons; and a sixth Act made it easier for the government to get criminals sentenced in court.

The Opposition to a Harsh Government

Ever since the death of Fox in 1806 (p. 37) the Whig Party had been a small, almost frightened, party. It was unable to make much of a protest against the way in which the country was being governed.

It was left to a small group of men outside Parliament to show that change and reform were needed. These men were called *Radicals* from the Latin word *radex* meaning root. They wanted to make very great changes – from the roots up. Robert Owen, a factory owner, wanted to bring in laws against the employment of young children in factories. Francis Place, a Charing Cross tailor, wanted to make it legal for men to form trade unions. Henry Hunt wanted to change the electoral system so that everyone had a vote. Maybe the most important Radical was William Cobbett, the son of a farmworker. In 1802 he started the *Weekly Register*, a Radical newspaper, but in 1810 he was fined £1,000 and sent to gaol for two years for having criticized flogging in the Army. In 1816 he reduced the price of his paper from 5p to 1p so that it escaped the stamp duty, and it became a widely read newspaper. He and other Radicals thought that the unreformed Parliament was unable to cope with the problems of a more modern Britain.

In February 1820 Arthur Thistlewood and some other extremists plotted to murder the whole Cabinet while the ministers were at dinner. These Radicals were arrested in Cato Street in Marylebone, London. Five of them, including Thistlewood, were hanged, five others were sent to prison for life in Australia. This was called the Cato Street conspiracy and was a last attempt at resistance by the Radicals who were suppressed by the working of the Six Acts.

Questions

Extract 8.1

The Speenhamland System 1795

Resolved.
... that the Magistrates will make the following allowances for the relief of all poor and industrious men

and their families, who endeavour (as far as they can) for their own support and maintenance.

That is to say,

When the Loaf weighing 8 lb 11 oz shall cost 1s. [5p] then every poor and industrious man shall have for his own support 3s. [15p] weekly, either produced by his own or his family's labour, or from the poor rates, and for the support of his wife and every other of his family, 1s. 6d. [7½p].

When the Loaf cost 1s. 4d. [7p]

Then every poor and industrious man shall have 4s. [20p] weekly for his own, and 1s. and 10d. [9p] for the support of every other of his family.

And so in proportion, as the price of bread rise or falls (that is to say) 3d. [just over 1p] to the man and a 1d. to every other of the family, on every 1d. which the loaf rises above 1s. [5p].

(*The Reading Mercury*, 11 May 1795.)

1. Why was there a rise in food prices after 1793?
2. Why did labourers' wages not keep up with this rise in prices?
3. How were the magistrates going to help the lowly paid workers and their families? How would this affect the level of the poor rates?
4. Why did this system encourage some employers not to put up their workers' wages? How did it affect the married man's decision on the number of children he would have?
5. Why did this system help the large-scale farmer more than the small-scale farmer?
6. Why was this system more widespread in agricultural areas than in industrial areas?

Fig. 8.1

1. What was the price of 1 lb of wheat in 1795? 1801? 1813? (One quarter equals 28 lbs.)
2. How do you explain these rises in the price of wheat after 1792?
3. How did Speenhamland affect the price of food (Extract 8.1)?
4. Why were there food riots during this period?
5. What was the aim of the Luddites?
6. What happened at Cato Street in 1820?

Worksheet

(A)

1. Make a list of the reasons why there was a rise in the level of unemployment in 1815. Show clearly (i) industrial development (ii) the end of the war. Which of these were a result of government policy?

2. Explain why some farmers did better during the war than they did in peacetime. (You might want to use the following words as guide-lines: marginal land; imports of food; high prices; government orders.)

3. Why were many working-class families living in poor housing conditions in 1820? Make a short list of the other ways in which the working class suffered at this time. (Wages? Diet? Prices? Taxes? Clothing? Employment? Unions?)

4. Why did the government have to collect more in taxation in 1820 than in 1790? Why did this affect the working class more than the richer people?

(B)

1. Write the letters that might have been sent by:
(a) a former soldier looking for work in 1815;
(b) one of the Blanketeers;
(c) Henry Hunt, after Peterloo.

2. Imagine that a child from a nineteenth-century working-class family has been brought into your home today. Make a list of the things that he would be surprised at. (Clothes; food; furniture; house; machinery in the home; your going to school, and so on.)

(C)

1. Write the headlines that might have appeared above reports on:
(a) the cancellation of a government order for clothing or munitions in the locality;
(b) the abolition of income tax – in papers controlled by the government and by the Radicals;
(c) the increase in taxes on goods (candles, salt, etc.);
(d) the Corn Laws – in papers controlled by factory owners, landowners, and by Radicals.

2. Draw posters that might have been used to:
(a) warn people about Captain Swing;
(b) inform people about the Corn Laws;
(c) inform people about the Game Laws;
(d) inform people about the Six Acts.

9 A New Approach, 1822-30

An Improving Economy

By 1822 there was a revival of foreign trade. Industrialists, mill owners, and others were busy producing the goods being sold to India, Canada, and the colonies in the West Indies. Trade with the United States of America recovered and there was a very great trade with the Spanish and Portuguese colonies in South America (Extract 7.1 on p. 41). A new colony grew in Australia as a result of trade. Once the home of 'convicts and kangaroos', Australia was becoming an important source of wool. The sheep farmers spent most of their money on goods imported from Britain.

Once industralists began to produce for the foreign market, they had to employ more workers. This meant more employment, higher wages – and a rise in the demand for goods at home. This had happened before (p. 2). This second revival in home trade was almost a repeat of the beginnings of the Industrial Revolution.

A More Contented People

A good deal of the unrest in the previous period (1815–22) had been the result of unemployment and low wages. After 1822 there was a slight improvement in people's living conditions, but this improvement must not be exaggerated. Many people still worked for low wages and lived in terrible conditions (Fig. 9.1). But there was a drop in the numbers out of work, and there was some improvement in the wages

Fig. 9.1 A family home at 12 Southern Street, Liverpool Road, Manchester. Millions of people lived in conditions like this.

being paid to certain workers – in the coal, iron, textile, and engineering industries.

At the same time there was a drop in the cost of bread and other goods. This meant that there was a rise in living standards. Even so, many workers still had a poor diet, worked long hours, and earned little money. But this was some improvement on the way they had lived in the years of heavy unemployment.

No Fear of Revolution

From 1793 onwards many people in Parliament and government had been afraid that there might be a revolution in Britain.

So the government passed a series of Acts to make it very difficult for leaders of popular discontent.

After 1820 there was a drop in the number of demonstrations and riots. Maybe this was because people now had work. Maybe it was because of their fear of the Six Acts and other repressive Acts of Parliament.

Whatever the reason, there were fewer signs of unrest. This gave some members of the government a chance to think about finding longer-term solutions to the many problems facing industrialized Britain.

Some of them could see that the government could not simply go on trying to hold down the people by the Six Acts. There had to be a better way of governing the country.

A New Government

Fortunately for the country's future, a number of new men were brought into the government in 1822. Sidmouth, the strict Home Secretary, resigned from office; and almost at the same time, Castlereagh, the Foreign Secretary, committed suicide. His successor was George Canning. We will see more of him in Chapter 10, but we ought to note here that he was more of a liberal than Castlereagh had been.

Lord Liverpool remained Prime Minister, but now he was influenced by Canning and not by the harsher Castlereagh. It was this new influence that helps explain why William Huskisson was asked to become President of the Board of Trade, Robert Peel was asked to become Home Secretary, and 'Prosperity' Robinson became Chancellor of the Exchequer.

The Death Penalty

One of Peel's first tasks was to tackle the system of law and order. In 1822 people could be hanged for over 100 crimes. Other people had tried to get Parliament to change this law. Samuel Romilly brought a Bill to Parliament in 1808 which would have changed the law that pickpockets should be hanged; but Parliament threw this Bill out. So people continued to be hanged for stealing articles worth about 25p, for scribbling on Westminster Bridge, and other minor offences.

In 1818 another M.P., James Mackintosh, took up the case for a change in these laws. He proved that many juries refused to find a man guilty because they did not believe that someone should be hanged for a small crime. He also showed that a man committing a minor offence might even murder if he thought that someone would give him away. 'As well to be hanged for a sheep as a lamb' was a proverb of the time.

So Peel had a lot of support when, in 1823, he proposed the abolition of the death penalty for over 100 crimes. Later on there were other changes in the law, and after 1838 people could only be hanged for murder and for treason.

Prison and Legal Reform

Peel also accepted the evidence that Elizabeth Fry and John Howard had produced about the harsh conditions in British prisons. They had shown that prisons were badly run and disease-ridden. Peel ordered that gaolers were to be paid by the government – so that they did not have to depend on money given by prisoners; magistrates were to inspect prisons; and women prisoners were separated from men. Each prison was to have a chaplain and teachers to give some basic education to prisoners.

The First Police Force

The government had previously relied on paid informers to spy on suspected people and to help get them arrested. Peel ended this system, but he was aware of the danger of popular unrest and of crime. There had been a number of risings and riots that had made life difficult in many towns. Outside the towns highwaymen attacked people moving from place to place. During elections there were many examples of the mob getting out of hand.

In 1829 Peel formed the Metropolitan Police Force with its headquarters at Scotland Yard, and appointed 3,000 policemen who were paid £1.05 each week. This reminds us of the value of money at the time. This force was allowed to work only in London; other boroughs could only form similar forces after the passing of the Act that reformed municipal corporations in 1835 (p. 73). However, the level of crime continued to increase in Britain's towns and cities. Some believed that this was a result of poverty; Peel believed that it was because of a few evil people.

Free Trade

William Huskisson, President of the Board of Trade, and George Canning (Fig. 11.2 on p. 61) were both M.P.s for Liverpool. They each knew about the importance of trade to the prosperity of that port (Extract 9.1).

Peel was the son of an important cotton manufacturer, and knew how important it was that Britain (and his father) should sell goods abroad.

We have already seen that Pitt tried to lower the level of import and export taxes (p. 25). By 1822 this was even more important than it had been in the 1780s. Britain was now the world's leading industrial country.

In 1824 the Chancellor, Robinson, brought in a budget which lowered import taxes on raw wool and raw silk. Later he lowered the import taxes on cotton, lines, woollen goods, coffee, cocoa, paper, lead, and iron. All this led to a fall in prices, which made it easier to sell British goods abroad. It also led to a rise in employment. As goods were cheaper, living standards in Britain rose.

Huskisson then brought in a series of Acts that reduced the tax on all imported manufactured goods to 20 per cent and the tax on raw materials to only 10 per cent. This lowered prices further.

Reciprocity Act 1825

We have seen that Pitt arranged a treaty with France by which both countries agreed to lower the taxes each charged on goods imported from the other one. Huskisson took this a stage further. He persuaded Parliament to pass an Act in 1825 which gave him the power to make similar arrangements with any other country. This Act also allowed him to negotiate a change in the Navigation Acts (p. 18), so that goods could be brought from foreign countries in foreign ships. This led to an increase in British trade with foreign countries; and this increase, like the others, led to increased employment, higher wages, larger profits – and a richer Britain.

Huskisson insisted that trade between countries in the British Empire was to be in British-owned ships only. He was not prepared to repeal the Navigation Acts altogether, and they were not abolished until 1849.

Huskisson and Trade Unions, 1824–5

Until 1824 British workmen were not allowed to

emigrate. The government was frightened that they might take abroad the secrets of the steam-engine and other machines. By 1824 Britain was confident enough of her lead in industry to think about changing this law.

Huskisson set up a Committee of the House of Commons to examine this law. Joseph Hume, M.P., and Francis Place (p. 46) persuaded him to allow the Committee to look also at the question of trade unions which had been made illegal by the Combination Acts of 1799 (p. 106).

The Committee decided that workmen should be allowed to form unions and the Combination Acts were repealed. However, there followed a rush of strikes in 1824, and this led the government to pass a law in 1825 that made strikes illegal.

Huskisson and Corn

Since 1815 there had been a campaign against the Corn Laws. Manufacturers argued that these laws kept the price of bread too high. This forced them to pay higher wages than they would have paid if there had been no such Acts. They also argued that if Huskisson was going to lower the duties on imports of manufactured goods and raw materials he ought, at least, to lower the tax on imported corn. Workmen's leaders, such as Place and Hume, argued that the high price of bread meant that working people had less money to spend on other things. This led them to have a lower standard of living, and meant that they had less money to spend on other goods – which meant a lower level of employment in other industries.

Huskisson knew this, but he was afraid to try to abolish the Corn Laws. After all, he was a member of a government that was controlled by a Parliament of landowners. He did suggest, though, that when the price of British corn rose (because of a poor harvest or a high demand for corn) the tax on imported corn should be cut. If the price of British corn fell (because of a good harvest in Britain) then this tax should rise. This would have given the British farmer a fairly safe market and sure income. It would also have led to a fall in the price of bread, at least during years of bad harvests.

But the landowners would not agree. So, in 1828 Huskisson resigned from the government.

Canning, Huskisson, and the Catholics

Corn was not the only major question of the time. We have seen that in 1801 (p. 27) and 1807 (p. 37) there had been attempts to allow Catholics the same rights as other people. However, these efforts had failed.

In 1827 Lord Liverpool died, and George Canning became Prime Minister. Canning let it be known that he would bring in a Bill to allow Catholics the same rights as other people.

The Chief Secretary in Ireland from 1812 until he joined the government in 1822 had been Peel. He had come under the influence of Protestants of Ireland who were frightened at the idea of freedom for Catholics. So he resigned from the government in 1827, as did the Duke of Wellington.

Huskisson, Canning's supporter, was delighted that the Catholics would have their freedom. Unfortunately, Canning died after only six months in office, and was succeeded by Robinson. After a short time Robinson resigned, and Wellington was asked to form a government.

Wellington and the Catholics

Wellington's family was a Protestant family which owned a lot of land in Catholic Ireland. Therefore, he was against Catholic Emançipation. Knowing this, Peel rejoined the government, and it seemed that Catholics would not get their rights. So Huskisson resigned, and when he did so he took with him a number of other men who had followed Canning. Lord Palmerston, (Chapters 16 and 17) and William Lamb, later Lord Melbourne, (Chapters 12 and 13) were two of the important Tories who left their party over the Catholic question in 1827–8.

Wellington did agree to the repeal of the Test and Corporation Acts. These stated that anyone who held a government job, or was a member of a town council, an Army officer, a lawyer, or a member of any such society, had to take communion in an Anglican church. This meant that Non-conformists, Jews, and Catholics could not get on in these societies and occupations. After 1828 these restrictions were lifted, but the law that stated that Catholics could not become M.P.s remained.

Daniel O'Connell and the Clare Election

In 1823 a Catholic lawyer, Daniel O'Connell, started a campaign for Catholic Emancipation, and formed the Catholic Association. Every Irishman was expected to join and to pay ½d each week to its funds. This money was collected at the Sunday masses in the Catholic churches in Ireland. This gave O'Connell

Fig. 9.2 Wellington, standing in the doorway of the House of Commons, urges the Speaker of the House to keep O'Connell (the shuttlecock) out of Parliament even though he has been elected as an M.P.

£1,000 a month to spend on pamphlets, speakers' expenses, and other things needed to run a campaign throughout Ireland.

In 1828 there was a by-election in County Clare in Ireland, and O'Connell put himself forward as a candidate. Not surprisingly the Catholic voters gave him a huge majority, but the law said he could not go to the House of Commons (Fig. 9.2).

Wellington, Peel and O'Connell

What was Wellington to do? If he refused to let O'Connell in, there was a danger of civil war in Ireland; Wellington had seen the cruelty and harm done by guerrilla wars in Spain (Chapter 7).

So, very reluctantly, he agreed that the law should be changed, and O'Connell allowed to take his seat as M.P. for Clare. In 1829 Parliament passed the Emancipation Act.

The Fall of the Tories

In 1828 Wellington had lost the support of Huskisson and other Canningites, by refusing to agree to Emancipation. In 1829 he also lost the support of those Tories opposed to Emancipation. One challenged him to a duel; others used their votes in the Commons to bring down the government. They had been unable to do this over Emancipation because Wellington's government had the votes of the Whigs and the Canningites. But on 15 November 1830 the government lost a vote on government spending and taxation. Wellington was forced to resign.

A New King, a New Age and a New Government

George IV died in June 1830, and was succeeded by his brother, William IV. It was William IV who had to accept the resignation of Wellington in November 1830, and it was William IV who had to ask the Whig leader, Earl Grey, to form a Whig government. This was the government that brought in a number of important reforms (Chapter 12), and began a new stage in British history.

In 1830 the Liverpool–Manchester Railway was opened (Fig. 9.3). This was the longest railway line ever planned at that time, and it linked two of the most important towns in the country (Extract 9.1). Its opening reminds us that the Industrial Revolution was also entering a new stage in 1830. Once again, politics and industrial development were marching hand in hand.

Fig. 9.3 Excavating at Olive Mount on the Liverpool–Manchester Railway.

Questions

Extract 9.1

Manchester and Liverpool, 1833

Manchester. The great manufacturing city is famous for cloth, thread, cotton ... as is Birmingham for iron, copper, steel. Favourable circumstances; ten leagues from the largest port in England, which is the best-placed port in Europe for receiving raw materials from America safely and quickly. Close by the largest coal-mines to keep the machines going cheaply. Twenty-five leagues away, the place where the best machines in the world are made. Three canals and a railway quickly carry the products all over England, and over the whole world.

The employers are helped by science, industry, the love of gain and English capital. So it is not surprising that Manchester already has 300,000 inhabitants and is growing at a prodigious rate.

Liverpool. Town destined to become the centre of English trade. A fisherman's harbour three centuries ago. A small town sixty years ago. The slave trade, basis of its commercial greatness. It carried slaves to the Spanish colonies at better prices than all the others. The foundation of the United States, the manufacturing

development of Manchester and Birmingham, and the spread of English trade over the whole world, have done the rest. Liverpool is a beautiful town. Poverty is almost as great as it is at Manchester, but it is hidden. Fifty thousand poor people live in cellars. Sixty thousand Irish Catholics.
(Alexis de Tocqueville, *Journeys to England and Ireland*, 1833.)

1.   Why was cotton manufacture concentrated in Manchester? What else helped the growth of Manchester? Why was Birmingham the centre of the metal trade?
2.   Which was the largest port in England? Which was the next largest? Which was the most important raw material received from America?
3.   Which was 'the place where the best machines in the world are made'?
4.   How do you account for the rapid growth of Liverpool?
5.   Why did people live in cellars in Liverpool? What effects did this have on their health and way of life?

Fig. 9.1

1.   Why did working people have to live near their place of work in the 1820s and 1830s?
2.   Why could they afford to pay only a low rent for their houses?
3.   How did this affect (i) the sort of housing a builder was willing to put up, and (ii) the overcrowding of these houses?
4.   How do you explain the presence of large numbers of children in the growing industrial towns?

Worksheet

(A)
1.   Explain why there were more people at work in 1822 than in 1816. Why did that lead to a rise in living standards?

2.   Make a list of the reforms by which Peel changed the criminal, legal, and prison systems.

3.   Explain how Huskisson's tariff cuts led to (i) more employment, and (ii) a rise in living standards.

4.   Give the arguments used (i) for, and (ii) against a change in the Corn Laws. Explain why Huskisson was unable to get the change he wanted.

5.   Give an account of Peel's attitudes towards Catholic Emancipation in (i) 1827, and (ii) 1829. Show that there was a difference in attitudes. Explain why he changed his mind.

6.   Write two sentences on each of the following: (i) Wellington's policies towards Catholics, 1827–9 (ii) Huskisson's hopes for Catholic Emancipation (iii) the 'Old Tory' attitude towards Emancipation 1829. Now show why the Tory Party was divided into three warring groups in 1830.

(B)
1.   Write the article (or obituary) that might have appeared in praise of Huskisson after his death. (The writer might have mentioned his work for trade, Corn Laws, trade unions, his friendship with Canning, his attitude towards Catholics, his resignation from Wellington's government, some of those who followed him into resignation.)

(C)
1.   Write the headlines that might have appeared above reports on:
(a) Castlereagh's death – in government, Whig, and Radical papers;
(b) the changes in the death penalty;
(c) the repeal of the Combination Acts – in papers controlled by the government, the Radicals, a manufacturer and a trade union;
(d) the cuts in import duties;
(e) the outbreak of strikes, 1824–5 – in papers controlled by the government, the Radicals, and the manufacturers;
(f) on Huskisson's resignation – in papers controlled by the government, the Irish Protestants, and Irish Catholics;
(g) O'Connell's election, 1828 – in papers controlled by the government, Irish Protestants, Irish Catholics, supporters of Canning and Huskisson.

2.   Draw the posters that might have been used to:
(a) advertise a public execution;
(b) warn people of the danger from highwaymen;
(c) invite recruits for the Metropolitan Police Force;
(d) advertise a meeting of the Anti-Corn Law Movement;
(e) advertise a meeting of the Catholic Association.

10 Ireland, 1760-1850

In this chapter we will look at the problems that were facing Ireland in 1760. A study of the history of Ireland since 1760 helps to explain some of the problems of Northern Ireland today. Until 1850, the British tried to tackle those problems – and failed. This meant that the Irish problem remained to make life difficult for politicians after 1850 (Chapters 23 and 27).

The Religious Problem, 1760

About three-quarters of the Irish people were Catholics. In the seventeenth century the British Parliament had drawn up a set of anti-Catholic *Penal Laws*, which meant that no Catholic could legally practise his religion; he was not allowed to send his children to school; he could not vote, own land, have a commission in the armed forces, become a Member of the Irish Parliament, become a lawyer, or have a post in the Civil Service. Edmund Burke (p. 14), a Protestant Irishman, said that these anti-Catholic laws were 'as well fitted for the oppression, impoverishment and degradation of a people as ever man thought of'. It is not surprising that the Catholic Irish never thought of themselves as 'British' people.

The Land Problem

Three-quarters of the land in Ireland was owned by landlords living in Britain. Some members of the House of Lords owned vast estates in Ireland; other Englishmen owned smaller estates. Few of them ever visited Ireland; instead, they appointed a bailiff to look after their estates.

These estates were split up into small plots rented out to the Catholic peasants. During the eighteenth and early nineteenth centuries there was a growth in the Irish population. Therefore, many people were anxious to get a plot of land to farm, and the bailiffs could charge very high rents. If someone failed to pay the rent, the police were called in to throw the family out of their hovel (Extract 10.1). There was always another family willing to pay the rent.

Fig. 10.1 Spinning thread in a cottage in Galway. The cottagers were so poor they could not afford to buy shoes.

The Irish peasants grew some corn on their small plot, and they sold this to pay the rent. This brought in a high income for the landlord living in England. The Irish themselves lived on a diet of buttermilk and potatoes, which were nourishing and cheap to grow.

The Economic Problem

There were a small number of Protestants living in Ireland; the majority of these lived in or around Belfast. They owned whatever industries flourished in that country. The flax or linen industry was found in the cottages of the peasants (Fig. 10.1) and in the homes of the people living in the small towns.

We saw in Chapter 4 that Britain would not allow any industry to develop in America if it was going to become a competitor for a British-based industry. The same was true of Ireland. The Irish were allowed to develop a linen industry, because Britain did not have one, but they were not allowed to develop a woollen industry – although they had the raw material and the skilled people to make the cloth.

Pitt had arranged a trade treaty with the French in 1786. The British Parliament refused to allow the signing of a similar treaty with Ireland. This angered the Protestants of Ireland. They owned the industries, and they had the money to develop newer and larger industries. But the British Parliament would not allow them to do so.

The Political Situation

There was an Irish Parliament in existence in 1760. Only Protestants were allowed to vote in elections and only Protestants could sit in the Parliament which met in Dublin.

But the Irish Parliament had little real power. Under the terms of an Act passed in 1494 no law passed by it could become law until it had been approved by the Westminster Parliament. Under the terms of an Act passed in 1714 every Act passed by the Westminster Parliament was law in Ireland – even if the Irish Parliament did not agree with it. That was why Britain could force the Irish to accept the terms of the Navigation Acts and the other laws that governed the development of trade and industry.

The Chief Secretary for Ireland was always a British politician. He and the Viceroy of Ireland paid little attention to the Irish Parliament, because they knew that the real power lay at Westminster. The Protestants did not like this; they wanted some chance of freedom.

Fear of an Irish Rebellion

The Irish felt that, like the Americans, they, too, were really being ruled by a British Parliament in which they had no representatives.

When France declared war on Britain in 1778 the Irish Protestants decided to raise an army so that they could defend their country if France invaded as part of an attack on Britain. The British government was frightened by the news of the formation of these Volunteer forces. It feared that this might be the beginnings of an Irish rebellion (Fig. 10.2).

So the British tried to put right some of the wrongs from which Ireland was suffering, and in 1777 they abolished some of the worst of the Penal Laws. Catholics now had some rights – although they still could not vote. The British also listened to the demands of the Protestant Irish Parliament, led by Henry Grattan. He asked that the British repeal the Acts of 1494 and 1714, and Britain agreed. So in 1782 the Irish Parliament became truly independent. At least the Protestant politicians could now claim that they governed Ireland, although the Chief Secretary was still a British politician.

In 1780 the British also abolished the worst features of the Navigation Acts as far as Ireland was concerned. Now Irish industry could develop. But, as we have seen, even the reforming Pitt was unable to get the British Parliament to pass a trade treaty with Ireland in 1786.

The French Revolution and Ireland

Many Irish people welcomed the news of the success of the French people's revolution in 1789. They had overthrown their king; they now had their own Parliament; every man was said to be 'equal' to every other man.

Wolfe Tone was a Protestant lawyer from Belfast. He wanted the Irish people to have the same rights as the French had won, and he wanted these rights for all Irishmen – Catholic and Protestant.

The British government saw that the Irish might be a danger to Britain once she started a war against France. Therefore, in 1792 there was a further relaxation of the Penal Laws; and in 1793 Catholics were allowed to vote in elections. But all this was too little and too late.

In 1791 Tone had founded a society called the United Irishmen. Both Catholics and Protestants joined it. Tone hoped to force Pitt to give more freedom to the Irish, but Pitt refused to do so. So in 1796 Tone went to France to ask for French help in case the Irish rose in rebellion against the British.

Tone's supporters throughout the country formed

Fig. 10.2 The Irish Volunteers meet at College Green, Dublin.

themselves into smaller gangs or societies. It is not surprising that the Catholics in their villages had their own such societies. Many of them had peculiar, even comical names. There were the Will-o'-the-Wisp Boys, the Peep-o'-day Boys, and the Whiteboys. They attacked Protestant homes, farms, and estates. This frightened the Protestants who formed their own Orange Society, named after the Protestant King William of Orange (p. 6).

It can be seen, then, that there was little unity in the so-called United Irishmen. Tone's hope of help from France came to nothing when the French fleets which sailed to Ireland in 1796 and 1797 failed to get through. The result was that it was only the Catholic peasants who rose in rebellion in the south and south-west of Ireland. The rising was easily but bloodily put down by the British Army.

The Act of Union, 1801

The Irish Protestants were frightened at the thought of being governed by a Catholic Parliament and government in Dublin. Pitt thought that this fear could be put to rest by the Act of Union. The Irish Protestants, joined by the British Protestants, would easily outnumber the Catholics in Britain and Ireland; the British Parliament would be controlled by Protestants; the majority of M.P.s would always be Protestants. So the Irish Protestants would have nothing to fear if Catholic Irish voters chose Catholic M.P.s.

The Protestant Irish M.P.s were not anxious to sign away their positions and powers. The Chief Secretary for Ireland was Lord Castlereagh, later to be the British Foreign Secretary. He had to deal with the bribery, the promises of titles, the offers of jobs and contracts, and the other methods of 'persuading' the Protestant M.P.s to agree to the Act of Union.

The Terms of the Union, 1801

The Act joined Ireland and Great Britain in a single kingdom, the 'United Kingdom of Great Britain and Ireland'. The Irish Parliament was abolished, and Ireland was split into 100 constituencies. The electors would send 100 M.P.s to sit in the House of Commons, and there would also be seats in the House of Lords for Irish Bishops, four Protestants, and twenty-eight Irish noblemen or peers. Trade between the two countries would be completely free, and Ireland would be treated in the same way as Wales and Scotland.

No Emancipation

Pitt had hoped that he would be able to please the Catholics of Ireland by getting Parliament to pass an Act to allow Catholics to stand at elections and, if elected, to sit in the House of Commons as M.P.s. But, as we have seen, George III refused to agree to this (p. 27).

O'Connell, 1828–9

We have already seen how a Catholic lawyer, Daniel O'Connell, managed to force an unwilling Duke of Wellington to agree to allow Catholics to sit in the House of Commons (p. 51–2).

The Irish saw O'Connell as the great liberator. He had, after all, won them their freedom – to sit in the House of Commons.

O'Connell and Home Rule

But O'Connell wanted more than that. He wanted the British to allow the Irish to have their own Parliament and their own government: he wanted Irish self-rule under Queen Victoria.

He hoped that the Whigs might give Ireland this self-rule, so between 1830 and 1841 he supported the Whigs. He played a part in helping to bring down Conservative governments in 1835 and 1839.

But O'Connell did not get what he wanted. All the Whigs did was to abolish the system of tithes in 1836. This system had forced Catholics to pay a tax to the local Protestant clergymen. Therefore, the abolition of tithes in 1836 was another small victory for the Catholics.

Peel and O'Connell, 1841–6

Peel became Prime Minister in 1841 (Chapter 14). He thought that the Irish problem was really a religious difficulty, and he hoped to solve it by helping the Catholic religion. There was a College at Maynooth, near Dublin, for the training of Catholic priests, and the British government had been paying £9,000 a year to the College authorities. Peel increased this grant to £26,000. More priests could now be trained and at less cost to their parents. Peel hoped this would please the Catholics. It did so, but it did nothing to solve the economic and political problems of Ireland: the question of land ownership and rents, and the demand for self-rule.

O'Connell and Clontarf

O'Connell knew this, and set off to tour Ireland to get backing for his demand for self-rule. Priests and many people turned out to support him; prayers were said for him in every Catholic church; and vast crowds came out to hear the Liberator.

Peel became frightened by this. He thought that O'Connell might turn out to be another Tone and there might be an Irish rising. In fact, O'Connell was opposed to violence, but Peel did not understand this. He banned a massive meeting due to be held at Clontarf in 1843. O'Connell agreed to call it off, but Peel decided to arrest O'Connell (Fig. 10.3). The House of Lords ordered his release from gaol, but he was a broken man by this time and died in Down on 15 May 1847.

Young Ireland

There were a number of young Irishmen who thought that O'Connell had failed Ireland. He had won a victory in 1829. But after that? Nothing! These younger men had their own newspapers, organizations, and supporters. They thought that the British would only give Ireland its self-rule when the Irish drove them out – as the Americans had. They wanted a revolution.

Between 1845 and 1849 Ireland suffered from a great famine. A potato blight destroyed most of the crop of 1845, and within six months most of the people were starving and over a million died. One result of this was the repeal of the Corn Laws (p. 84); another was a mass emigration from Ireland. Between 1846 and 1851 over 1.25 million people went to live in Canada and the United States of America and another 1.5 million left to live in England and Wales.

Fig. 10.3 A Punch *cartoon of O'Connell in gaol in 1843.*

THE PROBABLE EFFECTS OF GOOD LIVING AND NO EXERCISE!

It was these emigrants who sent back money to help the Young Ireland movement which grew in importance and size while O'Connell was in gaol. There was a half-hearted rising in 1848 which was easily suppressed. Maybe the people left in Ireland were too poor, too degraded, to rise. So in 1850 Ireland found itself with a smaller population, still governed by a British Parliament that did not understand the Irish problem (Chapters 23 and 27).

Questions

Extract 10.1

On the 13th March 1846 a Mrs Gerrard evicted 300 tenants from Ballinglass village, County Galway:
'On the morning of the eviction, a large detachment of the 49th Infantry and numerous police appeared . . . the houses were then demolished . . . the scene was frightful; women running wailing with pieces of their property and clinging to door posts from which they had to be forcibly torn; men cursing, children screaming in fright. That night the people slept in the ruins; next day they were driven out, the foundations of the houses were torn up and razed. . . .'
(Cecil Woodham-Smith, *The Great Hunger*, 1964, pp. 71–2.)

1. What was 'the eviction'?
2. Why would a landowner or his bailiff want to evict tenants?
3. Why were there more evictions during the Great Famine than in the years before 1845?
4. Why did the Army and the police go to the scene of evictions?
5. How did such evictions affect the relationship between the Catholic Irish and the British government?

Worksheet

(A)
1. Make a list of the ways in which Catholics suffered in Ireland in 1770.

2. How did the Protestants of Ireland suffer because of Britain's control of their island?

3. Write two sentences on each of the following: Grattan's Parliament; the Penal Laws; the Orange Society; Catholic Emancipation.

4. Wolfe Tone founded the United Ireland movement. Explain (i) what he hoped to achieve (ii) why it

had that name (iii) why the Catholics and Protestants quarrelled (iv) why the rising of 1798 failed.

5. Why was O'Connell called 'the Liberator'?

6. Write two sentences on the Maynooth Grant, 1843.

7. After 1845 Ireland suffered from 'the Great Famine'. Explain (i) why the potato was the main diet of the Irish peasants (ii) why the potato disease spread (iii) why the peasants did not buy the corn that was produced in Ireland – and exported to Britain (iv) why there was a mass emigration from Ireland.

(B)
1. Write the articles (or obituaries) that might have appeared on O'Connell's death in papers controlled by (i) Irish Protestants (ii) Wellington (iii) Irish Catholics.

2. Write the letters that might have been sent by:
(a) an English landowner to his bailiff in Ireland in 1820;
(b) an Irish M.P. in 1770 complaining of the limited power of his Parliament;
(c) an Englishman who had seen a meeting of Volunteers in 1778;
(d) an Irish Catholic who had been to one of O'Connell's meetings, 1840.

(C)
1. Write the headlines that might have appeared above reports on:
(a) the refusal to grant an Irish trade treaty, 1786 – in papers controlled by the government, Irish Protestant manufacturers, Irish Catholics;
(b) the first meeting of the Independent Parliament, 1782 – in English and in Irish newspapers;
(c) the 1798 rising – in papers controlled by the British government, Irish Protestants, and Irish Catholics;
(d) the Act of Union, 1801 – in papers controlled by the British government, Irish Protestants, and Irish Catholics;
(e) O'Connell's arrest, 1843 – in papers controlled by Peel, Irish Protestants, O'Connell's supporters, and supporters of Young Ireland.

2. Make a time chart for the years 1760–1848. Mark on it the main dates and events mentioned in the text. Add a line of explanation for each of the dates and events.

3. Draw the posters that might have been used to:
(a) forbid attendance at the Catholic mass;
(b) advertise a job with the Civil Service – 'No Catholic need apply';
(e) advertise the Clontarf meeting, 1843.

11 Foreign Policy under Castlereagh and Canning 1815-30

Industry and Foreign Affairs

In the nineteenth century Britain was the richest and most powerful country in the world. British Foreign Secretaries therefore played an important role in world affairs.

Castlereagh (1769-1822)

Robert Stewart Castlereagh was the second son of the first Marquess of Londonderry. The death of his elder brother meant that, on his father's death, he succeeded to the title and was the second Marquess of Londonderry.

He was elected to the Irish Parliament in 1790, and became a Member of the House of Commons in 1794. In 1798 he became Chief Secretary for Ireland, and helped Pitt to bring about the Act of Union in 1801 (p. 56).

Castlereagh was War Minister under Pitt and Portland. He and the then Foreign Secretary, George Canning, quarrelled about the failure of an invasion expedition in 1809. This dispute resulted in them fighting a duel, and this led to the resignation of both men.

But in 1812 Castlereagh was appointed Foreign Secretary by Lord Liverpool. It was Castlereagh who organized the Fourth Coalition in 1812, and he represented Britain at the peacemaking that ended with the Congress of Vienna in 1815.

Vienna, 1815

Castlereagh's main aim at Vienna was to make sure that Europe would enjoy a long period of peace. Europe and its people had suffered from over twenty years of fighting. Peace would help Britain in particular, because trade grew during peacetime but tended to drop off during times of war.

So he worked with the other Allies to make sure that France would never again be a threat to peace (p. 41). He also persuaded them to follow Britain's example and abolish the slave trade.

Unlike the other countries, Britain did not make any territorial gains at Vienna. Castlereagh said: 'It is not the business of England to collect trophies, but to restore Europe to peaceful habits.' But Britain had, in fact, made several important gains as a result of the Napoleonic Wars (p. 41).

Quadruple Alliance, 1815

Castlereagh organized the Quadruple (or Four-Nation) Alliance. Russia, Austria, Prussia, and Britain had already combined to defeat Napoleon, but in this new alliance they promised to co-operate so that Europe remained at peace (Extract 11.1 and Fig. 11.1). Representatives of the four countries would meet from time to time to make sure that everything was going well. This was the world's first attempt at international co-operation.

Castlereagh and the Europeans

Castlereagh had worked closely with the heads of other European countries since 1812. He knew the value of this co-operation, but some British people thought that he was too much under the control and influence of these Europeans.

Although this was untrue, Castlereagh did have a certain sympathy with the Tsar of Russia and Metternich, the Austrian Chancellor. They were both afraid that the ideas of the French Revolution were still important, and in 1814 Castlereagh himself wrote of 'a great moral change coming on in Europe. The danger is that the change may be too sudden to make the world better or happier.'

The Holy Alliance, 1815

By 1815 Tsar Alexander I of Russia had become a religious fanatic. He thought that ideas of liberty and democracy were wrong; he even believed they were sinful. He thought that by stamping out such ideas he

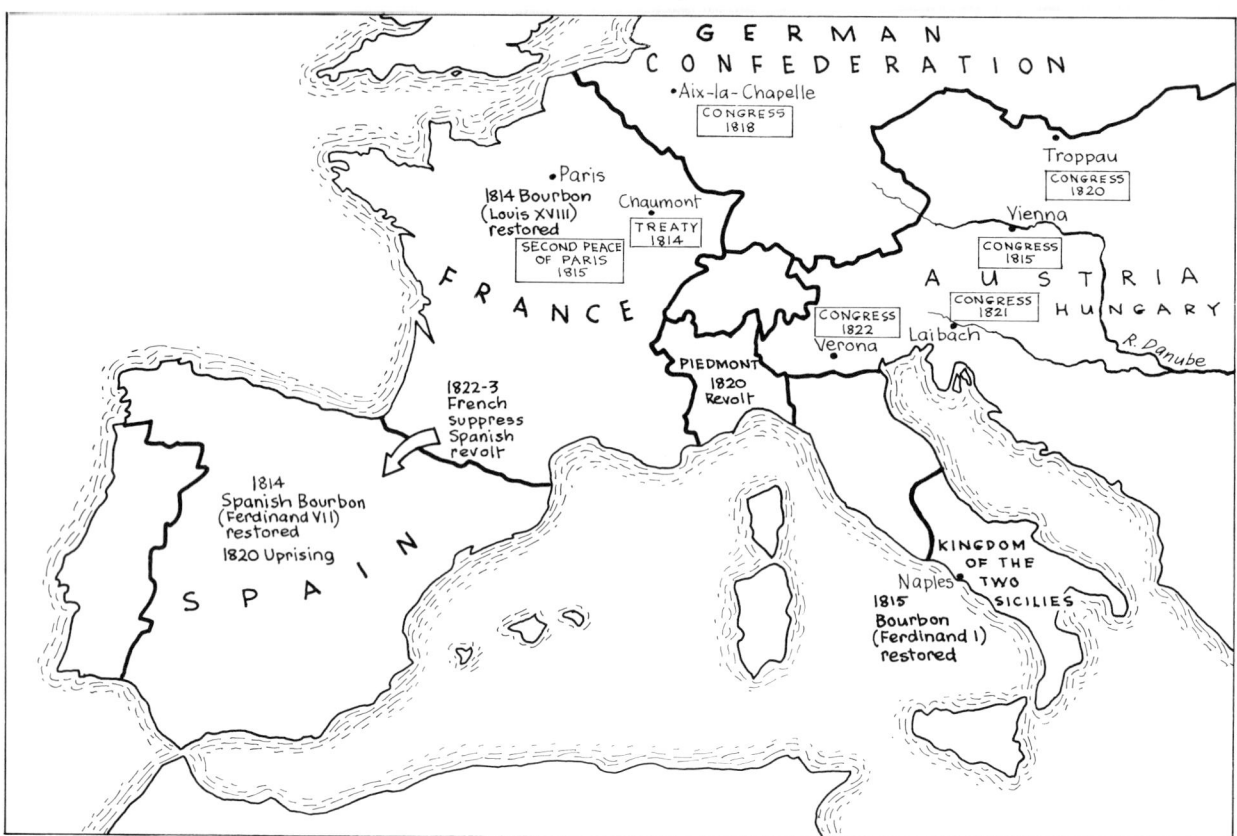

Fig. 11.1 The Congress System, 1818–22.

would be pleasing God and also keeping himself and his fellow-rulers on their thrones.

Alexander wrote a document in which he asked his fellow-rulers to agree to govern their countries in a spirit of Christian love and charity. He wanted them to agree to help each other to stamp out the anti-religious ideas of the French Revolution.

Castlereagh and Metternich thought that this document was a piece of 'sublime mysticism and nonsense', but every ruler in Europe signed it – except three. The Pope would not sign because his name did not appear at the top of the list; the Sultan of Turkey could hardly agree to govern in a Christian spirit – he was a follower of Islam; and the King of England, George III, was unable to sign because he had been declared insane. Castlereagh told Alexander that the Prince Regent did not have the power or right to sign such a document.

Aix-la-Chapelle

In 1818 the representatives of the Allied powers met for their first peacetime Congress at Aix-la-Chapelle (Fig. 11.1). They decided to take their armies of occupation from France, and allow her to join the Alliance, which now became the Quintuple (or Five-Nation) Alliance.

The American/Canadian Border, 1878

Castlereagh arranged with the government of America that both Britain and America would take their warships out of the Great Lakes. They also agreed that the boundary between Canada and America would be the line of the forty-ninth parallel of latitude. This ended the friction between the two countries, which in 1812 had led to war.

European Revolutions, 1818–22

Tsar Alexander I was right. The ideas of the French Revolution were still supported by many people in many European countries; they did not like the decisions of the Congress of Vienna. The Allies had put back the old rulers on their thrones. These rulers had old-fashioned ideas, while some of their people had learned the new ideas of liberty, equality, and fraternity. Many citizens wanted a share in the government of their countries.

There were uprisings in Spain, Portugal, Piedmont, and Naples (Fig. 11.1). Alexander wanted to send Russian troops to put down these uprisings against the Christian monarchs, but Metternich did not want to have Russian troops wandering around Europe.

He feared it might tempt Alexander to attempt to make his country even larger. Castlereagh also feared this and opposed the use of Russian troops.

Naples, 1820

Austria had a deep interest in Italian affairs: Lombardy and Venetia were part of her Empire. Also, the rulers of some of the smaller states were related to the Emperor of Austria.

In 1820 there was an uprising in Naples. This was led by the members of a secret society known as the *Carbonari* (or charcoal burners). They wanted to depose the cruel King Ferdinand and set up a republican, democratic form of government.

Metternich decided to send Austrian troops to put down this rising. Castlereagh agreed that Naples might almost be considered a 'domestic' problem for Austria, and did not object to Austrian intervention.

Troppau, 1820

The Allied powers had their next Congress at Troppau (Fig. 11.1), and Castlereagh sent the British Ambassador at Vienna as his representative.

Metternich persuaded the Russians and Prussians that there was a danger of a widespread European uprising by the liberals. Naples, he argued, was only the start.

The powers then signed a Protocol, or agreement. In this they declared that they would send troops to put down any rebellion, anywhere in Europe. Castlereagh protested, and withdrew the British representative from the Congress.

Laibach, 1821

In January 1821 Metternich invited the delegates to continue their discussions at Laibach (Fig. 11.1). Here they agreed to put down a rising in Piedmont, but again Castlereagh protested. His hopes of international co-operation had come to nothing.

Castlereagh's Suicide

Many British Radicals blamed Castlereagh for the government's repressive policy in Britain (p. 46); others attacked him for not stopping Metternich and Alexander from attacking liberals in Europe. In 1822 Castlereagh committed suicide. This led to a change in the law. Until his death a suicide had to be buried at a crossroads, but the government decided that this would be unfitting for a nobleman and a former minister. So the law was changed and it was decided that suicides could be buried in churchyards.

Lord Liverpool appointed George Canning to succeed Castlereagh.

Canning

Canning was the son of an actress who had married a rich man. Although he had been to school at Eton and to Oxford University many of the Tories looked down on him because of his mother's occupation.

But he was a very able man. He entered Parliament in 1794 and Pitt made him a junior minister in 1799. In 1807 he was Foreign Secretary in Portland's government, and was responsible for ordering the bombardment of Copenhagen (p. 34). In 1809 he had to resign after his duel with Castlereagh, but in 1822 he was appointed Governor-General of India. However, Castlereagh died on the day before he was due to sail for India, so he did not take up this position.

Canning and Liverpool

Canning, like Huskisson, was an M.P. for Liverpool (Fig. 11.2). He understood the importance of trade, and his main aim was to make Britain even greater, richer, and stronger. We have already seen that by 1822 Britain had begun to recover from the effects of the Napoleonic Wars, and by this time the fears of the revolution had begun to fade away in peacetime Britain. So Canning was more fortunate, in some ways, than Castlereagh had been immediately after 1815.

Fig. 11.2 Canning is cheered by the people of Liverpool after the 1812 election.

Verona, 1822

The Allied powers held a Congress at Verona (Fig. 11.1). The Duke of Wellington went as Britain's representative. Metternich and the Russians agreed to put down the uprising in Spain, but Metternich would not allow Russia to send an army across Europe. For his part, Alexander would not allow Austrian troops to be sent to Spain, in case Austria claimed Spain for itself. So they compromised and invited the French to send an army.

Canning ordered Wellington to withdraw from the Congress. The Congress system had broken down. But it is worth noting that Castlereagh might well have done the same; and it is also worth noting that Canning only protested about the French invasion of Spain. He did not send the Army or Navy to defend the liberals.

South America, 1823

Since 1809 the Spanish colonies in South America had been in revolt. Metternich, Alexander, the Spanish King, and his French ally wanted to send armies across the Atlantic once they had put down the Spanish uprising at home.

Canning let it be known that he would use the British Navy to prevent any troops landing in South America. He knew that many British merchants traded there (p. 38), and intended to help that trade to grow.

In 1823 he recognized the independence of the former colonies (Fig. 11.3). At the same time the President of America, James Monroe, said that his country would fight any European power trying to restore the old colonial system in South America. The *Monroe Doctrine* was a sign that America was beginning to think of herself as a world power.

So the Spanish and Portuguese colonies won their independence, and British trade grew. Canning boasted that, although he had failed to stop the French invasion of Spain, he had 'called the New World into existence to redress the balance of the Old'.

Portugal, 1826

Portugal had had a revolution in 1820, but the King had been wise enough to agree to give the people a democratic constitution. There were elections for a Parliament and the revolutionaries won.

In 1826 the King's brother was in Spain. He got the

Fig. 11.3 Canning's foreign policy, 1822–7.

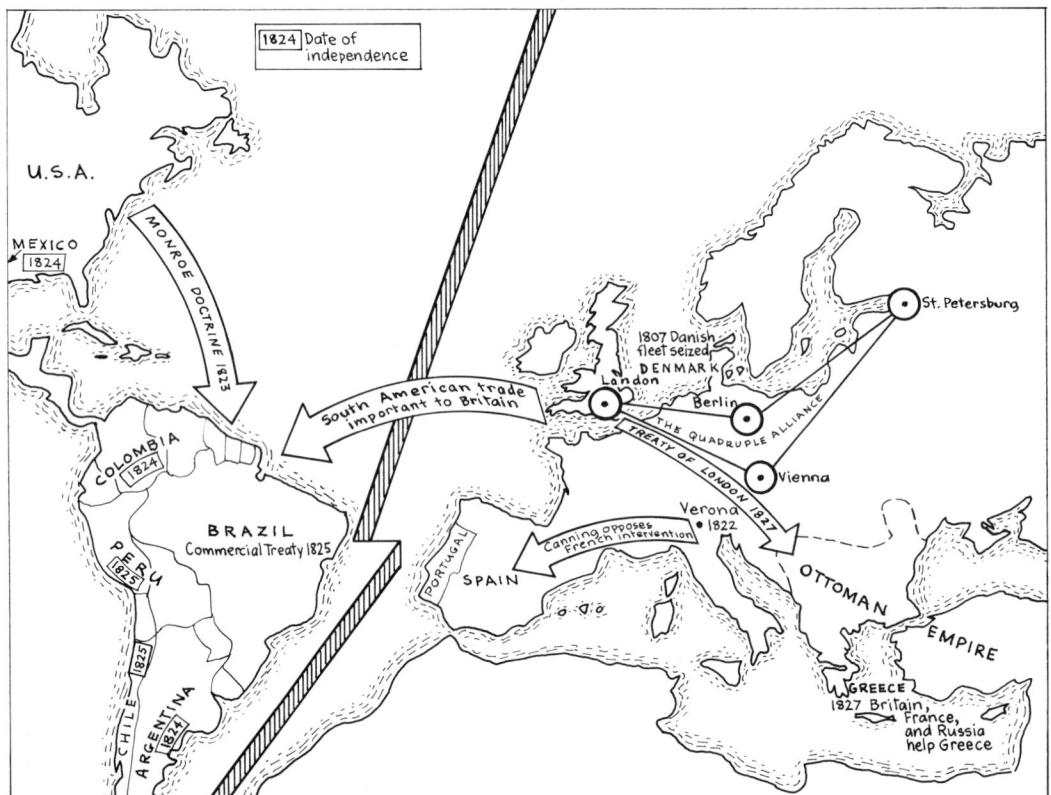

Spanish to promise to send an army into Portugal, and hoped to throw his elder brother off the throne and to dismiss the Parliament.

Canning had only protested when the French invaded Spain in 1820. In 1826 he sent a fleet and about 4,500 troops to Lisbon to help the liberal King. The Spaniards withdrew.

Greece, 1821–32

In 1820 the Turkish, or Ottoman, Empire was very large, but its rulers were weak and corrupt (Fig. 11.3). In 1821 the Greeks rose against their Turkish masters; they wanted to have their own independent government.

Most people in Britain were in favour of Greek independence. Metternich was against it, even though the Greeks were Christians fighting against an Islamic (Muslim) power. Alexander I was uncertain about what he ought to do.

In 1825 Alexander died, and the new Tsar, Nicholas I, wanted to help his fellow-Christians in Greece. The Sultan of Turkey asked one of his subjects, Mehemet Ali of Egypt, to come to his support. Ali sent a navy and an army and drove the Greeks back. By the summer of 1827 it seemed as if the Greeks would be crushed.

Navarino

Russia decided she would have to step in to help Greece. Canning did not want Russia to get any influence in this area, so in 1826 he persuaded the Russians and the French to sign a Protocol of St Petersburg. The three powers hoped to be able to persuade the Turks to agree to Greek independence, but the Sultan rejected their demands. These demands were renewed in the Treaty of London, 1827. Since the Turks still refused to recognize Greek independence, it was decided to send a joint British, French and Russian fleet to Greece. The fleet was commanded by Admiral Codrington. He found the Turkish and Egyptian fleets in the harbour of Navarino. On 20 October 1827 shots were exchanged. A battle followed and the Turkish and Egyptian fleets were sunk.

Wellington and Greece

The Battle of Navarino took place after Canning had died. Wellington became Prime Minister. He apologized to the Turks for the battle which he called an 'untoward event', and recalled the fleet. Russia, however, invaded Moldavia and Wallachia, part of the Turkish Empire, and in 1829 the Turks were forced to sign the Treaty of Adrianople. This gave the Greeks partial independence.

Wellington was frightened that Greece would become a pawn in Russia's hands. Britain and France therefore demanded the complete independence of Greece. In 1832 the Turks agreed to this.

Questions

Extract 11.1

The Quadruple Alliance, 1815

> To secure the execution of the present Treaty, and to consolidate the links which at present unite the Four Sovereigns, the Parties have agreed to renew Meetings at fixed periods, either of the Sovereigns themselves, or by their respective Ministers, for consulting upon their common interests, and for consideration of measures which at each of these periods shall be considered the most salutary for the prosperity of Nations, and for the Peace of Europe.
> (E. Hertslet, *The Map of Europe by Treaty*, 1875.)

1. What name do we usually give to 'the present Treaty'?
2. Who were the 'Four Sovereigns'?
3. Give the dates at which 'Meetings' were held between 1815 and 1822. Say briefly what was decided at each of these 'Meetings'.
4. Why had the events of the previous twenty years made diplomats anxious about 'the Peace of Europe'?
5. How was the peace of Europe threatened in 1820, 1825, and 1827?

Extract 11.2

Castlereagh and Canning compared, 1822

> That he was an amiable man in *private* life may or may not be true; but with this the public have nothing to do; and as to lamenting his death, it will be time enough when Ireland has ceased to mourn for his birth. As a minister, I, for one of millions, looked upon him as the most despotic in intention, and the weakest in intellect, that ever tyrannised over a country.
> Of the manner of his death little need be said, except that if a poor radical . . . had cut his throat, he would have been buried in a cross-road, with the usual appurtenances of the stake and mallet. But the minister was an elegant lunatic – a sentimental suicide – he

merely cut the 'carotid artery' (blessings on their learning!) and lo! the pageant, and the Abbey! In his death he was necessarily one of two things by the *law* – a felon or a madman – and in either case no great subject for panegyric. It may at least serve as some consolation to the nations, that their oppressors are not happy, and in some instances judge so justly of their own actions as to anticipate the sentence of mankind.

Canning is a genius, and no man of talent can long pursue the path of his late predecessor, Lord C. If ever a man saved his country, Canning *can*; but *will* he? I, for one, hope so.

(Lord Byron, *Preface to Cantos VI–VIII of Don Juan*, 1822.)

1. Why did Byron refer to Ireland in line 4?
2. What office had Castlereagh held in 1801?
3. Was Castlereagh as despotic as Byron suggested? Give reasons for your answer.
4. Explain 'buried in a cross-road'.
5. Why and how did Castlereagh's death lead to a change in the law?
6. Discuss Byron's opinion of Canning. Were his policies very different from Castlereagh's?

Fig. 11.1

1. Which countries were in the Quadruple Alliance? When and why was it formed?
2. Why did the Alliance break down after 1822? Who do you blame for this breakdown?
3. When did this alliance become the Quintuple Alliance? Which country joined the four original members?
4. Write three sentences on the issues discussed at the following places. Make sure that you say what decisions were reached at each place: Aix-la-Chapelle; Troppau; Laibach; Verona.
5. Who was British Foreign Secretary in 1820? What was his attitude towards the Troppau Protocol?
6. What action did Castlereagh take when the French threatened to invade Spain? How far, if at all, was his policy different from that of Canning?

Worksheet

(A)
1. Make a list of Castlereagh's aims at the Congress of Vienna. Explain how far he succeeded in achieving these aims.

2. Why did some people attack Castlereagh as being 'more European than English'?

3. Explain carefully the differences between the Quadruple Alliance and the Holy Alliance. (You might note the following: the members; meetings; aims; and attitudes of Castlereagh and Metternich towards each Alliance.)

4. Why did some people think that Canning was 'more English than European'?

5. What advantage did British industrialists gain from Canning's policies towards the states of South America?

6. Write two lines on: the Monroe Doctrine; the Battle of Navarino.

(B)
1. Write the articles (or obituaries) that might have appeared at the time of the deaths of:
(a) Castlereagh
(b) Canning
in papers controlled by the government, the opposition, and the Radicals.

2. Write the letters that might have been sent by:
(a) a Frenchman complaining of the restoration of the Bourbon King;
(b) Metternich, explaining why he had to interfere in Naples;
(c) Metternich, explaining why he did not want Russia to interfere in Naples;
(d) Canning, telling Wellington to oppose Metternich's policies, 1822.

(C)
1. Make a time chart for the years 1815–30. Mark on it the main dates and events mentioned in the text. Add a line of explanation on each of the dates and years.

2. Write the headlines that might have appeared above reports on:
(a) the formation of the Quadruple Alliance – in British, Russian, and French papers;
(b) the formation of the Holy Alliance – in British, Austrian, Russian, and Radical papers;
(c) the end of the Congress of Aix-la-Chapelle – in British and French papers;

12 The Reform of Parliament, 1830-32

The Old System

On pages 6–9 we studied the political and parliamentary system by which Britain was governed in 1760. We saw that the majority of people lived in new industrial areas where there were no constituencies (Fig. 2.2 on p. 8). There were more M.P.s elected for Cornwall than for Lancashire.

We saw that there was a bewildering mixture of qualifications for the vote. In some places only freemen could vote; in others only members of local councils (Extract 12.1); in others the franchise was given to certain taxpayers, owners of certain houses or, in a few towns, to every male resident.

We also saw that elections were surrounded by a good deal of bribery (Fig. 12.1) and violence. This

Fig. 12.1 How one candidate tried to win the support of the voters.

MR. MANGLES respectfully requests those of his worthy Friends, who may be disposed to celebrate his return to Parliament by their own fire sides as on the last occasion to send the inclosed Dinner Ticket, on or before THURSDAY the 2d of APRIL next, to his Agent MR. G. S. SMALLPEICE who will in exchange for such Ticket, give the Bearer thereof an Order for

TWELVE POUNDS OF BEEF,

ONE GALLON OF STRONG BEER,

TWO QUARTERN LOAVES,

THREE POUNDS AND A HALF OF FLOUR,

TWO POUNDS OF SUET,

TWO POUNDS OF RAISINS,

ONE POUND OF CURRANTS,

AND

TWO BOTTLES OF WINE, (PORT OR SHERRY).

MR. MANGLES also begs respectfully to inform those Friends who may not be disposed to dine in public, and may not wish themselves to exchange the Dinner Ticket, that the same is transferrable to any of their Neighbors.

An Answer is respectfully requested to be sent to MR. G. S. SMALLPEICE, on or before THURSDAY the 2nd of APRIL next.

Russells, Printers, Guildford

allowed the government to gain control of many seats. Even after M.P.s were elected there were many ways in which the government could bribe an M.P. to give it his support. This explains Walpole's power (Fig. 2.1 on p. 7).

There had been attempts to reform the old system. The Yorkshire Association had called for a national campaign. Pitt and Burke had tried, but failed, to get Parliament to pass a Reform Bill in the 1780s. However, in 1830 the demand for reform came to a head.

Who Supported Reform in 1830?

1. The Whigs. In 1830 Wellington's government was defeated in the Commons, and he resigned. In July 1830 King William IV asked Earl Grey, the leader of the Whigs, to form a government.

Grey wanted a chance to show 'that in these days of democracy, it is possible to find real ability in the high aristocracy'. He was certainly no Radical: he did not want to change things very much. Eleven of his thirteen ministers were landed aristocrats.

But the Whigs did appreciate that Britain was changing because of the Industrial Revolution. One of them, Henry Brougham, said, 'We don't live in the days of Barons. We live in the days of Leeds, Bradford, Halifax and Huddersfield.' A leading Whig M.P., Macaulay, wrote of the 'struggle of the middle classes against the aristocracy, the owners of a ruined hovel who have powers which are not given to cities famous for the marvels of their wealth and industry'.

2. The middle classes were the people who owned the factories, mills, mines, banks, shops, railways, companies, ships, canals and so on. They did not get their money from land, nor did they get their money in wages. They therefore came between the upper and working classes, so they are called the middle classes.

They were very rich – often richer than many landowners. They paid their taxes, but they did not have a vote because there were no boroughs in the new towns.

3. The working classes supported the calls for parliamentary reform. This is what had brought them to Peterloo in 1819. They hoped that a more democratic Parliament would pass laws about working conditions, housing, wages, education, the treatment of the poor, and so on.

Who was Opposed to Reform?

1. The Tories. In October 1830 Wellington said, 'I have never heard of anything which could improve

the parliamentary system. The country has a Parliament which has the full confidence of the country. M.P.s at present come from the people who own property and the landed interests have the largest influence.'

Wellington was right in his last sentence. The Duke of Norfolk had eleven boroughs in his pocket, Lord Lonsdale had nine, Lord Darlington seven and many other Lords two or three. The Duke of Newcastle argued that 'my boroughs are mine to do what I like with'. It is not surprising that he and other land-owners liked the old system.

2. Some Whigs thought that the system was a good one; they were among the many who did well out of it. Some of them thought that a reformed Parliament might become a people's Parliament. This, they thought, might pass Acts about taxation which would harm the better-off.

3. William IV had become King in 1830. In that year the people of France rose in revolt against their king and his government. They wanted a more democratic system, and they got what they wanted. The rich middle class were able to vote for the election of a French Parliament after 1830.

William IV was afraid that the call for a reform of the British Parliament might lead to a British revolution.

The First Bill, March 1831

On 1 March 1831 Lord John Russell introduced the first Reform Bill into the House of Commons. He was a younger son of the Duke of Bedford – a reminder that Grey's government consisted largely of land-owners.

There was a long debate on the Bill, and passions ran high. Reports of the debate appeared in news-papers up and down the country, and many people outside Parliament became excitedly interested.

After days of argument the Commons voted on this Bill. The representatives of the unreformed system voted in favour of reform – but by only one vote (Fig. 12.2).

After this success the Bill had to be considered by a Committee of M.P.s. Here the Bill was defeated and in April 1831 Grey told the King that there would have to be an election. The people would have the right to decide for or against reform.

The Election, 1831

Grey was supported by the Radicals, the working class, and the middle class who had organized

Fig. 12.2 The scene in the House of Commons while M.P.s waited to hear the result of the vote on the First Reform Bill.

political unions. Thomas Attwood had seen how O'Connell had united the Irish Catholics in his Catholic Associations (p. 51), and tried to do the same to win support for parliamentary reform. He organized local clubs around Birmingham. His Birmingham Political Union whipped up support for Grey who called for 'the Bill, the whole Bill, and nothing but the Bill'.

Bribery and corruption was at a high level. The Tories spent £400,000 on the election and complained that some voters asked 'as much as £10 before giving their pledge to support us'.

But the Tories lost many seats, and Grey's call for reform won.

The Second Bill, June 1831

On 24 June 1831 Russell introduced his Bill again. This time it was passed by a majority of 136 votes – a sign of the victory that Grey had won in the election.

The Lords

But before a Bill becomes an Act it has to be passed through the House of Lords, and on 8 October 1831 the Lords threw out Russell's Bill by 199 votes to 158. The majority of the Lords refused to see that Britain was changing. There were riots outside Parliament; the Duke of Newcastle was attacked by the London mob which broke the windows in Wellington's house in Hyde Park. The centres of Nottingham, Derby, Worcester, Bath, and Bristol were set on fire.

The Third Bill, December 1831

On 12 December 1831 Russell put his Bill before the Commons yet again, and this time it was passed by a majority of 162 votes. Once more it was sent to the House of Lords.

William IV had once promised Grey that he would create enough new Lords to make sure that the Bill would get through the House of Lords. But he changed his mind, and asked Wellington to try to form a government.

At first Wellington had an idea that he could govern the country 'by the sword', but he soon found that he could not get enough support in the Commons. So he told the King that he could not form a government. This saved the country from the danger of a civil war (Extract 12.2).

William IV sent for Grey again, and this time he had to agree that he would make new Lords if necessary. On 14 May 1832 Grey became Prime Minister again.

The Bill was put before the Lords and in June they gave in and passed it by 102 votes to 22. The majority of the Lords did not vote.

The Terms of the Reform Act 1832

1. The constituencies. The Act took away 143 seats from the south and distributed fifty-five among the towns where population was growing rapidly (Fig. 12.3). Sixty-five were distributed to the more populated counties, eight to Scotland, and five to Ireland.

67

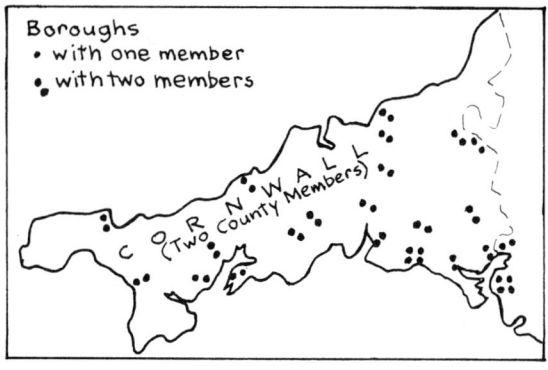

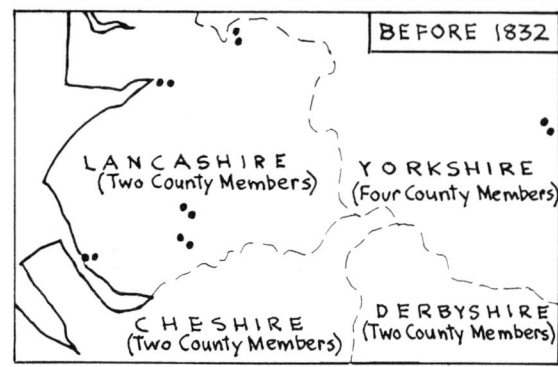

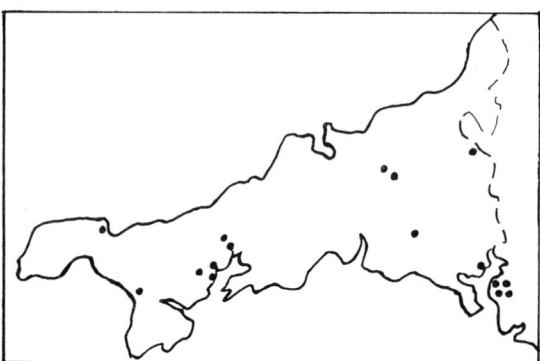

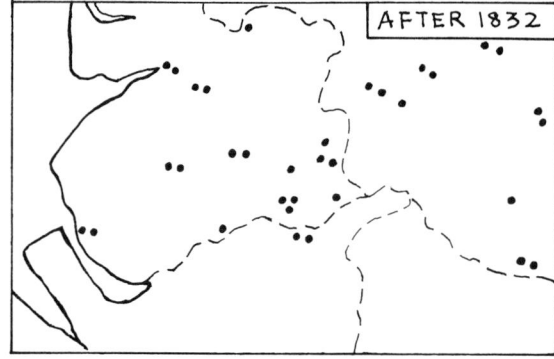

Fig. 12.3 The distribution of constituencies in Cornwall, Lancashire, Yorkshire, Cheshire and Derbyshire before and after the Reform Act 1832.

2. The franchise became much simpler. In the *counties* the owner of land kept his vote. But the franchise was also given to men who rented land – 'copyholders having property of the value of £10 a year and leaseholders paying a rent of £50 a year'.

In the *boroughs* the Act abolished all the old qualifications. After 1832 anyone who owned or rented a house rated at £10 a year was given the franchise.

Changes – for Good or Bad?

Before 1832 about 440,000 people had the vote. As a result of the 1832 Act about 217,000 were added to the electorate. The £10 household qualification meant that only the rich industrialists and merchants got the vote.

The working class, however, got nothing from the Act. We shall see later that this led to the development of the Chartist movement (Chapter 15).

The south and the south-west of England was still over-represented; there were still too many M.P.s from these agricultural areas.

The middle class now had a share in government. They had seen how the upper class had used their power to pass Corn Laws and Game Acts (Chapter 8). After 1832 the middle class used their newly won power to pass laws that benefited them. Thus they repealed the Corn Laws (Chapter 15) and Acts that made trade completely free from import and export duties.

Questions

Extract 12.1

Bath's Electorate before and after 1832

On Wednesday the election for this city came on, when Lord John Thynne and Lieut.-Col. Palmer were re-elected by the Mayor, ten Aldermen and twenty Common Councilmen.

During the election Mr Allen appeared in the Hall, insisting upon the right of the other eighty Freemen of the City to vote. But they ignored him and carried on chairing the two Members.
(*The Bath Herald*, October 1812.)

An analysis of the first reformed Parliament:
BATH: Population 38,063; number of £10 houses 7,314; the voters in the old constituency 33.

Bath has hitherto provided one of the most striking illustrations of the corrupt absurdities of our constitution. Through a long course of years for ten Parliaments, we find Lord John Thynne, brother of the Marquis of Bath, voting against Reform, against Catholic Emancipation and against every enlightened and patriotic measure.
(*The Weekly Dispatch*, January 1833.)

1. Which group of people had the right to vote in Bath in 1812? How many of them were there?
2. Which group of people actually elected the M.P.s in 1812? How many of them were there?
3. What proves that Lord Thynne belonged to the Tory Party? What did he think of Wellington's decisions on Emancipation in (i) 1828, and (ii) 1829?
4. How many people voted in Bath in 1833?
5. Draw two graphs to show the percentage of the population that had the right to vote in Bath in (i) 1812, and (ii) 1833.

Extract 12.2

The Army and Reform, 1832

> It was rumoured that the Birmingham Political Union was to march for London that night (Sunday 13 May 1832); and that we were there to stop it on the road. . . . We had been daily booted and saddled, with ball cartridge in each man's possession for three days. . . . But until this day we had rough-sharpened no swords. The purpose of so roughening their edges was to make them inflict a ragged wound. Not since the Battle of Waterloo had the swords of the Greys undergone the same process. Old soldiers spoke of it and told the young ones.
> (Private Alexander Somerville, *The Autobiography of a Working Man*, 1848.)

1. Who founded the Birmingham Political Union? Which classes of people joined it? Why?
2. Why did the members of the Union threaten to 'march for London' in May 1832?
3. Against which of the Houses of Parliament would they have directed their attack if they had got to London? Why?
4. What did William IV do that helped the passage of the Reform Bill and made it unnecessary for the Union to march?
5. What light does this Extract throw on the danger of a British revolution in 1832? In which country had the people risen to demand a more democratic government in 1830?

Fig. 12.3

1. How many M.P.s were elected for (i) Cornwall (ii) Lancashire before 1832?
2. Why might this have been fair in 1600?
3. Why had the population of Lancashire grown rapidly since 1760?
4. Name two large towns in Lancashire and three smaller towns.

5. How many M.P.s were elected for (i) Cornwall, and (ii) Lancashire after the passing of the 1832 Reform Act?
6. Do you think that after 1832 Lancashire was as fairly represented as Cornwall? Give reasons for your answer.

Worksheet

(A)
1. Write two sentences to show why each of the following supported parliamentary reform in 1830: Grey; Brougham; the middle classes in Bath and Liverpool; the middle classes in Manchester; leaders of the working class.

2. Write two sentences to show why each of the following was opposed to parliamentary reform in 1830: Wellington; the owners of rotten boroughs; King William IV.

3. Trace the course of the various Reform Bills 1831–2. You could do it as a series of entries in a diary or by a series of newspaper headlines.

4. Explain carefully the changes that were made by the Reform Act 1832 in (i) the franchise (or right to vote) in the county constituencies and in borough constituencies (ii) the distribution of seats.

5. Show how, if at all, the following gained or lost by the Reform Act, 1832: the landowning aristocrats; the manufacturing middle class; the working class.

(B)
1. Make a time chart for the years 1830–2. Mark on it the main dates and events mentioned in the text. Add a line of explanation for each date and event.

2. Write the extracts that might have appeared in the diaries kept by Russell OR Peel during the struggle over the Reform Bills 1831–2.

(C)
1. Write the headlines that might have appeared above reports on:
(a) the introduction of the first Reform Bill;
(b) the introduction of the second Reform Bill;
(c) the riots in Bristol, Nottingham, and Derby;
(d) the passing of the Bill, 1832.
(In each case you might care to produce headlines which might have appeared in Tory, Whig, and Radical newspapers.)

2. Draw the posters that might have been used to:
(a) advertise the holding of the election, May 1831;
(b) invite people to a Reform Meeting, October 1831.

13 The Work of the Whigs, 1833-41

The Great Reformers?

In the older history books, people used to describe this Whig period of government as one of 'Great Reform'. We will see later whether this title was deserved or not.

There were at least three quite separate groups of people in Parliament and in the government. There was a small group who wanted human life to be made better than it was. These people were called *Humanitarians*. In the eighteenth century some of these, such as Fry and Howard (p. 49), had tried to get prison conditions improved, and in the nineteenth century Humanitarians argued for a reform of factory conditions and the abolition of slavery.

Another important group was called the *Evangelicals*. They were the clergy and people in the Church of England who tried to give people an enthusiasm for their religion. One result of this was to make some people anxious to bring religion to the poor. This in turn led some of these people to become involved in the campaigns for making life better for the mass of the people. Wilberforce and Lord Shaftesbury were two leading Evangelicals.

There was a third important group of people in Parliament and in the government. These were the men who thought that the government should not play an important part in the economic or social life of the country and its people. Such people believed that no one should try to interfere with trade, business or the economy as a whole. So there was a strong belief in *laissez-faire* – or 'letting alone'. These people said that it was not the job of the government to do anything about factories, housing, sanitation, etc.

The Abolition of Slavery, 1833

In Chapter 5 we saw that Fox had persuaded Parliament to abolish the slave trade in the British Empire. We have also seen that Castlereagh managed to persuade the delegates at Vienna to abolish the trade elsewhere. This meant that there would be no more slave ships carrying people from the coasts of Africa to the West Indies or the United States.

But slavery continued to exist after 1807 and even after 1815. Men, women, and children in the West Indies or America continued to be bought and sold like so many heads of cattle.

Wilberforce and Pitt had taken up the campaign for the abolition of the slave trade in the 1780s (p. 26). The campaign, and that against slavery itself, was headed by members of the Society of Friends, or Quakers. The Quakers could not become M.P.s until the Test and Corporations Acts were abolished in 1828 (p. 51), so they had got Wilberforce to speak on their behalf. Wilberforce was on his death bed when he was told that Parliament had finally passed an Act to abolish slavery in the British Empire. The Act became law on 1 August 1834. On that day:

1. All slaves under the age of 6 were freed immediately;
2. Other slaves remained part-slave and part-free for four years. During that time they had to be paid a wage for their work during the one-quarter of the week when they were 'free';
3. Slave owners were compensated for the loss of their 'property' – the former slaves. The government paid £20 million in compensation. This worked out at about £37.50 for each slave.

Slavery and the Empire

The effects of abolition were most felt in the West Indies and in the former Dutch Colonies in the Cape of Good Hope in South Africa.

The sugar plantations of the West Indies depended on slave labour, but the freed slaves were unwilling to work for the low wages offered by their former owners. Although these owners received £15 million of the compensation money they were unable to make their plantations pay. The West Indies had once been a very important part of the British trading system, but after abolition they faded in their importance to Britain.

In the Cape, the Dutch settlers were already angered by the British government's treatment of black Africans. After abolition the Dutch packed up their possessions and drove on the Great Trek which took them away from the Cape. They crossed the Vaal River and went north. Here they founded two new states. The Transvaal and the Orange Free State were to be places where the Dutch could continue to own slaves. However, this was to lead to struggles between the Dutch and the British later in the century (Chapter 25).

Working Children, 1800–20

Children had always worked in the cottages of the domestic workers, and they continued to work in the factories of the industrialized towns.

Some of these children were sent to industrialized towns by Poor Law authorities looking after orphans (Extract 13.1). In 1802 Robert Owen, a factory owner, persuaded Parliament to pass an Act to limit the working day of these pauper children: their day was cut to twelve hours. In 1819, Sir Robert Peel, father of the future Home Secretary, persuaded Parliament to extend that Act to cover all children. After the 1819 Act no child under the age of 9 was to be employed in textile mills and no child aged between 9 and 12 was to be forced to work more than twelve hours a day.

But these Acts had very little effect. How were people to know the ages of children before the government had passed an Act forcing parents to register a child's birth (1836)? Who would go around the mills to make sure that owners were obeying the Act? The government left that task to local magistrates. Many of these were factory owners, others were related to factory owners; few of them bothered to summons anyone found guilty of breaking the law.

Sadler and Shaftesbury

In the 1820s Michael Sadler M.P., a Humanitarian, took up the cause of factory reform. Parliament set up a commission to investigate conditions in factories, and this reported to Parliament in 1831–2. It is from the details in this report that we know how badly children were treated in many factories (Extract 13.1).

However, Sadler lost his seat in 1832, and the case of factory reform was taken up by an Evangelical, Lord Shaftesbury. Many M.P.s argued against reforming factories. Some argued that the government ought to let owners get on with their own businesses. Others argued that, if factory hours were cut, British trade would be ruined.

The 1833 Act

Parliament passed a Factory Act which became law in July 1833. The really important part of this Act was that it allowed the government to appoint four Factory Inspectors. This was not a large number, but at least it was a beginning. And these Inspectors would be paid by the government. Therefore, they would not come under the influence of the owners. The reports of these Inspectors were to lead to other factory reforms in the 1840s.

But this Act was really a small step. It only applied to children in textile mills – and even then it excluded silk and lace-making factories. It did not apply to coal-mines – and many children went to work down in mines when they were not allowed to work in mills. Nor did it apply to brickyards, ironworks, engineering yards and other places where children continued to do dirty, hard, and dangerous work (Fig. 13.1).

Fig. 13.1 This engraving shows carding, drawing and roving. Can you find out what these processes are?

The Education Grant, 1833

One of the clauses in the 1833 Factory Act said that all children working in mills had to have two hours a day in school. This made the government take some interest in the question of children's schooling. The government decided to spend £20,000 a year on helping to find schools and teachers for the country's children, but in the same year it gave £50,000 for the rebuilding of the stables at Windsor Castle. Children were certainly not as important as horses in 1833.

The Poor Law Amendment Act, 1834

One of the effects of the increasing use of machinery was that there was a rise in the number of people out of work. These people had to go to the local magistrates and ask for assistance. This was provided out of money collected as a Poor Rate in each parish.

Other people also went to ask for parish assistance. First, there were the orphan children who had to be looked after; secondly, there were the old who could no longer work; and finally, there were the workers whose wages were too low to enable them to pay the high prices for bread. We have already seen that in 1795 the magistrates in Speenhamland near Newbury

had worked out a system of helping the workers to make ends meet (Extract 8.1 on p. 46). All these demands increased the Poor Rates.

In 1833 Parliament set up a Commission to examine the working of the Poor Law system throughout the country. It handed in a Report in 1834 and Parliament passed an Act that included most of the suggestions made by the Commission. This Act said:

1. No fit (or 'able-bodied') person was to receive money or other help from the Poor Law authorities except in a workhouse.

2. Conditions in workhouses were to be made very harsh to discourage people from asking for this help (Fig. 13.2).

3. Workhouses were to be built in each parish or, if a parish were too small, in a union of parishes. This gave the name Union to many workhouses.

4. Ratepayers in each parish or Union were to elect a Board of Guardians to supervise the working of the workhouse, the collection of the Poor Rate, and the sending of reports to the Central Poor Law Commission.

5. Three men should be appointed by the government to form a Poor Law Commission or Board. These would have an office in Whitehall in London. They would make sure that the system was working properly everywhere in the country.

Fig. 13.2 Inside a workhouse. Wives were separated from husbands, and children over five had their own wards away from their parents.

THE POOR MAN'S FRIEND.

Fig. 13.3 As this cartoon from Punch *shows, the only release from poverty for many was death.*

The Working People and the Poor Law Act

The people on the Commission and most M.P.s seemed to think that the poor were to blame for their own condition. They thought that if a man wanted a job and a living wage he could go and get one. This showed that they knew very little about the life of the mass of the people. Lowly paid for hard work and long hours, most had a poor diet, little furniture (Extract 14.1), and often became very ill (Fig. 13.3). Few, if any, of these people could change the conditions in which they lived and worked.

The workers were already angry because the 1832 Reform Act had done nothing for them, and now the middle-class Parliament had passed an Act which made life even harder for the workers. It is not surprising that many of them joined the Chartist movement which wanted more parliamentary reform (Chapter 15).

Others behaved as the Luddites had done. They attacked the new workhouses, attacked the Guardians going to and from their meetings, and tried to put a stop to the new Act. But they failed. They had to wait until they got the vote for a change in the Poor Law system.

Lord Melbourne replaces Earl Grey, 1834

In 1834 Earl Grey retired, and the new leader of the Whigs was Lord Melbourne. He had left the Tory Party in 1828 when Wellington refused to agree to Catholic Emancipation (p. 51).

In 1830 he was Home Secretary in the Whig government. It was Melbourne who sent troops to put down the rioters in the agricultural counties; and it was Melbourne who congratulated the magistrates at Dorchester who sent the Tolpuddle weavers to prison in Australia (p. 108).

So he, like Grey, was no Radical anxious to reform the country.

Town Councils

Today we expect to find a council wherever we live, and we expect it to do a number of things. The council organizes our schools, street cleansing, refuse collection, libraries, parks and, in many places, the water supply.

In 1835 there were only 178 councils in England and Wales. These were in the old boroughs which had, at one time or other, got a Charter to allow the townspeople to have their own councils (or corporation). There were no councils in the new and growing towns in the industrial areas.

Each of the 178 councils was controlled by a small number of people. Bath was typical of the rest. About 110 of the 38,000 people elected a council of 30 men. This, of course, was far from democratic, and the new middle class wanted a chance to have a vote in the election of their councils.

Municipal Corporations Act 1835

In 1835 all this was changed. The Act said:

1. All ratepayers should have a vote in council elections.

2. Each town should be divided into wards and councillors elected for each ward.

3. The councillors should choose aldermen; aldermen would form one-quarter of the council.

4. The council was to organize a police force.

Other Towns

The councils in the 178 reformed boroughs were not asked to do anything about housing, street cleansing, refuse collection, schools – or water supply. We will see later who handled all these services.

73

But at least the old boroughs had councils. The new towns did not. The 1835 Act had one clause that allowed people in such towns to ask Parliament to give them the right to elect a council of their own. So, for example, Manchester got its own council in 1839. Other towns did the same. But in some places important industrialists managed to stop such a move. So, for example, Merthyr, the 'iron city' of the world, did not get a council until 1907.

Minor Reforms

The 1835 Act was the last of the major reforms passed by the Whig government, although there were other, smaller, reforms. In 1836 there was an Act that compelled people to register every birth, marriage, or death. Today, each of us has a birth certificate issued by the Registrar-General. This system was started by the 1836 Act. Only after that date could people be certain of a child's age, and only then could the terms of Factory Acts really be made to work.

In 1840 the government set up a system of Penny Post. This had been proposed by Rowland Hill in a pamphlet published in 1837. In 1839 he was employed by the government to advise on how the system would work, and in 1840 the pre-paid postal system was introduced.

Queen Victoria

King William IV died just after midnight on 20 June 1837. Lord Conyngham, the Lord Chamberlain, and Archbishop Howley went from the King's deathbed to Kensington. Here, Princess Victoria, the dead King's niece, had to be woken up to be told that she was now Queen of Great Britain and Ireland.

On the following day she met Lord Melbourne and the other members of the Privy Council. She was only 18 years old. Therefore, it is not surprising that she asked Melbourne to help her in her new position, and it is no less surprising that the old man should have treated her as a daughter. There was a close relationship between the young Queen and her Prime Minister. This helped to make her dislike Robert Peel, Melbourne's political opponent.

Melbourne guided the young Queen through the first three years of her reign. In 1840 she married her cousin, Prince Albert, and he became her chief adviser, her 'permanent minister'. In 1841 the Whigs lost seats in the general election and the young Queen was forced to ask Peel to form a new government (Chapters 14 and 15).

Questions

Extract 13.1

Child workers, 1832

(a) Robert Blincoe, a Mill Worker:
I have had two hand-vices of a pound weight each, screwed to my ears. Then three or four of us have been hung on a cross-beam above the machinery, hanging on by our hands, without shirts or socks. Mind, we were apprentices, without father or mother to take care of us; I don't think they often do that now. Then we used to stand up, in a skip, without our shirts, and be beat with straps or sticks.

(b) John Moss, Apprentice Master:
What were the hours of work? From 5 o'clock in the morning till 8 at night, all the year through.
What time was allowed for meals? Half an hour for breakfast and half an hour for dinner.
Had they any refreshment in the afternoon? Yes.
Did they work whilst they ate it? Yes. They had no cessation after dinner 'til 8 o'clock at night.
Did any children work on Sundays as cleaners of the machine? Yes, every Sunday from six to twelve.

(c)
At what time in the morning, in the busy time, did these girls go to the mills? In the busy time, for about six weeks, they had gone at 3 o'clock in the morning and ended at 10, or nearly half-past, at night.
What was the wage in the short hours? Three shillings a week each.
When they wrought those very long hours what did they get? Three shillings and sevenpence halfpenny.
(*Report of Committee on Factory Children's Labour, 1831–2.*)

On Section (a)
1. Who looked after children when their parents died?
2. Why were many children sent away as 'apprentices'?
3. Where were they sent? Why were people willing to take them?
4. How were children punished? Can you suggest why they might have been?
On Section (b)
5. How many hours did these children work (i) each day (ii) per week?
6. What arrangements were made for them to have meals?
On Section (c)
7. How many hours did these children work?
8. Work out how much they received for each hour of work. (Remember that 5p is the same as 1 shilling or 12 old pence.)

Extract 13.2

Travelling by train, 1837

I resolved to run down here to see the Birmingham railroad, Liverpool, and Liverpool races. So I started at five o'clock on Sunday evening, got to Birmingham at half-past five on Monday morning, and got upon the railroad at half-past seven. Nothing can be more comfortable than the vehicle in which I was put, a sort of chariot with two places, and there is nothing disagreeable about it but the occasional whiffs of stinking air which it is impossible to exclude altogether. The first sensation is a slight degree of nervousness and a feeling of being run away with, but a sense of security soon supervenes, and the velocity is delightful. Town after town, one park and chateau after another are left behind with the rapid variety of a moving panorama, and the continual bustle and animation of the changes and stoppages make the journey very entertaining. The train was very long, and heads were continually popping out of the several carriages, attracted by well-known voices, and then came the greetings and exclamations of surprise, the 'Where are you going?' and 'How on earth came you here?' Considering the novelty of its establishment, there is very little embarrassment, and it certainly renders all other travelling irksome and tedious by comparison. It was peculiarly gay at this time, because there was much going on. There were all sorts of people going to Liverpool races, barristers to the assizes, and candidates to their several elections.

(Henry Reeve (ed), *The Greville Memoirs*, 4th ed., 1875.)

1. How far is it from London to Birmingham? Greville travelled from London by coach. Find the average speed of the coach.
2. How far is it from Birmingham to Liverpool? If the train travelled at 50 m.p.h. (80.45 km.p.h.) how long did it take to get from Birmingham to Liverpool?
3. How did the development of the railway industry affect the growth of the coal, iron, and engineering industries of Britain? How far is it right to talk of a second Industrial Revolution starting around 1830? Why?

Worksheet

(A)
1. Write two sentences on each of the following: Humanitarians; Evangelicals; *laissez-faire*.

2. Make a list of the main reforms passed by the Whigs, 1833–41. You might like to illustrate this list to show the importance of each reform.

3. Explain how the abolition of slavery affected white people in (i) the West Indies (ii) South Africa. (Why had they needed black workers? Where had these come from? What did the Abolition Act say about the future for former slaves? Why would this Act push up the cost of running plantations in the West Indies?)

4. Use the following names to write a series of short paragraphs on factory reform: Owen; Peel; Sadler; Shaftesbury.

5. Why did some owners become supporters of the movement for factory reform?

6. In 1834 the government passed the Poor Law Amendment Act. Explain (i) why some people thought that the Poor Law needed to be reformed (ii) how the Law was amended in 1834 (iii) who gained from these changes, and (iv) who lost by them.

7. Write a brief account of the career of Lord Melbourne using the following as guide-lines: (i) 1828–30 (ii) 1830 (iii) 1834 (iv) 1835–40 (v) Queen Victoria.

(B)
1. Write the letters that might have been sent by:
(a) an M.P. who had voted for Abolition of Slavery and who was writing to the dying Wilberforce;
(b) a Dutch farmer in South Africa after the passing of the Abolition of Slavery Act;
(c) a Radical opponent of the Poor Law Amendment Act.

(C)
1. Write the headlines that might have appeared above reports on:
(a) the 1833 Factory Act – in papers controlled by supporters and opponents of the Act;
(b) the riots against the new workhouses;
(c) the introduction of the system of Penny Post, 1840;
(d) the Accession of Queen Victoria.

2. Draw the posters that might have been used to:
(a) advertise the sale of slaves;
(b) advertise an outing by train.

14 Peel's Government, 1841-6

His Earlier Career

Sir Robert Peel became Prime Minister in 1841. He was the son of a prosperous cotton-manufacturer, so he knew something about the importance of industry and trade. His father had played a large part in the passing of the Factory Acts of 1802 and 1819 (p. 71). His son inherited his father's concern for people's well-being.

Peel had been educated at Harrow and Oxford: he had the sort of education that only the sons of the landed gentry had had until the Industrial Revolution. He became an M.P. in 1809 and Lord Liverpool appointed him to be Chief Secretary of Ireland.

Peel supported the Protestants and their Orange Order (p. 56), and this earned him the nickname of 'Orange' Peel. In 1822 he became Home Secretary (p. 49).

He opposed Canning's proposals for Catholic Emancipation in 1827 but supported Wellington's similar proposals in 1829 (p. 52).

Peel as Leader of the Tories, 1830–41

Peel opposed the Reform Bills in 1831–2. In 1834 Earl Grey resigned (p. 73), and King William invited Peel to form a government. This gave him the chance to write a letter (or 'Manifesto') to his electors in Tamworth, Derbyshire. In this he explained that he accepted the Reform Act as a 'final settlement' of the question of parliamentary reform. He also promised that he would make a 'careful review' of other organizations so that he could 'correct abuses and redress grievances' when necessary. This was the start of a new stage in the history of the Tory Party. People began to write about the 'Conservative' Party; they tried to forget the name Tory which reminded them of repression and an unwillingness to accept reform.

The Failure of the Whigs, 1830–41

The Whigs had carried out a number of reforms, but they had failed to understand the problems of Britain's growing towns. They had done nothing about the problems of housing, street cleansing, refuse collection, or water supply. Nor had they tried to solve the question of poverty (Fig. 14.1) which led to poor housing, poor diet and ill health (Extract 14.1). In 1838 there was a fall in the amount of trade, and the country suffered a depression. Thousands of workers were thrown out of work. But the Whigs offered no solutions to the trade problem.

Peel and Working Conditions

In 1840 Shaftesbury persuaded Parliament to set up a commission to examine conditions in the mines. The report of this commission gave many descriptions of the dirty, dangerous, and unhealthy work done by women and young children.

Shaftesbury introduced a Bill that became the Mines Act 1842. This stated that women and children under the age of 10 were not allowed to work underground.

In 1844 Parliament passed a Factory Act that compelled factory owners to put fencing around dangerous machinery. If they did not do so they could be fined or sent to prison. The Act also reduced the age at which children could be employed in mills from 9 to 8 years. You will remember that in 1836 Parliament had passed a Registration Act, and therefore in 1844 it was possible to know a child's age. The Act also reduced the hours of work for children aged between 8 and 12 to six and a half hours a day.

Peel and the Conditions in Towns

Peel set up several commissions to examine the conditions in Britain's industrial towns. The reports of these commissions make gloomy reading. They all tell of poor housing, an almost complete absence of any system of sanitation, street cleansing, or refuse collection. They found that most people got their water from some polluted source such as a river (Fig. 14.2).

A small number of people had become interested in this question of sanitary reform. They proved that a high death rate and a high rate of sickness were caused by poor sanitary conditions.

Fig. 14.1 The artist who drew this cellar home near St Giles, London, stressed that he had 'sketched it on the spot'. There were millions of people living in single rooms, but the thousands who lived in cellars were the poorest.

Fig. 14.2 The scientist Michael Faraday wrote a report on the pollution of the Thames. London's water supplies were taken straight from the Thames even though industries along the bank poured their untreated waste products into the river. Dead animals, floating in the water, were a common sight.

FARADAY GIVING HIS CARD TO FATHER THAMES;
AND WE HOPE THE DIRTY FELLOW WILL CONSULT THE LEARNED PROFESSOR.

The Cost of Poor Sanitary Conditions

Edwin Chadwick was one of the Poor Law commissioners who had to supervise the working of the Poor Law system, (p. 72). Chadwick and his fellow commissioners soon realized that a great deal of the money spent by the Guardians had to be spent because of the poor sanitary conditions in Britain's towns. They argued that if conditions were improved there would be a drop in the level of the poor rates.

This argument appealed to many people, and led to a demand for action by the government. In 1845–6 Britain was attacked by a massive outbreak of cholera. Thousands of people died, thousands more suffered long illness and made slow recoveries. This increased the demand for sanitary reform.

77

The Public Health Act 1848

Peel was defeated in 1846, and therefore was not Prime Minister when Parliament passed the first Public Health Act (1848). But the work of the various commissions had played a part in setting the stage for this Act.

The Act said:

1. A General Board of Health would be set up in London to give advice to towns.

2. Local Boards of Health *could* be elected by ratepayers in the towns.

3. A Local Board *had to be* elected if the death rate in the town rose to 23 per 1,000 of the population *or* if 10 per cent of the ratepayers signed a petition asking for such a Local Board.

A number of Local Boards were set up while people remembered the horror of cholera. But many people disliked what these Boards did. Local laws were passed to compel builders to put a water supply into new houses; all streets had to be drained, cleansed and swept; refuse had to be taken away; and the Board forced people to pay a Health Rate to provide the money needed to pay for this work.

The majority of M.P.s and local councillors supported the argument of *laissez-faire* (p. 70), and did not think it was the government's job to look after people's social conditions. So there was a growing opposition to Chadwick and his Board of Health, and in 1854 the Board was abolished. But its work continued. The Local Government Board was set up to supervise the work of the Local Boards of Health, and as time went by Parliament gave these even greater powers in the hope that this would make Britain a cleaner and healthier place.

The Railway System

The Stockton–Darlington railway was opened in 1825 (Fig. 1.3 on p. 4) amid scenes of great rejoicing. Even in 1837 a journey by train was something extraordinary (Extract 13.2 on p. 75). But in the 1840s more and more people became more and more used to seeing trains.

By 1850 Britain was covered in a network of railway lines. Trains carried the mail, food, coal and iron, manufactured goods, and building materials. Railway companies employed thousands of people and helped to provide employment for thousands of others – in the coal, iron, steel, and engineering industries.

Railway companies made high profits from carrying goods, so they did not want to carry passengers. But Peel realized the value of the railway system for the people and in 1844 he supported a Railway Act which forced every company to provide at least one passenger train a day on every line. The Act also said that passengers were not to pay more than one old penny (or two-fifths of a modern penny) for every mile they travelled.

This made it possible for many people to travel by train – to the seaside or work (Fig. 14.3).

Peel, Gladstone and Import Duties, 1841–5

When he became Prime Minister in 1841 Peel appointed William Ewart Gladstone to the post of President of the Board of Trade. Gladstone had been elected to the Commons in 1832. He was M.P. for one of those many rotten boroughs that continued to exist even after the Reform Act. Like Peel, Huskisson, and Canning, Gladstone knew a great deal about industry and trade. His family had made its fortune in the shipbuilding and shipping business. Their headquarters were in Liverpool which, as we have seen, was one of the first towns to show the signs of Britain's growth as an industrial power.

Peel, the son of a cotton manufacturer, and Gladstone, son of a shipowner, both believed in free-trade. In 1842 import duties were reduced to:

1. a maximum of 5 per cent on raw materials;

2. no more than 12 per cent on semi-manufactured goods; and

3. 30 per cent on manufactured goods.

So cotton manufacturers and others were able to get their raw materials more cheaply, and this enabled them to lower the prices of their finished goods. In turn, this meant that more people could buy the goods. The increased demand for goods led to more employment, better wages, higher profits, and a rise in the nation's prosperity.

In 1843 and 1844 some import duties were abolished completely, and in 1845 tariffs were lowered again so that the duty on manufactured goods fell to only 10 per cent. Some duties were abolished. This policy of Free Trade helped make Britain the 'Workshop of the World'. British factories used an increasing amount of foreign raw materials, and this meant that there was more work in the countries producing the raw materials. People in those countries had more money, and they spent some of it on British goods – clothing, furniture, pottery, and so on. There was a growth in the volume of British exports – and so more work, better wages, and higher profits.

The Corn Laws

Some of the manufacturers and other Free Traders argued that the Corn Laws ought to be repealed. We

Fig. 14.3 The arrival of the workmen's penny train at Victoria Station, London, 22 April 1865.

will see, in Chapter 15, how Peel dealt with this argument.

Income Tax

A cut in the level of import duties led to a fall in the amount of money coming into the Treasury, so Peel brought back the tax on incomes. Only people earning more than £150 a year had to pay it and even then they paid only a small tax of 7d [3p] in each £.

The Bank Charter Act 1844

Anyone could open a bank. They could ask people to lend them their gold, which was described as 'cash'. They could print their own banknotes to lend to other customers to build a factory, buy raw materials, or develop a firm.

In 1840 there were a very large number of small banks in Britain. Not all of them were properly run, many printed too many notes. The result was that they were unable to exchange the notes for gold when customers asked them to. When a bank went out of business (or 'bankrupt') local businesses suffered if they had been keeping their 'cash' in that bank. When one bank went down, there was often a rush to get money out of other banks. This drove some of these banks into bankruptcy also.

Peel knew that this financial uncertainty was not a good thing, so he brought in a Bank Charter Act in 1844. This stated that:

1. No new banks would be allowed to issue their own notes;

2. Existing banks could not increase the number of notes they printed;

3. When two or more banks amalgamated to make a larger firm, they would all lose their right to issue notes;

4. The Bank of England was to be split into two parts. One looked after the ordinary business of a bank – taking in money from some customers and lending it to others. The second (or *Issue*) section was to deal with the printing and issuing of Bank of England banknotes. All the notes issued had to be covered by an equal value of gold in the Bank's vaults – except for £14 million known as the fiduciary (or 'on trust') issue.

One effect of this Act was a fall in the number of note-issuing banks, but as industry grew there was a demand for large sums of money to finance the expansion. Small banks could not provide enough. Many of them amalgamated, and lost their right to issue notes. The last private note-issuing bank amalgamated with Lloyds in 1921.

Before 1844 the Bank of England had been only one out of hundreds of banks. The 1844 Act gave it a special position, and its notes became the normal currency of the country.

The Act halted the number of bank failures, although a few did fail after 1844. This gave a boost to business confidence. Men could rely on the banking system. This encouraged them to invest, to build up their firms – and so make Britain even more prosperous.

The Hungry Forties

In 1841 Britain was going through a trade depression (p. 82). Many people were out of work and living standards were very low (Extract 15.1 on p. 86).

During the 1840s there was a rapid growth in employment as a result of the development of the railways and of the Free Trade policy. More people were at work and earning money. The cost of goods fell because of Free Trade, and this led to a rise in living standards. People could afford better furniture, good clothing, and a varied diet.

The Co-operative Movement

Because of that improvement working people became more confident. One sign of that confidence was a decision made by a group of working men in Rochdale in 1844. They decided to run a co-operative shop rather than buy their goods from other shops. Instead of giving a profit to shopkeepers they would keep the profit for themselves, sharing it out as a dividend each year. This idea spread throughout the country. This 'dividend' was yet another form of saving for the working men and their families (Extract 14.2).

Peel and Ireland

Peel tried to help the education of Ireland's priests by giving more money to Maynooth College (p. 57), but the Irish problem was much greater than Peel and the British realized. In 1845 the Great Famine struck Ireland (p. 57), and Peel had no answer to this problem. However, the Famine forced him to re-examine the Corn Laws, and he was already under some pressure to repeal them. The Famine provided him with the excuse to do so (Chapter 15).

Questions

Extract 14.1

The effects of low wages and unemployment, 1838

In all I visited 83 dwellings. They were without furniture, only old boxes for tables, and stools, or even large stones for chairs; the beds were of straw and shavings, sometimes with torn pieces of carpet or packing canvas for a covering and sometimes without any kind of covering whatever. The food was oatmeal and water for breakfast; flour and water with a little skimmed milk, for dinner; oatmeal and water again for those who had three meals a day. I was informed by fifteen families that their children went without the 'blue milk', or milk from which the cream had been taken, on alternate days. I saw children eating decayed vegetables in the root-market. I saw a woman in the very last stage of hunger suckling an infant child which could scarcely draw a single drop of nutriment from her exhausted breast. I inquired of the child's age – 'fifteen months'. 'Why was it not weaned?' Another mouth would have been added to the number of those for whom the supply of oatmeal was insufficient. I was told that there had been several instances of death by sheer starvation.
(W. Cooke-Taylor, *Tour in the Manufacturing Districts of Lancashire*, 1838.)

1. What sort of furniture did these people have? How does this compare with the furniture shown in Fig. 14.1?
2. How many meals did they have? Make a list of the food described here. Compare this with the food which you eat. You might make illustrations to go with each list. (You could get cut-outs from coloured magazines.)

3. What is 'blue milk'? Why did poor people buy such milk? Why was it dangerous to the health of growing children?
4. How did hungry children manage to get food?
5. How does this extract help to explain the high rates of (i) death among babies and young children, and (ii) sickness among working people?

Extract 14.2

Founding a co-operative shop, 1865

The members held meetings and subscribed about £20. Two were sent to Newcastle to make the first purchases. They laid out the money to the best of their ability, buying a cask of herrings, a side of bacon, tobacco, etc. Their return was looked for anxiously. Cramlington being on a hill, with two roads leading from Newcastle, men were seen walking from one end to the other, like smugglers looking for a lugger. At last a little spring cart made its appearance, which caused some to come out and stand laughing at the madcaps. The cart having got to the little room, the shop was opened. The reader can imagine how the parcels would be made up by inexperienced men, but the purchasers had their weight. The stock was nearly sold out on the first Friday night and the two men went to buy more. They went on this way for the first three months, doubling and trebling their orders, till at last the dividend was declared. The number of members now rapidly increased. In the first quarter £450 was received, realizing a profit of £39. The receipts of the quarter ending March 1873 amounted to £23,000 of which £2,478 was profit. The members had increased from 80 to 1,688.
(J. Fynes, *Miners of Northumberland and Durham*, 1875.)

1. How did the working men get the money to start off their co-operative? What does this tell you about their standard of living and their wages?
2. Who ran the shop? How did that make it different from other shops?
3. When and why did the number of members increase?
4. What good habits did the co-operative encourage? How did (i) the Post Office Savings Bank (1861), and (ii) Building Societies also do so?
5. Why did the co-operative movement appeal to the skilled workers and mean very little to the majority of workers who were often out of work?

Fig. 14.1

1. How was this 'home' lit? Where did the mother cook the family's meals?

2. The family paid the equivalent of $12\frac{1}{2}$p a week in rent. Why did they not rent more than one room? Why did the landlord charge this rent and not a lower one? Why was the landlord unable to afford to pay for repairs to this room?
3. Why were people living in such 'homes' often ill?
4. Compare the furniture in this room with that listed in Extract 14.1. Compare the furniture of the Victorian poor with that in your own home. You might make coloured illustrations to go with the list of furniture.

Worksheet

(A)
1. Write two sentences (or more if you wish) on each of the following: (i) Peel and people's working conditions (ii) Peel and the conditions of British towns (iii) Peel and the Railway Act 1844.

2. Why were there more people at work in 1845 than in 1838? Why did that lead to a rise in living standards for some people?

3. Show how the development of a railway system affected: (i) employment – in that industry and other industries (ii) the distribution of food – and the health of the people (iii) the growth of towns.

4. Why did Peel cut the level of tariffs? Make a list of the cuts that he made. How did these affect (i) the cost of living (ii) the number of people employed in British industry?

(B)
1. Write the letters that might have been sent by:
(a) a manufacturer welcoming the cuts in tariffs;
(b) someone who wanted more sanitary reform in British towns;
(c) someone comparing life in 1838 with life in 1845.

(C)
1. Make a time chart for the years 1841–6. Mark on it the main dates and events mentioned in the text. Add a line of explanation for each of the dates and events.

2. Write the headlines that might have appeared above reports on:
(a) the Tamworth Manifesto;
(b) the trade depression of 1838;
(c) the outbreak of cholera, 1839;
(d) the setting up of the Board of Health, 1848;
(e) the Railway Act 1844.

15 The Chartists and the Anti-Corn Law League, 1838-50

Between 1837 and 1850 there were two nation-wide movements that wanted to get different laws changed: the Chartist movement and the Anti-Corn Law League. We will see that by 1850 the Chartist movement seemed to have failed while the Anti-Corn Law League had obviously succeeded. However, by the end of the century there was a movement to bring back import duties – on food and other imports; so maybe the success of the League was short-lived. On the other hand, by 1914 Parliament had passed a number of Acts that gave the country most of the reforms that the Chartists had asked for.

Their Common Origin – Trade Depressions

Between 1837 and 1841, and again in 1845 and 1847, there was widespread unemployment in Great Britain. The owners of the new and larger iron foundries could not sell their iron in Britain or overseas, so they closed down some of them. This led to a fall in the demand for coal, for transport workers to carry the coal and iron, and for the many unskilled men who worked on the docks loading and unloading ships. When these people had no work, they had no money to spend on food, clothing, furniture, and so on. This led to unemployment in textile mills (Extract 15.1), shops, flour mills – and among farmworkers.

A fall in the level of trade hurt the workman, but it also hurt the owners of industries. They had less profit when their works either closed or worked for only part of a week. Owner and workman were tied together.

The Workman in a Depression (Extract 15.1)

What happened to the families of the unemployed? They had a choice to make between begging and going into the new workhouses. Before 1834 they might have had a chance to get some money and help from the local magistrates, but after the passing of the Poor Law Amendment Act (1834) they had to go to the workhouse if they wanted money or help.

Here the men were separated from the women, children taken from their parents, and food, clothing, and bedding was of the lowest quality. It is not surprising that people were reluctant to go to the workhouses, nor that there were many attacks on these hated places by hungry people.

The new Poor Law was passed by a reformed Parliament. The Chartists wanted to make Parliament more democratic so that working people could become M.P.s and voters. They thought that a democratically elected Parliament would pass better laws about unemployment, housing, education, and other issues that concerned the working class.

It has been said that Chartism was a 'knife and fork' question. That is quite true. The Six Points (Fig. 15.1) were concerned with reforming Parliament, but the real aim of the Chartists was to get new laws passed about social questions.

Employers and the Depression

Most of the employers had a vote after the Reform Act of 1832, but Parliament was still controlled by the landowning aristocracy who had passed the Corn Laws in 1815. These landowning politicians seemed to be unable to do anything about the trade depressions which led some people to describe the period 1837–42 as 'the Hungry Forties'. Earl Grey and Lord Melbourne, the Whig Prime Ministers, did not seem to understand what was happening.

The employers – industrialists who sold their goods abroad – thought that they knew what ought to be done. They wanted to abolish the Corn Laws. They said that this would lead to a rise in the imports of food from France, Germany, Russia, and elsewhere, which meant that farmers in those countries would have money to spend. This money would be spent on British exports – clothing, kitchen utensils, and so on. There would then be a rise in the demand for more workmen in the factories making these goods (Extract 15.2).

The Six Points

OF THE

PEOPLE'S

CHARTER.

1. A VOTE for every man twenty-one years of age, of sound mind, and not undergoing punishment for crime.

2. THE BALLOT.—To protect the elector in the exercise of his vote.

3. NO PROPERTY QUALIFICATION for Members of Parliament —thus enabling the constituencies to return the man of their choice, be he rich or poor.

4. PAYMENT OF MEMBERS, thus enabling an honest tradesman, working man, or other person, to serve a constituency, when taken from his business to attend to the interests of the country.

5. EQUAL CONSTITUENCIES, securing the same amount of representation for the same number of electors, instead of allowing small constituencies to swamp the votes of large ones.

6. ANNUAL PARLIAMENTS, thus presenting the most effectual check to bribery and intimidation, since though a constituency might be bought once in seven years (even with the ballot), no purse could buy a constituency (under a system of universal suffrage) in each ensuing twelvemonth; and since members, when elected for a year only, would not be able to defy and betray their constituents as now.

Fig. 15.1 One of the many charters.

Protest Movements Start

Many local clubs were formed to protest against the unfair way in which the Reform Act had given the vote only to the better-off. In 1837 delegates from many of these clubs met at a National Conference at Birmingham. This drew up The National Petition (1837) which was presented to Parliament in 1838.

This was the first of the several Petitions which the protesters presented to Parliament. The protesters were given the name Chartists because of the wording of a poster (Fig. 15.1).

Middle-class manufacturers also formed their own local clubs and societies – but to protest against the Corn Laws. Delegates from many of these clubs met at the York Hotel in Manchester on 10 January 1839. Here they formed the Anti-Corn Law League.

Fig. 15.2 Cobden addresses a meeting of the Anti-Corn Law League Council.

The Difference in the Arguments and Appeals

The argument of the League was very simple. It wanted to abolish the Corn Laws. Everyone could understand that, and everyone could understand what would happen if these Laws were abolished. Food would be cheaper, and this would make life better for the working people. Food imports would rise but the countries that sold Britain the food would be able to buy British goods, so there would be more work in Britain, and both workers and employers would benefit.

The arguments of the Chartists were more complicated. First, there is some difficulty in understanding even the words of the Charter (Fig. 15.1). Secondly, it is even more difficult to see how *Equal Constituencies* would bring down the cost of living or increase the chances of finding a job. Of course, we know that a democratically elected Parliament has brought about a social revolution in this century. Today we have a state-provided system of social security – largely because the mass of the people voted for M.P.s who would pass laws to set up that system. But it must have been very difficult for the hungry working men of the 1830s and 1840s to see what benefit they would get from *The Ballot* or from the other Points of the People's Charter.

The Methods Used by the League

The League was led by rich industrialists (Fig. 15.2). They asked other rich industrialists to give them money to run a campaign. With this money they could pay for pamphlets, found newspapers, hire halls, pay speakers to go around the country, and so let people know the League's arguments.

After 1832 most industrialists had a vote. So the men who organized the League sent people out to make sure that these industrialists had their names on the electoral registers so that they could vote in elections. The League sent out leaflets to advise the middle-class voters to support candidates who would work for the abolition of the Corn Laws. So Cobden, Bright, Villiers, and other members of the League Council were elected to Parliament.

Inside Parliament these M.P.s argued in favour of the abolition of the Corn Laws. We shall see later that they were fortunate that Peel, the Prime Minister, believed in Free Trade.

The Methods Used by the Chartists

Few of the people who supported the Chartists had the vote, and when the Chartists handed in their National Petitions in 1838, 1842, and 1848, few M.P.s spoke in favour of the reforms demanded by the Six

Points. Most M.P.s were unlikely to be sympathetic to the demand to give the vote to all men over the age of 21 (Fig. 15.1). The M.P.s, as members of the wealthier classes, probably feared that if the electorate was altered so radically they might lose their seats in Parliament.

The Chartists were also unlucky outside Parliament, for they had few rich people among their supporters. Therefore, they could not afford to pay for the pamphlets, posters, and speakers as could the League.

An important weakness of the Chartist movement was a division among its leaders. The majority of them were men who hoped to be able to persuade Parliament to change its mind. Leaders such as William Lovett believed that peaceful persuasion would win the day. They knew that this meant that the reforms they wanted would not come for a long time. But they were prepared to wait – arguing their case from year to year.

Other leaders such as Feargus O'Connor were more impatient. They wanted the reforms to come about immediately. If Parliament would not listen to peaceful persuasion then the people would have to use physical force to make Parliament do what they wanted.

So there were Chartists who were armed – with guns, pikes, and other weapons. There were districts where Chartists went through a form of military training so that they could form part of a Chartist army.

Punch made fun of these physical-force Chartists (Fig. 15.3). But a rising by Welsh miners and ironworkers in 1839 was not at all funny. It led to an attack on Newport by men making their way to Monmouth where one of the Chartist leaders was in prison. Soldiers and workmen were killed – and many people who might have had some sympathy with the Chartists turned against them.

The End of the League's Campaign, 1846

In 1841 Sir Robert Peel became Prime Minister (Chapter 14). We have seen that he brought in a number of Budgets in which he lowered or abolished duties on imports into Britain. This freeing of trade from import duties was part of what we can call a 'Free Trade Stream' which was running strongly in the 1840s. Huskisson (Chapter 9) had been in at the start of that stream; he was the first minister to cut import duties. The Whigs did nothing about duties or about trade at all. Peel, another Tory Minister, took over where Huskisson left off.

But, as Cobden pointed out in Parliament, if Free Trade was good for industry and trade why was it not

A PHYSICAL FORCE CHARTIST ARMING FOR THE FIGHT.

Fig. 15.3 This cartoon, which appeared in Punch, *makes fun of the physical-force Chartists.*

good for corn? One day in Parliament Peel listened to a Cobden speech. He then turned to one of his ministers to say, 'You answer him for I cannot', and when the Corn Laws had been abolished Peel said that it was due to Cobden more than anyone else.

The League also benefited from an Irish tragedy. In 1845 and 1846 a blight attacked the potato crop in Ireland; the potato was the main food of the Irish peasant farmers. When this failed they had no food and no money to buy other produce. Peel decided to allow in, duty free, some cheap maize from Turkey. He hoped that this would be food for the starving peasants. It was ironic that while the peasants starved and maize was brought in, corn was being shipped from Ireland for sale in Britain.

But once Peel had allowed maize to come in duty free, he had made a hole in the tariff wall which had kept out foreign corn. The Duke of Wellington, Tory leader in the House of Lords, claimed that 'it was the rotten potatoes that did it'. Certainly Peel used the Irish famine as the excuse to ask for the repeal or abolition of the Corn Laws.

A few Tory M.P.s protested. They were led by Lord Stanley, the son of the Earl of Derby, by Lord George Bentinck and by Benjamin Disraeli. But all Peel's Cabinet agreed with their leader's proposal, as did the Whigs led by Lord John Russell. So in 1846 the Corn Laws were abolished. Foreign corn could now come in without having to pay any import duty.

The End of the Chartist Campaign, 1848

There was another trade depression in 1847, and this led to an upsurge in Chartism. Once again there were meetings. About 2 million people signed a National Petition to Parliament. O'Connor organized a march on Parliament in April 1848, and thousands of people met on Kennington Common. They were supposed to march to Parliament to hand in the Charter and the petition. Thousands of other Chartists were to march in from north of London.

The government, now led by Lord John Russell, was frightened that the physical-force Chartists might start their revolution. After all, there were revolutions in most European countries at the time – in Italy, Germany, France, Hungary, and so on. So the government made its preparations. Thousands of men were enrolled as special constables; the Army was brought into London; and the Duke of Wellington put in charge of the preparations to defend the capital.

The government did not allow the Chartists to come across the bridge into London, but they did allow a small number in a hansom cab to come with their Charter and to hand this in at the House of Commons. But the march never took place.

When Parliament examined the signatures on the petition, it found that surprising people had signed. There was 'Judas Iscariot', 'Queen Victoria' and 'Pug Nose' among other equally improbable names. The announcement of these findings in the newspapers caused the Chartists to lose much support and the movement soon faded out. Peel's Free Trade policy combined with a rise in the number of railway lines being built helped to make life better for the mass of the people. Once they were better fed and clothed, and once they had jobs and earned wages, few people wanted to get involved in arguments about parliamentary reform.

The Final Result – for the Corn Law League

Disraeli and his Tory followers had argued that repeal would lead to a flood of cheap food from Europe. This, said Disraeli, would ruin British farmers. Cobden and his supporters had claimed that repeal would lead to cheap food for the people. In fact neither Disraeli nor Cobden was right. European farmers had little food for export – they could hardly supply their own population which was continually increasing. It was not until the 1870s and 1880s when cheap food flooded in from America that British farmers were ruined (Chapter 21).

From 1846 to about 1875 British farmers went through what was called 'A Golden Age'. They used the railway network to sell their produce to a wider British market, and that market was a growing one. More people had work at higher wages – and so could afford to buy more and better food. Farmers learned to use machinery, chemicals, and other fertilizers and so made their farms more productive – and profitable.

The Final Result – for the Chartists

The Chartist movement collapsed after 1848. There were still Chartist Clubs which remained in existence in some industrial areas of South Wales and Yorkshire, and these formed the basis for the Labour Party when this got under way in the 1880s.

But if the movement collapsed, the same cannot be said for its Six Points. One by one, five of these have been granted by Parliaments over the years. Only the final point has not been achieved – and it is unlikely that it every will be (Fig. 15.1). We cannot say that the passing of the Ballot Act (1872) or the Payment of Members (1911) or a vote for every man (1867, 1884, and 1918) owes anything to Chartism. But the achievement of five of the Six Points ought to remind us that the Chartists were on the right track – but at the wrong time.

Questions

Extract 15.1

Chartists at Burnley, Lancashire, 1842

> Groups of idlers stood in the street, their faces haggard with famine. Each man had his own tale of sorrow to tell; their stories were complicated details of misery and suffering, gradual in their approach and grinding in their result. 'We want not charity, but employment' was their unanimous declaration. I found them all Chartists, but with this difference – that the handloom weavers united to their Chartism a hatred of machinery, which was far from being shared by the factory operatives. The latter also deprecated anything like an appeal to physical force, while the former strenuously urged an appeal to arms. I heard some openly advocating the burning down of mills in order to compel the factory hands to join an insurrectionary movement.
> (W. Cooke Taylor, *Tour of Lancashire*, 1842).

1. What was the main industry in Burnley? Why did that industry's development lead to a demand for coal?

2. What was meant by 'idlers'? Why were there many idlers in Burnley in 1842?

3. Why were 'their faces haggard with famine'? Where might they have gone to get help? Why were they unwilling to do so?

4. Why were the 'weavers' opposed to 'machinery'? Why did they want to use 'physical force'?

Extract 15.2

Free Trade – More trade

(A) I am a manufacturer of clothing, and I do not know why the making of clothes should not be as honourable as the manufacture of food. Did you ever hear any debates in the House to fix the price of my commodities in the market?
(*Speeches of Richard Cobden, M.P.*, 1870.)

(B) When I went into Brittany and Normandy in 1838 what said the Normans and Bretons? 'Why,' said they, 'admit our corn and then we'll see whether anybody can prevent the importation of your manufactures into France'. (CHEERS!) 'We are millions,' said they, 'willing to clothe ourselves in the garments you send us, and you have millions of hungry mouths to take our corn.'
(A. Prentice, *History of the Anti Corn Law League*, 1853.)

(C) To pay for that corn, more manufacturers would be required from this country; this would lead to an increased demand for labour in the manufacturing districts, a rise of wages, and would clear your streets of the two millions of paupers which now exist in the land.
(*Speeches of Richard Cobden, M.P.*, 1870.)

1. What had Huskisson and Peel done about the taxes paid on the raw materials used in the 'clothing' industry?

2. Why did Cobden think that it was unfair to help the farmer more than the manufacturer?

3. How would the abolition of the Corn Laws lead to an increase in exports to Brittany and Normandy?

4. Why and how would this help the working people of Britain?

Fig. 15.1

1. Which *twenty-one* year-olds are not mentioned? Why?

2. How would the *Ballot* help to *protect the elector*? Why was this more important for the working class than for the middle class?

3. Why did the middle class not ask for *Payment for Members*? Why was this important for the working class?

4. Why do we not have *Annual* elections?

Worksheet

(A)
1. Divide a page of your exercise book in two and then draw up lists to show (i) the advantages of the Anti-Corn Law League, and (ii) the disadvantages of the Chartist movement.

2. Why do we have more chance of unemployment in industrialized countries than in more primitive countries? How did a fall in trade affect (i) the employers, and (ii) the workers? Why were the effects of unemployment harsher in the 1840s than they are today?

3. What were the aims of the Anti-Corn Law League? How and why were they able to pursue those aims between 1829 and 1845? Why were the Corn Laws abolished in 1846?

4. Explain why and how the leadership of the Chartist movement was divided. How did this affect the progress of the movement?

5. Why did working people prefer to support the League rather than the Chartist movement?

(B)
1. Write the letters that might have been sent by:
(a) an unemployed workman explaining (i) why he is out of work (Extract 15.1) (ii) how he would have been treated by the magistrates before 1834 (iii) why he will not go into the workhouse;
(b) a farmer who benefited from the prosperity of the 1850s and 1860s;
(c) an unemployed workman complaining of his employer;
(d) someone who was frightened by the 'physical-force' Chartists.

(C)
1. Write the headlines that might have appeared above reports on:
(a) an attack on a workhouse;
(b) the publication of the Six Points;
(c) the formation of the Anti-Corn Law League (Fig. 15.2);
(d) news of the Irish famine;
(e) the vote that repealed the Corn Laws;
(f) the Chartist march of April 1848;

2. Draw or paint the posters that might have been used:
(a) to advertise a Chartist meeting;
(b) to advertise a meeting of the Anti-Corn Law League.

16 Palmerston's Policies, 1830-65

Palmerston had been a Tory minister from 1809 until 1828. He had admired Canning. In 1828 he resigned from Wellington's government, and he, Lord Melbourne, and other former Tories joined the Whigs. When they came to power in 1830 Palmerston became Foreign Minister.

By 1830 Britain's Industrial Revolution was entering on its second stage. We have already seen that the development of the railway system marks that second stage. Britain became even more industrialized, even richer. She became the 'Workshop of the World'.

Palmerston was able to be an active, energetic, even bullying minister because of Britain's industrial power and wealth.

An Englishman

Palmerston was once asked, 'If you had not been born an Englishman, what nationality would you have liked to be?' His reply showed his arrogant pride in the Englishness, 'If I had not been born an Englishman, I would have liked to have been born an Englishman!'

Like Canning he thought that the duty of the Foreign Minister was to pursue British interests abroad.

Belgium, 1830-9

In 1815 the Austrians had given up their territory in the Netherlands. The former Austrian Netherlands (or Belgium) was united with Holland to make a strong country.

But the Belgian people did not want to be ruled by the Dutch. In July 1830 there was a revolution in France; the new French King was Louis Philippe. The Belgians used this revolution as an excuse to drive out the Dutch.

Austria, Russia, and Prussia had signed the Troppau Protocol (p. 61). They offered to help King William of Holland. The Belgians asked the French to help them. They also offered the crown of their country to the son of the French King.

Palmerston did not want any European power getting control of Belgium, and by the end of 1830 he had persuaded all the powers to come to London for a conference to settle the Belgian affair.

This conference recognized the independence of Belgium, but in the summer of 1831 the Dutch invaded Belgium. The French sent an army to drive them out, and British and French fleets patrolled the northern coast (Fig. 16.1).

The Dutch withdrew from Belgium. It then seemed as if the French might stay in Belgium. Palmerston told the French King that he would not be allowed 'a cabbage-garden or a vineyard' in Belgium. He took the hint and withdrew.

Palmerston then persuaded the Belgians to choose a German prince, Leopold of Saxe-Coburg, as their King. He was Queen Victoria's uncle. The Belgians agreed. Britain now had a friendly nation in this new country.

In 1839 Palmerston organized the signing of the Treaty of London. France, Russia, Prussia, Austria, and Britain agreed that Belgium should be independent (Fig. 16.1). They also agreed that Belgium should be a neutral country. No one would invade Belgium during time of war. The Germans did so in 1914 – and Britain entered the First World War (p. 193).

Spain and Portugal, 1834

In 1828 Dom Miguel had illegally seized the throne of Portugal while the rightful Queen, Donna Maria, was still a baby. He ruled Portugal like a dictator; there was to be no Parliament and little freedom.

This pleased Austria, Prussia, and Russia. They also supported Don Carlos in Spain. He was the brother of the late King Ferdinand who had named his daughter, Isabella, as his successor. Don Carlos argued that only a man should rule – and as a dictator.

Palmerston sent armies to help both the female Monarchs. The Miguelists and Carlists were defeated, and Britain now had two allies to put into the

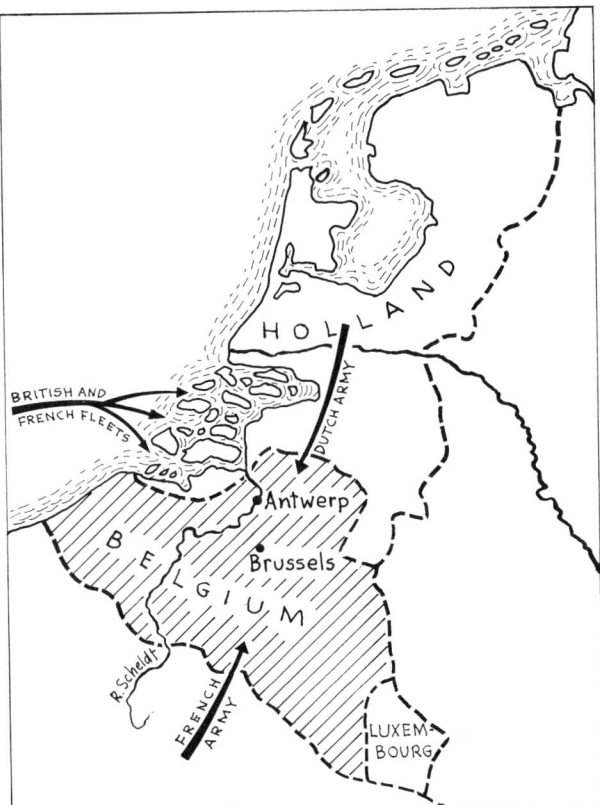

Fig. 16.1 Belgian Independence.

balance against the unfriendly nations of northern and eastern Europe (Extract 16.1).

The Chinese Opium Wars, 1839–42

In the 1830s the British government banned the sale of opium in India. Indian opium growers then sent their product to China. By 1839 the Chinese government had become opposed to this trade, because opium smoking was harmful, and was also costly. Chinese officials despised British traders, calling them 'barbarians'.

There were a number of clashes between Chinese customs officials and British merchants, and in 1839 the Chinese destroyed some ships carrying opium. This led to a war between the two countries. Canton was bombarded by the British Navy and Hong Kong was captured.

The Whigs went out of power in 1841 while this war was still going on. In 1842 Peel's Foreign Minister, Lord Aberdeen, signed the Treaty of Nanking. This stated that the Chinese had to give Hong Kong to Britain. They also had to open five ports – Canton, Amoy, Foochow, Nangpo, and Shanghai – to foreign trade. British traders gained a major share of Chinese trade. This further helped the growth of Britain's foreign trade and spurred on her Industrial Revolution.

The Eastern Question, 1833–41

One of Palmerston's main aims was to stop Russia getting too powerful. We will see how he managed to do this in Chapter 17.

The 1848 Revolutions

Palmerston was in office again in 1846. One of his first problems was the outbreak of revolutions throughout Europe.

Some people hoped that Britain might help the revolutionaries. But Palmerston was only a liberal when it suited British interests – as in Belgium, Spain, and Portugal. He did not send any help to the revolutionaries in Europe in 1848.

The Don Pacifico Affair, 1849–50

Greece had its share of revolution in 1847–8. During one rising the mob in Athens attacked shops and business property, including a shop belonging to Don Pacifico. He had been born in the British colony of Gibraltar and was therefore a British citizen. He asked the Greek government for £26,500 in compensation.

The Greek government turned down his claim, so he appealed to Palmerston. Relations between the Greek and British governments had been poor for some years, and in December 1849 Palmerston ordered a fleet to bombard Athens to bring the Greeks 'to their senses'.

Russia and France had signed the Treaty of London which recognized Grecian Independence. They objected to Britain acting on its own in 1849.

In Britain also there were many protests. Cobden and Bright thought that any war was wrong. Gladstone accused Palmerston of being a bully, but Palmerston defended himself in a speech – 'The Roman lived free from attack when he could say "*Civis Romanus Sum*" (I am a Roman citizen); so also the strong arm of England will protect a British subject against injustice; he will be able to say "*Civis Britannicus Sum*".'

Parliament cheered; the British people admired Palmerston more than ever. But the Greeks only paid £150 to Don Pacifico.

Palmerston and Louis Philippe of France

On p. 95 we will see that Palmerston opposed French ambitions in Egypt in 1839–41. When he got

89

Fig. 16.2 *A cartoon that appeared in 1847 in which Palmerston, as a showman, offers his policies to the people.*

back to office in 1846 he found himself once more opposed to Louis Philippe. Louis wanted Queen Isabella of Spain to marry his son, but Palmerston was opposed to this linking of the crowns of France and Spain. He wanted Isabella to marry a relative of Leopold of Belgium, but Louis would not agree.

Both governments then agreed that Isabella would marry her cousin, Don Francis. Then in the summer of 1846 Louis Philippe announced that while Isabella would marry Don Francis, her sister would marry Louis Philippe's son. It was thought that Don Francis would not be able to have children. So, in time, a child of the marriage of Louis Philippe's son would become King of Spain. Palmerston was furious and became even more an enemy to France (Fig. 16.2).

Palmerston and Louis Napoleon, 1848–51

In 1848 the French had another revolution, and Louis Philippe lost his throne. France became a republic. This meant that they had to elect a President as well as a Parliament, or Assembly. They chose Louis Napoleon, a nephew of the great Napoleon.

By 1850 the Assembly showed that it wanted France to become more democratic. Louis Napoleon used the French army and his own popularity to get himself elected 'President for Life'. Palmerston saw this as a move against the democratic leanings of the Assembly, and he told the French Ambassador in London that he approved of this. The Queen and Prime Minister, Russell, were furious with Palmerston. He had no right to offer this support without first consulting the Cabinet and the Queen. He was dismissed in December 1851.

Tit for Tat, 1852

Palmerston could not be kept out of office for long. He was very popular in the country, popular (only) in the Commons and disliked by the Queen. In 1852 several of his supporters in the Commons united with the Tories to force Russell from office. That, he said, was his 'tit for tat with Johnnie Russell'.

Aberdeen and Palmerston, 1852–5

The new Prime Minister was Lord Aberdeen; Palmerston became Home Secretary. During 1852 and 1853 the government slowly but unwillingly went down the road that led to the Crimean War (Chapter 17). Palmerston became unhappy about the government's policy, and in 1853 he resigned. But the government's conduct of the war was very poor, and in January 1855 Aberdeen was forced to resign. Palmerston became Prime Minister – and held on to that office for the next ten years, apart from a few months of Tory rule in 1859.

The Italian Question, 1858–60

In 1858 there was a growing demand in divided Italy that the country should become one country under the rule of one King. Piedmont became the leader in this unification movement.

Palmerston was in favour of this. He thought Austria had no right to be in Italy (Extract 16.2), but he did not want a war for Italian unification.

In 1853 Louis Napoleon had himself created Emperor Napoleon III. He supported Italian unification and seemed willing to make war to drive Austria out of Lombardy and Venetia, but was unwilling to take the final step and start the war. In January 1858 an Italian refugee, Felice Orsini, threw a bomb in Paris at Napoleon III. The Emperor was unhurt. The bomb had been made in Britain where most of the conspirators lived, and so French newspapers attacked the British government. Palmerston brought in a Conspiracy-to-Murder Bill. This would have allowed the government to arrest Orsini and other conspirators.

Palmerston's opponents accused him of 'truckling to France'. The Bill was defeated in the Commons, and Palmerston had to resign and the Tories formed a government. But in the general election of 1859 they failed to gain a majority and Palmerston became Prime Minister once again.

China again, 1856–60

The Treaty of Nanking satisfied neither the Chinese government nor the British traders, and there were frequent clashes between Chinese people and British merchants. Even as early as 1850 Palmerston saw that there would have to be another attack on China. From 1851 there was a widespread peasant rising against the Chinese government. While this was going on, some Europeans were murdered and in 1856 Chinese customs officers seized the Hong Kong ship, the *Arrow*, and accused the captain of piracy.

Palmerston ordered a fleet to bombard Canton, and a joint British and French army went out in 1857. This defeated the Chinese government's army – already weakened by its own civil war against the peasants. In June 1858 the Chinese signed the Treaty of Tientsin, but the peasants refused to allow the foreigners to use their ports. So the British and French continued to make war.

In 1860 they occupied the Chinese capital, Peking (Fig. 16.3). The government was then forced to sign the Treaty of Peking which confirmed the arrangements made at Tientsin. Eleven more ports were open to trade, including Shanghai and Tientsin.

Fig. 16.3 The Earl of Elgin leads the British troops into Peking on 24 October 1860.

The American Civil War, 1861

In 1861 the slave-owning states of America tried to break away from the Union, and this led to a civil war. Many people in Britain supported the Lincoln government which was trying to end slavery; others supported the slave-owning states which supplied Britain with most of its raw cotton.

In November 1861 a Northern warship stopped a British steamer, the *Trent*, and took off two Southern envoys. Many people in Britain were angry at this American interference with the freedom of shipping. Palmerston sent an angry protest to President Lincoln and the two envoys were released, but many people criticized Palmerston for appearing to support the Southern states.

In 1862 the government allowed the Southern states to build a warship in Liverpool. It was named the *Alabama*, and it destroyed or damaged a great number of ships sailing to northern ports. It was sunk in 1863 by which time it had done a great deal of damage, and the Lincoln government accused the British of having broken international law by allowing the *Alabama* to sail. America claimed compensation from Britain for the damage that the ship had done, but Palmerston refused to agree to this. There was a good deal of ill-feeling between the two countries. Gladstone later agreed to settle this claim when he was in power after 1868 (Chapter 19).

Palmerston and Bismarck, 1863–4

By 1861 Italians had won their struggle for a united Italy, and this increased the national feeling in Germany. From 1862 onwards the Prussian Chancellor, or Prime Minister, Otto von Bismarck, worked for German unification.

He thought that he would help his case if Prussia and Austria attacked Denmark to get back the two small duchies of Schleswig and Holstein. Palmerston threatened to stop Bismarck. 'If any attempt were made to interfere with the freedom of Denmark, those who made the attempt would find it would not be Denmark alone with which they would have to struggle.' Strong words. But Bismarck went ahead with his plans, and the Prussians and Austrians invaded and defeated Denmark and took the two duchies. Palmerston did nothing to stop them.

This was a sign that Britain was no longer the only industrial power in Europe. The German Industrial Revolution had begun and made Germany as strong as Britain. So Palmerston's power was no longer as great as it had been when Britain was quite easily the largest industial nation. His failure to stop Bismarck is a reminder that the power of a Foreign Minister depends on his country's industrial power; and by 1863–4 Germany was almost as strong as Britain. Palmerston's death in 1865 was the end of an era.

Questions

Extract 16.1

Palmerston, Spain and Portugal

> The Ministers had been accused of favouring revolution. They had, indeed, given their moral support to the great Spanish nation, which was endeavouring to imitate this country, by obtaining a representative Government.... They might boast that during the period they had been responsible for the affairs of this country Belgium had become free, independent, prosperous, and tranquil. That Portugal had at last established a free constitution, and was ready to profit by her alliance with this country and Spain.... Spain might yet follow the example set by Belgium and Portugal, and she might become, with the assistance of England, a great member of the European community.... If he could claim any part in such a triumph he should feel it a high honour.
> (Lord Palmerston, House of Commons, 10 March 1837.)

1. When and why had France crushed a rising in 'the great Spanish nation'?
2. How did Palmerston help the Carlists in Spain in 1834?

3. How had Canning helped the Portuguese in 1828? How do you explain Palmerston's admiration for Canning?
4. From which country had Belgium become 'free, independent'? When?
5. What treaty was Palmerston to organize in 1839 to help safeguard the independence of Belgium? How did this treaty affect Britain's entry into the First World War in 1914?

Extract 16.2

Palmerston and Italy

> I am very Austrian north of the Alps, but very anti-Austrian south of the Alps. The Austrians have no business in Italy, and they are a public nuisance there. They govern their own province ill, and are the props and encouragers of bad government in all the other states of the Peninsula (Italy), except in Piedmont, where fortunately they have no influence. Their claim of ancient rights of possession is groundless. Their title goes no further back than the Treaty of Vienna of 1815.... But ... the Austrians cannot be driven from their Italian provinces without a desperate struggle. However desirable their expulsion would be those who might make or recommend or encourage a war for that purpose would incur heavy responsibility.... A war to drive the Austrians out of Italy would succeed in its immediate object ... but if (Austria) was deeply engaged in a conflict with Italy, the Hungarians would rise and Russia would threaten the Galician frontier, and instead of seeing Italy freed, and nothing more, we might find Austria dismembered.
> (Palmerston, letter to Granville, 1857.)

1. Why was Palmerston 'very Austrian north of the Alps'? Which European country did he fear more than any other?
2. How far does this extract help to explain Palmerston's attitude towards the revolutionaries in 1848?
3. Which Italian 'province' was governed by Austria? When and why had she got this territory?
4. Which European ruler was preparing to go to war against Austria in Italy. What did Palmerston fear would happen if war broke out?

Fig. 16.1

1. When were Belgium and Holland united? Why? What gains had Austria made in return for giving up her Netherlands (Belgium)?
2. Why did the Belgians rise in 1830 and not, for example, in 1825 or 1835?

3. Which countries were opposed to Belgian Independence?
4. How did (i) France, and (ii) Britain help the Belgians?
5. Whom did the Belgians want to be their King? Whom did they agree to have as their King? Why was this a victory for Palmerston?
6. Why was Britain always interested in this area? How did it affect British policy in 1793, 1815, and 1914?

Worksheet

(A)
1. Explain the Belgian crisis of 1830–2 to show (i) why Belgium had been joined to Holland (ii) why and when the Belgians revolted (iii) why they asked France for help (iv) why some powers were opposed to Belgian Independence (v) how Palmerston helped Belgium and opposed France.

2. Give an account of Palmerston's relations with France in the following periods: (i) 1830–3 (ii) 1839–41 (iii) 1846–8 (iv) 1851 (v) 1854–6.

3. Write two sentences on Palmerston's relations with each of the following: Don Miguel; Don Carlos. Why did Palmerston's policies with Spain and Portugal lead to the division of Europe into Eastern powers and Western powers?

4. Give an account of Palmerston's policies in China in (i) 1839, and (ii) 1856–60.

5. What was the Don Pacifico affair? Why was Palmerston more popular in Britain because of this affair?

6. Write two sentences on each of the following: The *Arrow*; Orsini; the *Trent*; the *Alabama*.

(B)
1. Make a time chart for the period 1830–65. Mark on it the main dates and events mentioned in the text. Add a line of explanation for each of the dates and events.

2. Write the article (or obituary) that might have appeared after Palmerston's death. You might want to use the following dates as guide-lines: 1828–30; 1830–41; 1846–51; 1851–5; 1856–65.

(C)
1. Draw the poster that might have been used to recruit men to serve in the army sent to China, 1839 OR 1860.

2. Write the headlines that might have appeared

above reports on:
(a) the Treaty of London, 1839 – in British, Belgian, and French papers;
(b) the bombardment of Canton, 1839 – in British and Chinese papers;
(c) the Treaty of Nanking, 1842 – in British and Chinese papers;
(d) Palmerston's speech on *Civis Britannicus sum* – in papers controlled by the government, the Opposition, a Greek merchant;
(e) the question of the Spanish marriages – in British and French papers;
(f) Palmerston's appointment as Prime Minister – in government, Opposition, and Russian papers;
(g) Palmerston's resignation, 1859 – in government, Opposition, French, and Italian papers;
(h) the outbreak of the *Arrow* war – in British and Chinese papers;
(i) the *Trent* incident – in British and American papers;
(j) the Prussian attack on Denmark – in British, Danish, and Prussian papers.

17 Palmerston and the Eastern Question, 1830-56

What is the Question? – Part 1

Between 1760 and 1914 many governments were worried about what they called 'the Eastern Question'. There were, in fact, three smaller questions inside that bigger one. First, there was a question of the Turkish or Ottoman Empire (Fig. 17.1). It stretched across most of North Africa into south-east Europe; here, we will be concerned with the Turks in Europe. The Turks had won that large Empire in the fifteenth century, but by 1800 they found it increasingly difficult to govern such a huge Empire.

So they appointed Viceroys (or deputy Kings) to rule large areas; and some of their Viceroys became very powerful rulers of their own territories. One of them, Mehemet Ali of Egypt, almost overthrew the ruler of Turkey. So one question was 'Can Turkey continue to govern her Empire'?

The Question – Part 2

Some people thought that the answer to that part of the question was 'No' (Extract 17.1), and this led to a second small question: 'What would the peoples now ruled by the Turks do?' The Turks governed the countries that today are called Greece, Albania, Yugoslavia, Rumania, and Bulgaria. The people there were Christians, and they hated their Muslim rulers. They had also learned the ideas of nationalism. Most people thought that they would try to get their independence from Turkey. The Greeks did so between 1820 and 1832 (p. 63). The other peoples in the Balkans would follow the example of Greece if they could.

The Question – Part 3

That leads to the third small question: 'What would other countries do if Turkey started to crumble?' The British wanted to give the Turks a chance to recover their former strength (Extract 17.1), but the Russians wanted to take advantage of Turkey's weakness. Russia's leaders wanted to expand their power

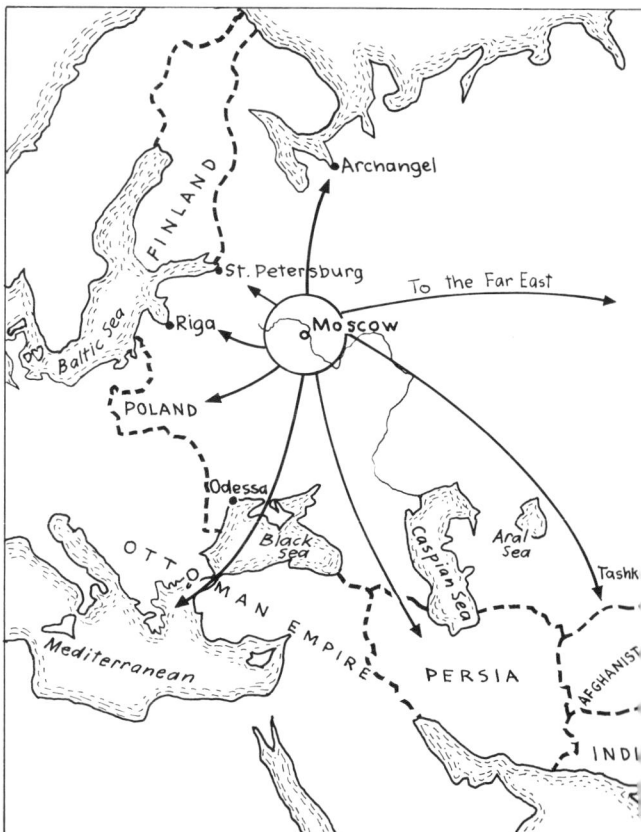

Fig. 17.1 The British view of Russian aims in the nineteenth century.

(Fig. 17.1), and the British thought that Russia wanted to get control of India – through Afghanistan and Persia. Britain was also worried about Russia's ambition to get into the Mediterranean. The Russians argued that they only wanted a chance to develop their trading, because their northern ports were ice-bound for eight months each year. So the expansion into the Black Sea and Dardanelles, Russia said, was only an attempt to find a warm water port. The British did not believe the Russians.

Mehemet Ali, 1820–30

In 1826 the Turks asked the Viceroy of Egypt, Mehemet Ali, to send an army and a navy to help defeat the Greeks (p. 63).

Mehemet Ali agreed, and the Turks promised to give him the area called Syria. But the Greeks were not defeated. Mehemet Ali's fleet was sunk at Navarino and the Greeks won their independence. So the Sultan (or ruler) of Turkey did not feel that Ali had earned his promised reward.

Mehemet Ali, 1831–3

When he did not get Syria, Mehemet Ali decided to take it. He sent an army from Egypt into Syria, and talked about founding an independent kingdom of his own (Extract 17.1).

The British Ambassador to Turkey was Stratford Canning, a nephew of the great Canning. He was afraid that Russia would take advantage of Ali's invasion to win some power and influence for herself. During 1831 and 1832 Britain was in a state of chaos because of the problems of the Reform Bills (p. 66). So Palmerston could not act as he wanted to.

Turkey asked for British help and got none, and this forced Turkey to turn to Russia for help. 'Like a drowning man clutching at a serpent' she asked for the help of the very power that was most interested in her collapse.

Unkiar Skelessi, 1833

Russia sent an army to help the Turks. The Russians forced the Turks to sign the Treaty of Unkiar Skelessi. This allowed Russian warships to sail from the Russian ports on the Black Sea through the Dardanelles and into the Mediterranean. The Turks would not allow warships of any other nation to sail from the Mediterranean into the Black Sea.

This gave Russia the exit from the Black Sea which was one of her main aims (Fig. 17.1).

Mehemet Ali, 1839–41

In 1839 a new Sultan decided to punish Mehemet Ali for having attacked in 1831–3, but Mehemet Ali's armies defeated the Turks.

In 1839 the French King, Louis Philippe, promised to support Mehemet Ali in his attempt to capture Syria. Louis Philippe hoped to become the 'guardian' of Mehemet Ali.

London Conference, 1840

Palmerston did not want to see Turkey broken up, and he certainly did not want to see French influence in this area.

So he arranged a conference in London in 1840. Austria, Russia, Prussia, and Britain agreed that Mehemet Ali would have to give up the territory he had captured from Turkey. France would not agree; neither would Mehemet Ali.

The British Navy was sent to bombard Beirut in northern Syria, and a British army defeated the Egyptians at the Battle of Acre (November 1840).

The Straits Convention, 1841

Mehemet Ali had to withdraw from Syria. France was disappointed, but Britain was more concerned with the Russian threat to the Mediterranean. In 1841 Palmerston got the Turks and the other powers to agree to sign a Straits Convention. This said that no foreign warships would be allowed to sail through the Straits of the Dardanelles. Palmerston had undone the damage of Unkiar Skelessi.

Turkey and the Holy Places

Palestine was part of the Turkish Empire. Each year thousands of Christians visited the Holy Places there.

Since 1300 the Turks had given the French the right to guard the Christians visiting the Holy Places. But in a treaty signed in 1774 the Turks agreed instead to make the Russians the guardians of the Holy Places.

Napoleon III and the Holy Places, 1853

Napoleon III wanted to win popularity among the Catholics of France. In 1853 he reminded the Turks of the old French claim to be guardians of the Holy Places. The British supported this claim – because it would help to lessen Russian influence in the area.

In February 1853 the Turks again said that Russia was to be the Christian guardian of the Holy Places. Canning went to see the Sultan of Turkey, and argued that this would make Russia too powerful. Nevertheless, Russia moved her army towards the border with Turkey.

The Vienna Note, September 1853

The British government was divided as to what to do about Russia's claims, but in June a joint British and

French fleet was sent to the Dardanelles. This was a sign that Britain and France were opposed to Russian advances into Turkey.

In June 1853 Russia invaded the Danubian provinces of Moldavia and Wallachia. Russia meant to get her own way. Palmerston wanted the British fleet to be sent into the Black Sea to threaten the Russian naval bases in the Crimea; other ministers hesitated and even Palmerston seemed unsure of what was happening.

In September the British, French, Austrians, and Prussians met at Vienna to discuss the Turkish problem. They issued a Note that asked Russia to withdraw her army and asked the Turks to agree to discuss the Russian claims to more influence.

Canning, in Constantinople (now called Istanbul), told the Turks to refuse the terms of this Note, and he promised British help in a war with Russia. So the Turks refused to accept the terms of the Note, and on 4 October 1853 Turkey declared war on Russia.

The British Cabinet was divided over the issue of providing help for Turkey. The Prime Minister, Lord Aberdeen, hoped that the problem could be settled by diplomatic discussions with the Russians and Turks.

He had the support of the majority of his ministers. Palmerston, on the other hand, thought that the issue would have to be settled by war. In November 1853 a Russian fleet destroyed a Turkish fleet at Sinope on the Black Sea (Fig. 17.1). Even then the British government hesitated. Palmerston resigned in anger. The government ordered the British fleet into the Black Sea in January 1854 but did not declare war until the end of March 1854.

The Crimean War

Another British fleet sailed off the northern coast of Russia, and attacked various fortresses. Troops were landed on the Finnish coast, but there seemed little chance of success in these northern waters.

The Crimea seemed to offer more of a chance. On 14 September 1854 troops landed at Calamity Bay to help in the capture of Sebastopol. They defeated the Russians in the Battle of the Alma and surrounded Sebastopol.

Allied fleets sailed to attack Sebastopol from the sea. General Menshikoff used the guns of his Russian

Fig. 17.2 The Charge of the Light Brigade at the Battle of Balaclava, 25 October 1854.

ships to help defend his besieged fortress, and the Allies were unable to capture Sebastopol from the sea.

In October Menshikoff met the Allied forces at Balaclava where there took place the heroic but useless Charge of the Light Brigade (Fig. 17.2). At the Battle of Inkerman the Russians were defeated after a very great struggle, and they retreated to Sebastopol.

Throughout the winter of 1854–5 the Allied armies besieged the town. British troops suffered heavy losses from the cold, lack of proper clothing and food, and the almost complete absence of medical and nursing services.

In June 1855 the Allies began an attack which lasted for three months. By September they had captured two of the principal strongpoints in Sebastopol – the Redan and Malakoff. The Russians then abandoned the town.

The Fall of the Aberdeen Government

News of the war had been quickly relayed to Britain by the newly invented telegraph. The best-known were the long reports sent by W. H. Russell, the correspondent of *The Times*. It was Russell who told the British people about the stupidity of the generals and other officers. Lords Raglan, Cardigan, and other noblemen had got their positions because they were wealthy – and not because they had any ability as soldiers.

Russell also wrote about the failure of the War Office to send out the right clothing, enough food, doctors, nurses and medicines. Because of this, there was an outcry in Britain in December 1854 and January 1855, and Parliament examined the government's handling of the war. Aberdeen was forced to resign and Palmerston became Prime Minister.

Sidney Herbert was War Minister in Aberdeen's government. He helped his friend, Florence Nightingale, to get together a group of dedicated women to go to nurse in the Crimea. Herbert and Florence Nightingale won the support of Russell who wrote about 'the Lady with the lamp' bringing order, cleanliness, and a slowing down of the death rate in the British hospitals in the Crimea.

The End of the War

Tsar Nicholas I died in 1855. The new Tsar, Alexander II, was anxious to make peace. So too

were Palmerston and Napoleon III. The three countries agreed on the terms of the Treaty of Paris, 1856. The Russians were forced to agree:
1. not to re-build Sebastopol as a fortress;
2. not to build a new fleet in the Black Sea;
3. to recognize a new state, Rumania, formed by uniting Moldavia and Wallachia.
Palmerston and the British could feel some satisfaction with this treaty. Russia would not now be so much of a threat to British power.

The Effect of the War

The war had a number of effects on British life. Some of these were less important – a new name for a woollen jacket (a cardigan), and a woollen helmet (a Balaclava). Some were long lasting; the Victoria Cross was made from the metal of the guns captured at the Battle of Sebastopol.

In India the war had an immediate effect; the British had brought many people from their Indian Army to fight in the Crimea. This lowered the number of British soldiers in India, and it also meant that Indian troops had to travel long distances, some overseas. Both of these were among the causes of the outbreak of the Indian Mutiny in 1857 (Chapter 18).

Questions

Extract 17.1

The decline in Turkish power

The Turkish Empire has reached, in its decline, that critical point, at which it must either revive or fall into a state of complete dissolution. To Great Britain, the fate of this Empire can never be indifferent. It would affect the interests of her trade and Indian Possessions, and the maintenance of her relative Power in Europe. More pressing duties may forbid H. M. Government to take an active part in the Contest which now agitates Turkey; but the issue of a struggle so likely to prove decisive of the Sultan's independence can hardly be overlooked and left to chance on any sound Principle of English Policy.

The difficulties with which the Sultan is faced against Mehemet Ali, arise from the distance to Egypt, the ease with which Syria can be defended against an army invading from the North, and the disadvantage of having a Fleet which, though superior in numerical Force to that of Egypt, is not so well manned.

In one respect, however, the prospect is clear. Let Mehemet Ali succeed in constituting an Independent State, and a great and irretrievable step is made towards the dismemberment of the Turkish Empire. That Empire may fall to pieces at all events, and he must be a bold man who would undertake to answer for its being saved by any effort of human policy. But His Majesty's Government may rest assured that to leave it to itself is to leave it to its Enemies.

(Stratford Canning to Palmerston, 19 December 1832.)

1.   What was 'critical' about the state of Turkey throughout the nineteenth century? How had her weakness been revealed by (i) the War for the Independence of Greece, and (ii) the events of 1831–2?

2.   Give the reasons given in the extract for British interests in the future of Turkey. Which country did Britain think would gain most if Turkey were broken up?

3.   What 'contest' was taking place in 1832? Explain how that 'contest' had its origins in 1825.

4.   Who was Mehemet Ali? How would his victory in 1832 affect (i) Turkey, and (ii) Britain?

Fig. 17.1

1.   Which three of Russia's aims were most feared by the British? Why?

2.   How did the Russians explain their need to expand into the Mediterranean?

3.   How did the Russians try to gain influence in the Mediterranean in 1833?

4.   Why was Britain afraid of this expansion of Russian influence?

Worksheet

(A)
1.   Why did Britain want to help the Greeks gain their independence after 1822?

2.   Why did Britain want to help the Turks to maintain their power, 1839–41?

3.   Explain Britain's fears of Russia, 1820–56.

4.   What part did Russia play in Turkish affairs during the following periods: (i) 1825–32 (ii) 1833–41 (iii) 1853–6?

5.   Explain the differences in the policies which Palmerston followed towards Mehemet Ali in (i) 1831–3 (ii) 1839–41.

6.   Trace the steps by which Britain went to war against Russia in 1853.

7.   Write two sentences on each of the following: Sebastopol; W. H. Russell; Lords Raglan and Cardigan; Stratford Canning.

8.   What were the results of the Crimean War for (i) Russian power in the Black Sea (ii) British political leaders (iii) the British Army?

9.   Write a paragraph on the work of Florence Nightingale for each of the following: The Crimean army; the nursing profession.

(B)
1.   Write the letters which might have been sent by someone visiting the Holy Places. He might have written about the various religious groups who had places of worship there (Catholics, Protestants, Orthodox Christians, Muslims, and so on. He might also have written about the Turkish rule, French and Russian attempts to be regarded as the Guardians.).

(C)
1.   Write the headlines that might have appeared above reports on:
(a) Mehemet Ali's invasion of Syria – in Turkish, Egyptian, Russian, and British papers;
(b) the signing of the Treaty of Unkiar Skelessi – in British, Russian, and Turkish papers;
(c) the signing of the Treaty of London, 1840 – in British, French, Turkish, Russian, and Egyptian papers;
(d) the Charge of the Light Brigade – in British, French, Russian, and Turkish papers.

18 The British Empire, 1760 – 1870

India, 1700–63

From 1600 onwards British merchants sent out ships to trade with the islands of the East Indies. These merchants formed the East India Company. They built warehouses, offices, and housing for their clerks and officials on various islands. They created an army to defend their property.

In the 1660s the British Company was driven out of the East Indies by the Dutch, so the British went to India. The Emperor of India, like the Sultan of Turkey (p. 94) had once been a powerful ruler, but by 1700 he was unable to control his people. Many local princes had become independent rulers of parts of India (Fig. 18.1).

The British Company took advantage of this. If they helped a prince to get control of the throne of some territory, he in return, would give them the right to trade in his area. So they helped one after another to get power – and won for the British Company a powerful trading position in India.

The Peace of Paris, 1763

The French East India Company also tried to do the same, and there was a long period of struggle between the two companies. Their governments sent armies to help and by 1763 the British had defeated the French. By the Peace of Paris, 1763 (p. 12) the British

Fig. 18.1 The growth of British power in India.

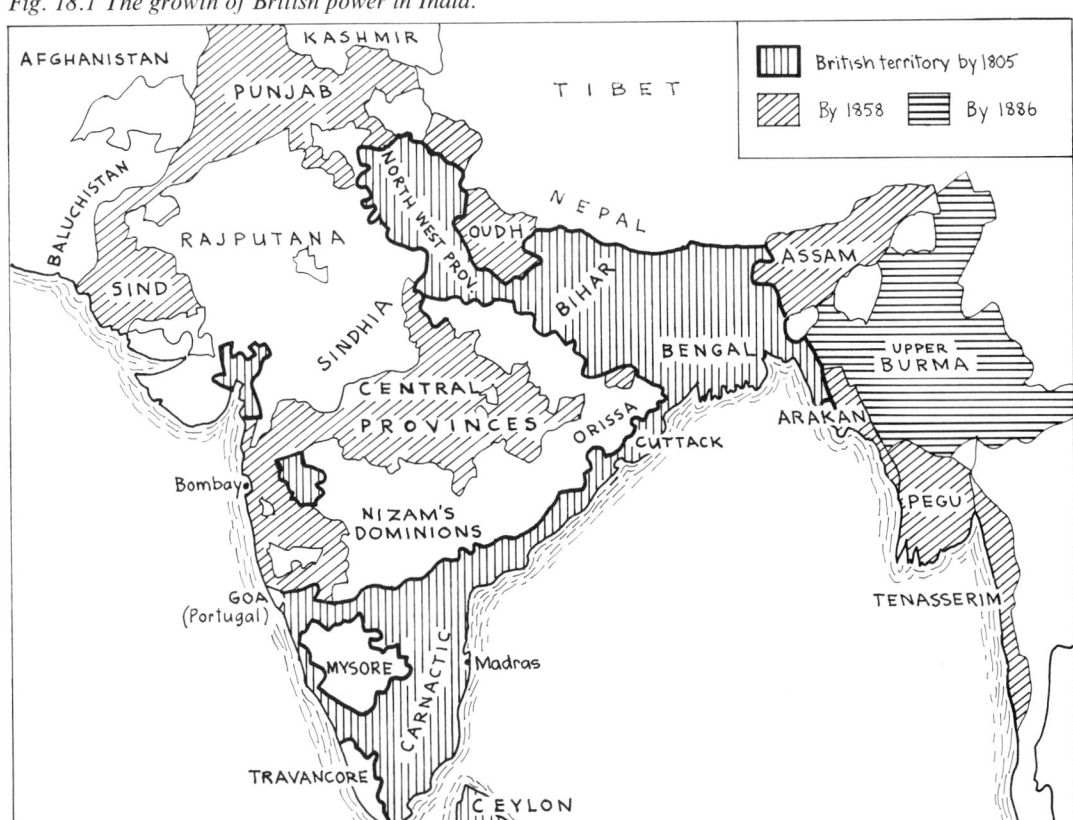

Company was left in control of part of the Carnatic, most of Bengal, and the island of Bombay. It might be thought odd that a trading company should be 'ruling' vast areas of territory.

The Regulating Act 1773

In 1773 Lord North's government decided that the government had to play some part in India. The Regulating Act allowed the British company to hold on to its control of the Indian trade and to appoint its employees as governors of Bombay and Madras. But the British government took the right to appoint a Governor-General, who would 'rule' the other two governors. It also appointed a Council of Four to help the Governor-General.

Warren Hastings, 1772–84

The first Governor-General was Warren Hastings; he had been the company's Governor of Bengal since 1772. The Council of Four which came out in 1774 thought that he must have been as corrupt as most other company officials. Many went to India as poor clerks but came back very wealthy people – nicknamed 'Nabobs'. They made their wealth by cheating the Indians, smuggling goods back home in company ships, looting after a victory, or accepting bribes from Indians anxious to win a contract or a position of power. Many people thought that they should use their positions to become richer. That is what British politicians did. Why not company clerks and officials?

Hastings in Power

So the Council of Four tried to catch Hastings out. They criticized everything he did and sent back unfavourable reports on his work. In fact he was an honest and very efficient official. His principal successes were to:
1. set up an efficient Civil Service to replace the company officials;
2. appoint British tax collectors to take the place of the less honest Indian collectors;
3. defend British interests in India during the period of the American Revolution (p. 22).

Indian Wars, 1780–4

The Mahrattas were a warlike tribe. In 1778 the French persuaded them that the British would not be able to fight in India because they were already losing in America. The Mahrattas attacked Bombay. Hastings sent an army across India, and the Mahrattas were defeated. Bombay was saved. Hastings took some land away from the Mahrattas and so extended British power.

In 1780 the King of Mysore, Hyder Ali, attacked the Carnatic. Hastings sent Sir Eyre Coote and an army from Bengal. Coote defeated Hyder Ali at the Battle of Porto Novo, and so Madras was saved for British trade.

Oudh

The ruler of Oudh had made a treaty with the company, which gave the company the right to trade in his province. In return the company helped him to maintain law and order. His female relations – the Begums of Oudh – seized his jewels and other treasures, fearing that the British would take them. The ruler asked Hastings to help him get them back. This was done; an army was sent in to invade the ladies' palaces, and the treasure was restored to the ruler.

But many people in Britain believed the Council of Four which said that Hastings was a dictator who ill-treated the native people and kept some of this money for himself. He was recalled from India in 1788 and put on trial. His trial lasted until 1795 – and although he was found innocent this was small consolation for seven years of uncertainty and so much money spent on his defence.

Pitt's India Act 1784

The Regulating Act had failed to settle the Indian problem, so in 1784 Parliament passed a new Act. This separated trading rights from the question of governing India, and the company was left to get on with trade. The British government set up a Board of Control in London. This Board had to appoint the Governor-General and other important officials; the Governor-General was given the right to overrule his Council if need be.

The Marquess of Wellesley, 1798–1805

During this period Britain was at war with France in Europe and elsewhere (Chapters 6 and 7). To safeguard British interests in India the government sent out armies to guard against the danger of native uprisings. Among the officers sent out was Arthur Wellesley, the brother of the Governor-General – and the future Duke of Wellington.

During this period the British:

1. made alliances with the weaker rulers. The British promised to defend them in return for the right to trade;

2. forced the Nizam (or ruler) of Hyderabad to disband his army and to make an alliance with the British;

3. conquered the whole of the Carnatic and much more territory around the mainland off Bombay;

4. took control of most of Oudh;

5. defeated the attempt of Tipoo of Mysore to control the Carnatic. Britain gained control of much of Mysore;

6. defeated the Mahrattas who tried to drive the British from the west coast.

The Marquess of Hastings, 1813–28

Hastings completed the work begun by Wellesley. He destroyed the power of the Mahrattas, took control of Poona, and captured Nepal (Fig. 18.1).

By 1823 most of India was under British rule or controlled by the British. Hastings then attacked Burma in the east and Afghanistan in the north. This led to a series of wars that did not end until 1849; by that time Britain had gained control of the Sind and the Punjab (Fig. 18.1).

Bentinck, 1828–35

Bentinck tried to make British rule in India a peaceful and efficient one. He stamped out the *thuggees* who, in the name of religion, murdered travellers along the long Indian roads. He also abolished *suttee*, or the burning of widows on their husband's funeral fire (Extract 18.1). Indian children were allowed to go to English-language schools so that they could get jobs in the government.

Dalhousie, 1848–56

Lord Dalhousie was Governor-General when Britain completed her work of controlling the Punjab (Fig. 18.1). He was a very active Governor-General, and seized territories when he thought the ruler was not governing wisely. He also invented the *doctrine of lapse*. This allowed him to take over a territory if a ruler died without an heir; seven states were seized under this doctrine.

The Indian Mutiny, 1857

1857 was the centenary of the Battle of Plessey. Many Indians had prophesied that India would get back its freedom in that year, and suspected that the attacks on the *thuggees* and the abolition of *suttee* was part of a British policy of stamping out their religions. Maybe the British wanted to make them Christians. Certainly missionaries were very active – in schools and churches. Indian pride was hurt by the way in which various Governors-General had annexed or conquered Indian territory.

But the Mutiny had several immediate causes.

1. In 1854–5 the government sent troops from India to the Crimea. This reduced the proportion of Europeans to native troops in India.

2. Many of these native troops (or *sepoys*) were opposed to being sent to foreign lands – such as Burma or the Crimea. The Hindus in particular thought that such travel offended their religious laws. They feared that if they went they might lose their traditional place in the *caste* or class system. No Hindu wanted to run the risk of his priests deciding that he had to move down a rung or more in this system – with the added danger of being classed as an untouchable, one of those millions of Indians who had no place in the caste system and were condemned to do only the lowest-paid, dirty and unpopular jobs.

3. Soldiers were issued with a new Enfield rifle. They had to bite the end of the cartridge before putting it into the rifle. Rumours swept through the ranks that the cartridges were covered in the grease of animal fat. Some said it was cow fat (which offended the Hindus); others said that it was pig fat (which offended the Muslims).

The Areas and Course of the Mutiny (Fig. 18.2)

In one way it is wrong to talk about an Indian Mutiny. It was largely a rising by troops and people in three regions. One centre was Meerut. Here the sepoys massacred the British and marched to Delhi where they proclaimed the re-establishment of the old Indian Empire.

A second centre was Cawnpore where a Mahratta chief led the massacre of the British. The third was Lucknow which underwent a long siege until it was relieved by Sir Colin Campbell.

Sir John Lawrence had kept the Sikhs of the Punjab loyal to the British. He led an army to recapture Delhi, and this marked the beginning of the end to the Mutiny. With the end of the Crimean War the British government had troops and time to spend on suppressing the scattered Indian rebels; by June

Fig. 18.2 A scene from the Indian Mutiny.

1858 these had been wiped out. British power was safe again.

The Government of India Act 1858

This abolished the East India Company and put India under the control of the British government. A Secretary of State for India took control of Indian affairs; he was helped by a Council of Fifteen which acted as a Cabinet.

In addition to this Act the government decided that reforms should be introduced more slowly and that more British troops should be sent to India. It is not surprising that many people believed that the Indians were not to be trusted, even though only a small number had taken part in the Mutiny. After 1857 all Indians were treated as if they were anti-British.

South Africa

By 1815 Britain had taken the Cape of Good Hope from the Dutch (p. 32), and the British settlers went out

to make a new life. British missionaries went there to try to make Christian converts among the native people.

The Dutch settlers, or Boers, hated the British settlers who took the land. They also hated the missionaries who treated the blacks kindly. They hated the British judges who gave black and white equal treatment if they were taken to court for a trial.

But the Abolition of Slavery in 1834 (p. 70) was the last straw. The Boers wanted to have their slaves to work their farms; now they could not do so. They decided to make a new life for themselves away from British rule. In 1836 about 5,000 Boers left on the Great Trek. They marched north to start two new states: these were called the Transvaal and the Orange Free State. By 1854 the British government recognized these two states as Boer Republics. There would be trouble between British and Boers later on in the century (Chapter 25).

Canada, 1791

Canada had been acquired by the British in the Peace of Paris, 1763 (p. 18). During the American

Revolution many colonists had worked for a British victory; after the war these *Loyalists* left America and made a new life in Canada.

In 1791 Parliament passed the Canada Act, which divided the region into two. One was called Lower Canada based on Quebec; this was French dominated. The French were allowed to practise their Catholic religion and use their own language, but they resented the presence of a British-appointed Governor. He had the power to overrule any decisions of the democratically elected Assembly (or Parliament). The second region – Upper Canada – was based on Ontario. This was English-speaking and occupied by the Loyalists. This also had an Assembly – but here again its decisions could be overruled by the Governor.

Canada, 1837–9

In 1837 there were rebellions in both provinces and the British government sent out Lord Durham to examine conditions there. He put down the risings and then sent back a report (1839) which was a major stage in the development of British policy. He said that the two provinces should be united. More importantly, he said that Canada should be given self-government; ministers should be chosen from the Parliament. If the British had done this in the American colonies maybe the American Revolution would not have taken place.

Canada, 1840

In 1840 the British government passed the Reunion Act which united the two provinces. In 1848 the Governor of Canada was Lord Elgin, Durham's son-in-law. He allowed the Parliament to choose its ministers, and he did not try to overrule any of their decisions. Canada had achieved *responsible government*.

Emigrants and Growth

Thousands of British people made a new life in nineteenth-century Canada. New provinces were founded in Nova Scotia (1848), New Brunswick (1848), and Prince Edward Island (1851). Railways pushed across the country to the Pacific Coast. In 1867 the British passed the British North America Act. This formed Ontario (or Upper Canada), Quebec (or Lower Canada), Nova Scotia, and New Brunswick into a federal union called the Dominion of Canada. Each province had a certain amount of self-government inside a union which preserved the unity of the whole country. This was the first of the British Dominions. Other white-settled colonies would achieve this status as time went on.

Australia

Captain Cook had claimed newly-discovered Australia during his voyages of discovery of 1768–79. Britain used the new country as a dumping ground for prisoners (Extract 18.2 and Fig. 18.3).

Convict settlements were opened at Botany Bay (1786) and Brisbane (1824). But in the 1820s Gibbon Wakefield and others in Britain encouraged people to emigrate to this new country, to farm and make a new life. By 1839 there were more free settlers than convicts in New South Wales. Wool became a major export to Britain (p. 48) and many Australians became wealthy farmers. In 1850 the British, following the principles of the *Durham Report*, gave the people of New South Wales, Tasmania, South Australia, and Victoria their own representative government, and in 1855 this became self-government. In 1900 the Commonwealth of Australia Act created a central government for the Dominion of Australia. As in Canada, each state had some powers while the central government dealt with defence, trade, the postal system, railways, immigration, and currency.

Fig. 18.3 The first Australia Day, 26 January 1788, when the British flag was unfurled at Sydney Cove.

New Zealand

Captain Cook had discovered New Zealand in 1769. By 1815 its Maori people had seen the arrival of a mixed group of white people. Settlers, traders, whalers and sealers, convicts escaped from Australia, and deserting sailors settled in the new country. Missionaries came to protect the Maoris and to try to make them Christians.

In 1839 Gibbon Wakefield founded the New Zealand Company. This landed 1,200 settlers on the south coast of North Island at Wellington. In 1840 the British government signed the Treaty of Waitangi with the Maori chiefs. They accepted British rule but were left in possession of their land, which was only to be sold to the British government. The number of settlers increased. These bought land from the Maoris – which was against the terms of the Treaty of Waitangi. Some Maoris resented this and this led to the First Maori War (1843) which was ended by Sir George Grey, Governor-General from 1848–53. He bought all the land not occupied by the Maoris in South Island and new settlers arrived at Otago and Canterbury. In 1852 the country was given representative government which in 1856 became responsible government. There was an increase in the number of settlers and a long period during which the Maoris tried to hold on to their land in North Island. The Second Maori War started in 1861 and lasted for several years, and Grey was brought back as Governor-General (1861–8). The Maoris were granted half the land in North Island while the rest was left for British settlers.

In 1907 New Zealand became the third Dominion in the British Empire. By then Britain had acquired large areas of land in Africa, where the British government showed no wish to follow the principle of the *Durham Report*. This was to lead to problems after 1945.

Questions

Extract 18.1

Burning a widow, 1799

> We saw a number of people assembled on the river-side to burn the body of a dead man. His wife was standing by the pile of wood on the top of which lay her husband's dead body. Her nearest relative stood by her; and near her was a basket of sweetmeats. I asked if this was her choice. They answered that it was voluntary . . . a great act of holiness. I was determined to stay and see the murder, against which I should certainly bear

witness at the tribunal of God. I exhorted the widow not to throw away her life . . . but in the most calm manner she mounted the pile and danced on it with her hands extended, as if in the utmost tranquillity of spirit. Previous to this, the relative whose office it was to set fire to the pile led her six times round it – thrice at a time. As she went round she scattered the sweetmeats among the people, who ate them as a very holy thing. This being ended, she lay down beside the corpse, and put one arm under its neck, and the other over it, when a quantity of dry cocoa-leaves and other substances were heaped over them to a considerable height, and then oil was poured on the top. Two bamboos were then put over them and held down fast, and fire put into the pile, which immediately blazed very fiercely. No sooner was the fire kindled than all the people set up a great shout of joy, invoking Siva. It was impossible to have heard the widow, had she groaned or even cried aloud, on account of the shouting of the people, and again it was impossible for her to stir or struggle, by reason of the bamboos held down on her, like the levers of a press.

(William Carey, letter from Calcutta, 1799.)

1. What was the Indian name for this practice? Which of India's two main religions used this practice? Why?
2. How and when did the British stamp out this practice?
3. Which governors were mainly responsible for stamping it out?
4. What other Indian customs and 'superstitions' were also attacked?
5. How did this affect the Indian attitude towards the British?
6. Why did Indians fear that the British were going to try to make them Christians?

Extract 18.2

Australia as a prison, 1786

> Heads of a Plan for effectively disposing of convicts and rendering their transportation reciprocally beneficial both to themselves and to the state, by the establishing of a colony in New South Wales, a country which by the fertility and salubrity of the climate, connected with the remoteness of its situation (from whence it is hardly possible for persons to return without permission) seems peculiarly adapted to answer the views of Government with respect to the providing a remedy for the evils likely to result from the late alarming increase of felons . . . more particularly in the metropolis . . . H.M. has thought it advisable to fix upon Botany Bay . . . which according to the accounts given by the late Captain Cook (and others), is looked upon as a place likely to answer the above purpose. I am therefore commanded to signify to your Lordships H.M.'s pleasure that you do forthwith take such measures as

may be necessary for providing a proper number of vessels for the conveying of 750 convicts to Botany Bay, together with such provisions, necessaries and implements for agriculture as may be necessary for their use after arrival.

(Lord Sydney, Home Secretary to the Lords Commissioners of the Treasury, 1786.)

1. To which overseas territory had prisoners been sent before 1783? Why was this no longer possible?
2. Read p. 35. For what crimes were men sent overseas to prison?
3. What evidence is there in this extract that such a sentence meant that men rarely came back to Britain after they had served their sentence?
4. How is Lord Sydney's name remembered in modern Australia?
5. What two economic developments best explain the growth of the rate of emigration to Australia in the nineteenth century?

Worksheet

(A)
1. Show how the British East India Company became ruler of parts of India in (i) 1700–63 (ii) 1780–4 (iii) 1798–1805 (iv) 1813–28 (v) 1848–56. You might want to make a list of the states conquered, treaties made, of British leaders and commanders.

2. Show briefly how the British government became involved with the ruling of India by Acts passed in (i) 1773 (ii) 1784 (iii) 1858.

3. Why did Hastings get involved in disputes with the Council of Four? Was it due to British suspicions of 'Nabobs'? Was it because of what he had actually done? Was Hastings a successful ruler from a British point of view?

4. Write two sentences on each of the following: Mahrattas; Hyder Ali; the Begums of Oudh.

5. Write a paragraph on each of the following: India during the American Revolution; India during the French Revolutionary Wars.

6. Write a paragraph on the work of each of the following: Wellesley (1798–1805); Bentinck (1828–35); Dalhousie (1848–56).

7. Write two sentences on each of the following: The Thuggees; suttee; the doctrine of lapse; sepoys.

8. Make a list of the reasons why a mutiny broke out in India in 1857. Why do some people think that it does not deserve the title of *Indian* Mutiny? (Was it a local mutiny? What were the main centres?)

9. Explain the reasons why the Boers went on a Great Trek in 1836. (Notice that your answer will have to do more than explain the effects of abolition of slavery.)

10. Explain carefully the differences between Upper and Lower Canada. (Where was each? Main language? Main religion?)

11. Why were there risings in both Canadas in 1837?

12. What was the *Durham Report*? Why was it important for the future of (i) Canada (ii) other countries in the British Empire?

13. Write two sentences on each of the following: Gibbon Wakefield and the British Empire; Botany Bay; the Treaty of Waitangi; the Maori Wars.

(B)
1. Write the letters that might have been sent by:
(a) one of Hasting's supporters;
(b) one of Hastings's critics;
(c) an Indian warning of the danger of a rising in 1857;
(d) a Scotsman who has emigrated to Canada;
(e) a soldier sent to serve in Botany Bay.

(C)
1. Make a time chart for the period 1760–1910. Mark on it the main dates and events mentioned in the text. Add a line of explanation for each date and event.

2. Write the headlines that might have appeared above reports on:
(a) the Regulating Act 1773 – in papers controlled by the government, an Indian, the East India Company;
(b) the Peace of Paris as regards India – in British and French papers;
(c) the abolition of suttee – in British and Indian papers;
(d) the horrors of Meerut – in papers controlled by the British and the Indians;
(e) the relief of Cawnpore – in British and in Indian papers;
(f) the Great Trek – in British and Boer papers;
(g) the *Durham Report* – in British and Canadian papers.

19 Trade Unions, 1760 – 1867

Trade unions play a most important role in today's society. But this was not always so. Trade unions and their members had to fight a long and hard battle before they became 'respectable'.

Industrialization and Unions, 1760–1820

One result of the Industrial Revolution was the increase in the number of workers. Few, if any of them, hoped to become industrialists or factory owners. So miners and other workers united to try to get better conditions or more pay (Fig. 19.1).

Owners and Unions

The first industrialists regarded their men as just another part of the process of manufacturing. The owner had a factory, machines, and workmen. All three were his to do with as he liked. If he wanted to make them work long hours, that was his right. It is little wonder that many workers saw themselves as 'slaves' to the owners. This helped to force men into some sort of union with their fellow-workers.

The Growth of Trade Unions

Workers in industrial towns lived close together. They found that they had the same complaints – about their hours, wages, and working conditions.

So there was a growth in the number of unions. Most of the early unions were formed from men in one craft or skill. The carpenters, file-grinders, and brushmakers each had their own union.

Until the coming of the railway system most of these unions were formed from men in one area. So the Sheffield file-grinders, Preston weavers, and Dorchester farm-workers each had their own local craft union.

The Combination Acts, 1799–1800

In 1797 the Navy mutinied (p. 33), and in 1798 the Irish rose in rebellion (p. 56). It is not surprising, therefore, that Parliament was afraid that the British people might imitate the French and begin a revolution.

In April 1799 Parliament was told that the journeymen millwrights of London were asking for a pay increase, and on 8 April 1799 Sir John Anderson, M.P. tried to bring in a 'Bill to prevent unlawful combination of workmen. . . .' Parliament agreed. Wilberforce (p. 26) asked 'whether it might not be better to extend the motion to make it general against unions of all workers', and so on 17 June 1799 Pitt, the Prime Minister, brought in a Bill to 'prevent the unlawful combination of all workmen'. This became known as the Combination Act. This forbade the formation of unions if these were going to try to improve wages or change the number of hours worked. A second Act (1800) forbade strikes, union meetings, and the collection of union subscriptions.

Friendly Societies and Uprisings, 1800–20

Many former unions continued – their leaders taking the chance of being caught and imprisoned. Many continued to exist, but only as Friendly Societies; they used the subscriptions to help members who were out of work, ill, too old to work and so on – as the Woolcombers did (Extract 19.1).

Repeal, 1824

In 1824 Huskisson set up a committee to examine the problem of workmen who wanted to emigrate (p. 50). Francis Place used this committee to help trade unionism. Place had been a journeyman in the breech-making trade, and in 1793 he had led a strike. But in 1799 he became a self-employed tailor. His shop at Charing Cross, London, became a meeting place for Radicals, free-thinking politicians and writers.

Fig. 19.1 The minutes of a meeting called to protest against the truck system of payment. ▶

SESSIONS-ROOM, BOLTON,
22d APRIL, 1818.

At a Public TOWN'S MEETING of the Land Owners, Leypayers, Manufacturers, and other Inhabitants of the Town of Great Bolton, in the County of Lancaster, held this day pursuant to a Requisition for the purpose of taking into Consideration the best Means of putting a Stop to the unlawful practice of Paying Wages to Labourers in Food and Raiment, instead of the Current Coin of the Realm,

Danl. Makinson, Esq. Boroughreeve,
IN THE CHAIR:
THE FOLLOWING
Resolutions
WERE UNANIMOUSLY CARRIED.

1st. That this Meeting views with the utmost Abhorrence the unlawful Practice of establishing Shops in large Works, for the purpose of paying Wages in Food and Raiment, instead of the Coin of the Realm.

2nd. That the Practice of suspending the Payment of Wages for a Month, and in many Instances longer, is highly injurious and oppressive to the poor Labourer, who is obliged to forego the many little Necessaries, in consequence of his lawful Wages being kept from him.

3rd. That the unlawful Practice set forth in the Requisition is injurious to all Trades, and to all property, particularly Property in Market Towns, inasmuch as it obstructs and monopolizes the free Circulation of Money.

4th. That such Establishments have a ten-fold Advantage over the fair Trader, by running no Risk, being paid beforehand, and disposing of Articles of inferior Quality, at such Prices as they think proper.

5th. That such pernicious Practices tend very much to the Increase of Pauperism, the Masters getting the Youth and Strength of their Servants, and the Town their old Age and Infirmities.

6th. That in casual or extreme Cases, such as the immediate Want of Medical Aid, it is reluctantly afforded, from a knowledge of the Inability of the Parties to pay for such Professional Assistance, except in Articles imposed upon them in lieu of their lawful Wages.

7th. That this Meeting recommends to all Masters employing Work-people, to pay Wages in the current Coin of the Realm every Week; and that Labourers and others, working for weekly Wages, are requested to demand the same as above, and in case of Refusal to summons such Defaulter before a Magistrate for the Recovery thereof.

8th. That this Meeting is determined, by every means in their power, rigorously to enforce the Penalty of £10. imposed for the Offence, by the Acts of the 12th Geo. I, c. 34, and the 22d Geo. II. c. 27, and to reward and protect, as far as they lawfully can, every Person giving Information of it; and every Friend to the existing Law of the Land is hereby invited to come forward for the same necessary Purpose.

9th. That One Thousand Copies of the 4th and 12th Sections of the above Acts be printed and posted in public Places at the Discretion of the Committee to be hereafter appointed.

10th. That the Petition now read be adopted by this Meeting, and transmitted to the County Members, to present to the House of Commons; and that Copies thereof, together with the Resolutions of this Meeting, be transmitted to such other Members as the Committee may think proper, and request their Support in carrying the Object of the Petition into Effect.

11. That Mr. Bowker, Mr. Woods, Mr. Brandreth, Mr. Cross, Mr. Gaskell, Mr. Blundell, Mr. Dobson, Mr. Brodbelt, Mr. Dawes, Mr. Griffiths, and Mr. Haselden be appointed a Committee to carry the above Resolutions into effect, with power to add to their Number; and that any Five of them be competent to act.

12. That these Resolutions be inserted in such London and Provincial Papers as the Committee in their Discretion may think proper. *DANIEL MAKINSON.*

The Thanks of the Meeting were given to the Chairman for his Readiness in calling the Meeting, and his impartial Conduct in the Chair.

One of his main supporters was Joseph Hume, M.P. He tried to bring in a Private Member's Bill to repeal the Combination Acts. Huskisson would not allow this, but he did appoint Hume to his committee in 1824. He also agreed to allow that committee to examine 'the law on workmen's combinations'.

The committee heard evidence from Place and other people sympathetic to trade unionism, and by the end of 1824 Parliament passed an Act to repeal the Combination Acts. Once again men were free to form trade unions.

No Strikes, 1825

Many new unions were formed; old ones came out into the open. There were many strikes and a good deal of violence as workers got their own back on some employers.

In 1825 Huskisson was forced by a frightened Parliament to bring in a Bill that forbade men to organize a strike. This was a step back for the trade unions.

One Big Union

Some people wanted to unite all British workers in one big union. In 1818 Lancashire spinners had formed the Manchester Philanthropic Society to act as a body to organize the workers in all trades. Another similar society was formed in London in 1819. But in the days of poor communication such schemes were over-ambitious.

In 1829 John Doherty formed the Operative Spinners of Lancashire – which was much bigger than a local union. He then tried to form the Grand General Union of Operative Spinners in the United Kingdom. In 1830 he organized the National Association for the Protection of Labour, with the support of unions in twenty different trades and a membership of 100,000.

He then set about trying to form a Grand National Consolidated Trade Union (G.N.C.T.U.) to bring together members of all trades from throughout the United Kingdom.

Robert Owen

Robert Owen, like Francis Place, was a self-made man. He had been a worker. He had married the daughter of a mill owner, but remembered the hardships suffered by his former fellow-workers.

In 1834 he took over the leadership of the G.N.C.T.U., and appointed four paid officials to run the union from its London headquarters. He claimed that he had 250,000 members – a workers' army that would force the government to pass laws about housing, and force employers to pay decent wages.

Employers and the G.N.C.T.U.

Many employers were frightened at such talk, and some of them got together to force their workers to sign a 'Document' or a promise not to support the Union. Others closed their works down until their starving workers agreed not to join the Union.

But the most famous case involved some workers in Tolpuddle in Dorset. In 1833 the wages of farm-workers were lowered from 40p a week to 35p – with the announcement that for 1834 the wages would be even lower – 30p a week. Some Tolpuddle labourers would not accept this, and one of them, George Loveless, sent for two members of the G.N.C.T.U. to ask them to help form a branch in Tolpuddle. An informer told the magistrates about this. On 21 February 1834 a warning notice was put up and on 24 February the six founders of the union branch were arrested.

During their trial it became clear that they had done nothing illegal; that is why, much later, they were pardoned. But the magistrates used the Mutiny Act of 1797 to find the men guilty. That Act had forbidden the taking of illegal oaths. When men joined a union they took an oath of initiation, and the Dorsetshire magistrates decided that this was illegal.

The men were sentenced to seven years' imprisonment on the island of Tasmania off Australia. Owen and the G.N.C.T.U. organized a series of protest meetings and marches – but the government took no notice. It was the continued protest of lawyers and M.P.s that convinced Melbourne that the sentence was wrong, and in 1836 the men were pardoned – although the government did not tell the men in Tasmania of this. Loveless accidentally read about the pardon in a newspaper which came out to Tasmania. In 1839 the men came home and were helped by money collected by union leaders and friendly M.P.s

Owen's Failure

The G.N.C.T.U. had hoped to force the government and employers to help workers, but the Tolpuddle case showed that the Union could not even help its own members. This was not the only weakness in Owen's scheme. The four largest unions – builders, potters, spinners, and clothiers – had never joined. Also, Owen never had enough money to support members who went on strike – so that they were driven back to work by hunger. Some of the money collected by the Union was stolen by dishonest officials – workmen who made off with the large sums paid in by the Union members.

Above all Owen found that men in one place or in one craft had little sympathy with workmen in another place and another craft.

The Hungry Forties

From about 1838 to 1842 Britain went through a trade depression (p. 82). One result of this was a growth in the number of the unemployed (Fig. 19.2). Another was the fall in the number of men in trade unions – which seemed unable to stop unemployment.

Some men imitated the Luddites, and set about destroying factories and mills. The Plug Riots at Preston (1842) saw an attempt by workmen to pull out all the plugs in all the steam-engines in the town. If they had succeeded they would have brought to a halt the town's factories and mills. The employers called in the police and the Army and there were many clashes between these and the angry workmen.

Other workers joined the Chartist movement (Chapter 15), but as we have seen, Chartism failed. So in 1850 many men turned to trade unionism again.

A New Working Class, 1840–60

The first workers in the industrial towns had been frightened 'immigrants' into a new society. By 1840 their grandchildren were the workers in the growing towns. They had been born in the towns and were a more confident breed of men.

Many of them had got on or had seen other workmen get ahead in the booming Britain of the late 1840s and 1850s. Some managed to save – in the Post Office, an insurance society, a sick club, or a friendly society. Thousands of workers formed their own Building Societies and bought their own homes. Rising wages and falling prices gave many workers a good standard of living.

Model Unions

So perhaps it is not surprising that when these men formed trade unions in the 1850s they formed a different sort of union to those formed by Doherty and Owen.

Once again they formed unions for each craft – the carpenters, millwrights, and engineers for example. But this time they formed national unions. These

Fig. 19.2 This Victorian painting shows the hopelessness felt by a family when the father lost his job. Before the introduction of the welfare state, unemployment meant poverty and hardship.

were made up from the joining together (or *amalgamation*) of local unions. It was easier to do this after 1850 because the railway system enabled leaders to travel about the country. It was now possible to hold national conferences and to send out literature to members throughout Britain.

Trade Councils

The leaders of various unions in the country realized that they had a good deal in common – although they were in separate craft unions. They all wanted a change in the law – to allow unions to strike, for example. They all wanted better wages and shorter hours.

So the national leaders of these national unions often met together to talk about their policies. In time they formed the London Trades Council, and branch officials of these unions in the industrial towns of Great Britain did the same. So there were Trades Councils in most industrial towns.

In London and elsewhere these Trades Councils

tried to persuade employers, journalists, and politicians that trade unionism was not about revolution (as Owen had said), nor was it about violence (as the Plug Riots had suggested).

Employers and Unions

However, employers refused to believe any of this. They thought that trade unionism was an interference with their right to do what they wanted, and so they locked out their men when they formed branches of unions.

In 1852 there was a nation-wide lock-out by engineering employers, and in 1853 there was a well publicized lock-out by the owners of textile mills.

When employers locked out their workers they tried to replace them with workmen brought in from other towns or countries. These 'blackleg' workers were protected by the police or the Army, and violence was common (Fig. 19.3).

The Unions and their Funds

In 1866 an official of the Boilermakers' Union ran away with the Union's money, but when the Union took him to court the judge decided that trade unions were not official (or corporate) bodies. As such they could not bring a case to court.

So the unions wanted a change in the law. In February 1867 the government agreed to set up a commission to examine the whole question of trade unionism. Many employers hoped that this would prove that unions were violent and dangerous, and some unions were frightened that the Commission might do just that. So the Salford Trades Council called for a meeting of the leaders of all the unions.

The Commission

The Commission heard the evidence of employers, politicians, and trade union leaders. The Amalgamated Society of Engineers showed that men joined the union to get the welfare benefits provided by the Union. The Commission decided that trade unionism ought to be encouraged. This obviously pleased the unions and their leaders, amazed the employers, and forced the politicians to pass new laws about trade unionism (Chapter 30).

We have seen that the death of Palmerston in 1865 marked the end of an era and the start of a new age. The report of this commission in 1869 showed that the new age would be one in which some workers would get a new deal from the politicians. But millions of unskilled workers would continue to be lowly paid and have a poor standard of living. Trade unionism only helped the few.

Fig. 19.3 A clash between strikers and blackleg workmen.

Questions

Extract 19.1

An early trade union

13 March 1794. Report on Woolcombers' Petition: William Gates being asked whether it was usual to go from place to place to seek employment, he said it was, and that their clubs or societies subsist them till they get work.... And being asked, whether there are any number of woolcombers who do not belong to the societies, he said, 'There are some, but not one in one hundred that does not belong to some society.'

Jonathan Sowton . . . was asked, of what nature the clubs were. He said, 'It is a contribution upon which every woolcomber (who is willing to be a member of a club) . . . the one end of it is to enable the woolcombers to travel from place to place to seek for employment, when work is scarce where he resides; and the other end of it is to have relief when he is sick wherever he may be; and if he should die, to be buried by the club; . . .'
(*The House of Commons' Journal.*)

1. Why did working men move 'from place to place'? Why was this more difficult in 1794 than in 1867?
2. List the ways in which the clubs helped their members.
3. Why were many of these clubs sometimes called Friendly Societies?

Fig. 19.1

1. What 'unlawful practice' was the subject of this meeting? Why was this practice illegal?
2. Why did some employers pay wages 'in food and raiment'? Why did their workmen have to accept this method of payment?
3. Why did this practice harm the 'Property of Market Towns'?
4. How does the fourth point show that many employers cheated their workers?

Worksheet

(A)
1. Why were more unions formed after 1800 than before 1700? Why were most of these unions 'local' and not 'national' in the 1820s and 1830s?

2. Explain why Parliament passed the Combination Acts. How did they affect the development of trade unions?

3. Explain why some people wanted to have one large national union for all working men. Make a list of the reasons why, in the 1830s, this was almost impossible. Make a second list of the reasons why Owen's G.N.C.T.U. did not succeed.

4. Make a list of the ways in which life became better for some working people after 1850. Why did this improvement not apply to the mass of the workers?

5. What evidence can you find of this improvement in living standards?

6. Why did Gladstone set up a Commission on Trade Unions in 1867? Explain (i) the fears that some trade union leaders had, and (ii) the hopes that some employers had when they heard about this Commission.

(B)
1. Make a time chart of the period 1760–1870. Mark on it the main dates and events mentioned in the text. Add a line of explanation for each date and event.

2. Write the letters that might have been sent by:
(a) a woolcomber looking for work in 1770 (Extract 19.1);
(b) a workman who had been forced to sign 'the Document';
(c) a Trade Council explaining why the aims of unions in 1867 were different from the aims of Robert Owen and the men who had organized the Plug Riots.

(C)
1. Write the headlines that might have appeared above reports on:
(a) the passing of the Combination Acts – in government and Radical papers;
(b) the repeal of the Combination Acts, 1824 – in government and Radical papers;
(c) the formation of the G.N.C.T.U. – in papers controlled by Owen and by the government;
(d) the Tolpuddle decision – in papers controlled by the government, by employers, and by Owen;
(e) the Report of the Royal Commission 1867 – in government, employers' and workers' papers.

2. Make posters to illustrate some of the following:
(a) a call to men to come to a meeting of an early union;
(b) the opening of the first Post Office Savings Bank;
(c) a meeting of a local Trades Council;
(d) the lock-out of 1853 – as seen by employers and by workers.

20 Gladstone's Great Ministry, 1868-74

His Early Career

William Ewart Gladstone was the son of a rich Liverpool merchant. The family fortunes had grown as that port had developed in the eighteenth and nineteenth centuries. He had the sort of education that had once only been given to the sons of the landed upper class. He went to Eton and then to the University at Oxford. In 1833 he became M.P. for the 'rotten' borough of Newark, and quickly made his mark in the House of Commons. Macaulay, a Whig M.P. and historian, described him as the 'rising hope' of the Tory Party.

Experience

In 1841 Peel appointed Gladstone to the post of President of the Board of Trade. Here he worked for the Free Trade policy (p. 78). This, as we have seen, led to lower prices, more employment, and a rise in living standards (Fig. 20.1).

Fig. 20.1 A middle-class family in their comfortable home.

Gladstone resigned over the grant to Maynooth College. In 1846 he supported Peel over the repeal of the Corn Laws (Chapter 15), and he, Lord Aberdeen, Cardwell, and other Tories became known as Peelites. They had nothing to do with the Tory Party and its wish to bring back the Corn Laws.

When the Whigs came to power, many of the Peelites were offered government positions. Gladstone was Chancellor of the Exchequer under Russell, Aberdeen, and Palmerston. During this long period he carried on with Peel's policy of lowering import duties. He abolished the taxes on newspapers – which helped to lower their prices. He set up the Post Office Savings Bank – which gave many workers a chance to save. In 1860 he sent Richard Cobden to work out a trade treaty with France.

At the same time Gladstone tried to lower the income tax and hoped that one day it would be abolished. But if the government collected less in taxation, it had to spend less. So Gladstone also had to make sure that little money was spent – on social reform at home or on war abroad.

Gladstone and Palmerston

Gladstone had little respect for Palmerston's vigorous foreign policy. He condemned the Foreign Minister's actions over Don Pacifico (p. 89). In 1861 he argued that Britain ought to support Lincoln and the North during the American Civil War (p. 91), whereas Palmerston tended to support the Southerners. During this Civil War in America the Lancashire cotton-workers suffered a great deal of hardship (Extract 20.1). Gladstone came to admire the way in which, in spite of this, the cotton-workers showed their support for Lincoln's government and their opposition to the owners of the cotton plantations on whose product their work depended. Gladstone's support for Lincoln's government won him many friends among the Radical Liberals; on the other hand, his admiration for the cotton-workers was one of the reasons why he came out in favour of extending the franchise in 1866.

Gladstone to the Top

Palmerston died in 1865 and Russell became Prime Minister. Gladstone became leader of the House of Commons. Most of the Whigs admired him – for his intelligence, his work as Chancellor, his honesty and courage against Palmerston, and for his obvious ability. When Russell became too sick and old to carry on Gladstone became Prime Minister and head

Fig. 20.2 Gladstone attacks Disraeli's first budget in the House of Commons.

of his party, which some people now called the Liberal Party.

Before he did so he clashed with the man who was to prove to be his main rival – Benjamin Disraeli (Fig. 20.2). In 1866 Gladstone, as Leader of the House of Commons, brought in a Parliamentary Reform Bill. Some Whigs sided with the Tories to defeat Gladstone's proposals. Russell resigned, and the Tories formed a government. Disraeli then 'stole the Whigs' clothes' by bringing in his own Reform Bill. This got through the Commons – because Gladstone could not honestly oppose something which he had proposed himself (Chapter 29).

In Power

Disraeli's success was short-lived, for in the general election of 1868 the Liberals won a sweeping majority. The middle classes – industrialists, merchants, bankers, and so on – preferred Gladstone to Disraeli. He had, after all, lowered taxes, helped to improve trade, and provided them with the chance to get on. They wanted the chance to help themselves to make even more money and create even more jobs (Extract 20.2).

Gladstone understood these ambitions, for he was himself the son of just such a middle-class family. He also received the support of most of the new working-class voters. They also liked the idea of self-help. That, after all, was what they were doing in their trade unions.

New Demands from a New Society

Gladstone came to power as Britain was ending the second stage of its Industrial Revolution and just entering a third stage. This, as we shall see, was based largely on the development of the steamship. After 1870 Britain became just one industrial nation in a world where other industrialized countries were also growing up. The older industries – coal and cotton – had depended on strength or on the nimble fingers of women and children. The new industries – chemicals, electrical engineering, and so on – depended on the technical skills of better-educated workers and managers. Already by 1867 there was evidence that Britain was falling behind in the industrial race. This would lead to the need for a development of Britain's educational system (Chapter 32).

The middle class had won their share of the political system in 1832. By 1868 they wanted more of the privileges that only the upper class had once had. They wanted a change in the way that universities, the Civil Service, and the Army were run. As we shall see,

Gladstone passed laws on all these things.

He also tried to satisfy the demands of the working class; there was legislation to help trade unions for example.

But Gladstone could not forget that one of his main aims was to keep down the level of taxation. This meant that he would not agree to the government spending much money.

The Torrens Act 1868

In 1868 Parliament passed an Act that allowed local councils to deal with slum housing. It was taken through Parliament by one of Gladstone's ministers, Torrens. A council could decide that a house was 'unfit for human habitation' – because it had no water supply, no drains, or was badly constructed. It could ask the owner to repair the property. If he would not, the council could condemn the property and order that it be pulled down.

This meant that when councils acted there was even less housing available for the working class, who then crowded together in other, often inadequate, housing. So this Act did very little to help the poor. Also it was opposed by property owners who thought that it was an interference with their right to do what they wanted.

Few councils did much about this Act. After all, many councillors were property owners. Others were frightened at the possible increase in the local rates if they employed people to pull down houses.

Education

In Chapter 30 we will see that W. E. Forster brought in an Education Act (1870) which laid the base for the state education system that we have today.

Until 1871 only Anglicans could go to the universities of Oxford or Cambridge. Religious tests had been imposed during the seventeenth century, and only members of the Church of England could have a university education. By 1871 many people in the middle classes wanted to send their sons to universities, for they were able to afford to pay the high fees. But many of them were members of one or other of the many non-Anglican Churches.

Gladstone pleased them by abolishing the religious tests in the University Test Act of 1871. This Act gave the rich a chance to have a university education, and it cost the government nothing – which pleased Gladstone.

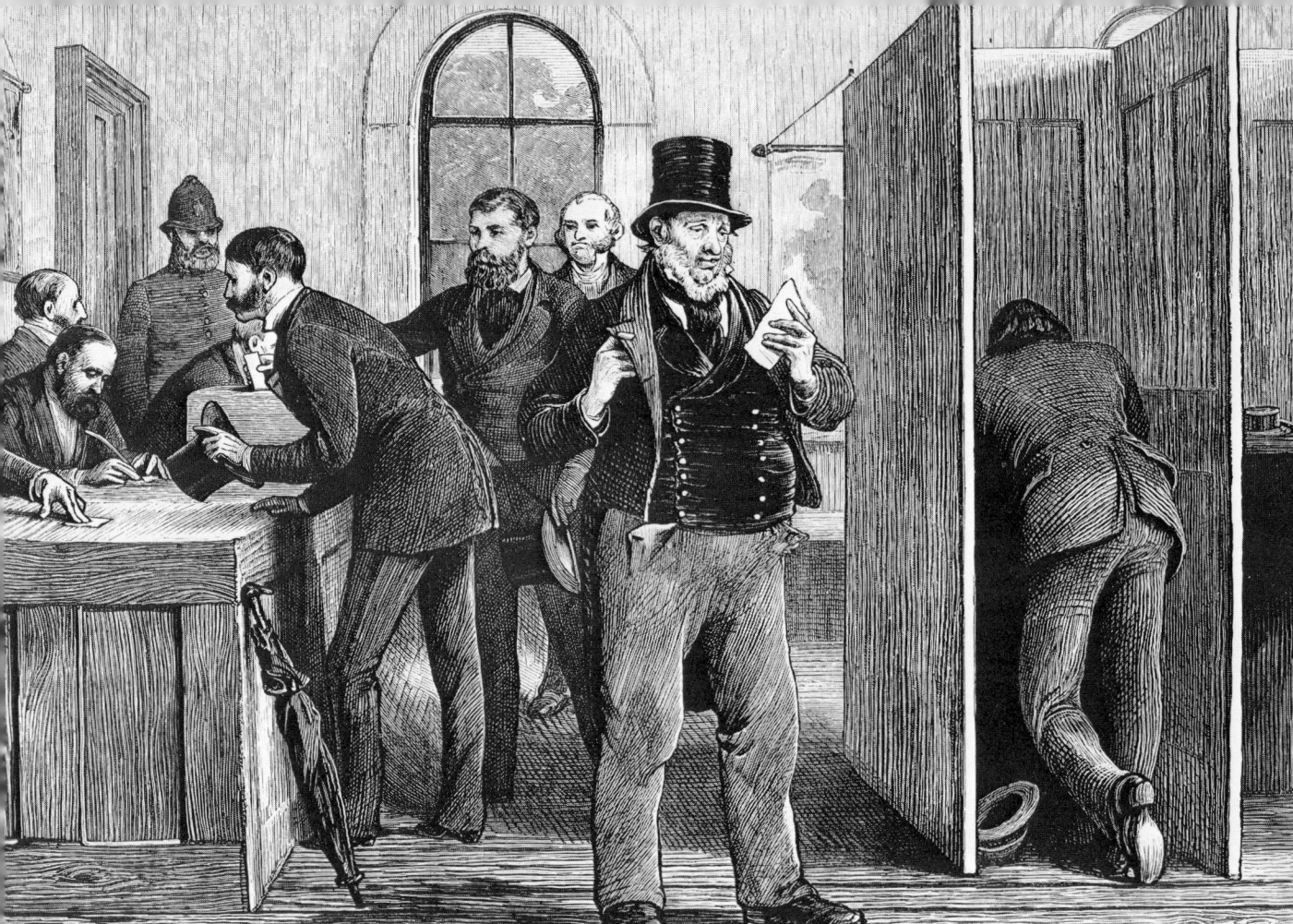

Fig. 20.3 Voting by secret ballot.

Civil Service Reform, 1871

The Crimean War had shown that the Civil Service was inefficient. One reason for this was the system of recruitment to and promotion in the Service. Politicians could get jobs for their relations and friends – whether they were clever or not.

In the 1850s the British had taken over the government of India (Chapter 18), and Sir Charles Trevelyan had gone out to examine the way in which the Indian Civil Service was organized. He reported on the need for a better system, and proposed that no one should be allowed into the Service unless they passed an entrance examination. He also proposed that promotions to higher positions should only go to people who passed other examinations.

In 1871 Gladstone introduced these reforms into the British Civil Service. Only people who passed an examination could be taken on. The entrance examinations varied for different grades of the Service. Only men of high educational standard could pass the examinations set for people who wanted to enter the Administrative Grade. These were the men who would, in time, become the Heads of government departments. They would advise ministers and suggest new laws.

This reform pleased the middle classes. Their sons were as educated as the sons of the landed upper class. Now, after 1871, they would be able to get jobs in the Civil Service even if they had no relative to help them on their way. The reform also pleased people who wanted the Service to become more efficient. This would lead to a fall in the money spent by each department. Again, the reform pleased Gladstone – because it cost the government nothing. Taxation would not have to be increased.

The Ballot Act, 1872

In Chapter 27 we will see that some workers got the right to vote in 1867.

In the open system of voting employers could check on the way a man had voted. If he did not do as he was told he could be sacked.

In 1872 Gladstone brought in the Ballot Bill. After

this, men voted in secret (Fig. 20.3). The employer could not control his men's voting, and this of course pleased the workers. It was yet another measure that did not lead to any increase in taxation.

The Licensing Act 1872

Drunkenness was one of the main problems in most industrial towns. Men, women, and children who lived in very poor housing conditions spent a good deal of time in the many ale-houses or beer shops. These were well-lit, warmer than their cold, damp homes, and somewhere where people could forget their real conditions.

Churches formed Temperance Societies to try to bring an end to drunkenness, and the Liberal Party had many members from the Nonconformist Churches which wrote and spoke against 'the demon drink'. These approved of the Licensing Act. This measure was intended to cut down on the number of places where intoxicating drink could be sold. It also limited – but very slightly – the hours during which such places could stay open.

But brewers and the owners of ale-houses were annoyed at this interference with their freedom. In the House of Lords, a Bishop said that he would prefer to see 'England free and drunk rather than England sober by law'. There was rioting against the Act in many towns. In the election campaign of 1874, Gladstone declared that 'every publican became a Tory election agent and every saloon a Tory committee room'. It was one reason for the Liberal defeat in that election.

Army Reform

The Crimean War had shown that the Army was badly in need of reform. Officers could buy their way to promotion, even if they had no ability. Few ordinary men willingly joined a force that insisted on a man joining for life. Conditions in the Army made many of them hate it; there was the flogging of offenders, low pay, poor housing, and the danger of a long period of overseas service – in India or Hong Kong for example.

Gladstone appointed Edward Cardwell to undertake a reform of the Army. He abolished the buying of commissions, and in future a man's promotion would depend on his ability and length of service. He also abolished flogging.

He tried to make the Army more attractive to ordinary people. He ended the system whereby a Regiment was known either by a number ('Fifty-first of the Line') or by the name of its founder ('Cooper's Horse'). Instead, Regiments were linked to one of the English counties, so there were Regiments with Yorkshire, Lancashire, Sussex and so on, in their names. This, he hoped, would attract recruits from the various counties. Each Regiment was divided into two battalions. One would serve overseas while the other would stay in its Regimental base at home. This guaranteed the men a period of service in Britain – and a chance to get home. The period of service was cut, and in future a man could join for six years with another six years spent in the reserve.

This reform pleased many people. Men who were ambitious for their sons' progress as officers could now look forward to their having a chance. Local pride was satisfied by the naming of the county Regiments, and Gladstone was pleased still further because a more efficient Army would cost the country less money – and so lead to a fall in taxation.

Other Reforms

We will see that Gladstone pushed through important Acts concerning trade unions (Chapter 28), and in doing so he aroused a great deal of opposition. Employers thought that he was a supporter of trade unions, but when he forbade picketing, trade unionists thought that he had taken a hard line. So he pleased few.

He also supported a number of Acts concerning Ireland (Chapter 24). Here again he lost much support. The Irish Catholic voters thought that he did not give them what they wanted, but on the other hand, many landowners and non-Catholics thought that he had given away too much.

Foreign Affairs

Gladstone followed a very different foreign policy from Palmerston. When Germany and France fought a war (1870–1) he stayed neutral – even though the growth of Germany meant a threat to Britain's industry and power. During the war, Germany gained Russia's support by suggesting that Russia ignore the Treaty of Paris (p. 97). In 1871 Russia started to rebuild both her fortresses and her fleet, and Gladstone took no action.

He settled America's claim for damages done by the *Alabama* (p. 91); he agreed to pay £3¼ million to the American government.

None of this pleased the British people who had become used to seeing Britain's Foreign Ministers doing whatever they wanted to. They failed to realize that by 1871 Britain was no longer able to behave as she had done in the 1830s and 1850s. They blamed

Gladstone for being weak, and preferred Disraeli's policy.

A Divided Liberal Party

By 1872 Gladstone realized that his government had done as much as it could, and he wanted to resign. But Disraeli refused to form a government unless there was an election. Gladstone did not want to have one, so he had to carry on.

But he now had a divided party. Lord Hartington, son of the Duke of Devonshire, thought that he had gone too far. He had interfered with property owners in slum areas, with landowners in Ireland (p. 186), with brewers, licensees, and employers. He had started a national system of state education (p. 174) and made the Civil Service more open to 'ordinary' people. All this was, in Hartington's opinion, 'too much' and 'too radical'. And many old-fashioned Whigs supported him.

On the other hand, there were many people who thought that Gladstone had not gone far enough. He had done little to help the mass of the people. They still had low wages, and lived in appalling conditions. Some Liberals wanted Radical reform – on housing, pensions, and education.

Gladstone argued that the Liberals ought to follow policies of PEACE (to avoid war and taxation), RETRENCHMENT (or a cut in government spending), and REFORM (provided this cost the government nothing). But the Radical Liberals wanted more.

The General Election, 1874

During this election many former Liberal voters deserted their party and supported Disraeli and the Tories. Some middle-class people did so because they wanted the government to follow a vigorous foreign policy; some did so because they feared that Gladstone was going 'too far'; others because they liked Disraeli's promise of social reform (Extract 21.1 on p. 123).

Many working-class voters also deserted Gladstone. They preferred the Tories who they thought might do something about their social conditions – and about their trade unions.

The result was that the Tories won a majority in the 1874 election; this was the first time since 1841 that they had done so. So Disraeli came to power. In January 1875 Gladstone decided to give up the leadership of the Liberal Party, and Lord Grenville succeeded him. Gladstone's career seemed to have come to an end, but we will see later that this was not to be the case.

Questions

Extract 20.1

The cotton famine

It has been a poor time for me owing to the American War which seems as far off being settled as ever. The mill I work in was stopped all last winter, during which time I barely kept alive. When we started working again it was with Surat cotton and weavers can only mind two looms. We can earn very little. I have not earned a shilling a day this last month. My clothes and bedding is wearing out very fast and I have no means of getting any more, as what wages I get does hardly keep me, after paying rent, rates and firing. The principal reason why I did not take any notes these last two years is because I was sad and weary. One half of the time I was out of work and the other I had to work as hard as ever in my life and can hardly keep myself living. If things do not mend this summer I will try somewhere else or something else, for I cant go much further with what I am at.

(John Ward, *The Diary of John Ward of Clitheroe, Weaver, 1860–4*.)

1.   Which American war is referred to here? Why were many mills stopped because of that war? Which area suffered most heavily because of this?
2.   Where did 'Surat' cotton come from? How did it compare with American cotton?
3.   How long did Ward suffer great poverty? What evidence is there in this extract that he had been used to a reasonable standard of living?

Extract 20.2

Self-help

The spirit of self-help is the root of all genuine growth in the individual, and . . . it constitutes the true source of national vigour and strength. Help from without is often enfeebling in its effects. Whatever is done for men or classes takes away the stimulus and necessity of doing for themselves.

National progress is the sum of individual industry, energy and uprightness, as national decay is of individual idleness, selfishness, and vice. What we are accustomed to decry as great social evils will, for the most part, be found to be but the outgrowth of a man's own perverted life . . . (thus) the highest patriotism consists, not so much in altering laws and institutions as in helping and stimulating men to elevate and improve themselves by their own free independent individual action.

(Samuel Smiles, *Self-Help*, 1859.)

1. How far does this extract explain why Victorian politicians were unwilling to tackle the social problems of housing, poverty, and unemployment?
2. Why did this policy of self-help lead to lower taxation? Why did this please the middle classes?
3. How else did the middle class benefit from following this policy?
4. How were working people able to follow this policy? Give two examples of ways in which they did so. Explain why the poorer working people were unable to do so.

Fig. 20.1

1. How did the father of this family benefit from the fall in (i) income tax, and (ii) indirect taxes?
2. Why did many such fathers send their sons away to boarding schools?
3. Why were many such fathers pleased by Gladstone's reforms of (i) the Civil Service, and (ii) university admissions, and (iii) the Army?
4. Why were some fathers annoyed by those reforms?
5. Why were many such fathers annoyed by Gladstone's policies on (i) licensing, and (ii) foreign affairs?
6. Many middle-class families voted for Gladstone in 1868. Give four reasons why many of them did not do so in 1874.

Worksheet

(A)
1. Make a brief summary of Gladstone's career (i) before 1841 (ii) 1841–6 (iii) 1846–65, to show the way in which he became increasingly important.

2. Who were the 'Peelites'? Explain why they broke from the Conservative Party in 1846. Why, in time, did most of them join the Whig Party?

3. How had Lancashire workers suffered during the American Civil War? Why?

4. Trace the course of the argument over parliamentary reform between 1865 and 1867.

5. Why did Gladstone win the 1868 election?

6. Make a list of the major reforms passed during the 'Great Ministry'. Show which of these reforms (i) pleased the middle class (ii) annoyed the middle class (iii) pleased the working class (iv) annoyed the working class.

7. Explain the argument in favour of a Licensing Act in 1870. Why was Gladstone's Licensing Act so bitterly opposed? What effect did it have on the 1874 election?

8. Make a list of the ways in which Cardwell reformed the Army at this time. Why were these reforms needed?

9. Give four reasons why Gladstone lost the election of 1874.

(B)
1. Write the letters that might have been sent by:
(a) the owner of slum property who had heard about the Torrens Act;
(b) a Nonconformist whose sons go to Oxford or Cambridge University after 1872;
(c) a brewer after the passing of the Licensing Act.

(C)
1. Write the headlines that might have appeared above reports on:
(a) the cut in the newspaper tax;
(b) the result of the election of 1868 – in Whig and Tory papers;
(c) the Ballot Act;
(d) the Licensing Act – in papers controlled by brewers and by a Temperance Society;
(e) the results of the election of 1874 – in Whig and Tory papers.

2. Draw the posters that might have been used to:
(a) call a meeting to protest against the new licensing laws;
(b) protest about Gladstone's handling of the *Alabama* affair.

21 Disraeli, 1874-80

Background

Benjamin Disraeli was born in 1804. His father was a Jewish immigrant who had become a successful businessman. He wanted his son to enjoy all the privileges of having been born in England, so he changed the family name from D'Israeli which looked and sounded very Jewish. He had his son baptized in the Anglican Church, and sent him to a private school.

A Novelist

In 1826 Disraeli wrote his first novel, *Vivian Grey*. His best-known novels, *Coningsby* (1844) and *Sybil* (1845), were published after he had become an M.P. In these novels he showed that the industrialists and merchants were treating their workpeople very badly. He wanted the landed upper class to act as protectors of the working class.

He had ambitions to become more than a novelist, and stood in several elections in the 1830s – as a Whig, as a Radical, and as an Independent candidate, but few people took him seriously. He also offended serious-minded people by his clothes. He liked to dress up in yellow waistcoats, red velvet jackets, and blue trousers. This was certainly not the stuff of which Victorian politicians were supposed to be made!

In 1837 he made friends with Mrs Wyndham Lewis whose husband, a Tory, controlled the rotten borough of Maidstone. She persuaded her husband to let Disraeli have this seat when it became vacant in 1837. In 1839 he married Mrs Lewis – by now a very wealthy widow. Her money allowed him to devote most of his attention to politics.

Disraeli and Peel

Disraeli entered Parliament as a Tory, and when Peel came to power in 1841, Disraeli expected to be given a Cabinet post. Gladstone had one; Disraeli did not. He did not forgive Peel for this.

In 1845 and 1846 he opposed Peel's decision to repeal the Corn Laws (Chapter 15). He said that repeal would mean ruin for the British farmers and for their landlords – the majority of whom were Tories. The majority of Peel's party supported their leader and the Corn Laws were repealed. Disraeli, Lord George Bentinck, Lord Stanley (son of the Earl of Derby), and a small number of Tories were unable to prevent this 'betrayal of the gentlemen of England' as Disraeli described it.

In fact, British farmers became very rich after 1846. British workmen had more money to spend, and they spent much of it on home-grown food. But Disraeli proved to be right after 1873. Massive imports of food led to a great fall in food prices.

1846–67

In June 1846, just as the Act repealing the Corn Laws received the royal assent, Peel was defeated in the House of Commons over an Irish Coercion Bill. He resigned (Fig. 21.1) and was succeeded by Russell and the Whigs. Peel led his former colleagues on the Opposition benches, until his sudden death in July 1850, a few days after falling from his horse.

Disraeli was the leading member of the small number of Tory M.P.s in the Commons. He was faced with so many great men on the government benches: Palmerston, Russell, and other leading Whigs had been joined by Aberdeen, Gladstone, Cardwell and other 'Peelites', and the voters supported the policies of the Whig–Peelite governments.

Disraeli had a hard job to do. He had to show the few remaining Tory M.P.s that they had to give up arguing in favour of Corn Laws; he also had to show the British voters that the Tory Party was a party that deserved their support.

A New Party

Lord Derby, the Tory leader, was Prime Minister three times between 1846 and 1868, and Disraeli was a Cabinet minister in each of those governments

119

Fig. 21.1 Sir Robert Peel leaves the House of Commons after his resignation on 29 June 1846.

Fig. 21.2 Gladstone (left) and Disraeli (right) offering the British voter a choice of policies. Disraeli promised a larger empire. This cartoon in Punch *suggested that Gladstone's alternative to this was prosperity.* ▼

(Fig. 20.2 on p. 113). But these governments were only in office for very short periods.

The only important thing that a Tory government achieved was the passing of the Second Reform Act 1867 (p. 155), but even that got no reward from the voters. In the 1868 election Gladstone came back to power.

In the 1870s Disraeli appointed a friend, J. A. Gorst, to set up a Tory Party organization. This had its headquarters at the Carlton Club in London, but branches were set up in each town. Agents were appointed to organize each constituency; voters were contacted, supporters recruited, and meetings held to explain party policy.

He toured the country in 1872 making a series of speeches in which he argued for a stronger foreign policy. He hoped to win the support of people who remembered Palmerston and were angry with Gladstone's weaker policy (Fig. 21.2).

But he also argued for social reforms (Extract 21.1). This was very different to the policy of the Gladstone government.

In 1874 when the Tories won a majority of the seats in the general election, Disraeli appointed R. A. Cross as Home Secretary. He was to put Disraeli's ideas on social reform into law.

THE CHOICE OF HERCULES.

Housing Act 1875

The Torrens Act (1868) was a first step to slum clearance. In 1875 Cross persuaded Parliament to pass the Artisans' Dwellings Act. This gave councils powers to deal with whole areas at the same time.

There was a major weakness in this Act: it was an *adoptive* Act. Councils could, if they wanted, use the powers given them by the Act, but most councils did not adopt these powers. They were frightened at the thought of the increases in rates.

In Birmingham Joseph Chamberlain had become leader of the Liberals and Lord Mayor. He forced the Council to use all the powers of the Act.

He boasted that in three years, 1873–6, he had transformed Birmingham. It had been a dirty, unhealthy city, but Chamberlain cleared many thousands of slum houses, paved the streets, laid drains, provided a water supply for each house, and built new roads through what had been slum property.

However, even this was of no real value to the really poor. The better-off workers were able to afford to buy their own homes or to rent a decent house, but the poor had to live together in over-crowded houses. When these were pulled down they crowded together in some other area. The problem of housing would not be solved merely by knocking down slum property.

The Public Health Act 1875

The first Public Health Act had been passed in 1848 (p. 78), and since then there had been a number of Health Acts. Most of these dealt with only one part of the problem of Public Health. There were Nuisance Removal Acts, Burial Acts, Refuse Disposal Acts, and so on.

In 1875 the Civil Servants persuaded Cross to bring all these small Acts into one large Public Health Act. This *compelled* each local council to appoint a Medical Officer of Health. He would have the power to make the town healthier – by insisting on drains, clean shops, decent water supplies, and so on. To help the Medical Officers, the 1875 Act also *compelled* the local councils to improve the sanitary conditions of their towns or cities.

The Factory Act 1875

Since 1833 there had been a large number of Factory Acts. Some referred to children, others to women workers; some to the number of hours worked, others to conditions in mills; some dealt with coal-mines, others with factories.

The Civil Servants persuaded Disraeli to put all these smaller Acts into one large Act. The 1875 Act limited the number of working hours of young people and women to fifty-six hours per week.

Pure Food and Drugs Act 1875

One of the worst features of life in Victorian towns was the way in which shopkeepers cheated their customers. They mixed sand with the brown sugar, chalk with white sugar, and splashed water on the sacks of tea to make them heavier. Parliament passed an Act that outlawed such practices, and Disraeli's Act, 1875, extended the powers of Food Inspectors.

The Merchant Shipping Act 1876

Many shipowners made a lot of money if their ships sank. This was because they were paid compensation by insurance companies for the loss of the ship and its cargo. There was evidence that many owners sent out their ships when they were overloaded or unfit to go to sea.

Samuel Plimsoll, a backbench M.P., took up the case of the widows of the sailors who died in the many shipwrecks. They received no compensation. It was Plimsoll who demanded that each ship should have a load-line – now known as the Plimsoll line. This would show when the ship was carrying just the right amount of cargo.

Climbing Boys' Act 1875

Boys were used as chimney-sweeps in the huge chimneys of the large Victorian houses. Many of them had been burnt to death; others suffocated to death. There had been a number of Acts to stamp out this dangerous and dirty work, and the 1875 Act was the last. As children were forced to go to school, there was less chance of their being employed as sweeps.

Other Reforms

In Chapter 30 we will see that Disraeli's government helped pass important Acts to help trade unions and their members. It also supported an important Education Act in 1876. This we shall study in Chapter 32. This was yet another sign that the government was beginning to understand the connection between the country's educational system and the development of industry.

The Suez Canal Shares, 1875

The Suez Canal had been opened in 1869 (Fig. 22.1 on p. 125). It had been built by a French engineer, Ferdinand de Lesseps. The British government had refused his request to help in its building, and after 1869 France had a great deal of influence in Egypt, whose ruler, the Khedive, owned half the shares of the Suez Canal Company – his reward for allowing the Canal to be built through his country.

But the Canal was very important for British merchants. They had once had to send their goods around the Cape of Good Hope on the way to India and Australia. The Canal cut the journey to Australia by 1,000 miles (1,600 kilometres) and to India by a staggering 4,000 miles (6,400 kilometres).

Sailing ships could not use the Canal; they needed room to tack (sail in different directions) to take advantage of the wind. Only steamships could use the Canal, and this gave a great boost to the development of better, larger, cheaper, and more efficient steamships.

In 1875 the Khedive of Egypt became bankrupt, and wanted to sell his Canal shares. Disraeli heard about this, and in a secret deal and without Parliament's permission, he bought the shares (Extract 21.2). This gave Britain control of the Canal. It also meant that Britain would have to play a large part in Egyptian affairs in the future.

India

Disraeli dreamt of creating a large Empire out in the East. In 1876 he persuaded the Queen to accept the title of Empress of India (Fig. 22.3 on p. 128). This helped to impress the rulers of the Princely States of India.

He needed their support because Russia seemed to be advancing on India. They had been defeated in the Crimean War in 1856, but then they tried to expand their Empire in Asia. By 1875 they had reached the border of Afghanistan, and tried to gain control of this kingdom which borders on India.

Disraeli sent an agent to Kabul, the capital of Afghanistan, to look after British interests. He was murdered. Disraeli then sent an army to take revenge – and maybe control of the country. Unfortunately, the Afghans were better-led and better-armed, and the British lost thousands of men at the Battle of Maiwand. In August 1880 Sir Frederick Roberts (later Lord Roberts) won a victory at Kandahar, but it was obvious that the British would have to give up their ambitions of taking control in Afghanistan.

Transvaal

The Boer settlers had left the Cape of Good Hope on their Great Trek in 1836 (p. 71). By 1877 they had developed their own Boer Republics of the Transvaal and the Orange Free State. Here they clashed with the Zulus.

In 1877 Disraeli sent a British army into the Transvaal, and announced that Britain had taken over (or *annexed*) that Republic 'to protect the Boers from the Zulus'. The British had to fight a series of wars against these black warriors, and at the Battle of Isandhlwana the Zulus inflicted a heavy defeat on a small British force. However, the British got their revenge at the Battle of Ulundi (1879).

The Boers argued that they did not want British protection; and they certainly did not want Britain to annex their Republic. This led to the first of the Boer Wars which had to be settled by Gladstone in 1884 (Chapter 23).

Foreign Policy

Disraeli had a 'forward' policy – in Afghanistan, the Transvaal, Egypt, and above all, in the Balkans. He saw himself as Palmerston's successor. Gladstone had shown that he did not want to get involved in a vigorous or 'forward' foreign policy, but Disraeli thought that the British people would welcome such a policy (Chapter 22).

1880 and the Election

In 1876 Disraeli had accepted the title of the Earl of Beaconsfield (Fig. 22.3 on p. 128); he had wanted his dying wife to enjoy a brief period as a countess. Queen Victoria was pleased to give him that honour. She liked Disraeli who called her 'my Faery' and treated her as a lady, whereas Gladstone, she stated, 'treats me as if I were a public meeting'.

But in 1880 Disraeli lost the general election. The British people may have approved of his 'forward' policy in 1878; they certainly did not do so in 1880. They were concerned at the way in which British farming was suffering because of the imports of cheap foreign food (Fig. 21.3). Disraeli did nothing to help the farmers and landowners whom he had defended in 1846. Nor did he do anything to help British industrialists who by 1880 were beginning to suffer from the flood of foreign goods. Britain was certainly no longer the only industrialized country in the world. One sign of this was the flood of foreign food; another was the rise in the level of unemployment. Disraeli's government was unfairly blamed for this change in British fortunes.

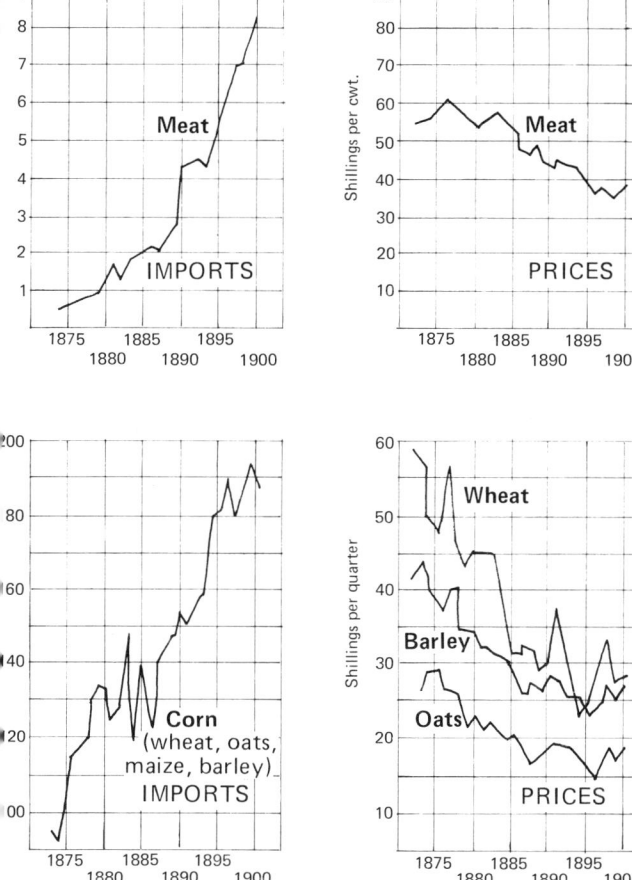

20 shillings = £1   1 cwt (hundredweight) = 50.8 kg

Fig. 21.3 Rising imports and falling prices.

Questions

Extract 21.1

Disraeli and public health

I am not here to maintain that there is nothing to be done to increase the well-being of the working classes of this country; but in attempting to legislate upon social matters the great object is to be practical – to have before us some distinct aims and some distinct means by which they can be accomplished.

I think public attention as regards these matters ought to be concentrated upon sanitary legislation. . . . Pure air, pure water, the inspection of unhealthy habitations, the adulteration of food, these and many kindred matters may be legitimately dealt with by the legislature.

A great scholar and a great wit . . . said that in his opinion there was a great mistake in the Holy Scriptures, and that, instead of saying 'Vanity of Vanities, all is Vanity' – *Vanitas Vanitatum, omnia vanitas* – the wise and witty king really said *Sanitas sanitatum, omnia sanitas.* It is impossible to over-rate the importance of the subject. After all, the first considerations of a minister should be the health of the people. A land may be covered with historic trophies . . . with universities and with libraries; the people may be civilized and ingenious; the country may even be famous in the annals and actions of the world, but if the population every ten years decreases, and the stature of the race every ten years diminishes, the history of that country will soon be the history of the past.

(Benjamin Disraeli, Speech at Manchester, April 1872.)

1. When and how did Disraeli first show an interest in the question of public health and sanitary reform?
2. When and by what Acts did Disraeli get his proposals approved by Parliament?
3. Why were his proposals opposed by many Liberals?

Extract 21.2

Purchase of Suez Canal shares

I had heard that shortly the Khedive's canal shares, which amounted to nearly half of them, would pass into French hands. Many politicians in this country had always disliked or mistrusted the Suez Canal scheme. At that time about 86 per cent of the tonnage that passed through the canal was British. The British merchant was paying the dividends, the French public was receiving them. The consequence of this was that the canal dues were kept very high. . . .

I asked Lord Derby to consider the chances of getting the canal dues lowered if the whole of the property passed into the hands of the French. . . . Then arose another question. What authority or what means had the Government for buying shares in a commercial company? Parliament was not sitting, and even if it was and the House of Commons were asked for this £4,000,000, 'the gaff would be blown' to use Lord Derby's own phrase. (Laughter.) The French would immediately be on the qui vive. . . . Lord Rowton was sent by Mr Disraeli to Baron Rothschild; although at first the Baron must have been rather staggered at being asked to supply four millions in a very few days without any security. (Laughter.) But the money was furnished, though not all at once. I believe it was paid in instalments. The whole business occupied no more than eight or ten days. Not a whisper got out, nobody heard a word of what was going on, and there came a Friday when the air of England was filled with thrown-up hats. (Cheers.) All England acclaimed the great achievement which would redound for ever to the honour of Mr Disraeli.

(Mr Greenwood's Speech in Honouring Frederick Greenwood, being speeches delivered in praise of him at a dinner held on 8 April 1905, Privately Printed, 1905.)

1.   Who was the Khedive? Why did he have a large number of shares in the Suez Canal Company?
2.   Why should the British have taken an interest in the Canal?
3.   How might British merchants benefit if Britain gained control of the Canal?
4.   Why did the purchase of these shares have to be done in great secrecy?
5.   Explain the importance of the Canal for British trade with (i) India (ii) Australia. (Other routes? Costs? Prices of goods in Britain?)

Fig. 21.3

1.   Name two countries from which Britain imported wheat after 1873. Why had these countries not been able to sell wheat in Britain before 1870? Why could they do so after 1873?
2.   Why did foreign farmers make a profit even though the price of wheat fell in Britain? Why could British farmers not compete with them?
3.   Why was this price fall good for (i) some British industrialists, and (ii) most British families?
4.   From which countries did Britain import large quantities of meat after 1875? What industrial developments enabled this trade to be carried on?
5.   Why was this increased import of food good for the nation's health?

Worksheet

(A)
1.   Make a summary of Disraeli's career from (i) 1830–46 (ii) 1846–66 (iii) 1866–8 (iv) 1874–80 (v) 1880–1.

2.   Make a list of the main reforms introduced by the Disraeli government 1874–80. Write two sentences on each of these reforms.

3.   Write two sentences on each of the following: Medical Officers of Health; the Plimsoll line; climbing boys.

4.   Write two sentences on each of the following: Kabul; the annexation of the Transvaal.

(B)
1.   Write the letters that might have been sent by:
(a) Peel, explaining why he offered a government post to Gladstone but did not offer one to Disraeli;
(b) a sailor, in favour of the arguments being used by Samuel Plimsoll;

(c) a housewife after she had bought food at the lower prices.

(C)
1.   Write the headlines that might have appeared above reports on:
(a) the result of the 1868 election – in papers controlled by the Tories, Whigs, and Radicals;
(b) Disraeli's speech on foreign policy;
(c) Disraeli's speech on public health (Extract 21.1);
(d) the result of the 1874 election – in papers controlled by Tories, Whigs, and Radicals;
(e) the buying of the Suez Canal Company's shares – in papers controlled by merchants, Tories, Whigs and shipowners;
(f) the granting of the title of Empress of India (Fig. 22.3 on p. 128).

2.   Make a poster on ONE of the following:
(a) an advertisement for cheaper food now in the shops;
(b) a council's intention to clear a slum area;
(c) a meeting called by Samuel Plimsoll.

22 The Eastern Question, 1875-8

Gladstone and Disraeli differed over many things, but their greatest clash concerned British policy towards Turkey.

The Eastern Question

We have already seen that this question contained three smaller questions (p. 94). These were the future of Turkey, the policies of the great powers, and the spread of nationalism among the Christian people living in the Turkish Empire.

Britain and Russia had clashed over this question in 1827 (p. 63) and 1839 (p. 95), and in 1854 Britain had gone to war against Russia (p. 96).

In 1856 Palmerston and his fellow ministers hoped that Turkey would be able to make the reforms needed if it were to continue to rule a large Empire. These hopes were to be disappointed.

Pan-Slavism

The word *pan* comes from a Greek word meaning *all*. The Slavs are one of the races living in Eastern Europe. These include the people we call Yugoslavs, Bulgarians, and Poles, as well as the people living in Bohemia in Czechoslovakia.

The largest group of Slavs are the Russians. After the military defeat in 1856 the Russians changed their policies in the Balkans. They thought that they would get more advantages if they tried to help their fellow-Slavs to get their independence from Turkey. This might be done without Russia being involved in a war. It might also be done without rousing the suspicions of Britain or other powers such as Austria or Germany.

This was less likely after Britain gained control of the Suez Canal (Fig. 22.1). The Canal was 'the lifeline of the Empire', and a Russian advance into the

Fig. 22.1 The opening of the Suez Canal, 1869.

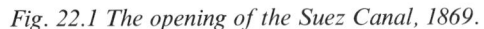

Mediterranean would be seen as a threat to that lifeline.

The Bosnian Rebellion, 1875

In 1875 the Christian Slavs living in Bosnia rose in rebellion against their Turkish masters. They had seen how weak the Turks were in 1856 – only Britain and France had stopped Russia from defeating Turkey. Even so, the Slavs had seen Rumania gain self-government as a result of that war.

The Turks had promised that they would reform their system of governing their Empire, but they did not so do. They remained what they had been for many years – cruel, greedy, and inefficient (Extract 22.1).

In 1875 the people of Bosnia and Herzegovina rebelled. Russia, Germany, and Austria wanted to force the Sultan of Turkey to agree to home rule for the Bosnians, But Disraeli would not agree. He was afraid that this would further weaken Turkey. A weaker Turkey would be even less of a barrier to Russian advance into the Mediterranean.

The rebellion spread from Bosnia. The Bulgarians, the Serbs, and the people of Montenegro joined in, and the Turks were frightened that the whole of their Mediterranean Empire would become involved. They realized that they might lose all that Empire.

In 1876 the Turkish army took its revenge on the ordinary people in Bulgaria – the state nearest to mainland Turkey. The world was horrified. Gladstone wrote a number of pamphlets and made many speeches about the Bulgarian massacres (Extract 22.1), but Disraeli refused to side with the Christians in a war against Turkey. He was more concerned to prevent the collapse of Turkey, and so hold back the Russian threat.

Russia makes War, 1877

While the other powers argued among themselves Russia sent an army to help the Bulgarians. In May 1877 Russian troops crossed the Danube, and by July they had reached Plevna where the Turkish army held them at bay until December 1877. The fall of Plevna allowed the Russians and Bulgarians to sweep on towards Constantinople and in January 1878 the Turks agreed to an armistice which brought the fighting to an end.

The Treaty of San Stefano, 1878

The Russians and the Turks negotiated the terms of a peace treaty once the armistice had been signed. These negotiations led to the signing of the Treaty of San Stefano (Fig. 22.2). This said that:

Fig. 22.2a The arrangements proposed at San Stefano, 1878.

Fig. 22.2b The Balkans and the Treaty of Berlin, 1878.

1. Turkey was to lose most of her territory in Europe. She would keep only four portions of her original dominions. If you look at the map you will see that these were separated from Turkey itself by independent Bulgaria. The Russians, the Serbs, and other Slavs hoped that Turkey would be unable to rule these provinces properly. After all, she had been unable to control Bulgaria. She was probably not going to be able to govern Bosnia and the other separated provinces. These might then fall into Slav hands.

2. A large new state of Bulgaria was created. As you can see from Fig. 22.2 this country stretched from the Danube to the Aegean Sea. This gave it a long sea coast along which to build ports and harbours. Russia wanted this as an outlet into the Mediterranean. She could send her wheat and other exports overland through a friendly Bulgaria.

3. Rumania, Serbia, and Montenegro were made larger. They were also given their complete independence from Turkish rule. This pleased the Slav peoples. It also encouraged Serbia to think about gaining control of Bosnia (Fig. 22.2).

4. Russia gained Kars and Batoum in the Caucasus from Turkey and also recovered part of Bessarabia which she had lost to Rumania in 1856.

5. In return Rumania was given Dobruja which had been part of Turkey.

Britain, Austria, and the Treaty

Britain was alarmed at these arrangements. Disraeli feared that Bulgaria would be a puppet in the hands of Russia. This would mean a Russian threat to the Turks at Constantinople and to British interests in the Mediterranean.

The Austrian Empire included many Serbs and other Slavs. The Austrians were afraid that Serbia's ambition might grow to the point where Serbia might think of attacking Austria, so Austria did not want to see Serbia grow any larger. On the contrary, Austria had ideas of advancing into the Balkans to replace the weakening Turkey as the great power of that area.

Germany, under Bismarck, had no interest in the region, but she did not want to see Austria and Russia (her Allies) fighting over the Eastern Question. So Bismarck, Disraeli, and Austria forced the Russians and the Turks to tear up the Treaty of San Stefano and come to Berlin to make a new treaty.

The Treaty of Berlin, 1878

In Berlin the powers redrew the map (Fig. 22.2). These new arrangements were very different to those made at San Stefano. The main terms of the Congress of Berlin were:

1. The proposed State of Bulgaria was split into three. One part was still called Bulgaria; this was granted self-government but remained under Turkish control. Another part, eastern Rumelia, was to be governed by a Christian governor appointed by the Turks. The third part, Macedonia, was restored to Turkey.

2. Bosnia and Herzegovina were handed to Austria – not as part of her Empire but to 'administer'. This meant, in fact, that Austria ruled these regions. In 1908 she formally announced the annexation of these Slav regions as part of her advance to the south-east.

3. Serbia and Montenegro were still recognized as independent, but they had to hand back some of the territory they had claimed at San Stefano.

The effects of these arrangements were that Turkey-in-Europe was now a compact piece of territory. It also meant, though, that Austria was now involved in the Balkans – and opposed to Russia's claims to be the great power of the region. Britain liked this. It meant that the Russians would be held in check.

Britain took possession of the island of Cyprus. This would be a base from which the British could keep an eye on Russia to the north and the Suez Canal to the south.

Disraeli and the Congress

Disraeli, now the Earl of Beaconsfield (Fig. 22.3), played a large part in the Congress. Bismarck said of him, 'Watch the Jew. He's the one', but the Foreign Secretary, Lord Salisbury, did most of the work since Disraeli was now very old, partially deaf, and easily tired.

On their return from Berlin they received a great welcome (Extract 22.2). This further example of Britain's power to decide the future of Turkey was popular with the British people.

Turkey and the Congress

Once again, Turkey had been kept in being by the actions of Britain – and Austria. Once again, the Turks were forced to promise that they would reform. But they failed to do so. This led to further crises in this region, and this, as we shall see, led to the outbreak of the First World War.

Fig. 22.3 Having persuaded the Queen to accept the title of Empress of India, Disraeli accepted the reward of the Earldom of Beaconsfield.

Gladstone and the Congress

Gladstone condemned Disraeli's policy towards Turkey. He had wanted Britain to make war on the cruel Turks, and wanted Turkey driven out of Europe 'bag and baggage' (Extract 22.1). Disraeli had sided with the Turks against the Christians, so it is not surprising that Gladstone attacked Disraeli.

This Balkan policy was just one more example of that 'forward' policy that Gladstone condemned. In the winter of 1879 Gladstone went on a long tour of Midlothian in Scotland, speaking to vast crowds about Disraeli's wickedness. He called on the British voters to condemn the policy that led to war in Afghanistan, the Transvaal and elsewhere (Extract 23.1 on p. 134).

Meanwhile Disraeli spoke of the need to make the Empire even larger and more powerful. Neither he nor Gladstone seemed to understand the real problems of Britain. Farmers were being ruined; British industries were unable to meet the challenge of Germany and America; industrial workers faced unemployment; and poverty was a real problem for millions of people in a country whose leaders seemed to care more about foreign and imperial affairs than about their own people.

Questions

Extract 22.1

Gladstone on the Bulgarian horrors

We know that there have been perpetrated, under the authority of a Government to which we have been giving the strongest support, outrages, so vast in scale as to exceed all modern example. These are the Bulgarian horrors. What can be done to punish, or to prevent? . . .

The Turkish race was from the black day when they first entered Europe, the one great anti-human specimen of humanity. Wherever they went, a broad line of blood marked the track behind them. They represented everywhere government by force, as opposed to government by law. . . .

Twenty years ago, France and England determined to try a great experiment in remodelling the administrative system of Turkey, with the hope of curing its intolerable vices, and of making good its not less intolerable deficiencies. . . .

At vast expenditure of French and English life and treasure, gave to Turkey twenty years of a repose. . . . The insurrections of 1875 . . . have disclosed the total failure to fulfil the promises. Even these miserable insurrections, she had not the ability to put down. . . . A lurid glare is thrown over the whole case by the Bulgarian horrors. . . .

I entreat my countrymen . . . to require and insist, that our Government, which has been working in one direction, shall work in the other, and shall apply all its vigour to concur with the other states of Europe in obtaining the extinction of the Turkish executive power in Bulgaria. Let the Turks now carry away their abuses in the only possible manner, namely by carrying off themselves. Their Zaptiehs and their Mudirs, their Bimbashis and their Yuzbachis, their Kaimakams and their Pashas, one and all, bag and baggage, shall, I hope, clear out from the province they have desolated and profaned.

(W. E. Gladstone, *The Bulgarian Horrors and the Question of the East*, 1876.)

1. To which country had 'we been giving our strongest support'? Why did Britain have such an interest in that country? Of whom was Britain afraid?
2. What war had ended 'Twenty years ago'? Which countries had Britain (i) helped (ii) opposed during that war?
3. What evidence is there in this Extract to suggest that Turkey was too weak to govern her Empire?
4. Who was Prime Minister in 'our Government'? In what 'direction' had this government 'been working'? Did this policy change because of Gladstone's appeal?
5. Which country came to the aid of Bulgaria in 1877? How was she rewarded in 1878?

Extract 22.2

'Peace with honour'

As soon as the packet which was bringing back the two English plenipotentiaries touched the pier at Dover, the Mayor and Corporation stepped on board to present the Premier with a congratulatory address. The Premier in making his acknowledgements, claimed to have brought back 'Peace with Honour' . . . and demanded recognition for Lord Salisbury's share in this result as equal to his own.

Other addresses of welcome and congratulation followed, and Ministers proceeded by special train to London. The Charing Cross Station had been decorated in their honour, and was crowded with spectators who closely packed the tiers of seats which had been erected. The arrival of the Ministers was greeted with ringing cheers. They were received upon the platform by the Lord Mayor and Sheriffs, in their robes of office, and a distinguished company. Something of the air of a triumph was given to their progress along the crowded way to Downing Street.

In response to the cheers of the throng Lord Beaconsfield appeared at a window, and repeated the phrase which he had used at Dover. . . .
(Geo. Carslake Thompson, *Public Opinion and Lord Beaconsfield, 1875–1880*, 1886.)

1. Who were the 'two plenipotentiaries'?
2. What 'phrase' did Beaconsfield repeat 'at a window' in Downing Street? From which house did he make that statement?
3. Pick out three words that show that the British approved of Disraeli's success at Berlin.

Fig. 22.1

1. When was the Canal opened? Who was the engineer in charge of its construction? Which country got most of the financial benefit from the Canal from 1869 to 1875?
2. How did this Canal affect the British trade to (i) India (ii) Australia?
3. Why did the opening of the Canal help in the development of steamships?
4. How did the opening of the Canal affect (i) the prices, and (ii) the amount of meat coming into Britain from abroad? Who gained and who lost by that increase in imports?

Worksheet

(A)
1. Make a list of the various Slav people mentioned in the chapter. Why were some of these described as Southern Slavs while others were called Northern Slavs?

2. Make a list of the complaints that Christians might have made against their Turkish rulers (see Extract 22.1 also).

3. Make a summary of the main changes proposed in the Treaty of San Stefano. Show in a separate column how these were altered by the Treaty of Berlin.

4. Write two sentences on each of the following: (i) the attitude of the Serbs to the Slavs who lived in the Austrian–Hungarian Empire (ii) the attitude of the Austrian–Hungarian government towards the Serbs and other Slavs in the Balkans. Show why the differences between the Serbs and the Austrian–Hungarian government led to war in 1914.

5. Explain the policies of (i) Gladstone, and (ii) Disraeli towards Turkey, making sure that you show and explain the differences between them.

(B)
1. Write the letters that might have been sent by:
(a) a Russian explaining the change in Russian policy towards Turkey from 1833 to 1853;
(b) one of Disraeli's friends explaining why he would not help the Christians against their Turkish rulers, 1875–6;
(c) a Russian explaining the value of the Big Bulgaria created at San Stefano;
(d) a Serb complaining of Austria's annexation of Bosnia and Herzegovina.

(C)
1. Write the headlines that might have appeared above reports on:
(a) the Bosnian uprising, 1875 – in Russian, Slav, Austrian, and British papers;
(b) the Bulgarian massacres – in Turkish, Slav, Tory, and Liberal papers;
(c) the fall of Plevna, 1877 – in Turkish, Russian, Slav, Tory, and Liberal papers;
(d) the Treaty of San Stefano, 1878 – in Tory, Liberal, Turkish, Serb, Russian, and Austrian papers;
(e) the Treaty of Berlin, 1878 – in Tory, Liberal, Turkish, Serb, Russian, Austrian, and German papers;
(f) the acquisition of Cyprus by Britain – in Greek, Turkish, Tory, and Liberal papers;
(g) the return of Disraeli and Salisbury from Berlin – in Tory, Liberal, and Radical papers.

2. Make a poster that might have been used to advertise one of Gladstone's meetings during the Midlothian Campaign.

23 Gladstone's Later Career, 1880-95

Back into Action, 1879

In 1875 Gladstone gave up the leadership of the Liberal Party (p. 117). But the pull of politics was too strong, and anger at Disraeli's policies drew him out of retirement. In the winter of 1879 he went on a long tour of Midlothian in Scotland (Fig. 23.1).

He condemned Disraeli's policies in Africa, Afghanistan, Cyprus, and Egypt, and appealed to the conscience of the British people against the aggressive warlike policies followed by Disraeli (Extract 23.1).

In 1880 Disraeli called a general election. He hoped that the people would support his Palmerstonian policies. He had, after all, made Britain great once again, but he had forgotten that most people are more interested in their standard of living than in glorious foreign policies. Napoleon had said that 'An army marches on its stomach'. John Burns, a Labour leader went further; he said that 'the world moves on its belly'.

By 1880 the British people were suffering the first bad effects of the depression in agriculture and industry which were the outward signs that Britain was no longer the world's leading industrial power.

Back in Power, 1880

The Liberals came back with a majority of 120. It

Fig. 23.1 Gladstone leaves West Calder railway station during his tour of Midlothian in 1879.

seemed as if Lord Grenville would become Prime Minister (p. 117), and he asked Gladstone if he would join his government. Gladstone said that he could not possibly take a junior position in a government after he had been Prime Minister. Grenville knew that the Liberals could not form a government without Gladstone, so he stood down and the Queen sent for Gladstone and asked him to form a government.

The Questions

But within five years his government was in ruins. How did it happen? What had he done to bring about this unexpected turn of events?

Gladstone's Divided Party, 1880

In 1880 Gladstone had to deal with two or maybe three different groups inside his own party. There were the old-fashioned Whigs, led by Lord Hartington, the son of the Duke of Devonshire. They thought Gladstone was a Radical. He seemed to be willing to 'trust the people'; willing to appeal for their support as in Midlothian; and willing to promise to pass laws to please them. All this, said the Whigs, was too much. They feared that Gladstone would lead the party down a socialist path.

Others realized that he was not a Radical at all. Indeed the leading Radical, Chamberlain, thought that Gladstone was much too conservative in his thinking and his policies. Chamberlain wanted the Liberals to deal with the many problems of the time – housing, unemployment, old age, education, and so on. All this would need more government action, more laws, higher taxation (Fig. 23.2), and Gladstone would have none of it. He refused to do what Chamberlain wanted, which led Chamberlain to attack Gladstone as a Rip Van Winkle (Extract 23.2).

The Fourth Party

Gladstone was 71 years old in 1880. Perhaps he ought to have retired. Maybe, as Chamberlain suggested, he was too old to understand the problems of Britain as it moved into the third stage of its Industrial Revolution.

He had earned the name of the Grand Old Man of British politics. But three Tory M.P.s refused to treat him with the respect he felt he had gained. Lord Randolph Churchill, J. A. Gorst (p. 120), and Salisbury's nephew, A. J. Balfour, formed a group that was annoyed at the way in which the Tory leaders seemed unwilling to attack Gladstone. They worked closely together to make life uncomfortable for Gladstone. Some people called them the Fourth Party – after the Tories, the Liberals, and the Irish Nationalists.

Gladstone's policies gave Churchill and his friends plenty of ammunition to play with.

Charles Bradlaugh

Charles Bradlaugh was an *atheist* – a man who does not believe that God exists. In 1880 he was elected M.P. for Northampton. When he went to the House of Commons he refused to swear the usual oath of allegiance to the Queen. Every other M.P. took the oath, their hands on the Bible. Bradlaugh did not believe in God – or the Bible. So he asked to be allowed to *affirm* – to give his word that he would be loyal to the Queen.

Fig. 23.2 This cartoon entitled 'Sowing Tares' appeared in Punch *in 1886 when Chamberlain was arguing that the Liberal Party ought to adopt new, socialist and radical policies to help the sick, unemployed, homeless and old.*

Gladstone was caught in a trap. If he refused to allow Bradlaugh to take his seat without taking the oath, he would be acting like George III over the Wilkes election in 1768. Churchill would then accuse him of being illiberal. But if he allowed Bradlaugh to affirm, then Churchill would accuse him of being a friend to people who did not believe in God.

Gladstone was in fact prepared to let Bradlaugh affirm, but the Commons decided that Bradlaugh could not enter the House without taking the oath. The affair dragged on for six years, and Bradlaugh was re-elected three times by the voters of Northampton. He was eventually allowed to affirm and take his seat in 1886. By that time Gladstone and the government's position had been severely weakened.

Egypt 1881–2

Disraeli had bought the Khedive's shares in the Suez Canal Company, and Britain and France had to make sure that the shareholders received their dividends each year. This meant that both countries had to have officials stationed in Egypt.

In 1881 an Egyptian nationalist, Arabi Pasha, led riots against these foreigners, and the French government quickly withdrew their officials. Gladstone decided that he had to look after the interests of British shareholders, so he sent an army under Sir Garnet Wolseley to restore order. In 1882 Wolseley defeated Arabi Pasha's army at the battle of Tel-el-Kebir.

Many Liberals felt that Gladstone had behaved just as Disraeli would have done. They feared that this attack on Egypt could be condemned as a 'most wanton invasion' – the words Gladstone had used about Disraeli in 1879 (Extract 23.1). Churchill used the Egyptian affair to show that Gladstone had been a hypocrite.

The Sudan

The Sudan was under the control of the ruler of Egypt. In 1882 Gladstone sent officials to govern Egypt, but he refused to send any to the Sudan. In 1883 a religious fanatic, the Mahdi, led the people of the Sudan in a revolution against the Egyptians.

At first Gladstone refused to do anything, saying this was an Egyptian affair. But Britain was really in control in Egypt, so in 1884 Gladstone was forced to give in to the demands made by Churchill and other Tories. He agreed to send a British army to bring out the Egyptian officials and their families.

General Gordon was sent to take charge of this operation. However, when he got to Khartoum, the capital of the Sudan, he decided to try to defeat the Mahdi before withdrawing. He was defeated by the Mahdi's forces and besieged in Khartoum.

At first Gladstone refused to send in an army to help Gordon out of his difficulty, but in 1885 he gave way to public demand to do so. But the relief force arrived two days after Gordon had been killed.

Gordon had been 'insubordinate' and had not done what he was supposed to do. But the majority of people in Britain blamed Gladstone for Gordon's death. His nickname of the 'Grand Old Man' was changed, by some, to 'Gordon's Own Murderer'.

Afghanistan

Gladstone ordered General Roberts to bring the British Army out of Afghanistan. The Russians then sent an army in and defeated the Afghan army at Pendjeh in 1885. Gladstone's withdrawal had allowed the Russians to draw nearer to India, the 'biggest jewel in the British Crown'. This angered many people.

The Transvaal

Gladstone had condemned Disraeli's annexation of the Transvaal, but he hesitated about giving the Boers their independence when he got to power. In 1881 the Boers defeated the British in the battle of Majuba Hill. Gladstone then withdrew the Army and invited the Boers to a conference. This led to the signing of the Convention of London (1884). This gave the Boers their independence. Once again, some people said, Gladstone had withdrawn and allowed Britain to be humiliated.

Ireland

Ireland caused Gladstone more problems than any other single issue. We will see more of this in Chapter 24.

Here, though, we ought to note three things. First he tried to stamp out the murderous attacks on landlords and their farms, animals, and buildings. This led him to pass a Coercion Act that allowed the Chief Secretary of Ireland to order the arrest of people and their imprisonment without trial. This angered the Irish and was condemned by many people in Britain as being illiberal. Secondly, he tried to please the Irish by a new Land Act (p. 138). But in the 1880s the Irish Nationalists were led by a strong man, Parnell, who wanted home rule for Ireland. When he could not get that from Gladstone he organized his followers in the House of Commons to make life difficult for the government. One after another they got up to speak – for hours at a time – so that the Commons could not get on with its ordinary work. This forced Gladstone to bring in a new way of running the affairs of the House of Commons. This became known as the closure, or the guillotine. It meant that the government would bring in a Bill and say that it would allow two, or three, or four days for debate on the Bill. At the end of that time a vote would be taken – even if the Irish had prevented any discussion or debate. Many M.P.s thought that this was an interference with free speech, but it was the only way in which the Commons could have got through its business.

Some Reforms, 1880–5

This ministry earned the nickname 'The Ministry of all the Troubles', but despite this Gladstone did manage to get some reforms through Parliament. In 1882 there was the Married Women's Property Act. Up until 1882 a married woman's property became her husband's – even if it was a gift given her by a rich father. Gladstone's Act allowed women to keep their own property – a sign that some women, at least, were demanding equality with men.

In 1883 there was the Corrupt Practices Act. This laid down how much money a candidate could spend during an election campaign. It made it illegal for a candidate to 'treat' electors by buying food or drink for them. This was a small step along the road of parliamentary reform. Rich people would not be able to have quite so much influence as they once had.

In 1884 and 1885 there were very important Parliamentary Reform Acts (Chapter 29). The 1884 Act gave the franchise (or right to vote) to millions of men living in the county constituencies, and after 1884 they had the same rights as adult males living in the boroughs. The electorate now shot up to about 5 million (Fig. 23.3).

The 1885 Act ordered a redrawing of the boundaries of the constituencies and a redistribution of seats so that there were, roughly, the same number of voters living in each constituency. This meant that there had to be new electoral registers for all the new constituencies.

Gladstone Defeated in the Commons, June 1885

In June 1885 Gladstone was defeated by a combination of the Tories and the Irish Nationalists led by Parnell. In this vote about 70 Liberal M.P.s led by

Hartington abstained – to show their displeasure with Gladstone.

Gladstone resigned, but there could not be an election because the new electoral arrangements had not been completed.

The Queen asked Lord Salisbury to form a temporary government. Lord Randolph Churchill was a member of that government. He persuaded Parnell that the Tories would end coercion in Ireland.

Election, November 1885

By November 1885 the electoral registers were ready and the boundaries of the constituencies had been drawn. In the election campaign there were four major groups. Gladstone led the majority of Liberals. He put forward a programme that promised lower income tax, more education, and a chance for the people to help themselves to a better life. Chamberlain led a small number of radical Liberals. They put forward what became known as the unofficial programme. In this they promised to deal with the real social issues of the time – unemployment, poverty, old age, and slum housing.

Salisbury and the Tories promised in their campaign to restore Britain's name abroad.

The fourth group was led by Parnell, who demanded Home Rule for Ireland. Parnell and his followers won eighty-six seats in Ireland itself, but

Fig. 23.3 John Bright speaking in favour of Parliamentary reform to the electors of Birmingham.

more importantly, Parnell had an influence among Irishmen living in Britain. There were many cities and towns where there were thousands of Irishmen, and the large number of Irish voters would be an important minority during the election. Parnell advised them to vote for the Tory candidates in their constituencies. It is reckoned that this was responsible for Tory victories in about forty seats.

The Election Result

The Liberals won 335 seats, the Tories 249, and the Irish (in their Irish seats) 86. The Irish now held the balance between the two major parties. What would Parnell do when Parliament came together again in January 1886? Would he support Salisbury and the Tories, or Gladstone and the Liberals?

Gladstone and Home Rule

Gladstone decided to try to win Parnell's support. On 17 December he announced that he now thought that Ireland ought to have Home Rule.

Chamberlain was very angry. He had won the support of many of the working-class voters by his 'unofficial programme', and resented the way in which his ageing leader now ignored him. He realized that if the party went for Home Rule there would not be time to deal with the social problems that he wanted to tackle.

Parliament met in January 1886, with Salisbury continuing as Prime Minister. His government's future policy was outlined in the usual Queen's Speech. Jesse Collings, a supporter of Chamberlain's, protested that the programme made no mention of the distress in agriculture, and he brought in an amendment that was supported by the Irish. Salisbury's government was defeated and he resigned. Gladstone became Prime Minister in February 1886.

In April 1886 he brought in his Home Rule Bill, and Hartington and his followers immediately went over to the Tory side. Chamberlain and his supporters stayed on the Liberal side trying to get Gladstone to give up the Irish Bill. But in March 1886 he and his followers announced that they would take the name of Liberal Unionists and would vote against Home Rule.

In June 1886 the Bill was defeated in the Commons and Gladstone resigned. Once again, Salisbury became Prime Minister. Hartington supported the new government, but Chamberlain did not do so at first. He hoped that Gladstone might resign and that the party might then give up its Irish Bill. If it had

done so he could have come back into the fold – and maybe have become leader. If this had happened the Liberals might have tackled the social problems of the time.

Home Rule Again, 1893

In 1892 the Liberals won a majority of the seats in the election. Gladstone, now 83 years old, brought in a second Home Rule Bill. This passed through the Commons but was defeated in the House of Lords. Gladstone wanted to resign and have another election on the Irish issue. His Cabinet did not agree and in 1894 Gladstone resigned. He was succeeded by Lord Rosebery.

Questions

Extract 23.1

Gladstone attacks Disraeli

> But what has been the course of things for the last three years? . . . They have annexed the Transvaal territory, inhabited by a free European, republican community, although out of 8,000 persons in that republic qualified to vote, we are told . . . that 6,500 protested against it. We have made war upon the Zulus. We have thereby become responsible for their territory; and we are now, as it appears from the latest advices, about to make war upon a chief lying to the northward of the Zulus. In Europe we have annexed the island of Cyprus. . . . We have assumed jointly with France the virtual government of Egypt. . . . We have undertaken to make ourself responsible for the good government of Turkey in Asia. . . .
>
> Well, and as if all that were not enough, we have, by the most wanton invasion of Afghanistan, broken that country into pieces, destroyed whatever there was in it of peace and order, caused it to be added to the anarchies of the Eastern world.
>
> (Gladstone, Speech at Edinburgh, 1879.)

1. Which people lived in the Transvaal? Why, when, and by whom was this country 'annexed'?
2. How did Gladstone deal with the Transvaal in 1881 and 1884?
3. Why did Britain make war on the Zulus? Write a line on the battles of Isandhlwana and Ulundi.
4. When and by whom was Cyprus 'annexed'? Why?
5. When and why did Britain become responsible for 'the government of Egypt'? What was Gladstone forced to do in Egypt in 1881–2? Why?
6. Explain the reference to Afghanistan. How did Gladstone deal with this problem after 1880?

Extract 23.2

Gladstone v. Chamberlain, 1884–5

(A)

There is a disposition to think that the Government ought to do this and that, and that the Government ought to do everything. If the Government takes into its hand that which the man ought to do for himself, it will inflict upon him greater mischiefs than all the benefits he will have received. . . . The spirit of self-reliance should be preserved in the minds of the masses of the people, in the minds of every member of the class.
(Gladstone speaking at Edinburgh, September 1884.)

(B)

It is therefore perfectly futile and ridiculous for any political Rip Van Winkle to come down from the mountain on which he has been slumbering and to tell us that these things are to be excluded from the Liberal programme. . . . We have to account for and to grapple with the mass of misery and destitution in our midst. . . . I shall be told tomorrow that this is Socialism. Of course, it is Socialism. The greater part of municipal work is Socialism, and every kindly act of legislation by which the community has sought to discharge its responsibilities and its obligations to the poor is Socialism, but it is none the worse for that.
(Speech at Warrington, 8 September 1885, from W. H. Lucy (ed), *Speeches of Rt Hon Joseph Chamberlain*, 1885.)

1. Why would Gladstone's policies keep down the level of taxation? Why would Chamberlain's policies lead to a rise in taxation?
2. What did 'socialism' mean to Chamberlain? Name three ways in which 'the poor' needed government help in 1885.
3. Which of these two had his way in 1885–6? With which one do you agree? Why?

Fig. 23.2

1. How did the cartoonist show that socialism was something evil?
2. How did he show that Englishmen were opposed to socialism?
3. Which social class, according to the cartoon, might be most influenced by socialism?
4. Which of the following was the cartoonist attacking: Bright; Chamberlain; Disraeli; Samuel Smiles? Explain your choice, and why you rejected the other three names.

Worksheet

(A)
1. Write two sentences to explain why (i) Harting-

ton disagreed with Gladstone in 1880, and (ii) Chamberlain disagreed with Gladstone in 1886.

2. Write a short paragraph on EACH of the following: the Fourth Party; Bradlaugh; affirmation by M.P.s; the closure.

3. Write a brief account of the career of Lord Randolph Churchill to show (i) why and how he tried to be Disraeli's successor (ii) his relations with Gladstone (iii) his dealing with Parnell (iv) his resignation.

4. Write a short paragraph on EACH of the following: Arabi Pasha; the Mahdi; Khartoum.

5. Make a list of the countries in which Britain suffered defeats between 1880 and 1885. Write a brief note on each of the defeats you have mentioned.

6. Give an account of the ways in which the electoral system was changed in (i) 1883 (ii) 1884, and (iii) 1885.

(B)
1. Write the letters that might have been sent by:
(a) Parnell advising Irish voters in Britain to vote for the Tory candidate, 1885;
(b) an M.P. after seeing Bradlaugh's first attempt to take his seat in the Commons;
(c) a British officer in Egypt, 1882;
(d) one of Gladstone's supporters, explaining the difficulties facing the Ministry in 1884–5.

(C)
1. Write the headlines that might have appeared above reports on:
(a) Gladstone's return to power, 1889 – in Tory, Whig, Liberal, and Radical papers;
(b) Chamberlain's attack on Gladstone (Extract 23.2) – in Tory, Liberal, Radical, and Irish papers;
(c) Bradlaugh's refusal to take the oath – in Tory, Liberal, Anglican, and Irish papers and in a newspaper which supported Bradlaugh's atheistic views;
(d) the news of the Battle of Tel-el-Kebir – in Liberal, Radical, Tory, and Egyptian papers;
(e) the outbreak of the Mahdi's revolt – in Liberal, Tory, Egyptian, and Sudanese papers.

2. Make a poster on ONE of the following:
(a) the depression in the agricultural industry;
(b) a meeting to protest about Gordon's death.

24 Ireland, 1850-1900

The Fenians

In Chapter 10 we looked at the Irish problem. We left our study at the point where millions of Irish people had to leave their country because of the Great Famine. Some of them settled in Britain, and a number became voters in British constituencies. As we have seen, they were used by Parnell in his struggle with the British governments. But many others went to America. They took with them their own memories of the way in which the British treated Ireland. They continued to hope for an independent Ireland.

In 1858 a group of Irishmen in America, founded the Irish Republican Brotherhood. They wanted to help Ireland to get its independence. The Irish word for independence is *fein* and the Brotherhood became known as the Fenians.

They collected money from the Irish–Americans. They had their own newspaper in America which kept alive memories of Ireland. Some of the Irish took part in the American Civil War (1861–5), and after the war they used their knowledge to set up training camps for young Fenians. Some of these formed small armies that raided across the border into Canada. Some of them came to Britain and set up bombing gangs. They tried to seize Chester Castle and to blow up Clerkenwell Gaol.

Some of the Fenians went to live in Ireland itself where they tried to rouse the peasant farmers against their landlords. There was a great deal of violence – landowners and their bailiffs being shot, animals and crops being destroyed (Fig. 24.1).

Gladstone, 1869–84

When Gladstone was told that he had won the 1868 election his first words were 'My mission is to pacify Ireland'. Like most of his supporters he thought that the real problems of Ireland were connected with the Protestant Church and landownership (Extract 24.1).

In 1869 Parliament passed the Irish Church Act. This said that the Protestant Church was no longer the official Church. Farmers did not have to pay their tithes to the local Protestant clergymen, and the

Fig. 24.1 A scene drawn at a trial of Fenians in Dublin, 1867.

Church itself had to give up about £25 million of land and other wealth which it had collected in the past. Some of this money was used by Gladstone to help found schools in Ireland.

But this Act pleased no one. The Catholics were not grateful, and wanted many more important reforms. The Protestants – in Ireland and Britain – were angry at the way in which 'godless Gladstone' had dealt with the Protestant Church.

In 1870 Gladstone tackled what he thought was the second main problem – the land. The Irish Land Act said that no tenant could be evicted provided he paid his rent on time. It also said that when a tenant gave up a farm – at the end of a lease – he was to be paid (or compensated) for any improvements he might have made to the farm. But this Act did very little for the tenants. There was nothing to stop a landlord putting up the rent at the end of a lease. If the tenant could not pay then he could be evicted, and if landlords did not agree to pay the compensation for improvements, the tenant might have to go through a very expensive trial to get what he deserved. A great number of tenants could not afford to do so. Many who went to court found that the judges favoured the landlords and gave unfair decisions (Extract 24.2).

Also, the Act said nothing about the problem facing the tenant who got into arrears with his rent. During the 1870s there was a sharp drop in the price of wheat and other produce (Fig. 21.3 on p. 123). Tenants received a smaller income when they sold their crops, and this meant that some of them could not pay the yearly rent. The landlord was then free to evict the tenant.

So Gladstone had tried to 'pacify Ireland' by doing what Bright had suggested (Extract 24.1). But the Irish were still not satisfied.

Parnell

Charles Stuart Parnell was a Protestant landowner from County Meath in Ireland. He became convinced that the problems of Ireland would only be solved when the Irish had their own Parliament. In 1875 he was elected to the House of Commons. Here he joined the other Irish M.P.s who were led by an Irish lawyer, Isaac Butt. Butt's policy was to ask each year for Home Rule. When Parliament turned down this demand, Butt and his followers decided that there was nothing more they could do. Parnell decided that there was a good deal that could be done. By 1877 he had been chosen leader of the Irish M.P.s and had

begun a policy of preventing Parliament discussing anything if it would not try to deal with Ireland. This policy of *obstruction* led to the introduction of the closure, or guillotine (p. 133). But Parnell knew that he had to rouse the Irish people if he was going to have any real influence on the British government.

Davitt and the Land League

Michael Davitt had been a Fenian in the 1860s. He had believed that the British could be bombed out of Ireland, but a long term in prison had helped him to see that this policy would not succeed. In 1879 he founded the Land League in Ireland. The League was sent money from America, and recruited members from among the tenant farmers and their families. Its policy was to force the government to allow the Irish tenants a chance to own their own farms.

In 1879 Parnell, the 'uncrowned King of Ireland', became President of the Land League. He went on a speaking tour of Ireland, and told his followers not to pay their rents. He asked them to treat 'as a leper' anyone who took over a farm from which a tenant had been evicted. The first person to be treated in this way was Captain Boycott of County Mayo (Fig. 24.2). His servants and workers left; shop-

Fig. 24.2 Captain Boycott and his family are guarded by soldiers as they bring in the harvest on their farm.

keepers would not serve him; postmen would not deliver his mail; blacksmiths would not shoe his horses; and he had great problems getting in his harvest. His name added a new word to the English language.

Although Parnell did not tell his supporters to become violent, many of them adopted the tactics of the former Fenians. They burned hayricks, maimed cattle, and burnt farmhouses and owners' homes. Ireland was far from being pacified by the time Gladstone came back to power in 1880.

Gladstone's Ministry of All the Troubles, 1880–5

In 1880 Gladstone's Liberals won 347 seats and the Tories won 247. Parnell led a group of sixty-five Irish M.P.s who wanted Home Rule for Ireland. Gladstone hoped to 'pacify Ireland' without allowing its independence.

He appointed W. E. Forster to the post of Chief Secretary for Ireland, and to try to deal with the violence that was common in the west and south of Ireland Gladstone helped pass a Coercion Act (1881) The Irish in the Commons did their best to prevent this Act getting through. They kept the Commons in session for forty-one hours without a break, but the Act was still passed. It gave Forster and his officials the right to arrest and imprison anyone without bringing them to trial.

But Gladstone knew that Ireland could not be held down by coercion alone, so in 1881 Parliament passed a second Irish Land Act. This was a great improvement on the 1870 Act. It said that:

1. *Fair rents* would be fixed by judges appointed by the government.

2. *Fixed tenancies* would have to be arranged between tenants and landowners. This would put an end to evictions.

3. *Free sale* of a lease would be allowed to a tenant who wanted to give up farming during the period of his tenancy.

This gave the Irish tenants the 'three F's' they had been demanding. However, Parnell and his followers wanted much more than a solution to the land problem. They wanted Home Rule.

Parnell Again, 1881–2

Parnell (Fig. 24.3) told the tenants to carry on with their policy of not paying rents, and so violence continued and evictions were carried out by the police and the Army. Gladstone decided that Parnell was responsible for this unrest. He said that 'the resources of civilization are not exhausted' – and arrested Parnell under the terms of the Coercion Act. He was imprisoned in Kilmainham Gaol in Dublin.

But the violence only increased. More people were killed; more bomb outrages took place. In May 1882 Gladstone sent Joseph Chamberlain to see Parnell in

Fig. 24.3 Parnell was ejected from the House of Commons in 1881.

gaol; Gladstone promised that the government would pay off all the past rent owed by the thousands of tenants. This would save them from eviction. Parnell on his part agreed to put an end to the violence in Ireland. This 'Kilmainham Treaty' was agreed and Parnell came out of gaol in May 1882.

Phoenix Park Murders

Forster resigned in protest at the release of Parnell. At the same time Lord Cowper, Viceroy in Dublin, resigned on the grounds of ill health. They were replaced by Lord Spencer and Lord Frederick Cavendish. On 6 May, the day after his arrival in Dublin, Cavendish went for a walk through Phoenix Park with his Under-Secretary, T. H. Burke. Burke, an Irishman, was attacked by a gang armed with knives. Cavendish tried to defend his Under-Secretary, and both men were brutally murdered.

Parnell, Davitt, and Fenians, and other Irish leaders condemned the murders. Gladstone was the uncle of Lady Frederick Cavendish, and he could not ignore this murder of his niece's husband. The Coercion Act was therefore reintroduced. The agreement on arrears was modified to bring less relief to the tenants and so violence continued throughout Ireland.

Ireland and British Politics, 1885

In Chapter 23 we have already seen something of the way in which Irish affairs affected British politics in 1885. In this chapter we will look at this question again – but from a slightly different point of view.

Parnell and his Irish Nationalist M.P.s were angry at the way in which Gladstone was dealing with Ireland. In June 1885 Lord Randolph Churchill for the Tories promised Parnell that a Tory government would end coercion, and so Parnell and his followers voted with the Tories in a vote in the House of Commons. Gladstone was defeated. As we have seen (p. 133) Salisbury became the Prime Minister in a temporary government until the general election which was held in November 1885, and it was during this election that Parnell advised Irish voters in Britain to vote for Tory candidates. When all the results were in, the Liberals had 335 seats, the Tories 249 and Parnell's Nationalists had won eighty-six seats in Ireland.

Gladstone and Home Rule

We have seen that in December 1885 Gladstone

decided that Ireland ought to have its independence (p. 134). When Parliament met in January 1886 Salisbury continued as Prime Minister, and he put forward his proposed programme in the Queen's Speech with which Parliament opens. This said nothing about the agricultural depression. Jesse Collings, one of Chamberlain's supporters, brought in an amendment, usually known as 'the three acres and a cow' amendment. The Liberals and the Irish voted for this. The Tory government was defeated, Salisbury resigned, and Gladstone was in power again.

In April 1886 Gladstone brought in his Home Rule for Ireland Bill. He showed that Ireland was not satisfied by Land Acts or Church Acts or Education Acts. Ireland wanted the same rights as the British had already given to Canada and other 'colonies'.

But this Bill was defeated (p. 134), when Chamberlain led ninety-three Liberals to side with the Tories against the Bill.

Salisbury and Ireland

After Gladstone's resignation in June 1886 Salisbury became Prime Minister for the second time. He appointed his nephew, A. J. Balfour, to the post of Chief Secretary for Ireland. Salisbury and Balfour meant to govern Ireland 'firmly' and to win the support of the tenants with a series of Land Acts. They also hoped to destroy Parnell's reputation.

As part of the policy of firmness, the government brought in a number of Coercion Acts. When the Land League ordered tenants only to pay what they thought of as a 'fair rent', Balfour ordered the eviction of any offenders and their imprisonment. There was a good deal of violence on both sides. The Irish soon came to hate 'Bloody Balfour' and his policies.

However, Parliament brought in the Land Purchase Acts. The government would lend money to tenants who wanted to buy their farms from the British landowners; many tenants took advantage of these Acts. They became farm owners and not mere tenants. Instead of paying a rent they had to pay back – over forty-nine years – the money which they borrowed from the British government. Balfour and Salisbury hoped to create a large body of Irish farm owners. They hoped that these would not want to follow Parnell and the Land League. This, said Balfour, would 'kill Home Rule by kindness'.

Salisbury and Parnell

In 1887 the leading English newspaper, *The Times*,

published a series of letters that were supposed to have been written by Parnell, and which showed that he had ordered the Phoenix Park murders in 1882. Most people believed that these letters were Parnell's, and British opinion of the Irish leader became increasingly hostile. There was a good deal of support for Balfour's policy of 'firmness'.

But in 1889 Parnell brought a libel case against *The Times*. He wanted to prove that he had not written the letters and that *The Times* had lied (or committed a *libel*). The government allowed its leading lawyer, the Attorney-General, to help *The Times* to fight the case against Parnell. But in 1890 the case came to a sudden end, when a journalist, Richard Piggott, admitted that he had forged the letters. The libel was proved and Parnell won a great victory. This made him even more popular in Ireland. It also gave him a great deal of respect in Britain where people turned against the government which had supported *The Times*.

But Salisbury was not finished. In 1890 Chamberlain was well on his way to becoming a member of the Tory Party. He had met Parnell in Kilmainham Gaol in 1882. At that time he had used an Irish M.P., Captain O'Shea, as a go-between to arrange his meetings with Parnell. He and most other politicians knew that Parnell and O'Shea's wife, Kitty, were living together. He had used this as a bargaining counter in his dealings with Parnell in 1882.

In 1890 Chamberlain persuaded O'Shea to bring a divorce case against his wife and to name Parnell as the co-respondent (or 'other man') in the case. Parnell offered no evidence during the divorce hearing. O'Shea's lawyers were free to make whatever accusations they wanted to, and Parnell's character was torn to shreds.

Parnell and the Voters, 1890–1

British voters were shocked by the stories brought out during the divorce case. Gladstone had known since 1880 that Parnell and Mrs O'Shea were living together, and this had not prevented him from dealing with Parnell in 1882. But he could not ignore the way in which newspapers, Non-conformist preachers, and societies condemned the adulterer. He realized that if he continued to co-operate with Parnell, he would lose votes in Britain. So he asked the Irish Nationalist M.P.s to throw Parnell over as leader and choose a new one.

The Irish M.P.s had known about Parnell's relationship with Mrs O'Shea, but when they saw that Gladstone would not deal with Parnell they realized that Ireland would not get Home Rule as long as Parnell remained the leader of their party. So some

of them wanted to get rid of the man who called himself 'master of the party' – because of his mistress. The Irish Party split. Twenty-six M.P.s remained loyal to Parnell, but forty-four followed a new leader, Justin McCarthy.

It was fortunate for the future of Ireland that Parnell died in October 1891. If he had lived there would have been a continued bitterness between the two sections of the Irish Party. His death removed the cause of that bitterness and allowed the two sides to come together again.

Home Rule 1893

We have already seen that in 1893 Gladstone brought in a second Home Rule Bill. This one passed through the Commons but was defeated in the House of Lords. The problem of Ireland remained to bother British politicians, and in Chapter 31 we will see how it played a large part in British politics in 1909–14.

Questions

Extract 24.1

My Dear Sir, . . . For twenty years I have said that the only way to remedy the evils of Ireland is by legislation on the Church and land. But the legislation must come from and through a Parliament which is not Irish. . . . The Whigs are as afraid as the Tories are of questions affecting the Church and the land, and they seem to have almost no courage.

Lord Russell is old, and cannot grapple with a great question like this. Mr Gladstone hesitates, and hardly knows how far to go. . . . I suspect he has not studied the Land Question, and knows little about it. . . . The Liberal Party is not in a position for undertaking any great measure of statesmanship. Some Whigs distrust Mr Gladstone, and some, who call themselves Radicals, dislike him. He does not feel himself very secure as leader of a powerful and compact force.

I am, very sincerely yours, John Bright.
(R. Barry O'Brien, *John Bright*, no date.)

1. Why did Bright think that 'the Church' in Ireland was one of the 'evils'?
2. Why were English politicians 'afraid' to deal with the problem of the Irish Church?
3. What position was occupied by 'Lord Russell' in 1868? Write a sentence to show Russell's connection with (i) the 1832 Reform Act (ii) Palmerston's resignation in 1851, and (iii) Chartism in 1848.
4. Why did Gladstone 'not feel very secure'?
5. Write a sentence on each of the following: (i) Bright and the Corn Laws, 1845–6 (ii) Bright and the Reform Act 1867, and (iii) Bright and Home Rule, 1886.

Extract 24.2

Tenants v. Landlords, 1877

A twenty-one years' lease granted to the present tenant's father in 1860 fixed the rent at £410. The son succeeded while this lease was running, and in 1877 became anxious for a new lease.... The new lease was not granted, and the tenant sought to register under the Land Act of 1870 his permanent improvements. These improvements were mainly under the following heads: Blasting and removing stones; levelling old ditches and making new ones; building sewers; making drains; sinking wells and repairing roads. There were also building improvements... there was an enclosure wall, a new granary and cowsheds, workmen's lodge and piggeries. The tenants' accounts showed an expenditure on these and other items of over £2,000. But the landlord contested the right to register these improvements. A lawsuit arose, which ended with the decision that the improvements could be registered, but not the amount of money spent on them. The lawsuit cost the tenant £500. This lease expired a few months before the Land Act of 1881 was passed. No renewal had taken place, and the tenant was served with a notice of eviction, under the pressure of which he accepted a sixty years' lease, at a rent of £380.
(H. S. Wilkinson, *The Eve of Home Rule – Impressions of Ireland in 1886*.)

1. When was this lease due to finish?
2. Find three words that help you to understand the sort of farming practised by this tenant-farmer.
3. Why did the tenant wish to 'register under the Land Act of 1870'?
4. What happened to food prices in the 1870s? How did this affect the income of this tenant?
5. Why did few tenants try to challenge their landlords in the law courts?
6. How would the Land Act 1881 have helped this tenant?
7. Why was the landlord willing to accept a lower rent in 1881 than he had received in 1860?

Fig. 24.3

1. Who was the Prime Minister in this Parliament?
2. What had he done to help the Irish peasants in 1881?
3. How did he treat Parnell in (i) 1881, and (ii) 1882?
4. Why did Parnell advise Irishmen living in Britain to vote for the Tories in 1885?
5. Why did he wish that he had not done so in January 1886?

Worksheet

(A)
1. Write a short paragraph on EACH of the following: Fenianism; obstruction in Parliament; the Land League; the Phoenix Park murders; Kitty O'Shea; Richard Piggott.

2. Explain how and why the Irish Americans help Irish nationalism.

3. Make a list of the ways in which the first Land Act helped the Irish tenant. Show why the second Land Act was an improvement on the first.

4. Give an account of the main events in Parnell's career from 1877 to 1891. You may want to write about (i) the Irish Party in the Commons (ii) the Land League (iii) the Kilmainham Treaty (iv) the 1885 election (v) Home Rule 1886 (vi) *The Times* libel case (vii) the O'Shea divorce case.

5. Write a series of paragraphs to show how Gladstone dealt with the Irish question between 1880 and 1885. You might use as headings: (i) Coercion (ii) the second Land Act (iii) Kilmainham (iv) Phoenix Park murders (v) Parnell in the Commons.

(B)
1. Write the letters that might have been sent by:
(a) an English landowner complaining of attacks on his estate by Fenians;
(b) one of Parnell's supporters explaining these attacks;
(c) a bailiff explaining why and how a tenant had been evicted;
(d) an evicted tenant describing the eviction;
(e) one of Boycott's relatives describing the difficulties he faced.

(C)
1. Write the headlines that might have appeared above reports on:
(a) an eviction – in papers controlled by the government, Parnell, Irish landowners, and the Tory opposition;
(b) the treatment of Boycott – in papers controlled by Parnell, landowners, and the government;
(c) Parnell's arrest – in papers controlled by the government, Parnell, the Tories, and Irish landowners;
(d) Parnell's release – in papers mentioned in (c);
(e) the result of *The Times* libel case – in papers controlled by Parnell, the government, the Liberals, Irish landowners – and in *The Times* itself;
(f) the result of the divorce case – in papers controlled by the government, Tories, Nonconformists, Liberals, Irish Catholics, Parnell, and Irish landowners.

25 Lord Salisbury, 1867-1902

Disraeli's Successor

In 1867 Lord Salisbury (then Viscount Cranborne) was a member of the Conservative government which brought in the 1867 Reform Bill. He resigned from the government because he disagreed with this Bill.

In 1868 he became the Marquess of Salisbury when his father died. When Disraeli became Prime Minister in 1874 Salisbury became Foreign Minister, and played a major part in the Congress of Berlin. In 1881 Disraeli (the Earl of Beaconsfield) died, and Salisbury became the leader of the Conservative Party.

Salisbury Defines His Policies, 1885-6

In June 1885 Salisbury became Prime Minister for the first time. Parnell, Randolph Churchill, and Gladstone hoped that he would deal with the Irish problem. However, he refused to do so (Fig. 25.1). In later years he was to try to 'govern Ireland with firmness' while trying to 'kill Home Rule by kindness'. But he was never prepared to give Parnell and his followers the Home Rule which they wanted (Chapter 24).

In 1886 Salisbury became Prime Minister for the second time, and Lord Randolph Churchill became leader of the House of Commons and Chancellor of the Exchequer. He was only 37, the youngest Chancellor since Pitt. Churchill wanted the party to follow Disraeli's ideas of social reform; he wanted to win the votes of working men.

But Salisbury did not think that all of Disraeli's ideas were very good. For instance, he did not think that the government should play a part in people's social or economic life. So Salisbury was not very happy with Churchill's plans. In the winter of 1886 Churchill planned his budget. He wanted to cut income tax, lower the import taxes on tea and tobacco, and give local authorities an extra £5 million to spend on social reform. But he wanted a cut in the money spent by the War Office. W. H. Smith, Secretary of State for War, refused to agree to such cuts, and Salisbury supported him. Churchill then wrote a letter in which he offered to resign. He

thought that no one could take his place and that the Prime Minister would have to allow him to do what he wanted. Salisbury allowed Churchill to publish his letter in *The Times*. He then appointed a Liberal Unionist, G. J. Goschen, to the post of Chancellor. As Churchill said, 'I forgot Goschen', but Salisbury had not – and Churchill never held office again.

Salisbury's Domestic Policies

The most important Act passed by Salisbury's government was the Local Government Act (1888).

Fig. 25.1 Neither Gladstone (left) nor Salisbury was anxious to deal with the Irish question in 1885–6. When Gladstone did so, in 1886, the 'shell' blew up and split the Liberal Party.

The Municipal Reform Act of 1835 had dealt with the question of the government of towns, but the 1888 Act dealt with the government of the countryside. It created sixty-two county councils and made separate county borough councils for towns with populations over 50,000. The Greater London area was to be governed by the London County Council, the forerunner to the modern Greater London Council.

In 1891 the government abolished school fees; for the first time children and their parents did not have to pay to go to the Board Schools. In the same year there was a Factory Act. This said that no child below the age of 11 could go to work, and women workers were not to work more than twelve hours a day.

In 1897, during his third ministry, Salisbury passed the Workmen's Compensation Act. It stated that workers who were injured while at work or who caught a disease because of the work they did could claim compensation from their employer. This was a first step along a long road of workmen's compensation.

Salisbury's Failure

In 1892 Parliament passed a Smallholdings Act. This was an attempt to deal with the unemployment in the agricultural sector. But this Act did not work properly and little improvement took place, although it shows that Salisbury was aware of the conditions in which people worked and lived.

However, he ignored the terrible poverty revealed to a Royal Commission on Labour in 1892. This showed that about half the country's workers earned about 75p a week but that they needed about 150p if they were to have enough to live on (Extract 25.1). He ignored the growth of the new, militant, and large trade unions which grew up after the London Dockers' Strike of 1889. He ignored the growth of the Labour Party which came into existence because neither of the two older parties were willing to tackle the social problems of the late nineteenth century.

Salisbury's Foreign Policy

Salisbury was his own Foreign Minister, and although unwilling to follow Disraeli's social policy, he did follow his old leader's ideas on foreign affairs.

He thought of France as Britain's main enemy. This led him to be friendly to Bismarck of Germany who had created a Triple Alliance of Germany, Austria, and Italy. In 1887 Salisbury signed a naval agreement with Italy, in which both countries agreed that no country should be allowed to take over any of the islands in the Mediterranean or any of the countries bordering on that sea.

In 1885 Salisbury agreed to the reunion of Rumelia with the Kingdom of Bulgaria, and in 1895 he tried to get the other powers to agree to act together against Turkey after a series of massacres carried out against the Christians of Armenia. But no one was willing to act. The Turkish question was to trouble Europe again (Chapter 34).

In the 1890s the European powers began to take an increasing interest in China, and there was a danger that they might get involved in a war as each tried to extend its own influence on that vast country. Salisbury persuaded Russia, Germany, and France to agree that they and Britain should have certain areas of China as their own 'spheres of influence'.

Salisbury and Africa (Fig. 25.2)

In the middle of the nineteenth century British explorers had gone into previously unknown parts of Africa, the 'Dark Continent'. Livingstone was one of the most important of these explorers. He hoped that British people would go into Africa to bring Christianity as well as trade.

In the 1880s it seemed as if Livingstone's wish was being realized, but at first the government played no part in this development. Salisbury knew that the East India Company had been responsible for the development of India in the eighteenth and early nineteenth centuries, and he wanted the development of Africa to be left to similar trading companies. In

Fig. 25.2 The division of Africa.

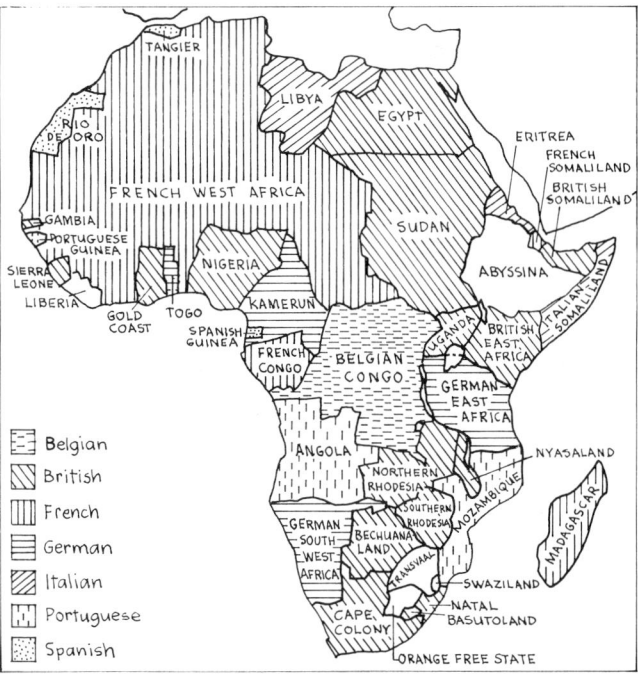

1886 a group of merchants formed the Royal Niger Company; in 1888 a second group formed the British East Africa Company; and in 1889 a third group formed the South Africa Company. Each of these companies was granted a government Charter. This detailed the territory in which the company had the sole right to trade. Agents for the various companies went out to sign agreements with chiefs and kings in their territories, and there was a growth in British trade in these regions.

The government did not play a large part in this development, but Salisbury made it clear that Britain would not stand aside if her interests were threatened by other powers. In particular, he regarded the Nile Valley as belonging to Britain's sphere of influence. In 1890 Germany agreed to recognize Britain's take-over of Zanzibar in exchange for Britain's handing back of the island of Heligoland in the Baltic (Fig. 7.1 on p. 37). In the same year France agreed to Britain's position in Zanzibar while Britain recognized French control of Madagascar. In 1891 Britain and Portugal signed an agreement that recognized the Zambesi as the boundary between British and Portuguese interests in East Africa.

The Increase in Government Interest

In 1892 the British East Africa Company faced bankruptcy, and it seemed as if it would have to give up its trade in Uganda and Kenya. It seemed likely that the French would move in. This would give them some control of the Nile Valley. Britain could not allow this. So, unwillingly, the government annexed the regions. In 1900 Britain also annexed Nigeria in order to protect British interests in West Africa. Once again, as in India, the flag followed trade.

After 1895 the Colonial Secretary was Joseph Chamberlain, the former Radical Liberal. He used his energies and abilities to help develop the British colonies in Africa, realizing that the growth of trade would increase employment in Britain. But this development would need a great deal of money. There would have to be railways, harbours, and roads. Someone would have to spend money on research into tropical diseases which killed men and animals and so made these colonies less valuable than they might have been.

Chamberlain agreed to provide government money for these projects (Extract 25.2). This was a major shift of policy – for now the government was taking an active part in developing trade.

The Sudan

British interests in the Nile Valley led Salisbury to agree to the reconquest of the Sudan, lost to the Mahdi in 1884 (p. 132). In 1898 Kitchener led an army into the Sudan, and defeated the Mahdi's successor at the Battle of Omdurman. Kitchener ordered that the Mahdi's grave should be ransacked. He used the Mahdi's skull as an inkstand.

Kitchener moved on from Omdurman, and at Fashoda he met a French armed force led by Captain Marchand. France intended to create a French Empire stretching across North Africa. For a time it seemed as if France and Britain would go to war. The Royal Navy was put on a war footing; politicians in both countries made warlike speeches. But the French withdrew in November 1898 and the Sudan was safely in British hands.

The Boers

In 1886 gold was discovered in the Witwatersrand in the Transvaal, and thousands of British prospectors flooded into the region. The Boers were farmers; they had no interest in gold-mining. They despised the newcomers, or Uitlanders. By 1888 there were more Uitlanders than Boers in the Transvaal. But the Boers, led by their President, Kruger, did not give the Uitlanders any rights. They could not vote in elections; they were heavily taxed; and the railways charged very high rates to bring machinery into the Transvaal or take material out.

So there was a good deal of hostility between Boers and Uitlanders. This brings us to consider the position of Cecil Rhodes. In 1884 he had got a British protectorate over Bechuanaland, and in 1889 his British South African Company was given the right to develop the Zambesi valleys and the territory formerly called after Rhodes – Rhodesia – and now Zimbabwe. He was chairman of the company that owned the Kimberley diamond mines, and by 1890 he was a multi-millionaire. He was Prime Minister of the Cape from 1890 to 1896, but his ambition was to see a growth of British influence throughout Africa. In particular he wanted to build a railway from the Cape of Cairo which would run, he hoped, through British territory and through the Boer Republic (Fig. 25.2).

The Jameson Raid, 1896

In 1896 Rhodes planned an invasion and conquest of the Transvaal. Dr Jameson was the administrator of Rhodesia. Rhodes advised him to plan an invasion of the Transvaal from the north while the Uitlanders would rise in revolt inside the Transvaal. But the raid was a disaster. Kruger halted the invading forces, arrested Jameson, and let the world know the British plans; Rhodes was forced to give up his position in the Cape. The British government, and in particular, Joseph Chamberlain, appeared as warmongers in the world's eyes. And the Kaiser of Germany sent a telegram to congratulate Kruger for having stopped the British advance.

The Boer War, 1899–1902 (Fig. 25.3)

The Uitlanders in the Transvaal continued to ask for an improvement in the way in which Kruger treated them, but he refused to change his policies. In 1899 the Uitlanders sent a petition to ask the Queen to help them, as a result of which Chamberlain sent an army to the Cape. Kruger regarded this as a threat to the Boers, and demanded that it be withdrawn. Chamberlain refused and in October 1899 the Boers declared war on the British.

The war fell into three periods:

1. From October 1899 to January 1900 the Boers were very successful. They had larger forces than the British and they took the offensive. They besieged the British forces in Ladysmith (in Natal), Kimberley (in the Cape) and Mafeking (in Bechuanaland). In December 1899 there was a 'Black Week' when British attempts to relieve these towns failed.

2. From February 1900 to August 1900 Lord Roberts and Lord Kitchener led large armies which relieved the besieged towns and captured Johannesburg and Pretoria, the capital of the Transvaal.

3. Many people thought that the Boers would now give in. But the war continued, mainly as a guerrilla war. Kitchener enclosed large areas inside lines of barbed wire guarded by blockhouses. Behind the wire he destroyed farmhouses where friendly families might have helped the Boer guerrillas. Women and children were interned in concentration camps where bad hygiene and poor administration caused thousands of deaths among the civilians. This period came to an end when the Boers agreed to the Treaty of Vereeniging (1902). The Transvaal and the Orange Free State were annexed but the Boers were promised that they would, one day, get self-rule. The British government gave £3 million as compensation for the damage done to Boer farms during the fighting.

The Significance of the Boer War

In 1900 Salisbury gave up the post of Foreign Secretary. His successor was Lord Lansdowne, who appreciated that Britain would not be able to fight a

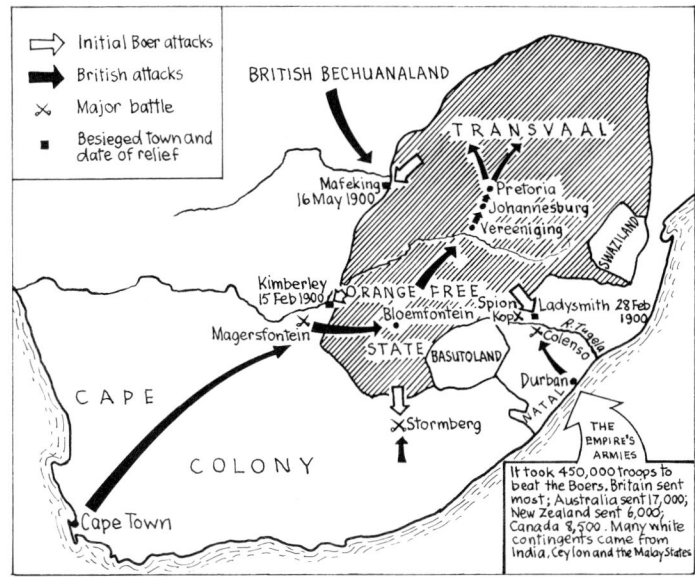

Fig. 25.3 The Boer War, 1899–1902.

war against a major power. So he worked to find some allies for Britain, and in 1902 he signed an alliance with Japan that would help guard Britain's interests in the Far East where Russia was showing herself as a threat.

In 1900 the government called a general election. The British people voted for the government in this wartime – or 'khaki' – election. The Tories won 402 seats and an over-all majority of 134. But after 1902 the people had more chance to think about the Boer War, and this was one of the reasons for the Tory defeat in the 1906 election.

In 1902 Salisbury resigned, and his nephew, Balfour, became Prime Minister. He, like his uncle, had little sympathy for the working class. He refused to intervene over the Taff Vale dispute (p. 163), and this was a major reason for the growth of the Labour Party. This grew (Chapter 29) because the other parties failed to act or, when they acted, behaved very foolishly.

Questions

Extract 25.1

Working-class poverty, 1892

A Royal Commission on Labour, set up in 1892, heard evidence that the minimum wage required for a man, wife and two children, was 30s [£1.50] a week. This argument was put forward by H. M. Hyndman, an old Etonian who had become a Marxist Socialist. He outlined a budget for this ideal family [5p = 12d or 1s, and 1lb = 0·45kg]:

	s.	d.
Rent	5	3
(three rooms if lucky)		
Firing	2	9½
Light		8½
Soap, soda, etc.		10
Bread	1	8
(slightly under four quartern loaves at 5½d)		
Oatmeal		4
Grocery	2	6
(tea at 4s a lb; sugar at 2d)		
Butter, cheese, etc.	1	0
(cheese at 7¼ a lb; butter at 1s 3d a lb.)		
Flour		4
Meat	3	0
Vegetables and fruit	2	6
(potatoes at ½d a lb.)		
Club, union, sickness and death benefit	3	3
Total	24	2

Over half the workers in the country were paid about 15s in 1886.

1. How much was paid for the rent of three rooms? Why did many working-class people live in only one or two rooms? What effect did this have on (i) the danger of disease (ii) a child doing homework?
2. What was the meaning of 'Firing'? Why does a modern family spend a high proportion of its income on firing and 'Lighting'? What does this tell you about modern day living standards?
3. How were working-class families helped by the fall in import prices after 1873? If this fall had not taken place, what would have changed in this budget? How would that have affected the living standards of the working class in 1892?
4. Why did working-class families spend so much on 'club . . . death benefits'? Why were thousands of such families unable to keep up these payments for the whole of their lives? Why did many families never begin to make such payments?
5. What items appear in a modern family budget but do not appear here? What does this tell you about the change in living standards since 1892?

Extract 25.2

Chamberlain and the British Empire

'I regard many of our colonies as being underdeveloped estates, which can never be developed without Imperial assistance. . . . I shall be prepared to consider . . . any case in which by the investment of British money those estates which belong to the British Crown may be developed for the benefit of their population and for the benefit of the greater population which is outside.'
(Joseph Chamberlain, speech, 1895.)

'It is only in such a policy of development that I can see any solution of those great social problems by which we are surrounded. Plenty of employment and a contented people go together. . . . It is a great policy. It is open to criticism, for you cannot undertake a policy of this kind without a certain amount of risk. But if the people of this country are not willing to invest some of their superfluous wealth in the development of their great estates, then I see no future for these countries, and it would have been better never to have gone there.'
(Joseph Chamberlain, Speech to West African Railways Deputation, 1895.)

1. When did Chamberlain become Colonial Secretary? Why did some Liberals find this an extraordinary appointment?
2. What was meant by 'Imperial assistance'? How do you think the government might have helped merchants in areas such as Nigeria, Kenya, or Uganda?
3. Why did Chamberlain offer more help to Africa than to Australia or Canada?
4. How would government aid help (i) the local people of Africa (ii) British trading companies, and (iii) British working people?

Fig. 25.2

1. Which was the first British colony in Africa? When did Britain occupy it for the first time?
2. Which company developed North and South Rhodesia? Explain the names given to these territories.
3. Write two sentences to show the link between the Sudan and (i) Gladstone, and (ii) Kitchener.
4. Through which territories might the British have built a railway from the Cape to Cairo? Why did such a project mean that the British would have to fight the Boers?

Worksheet

(A)
1. Write two sentences to show (i) the cause, and (ii) the effect on the Tory Party of Churchill's resignation in 1886.

2. Write a paragraph on the Local Government Act 1888.

3. What were the successes and failures of the Salisbury governments in (i) domestic politics (ii) foreign affairs (iii) imperial affairs?

4. Explain (i) why, and (ii) how the government took responsibility for Uganda and Kenya.

5. Explain why and how the government helped the development of the British Empire in Africa.

6. Why did the British become interested in the Transvaal in 1886? How did they try to gain control of that state in 1896?

7. Show the differences between (i) the short-term, and (ii) the long-term causes of the quarrel between the British and the Boers which led to the Second Boer War, 1899.

8. Why did Britain do so badly in the first years of that war? Why did Britain finally win?

(B)
1. Write the letters that might have been written by:
(a) one of the low paid (Extract 25.1) after reading Salisbury's speech on self-help;
(b) an agent of the Royal Niger Company on his success;
(c) a Sudanese after the capture of Khartoum in 1898;
(d) a Uitlander in (i) 1890 (ii) 1896 (iii) 1899;
(e) a Boer complaining of Kitchener's tactics during the Boer War.

2. Write the notice (or obituary) that might have appeared after the death of Rhodes.

(C)
1. Write the headlines that might have appeared above reports on:
(a) Churchill's resignation, 1886;
(b) the formation of the British East Africa Company, 1888;
(c) the appointment of Chamberlain, 1895;
(d) the Fashoda crisis;
(e) the discovery of gold in the Transvaal, 1886;
(f) the Jameson raid, 1896;
(g) Black Week, 1899;
(h) the signing of the Treaty of Vereeniging, 1902;
(i) the general election, 1900.

2. Make a poster that might have been used for ONE of the following:
(a) to advertise a meeting in honour of Kitchener after the capture of Khartoum;
(b) to ask people to vote (i) for (ii) against the government in the 1900 election.

26 Tariff Reform, 1881-1906

The Lost Leadership

Until about 1870 Britain was easily the world's greatest industrial power, but by 1900 other countries had overtaken Britain in the industrial race. America was producing more coal and steel than Britain; and Germany was producing more steel and almost as much coal. The situation was the same in many industries; and we shall see, the position was even worse in some industries. What could the British government do to try to change things?

Reasons for Britain's Failure

Before trying to change things, the government had to find out what had gone wrong. Salisbury thought that the decline was due to a failure on the part of Britain's industrial owners. They had learned to live on the money made by their fathers' efforts and made no effort themselves.

Marshall, an economist, said that Britain lost her lead because other nations had bought industrial machinery and learned to do things for themselves.

Certainly India, Hong Kong, and Japan had taken away a great part of Britain's textile market in Asia, but America, Germany, France, and Switzerland had done more than that. They had become industrial giants. Their ambitious industrialists built large factories where they installed the very latest machinery. They produced better quality goods at a cheaper price than British factories. Consequently, they drove British goods out of markets in America, Canada, South America, and Europe (Fig. 26.1).

New Industries

Britain had most of its investment in industries that had almost stopped expanding – coal, cotton, and shipbuilding. The Germans had most of their finance in industries that were growing fairly rapidly; and the Americans had over a quarter of their investment in industries that would expand very rapidly.

British industrialists had failed to maintain an interest in the new industrial world. In 1896 a book called *Made in Germany* showed that German goods were now flooding into the British home market. Germany led the world in metals' technology, in mining technology, electrical engineering, and the chemical industry (Extract 26.1).

Some people thought that Britain had failed to develop these new, expanding, technological industries because her educational system did not produce the right sort of workers, managers, or industrialists (Extract 26.1). Others claimed that British goods were not selling abroad because other countries had put import taxes, or tariffs, on such goods. On the other hand, because Britain had no tariffs, foreign goods could come into Britain quite freely.

Fig. 26.1 This cartoon was captioned: 'The Uncommercial Traveller'. Mr Punch: 'Now, Mr Bull, wake up! You'll have to keep your eye on that chap. He's always at it, speaks their languages, and knows their money.' John Bull: 'Pooh! My goods are better than his!' Mr Punch: 'I daresay – but you've got to make them understand it!' The artist thought that British merchants had lost the will to sell their goods.

Britain Lends Money to Foreigners

During the earlier part of the nineteenth century Britain sold more goods abroad than she bought. Foreigners paid more gold to Britain than the British paid to foreigners for her imports. This gave Britain a surplus in her balance of trade.

If Britain had held on to that money, world trade would have dropped sharply. The world would not have had enough money to continue trading at a high level. Instead, the British loaned much of that money to foreign countries to help them become industrialized although most of the money was in fact spent in Britain itself. Her coal, steel, and engineering industries benefited from the building of railways overseas, and British textile machines were bought by foreign companies with money borrowed from British banks and lenders.

By 1914 Britain had loaned about £3.5 billion overseas. Each year after 1905 foreigners paid about £120 million a year interest on this money.

The Balance of Trade and Balance of Payments

From 1880 onwards there was a growth in the amount of foreign goods coming into Britain. At the same time there was a slow-down in the quantity of produce being exported from Britain. Britain was not earning a surplus of gold in her trade. Indeed, she was paying more than she earned. But this was covered by the income from interest on overseas investments. The £120 million coming in each year more than covered the difference between what Britain spent on foreign goods and what she earned by selling abroad.

The Results of the Decline

But there was no hiding this fact from some workers and their employers. Britain lost some of her markets to foreigners, and foreign goods poured into Britain. There was, obviously, a lower demand – overseas and at home – for British goods. Employers who could not sell their products had to close their factories and dismiss their workmen; unemployment became a fact of life for thousands of people. Many of these were men with skills that had once earned them high wages. They had been the confident members of the self-helping trade unions (p. 110). They had formed Building Societies and bought their own homes, but from 1880 onwards about 12 per cent – or one in every eight – of British workmen were unemployed each year. Many men were out of work for a long period.

Fair Trade, 1881

Some people thought that Britain should give up its policy of Free Trade. Foreigners did not allow British goods to go 'freely' into their countries; they had their systems of tariffs. It seemed only fair to the Fair Traders that Britain should have a system of tariffs of her own. These could be used to keep some foreign goods out – and so help employment in Britain. They could also be used to make bargains with foreigners. If they lowered their tariffs on some of our goods, we would lower our tariffs on some of their goods. This is what Pitt had done in the 1780s (p. 25), and Huskisson in the 1820s (p. 50).

But Free Trade was part of the Liberal Party's 'gospel'. John Bright was one of those who fought for Free Trade and for the repeal of the Corn Laws (p. 84). Bright came out very strongly against proposals for Fair Trade, and claimed that Britain and her workers had gained from Free Trade and would lose from a system of tariffs. Most people agreed with Bright.

Imperialism and Chamberlain

We have seen in Chapter 25 how Chamberlain tried to develop British colonies in Africa. This was an attempt to find new markets for British goods – and so provide more employment.

In 1887 and 1897 Queen Victoria celebrated two Jubilees. During the celebrations ministers came from Australia, Canada, and New Zealand to play their part in honouring the ageing Queen. In 1897 Chamberlain had discussions with ministers from the 'white colonies', for he wanted them to agree to take more British goods and fewer goods from America, Germany, and Japan.

Colonies and Their Tariffs

The colonial countries had their own systems of tariffs. They used the money they got from these taxes to help run their countries. Their tariffs applied to goods coming from overseas – to German, American, Japanese, and British goods.

Chamberlain wanted these colonial countries to put a lower tariff on goods coming from Britain than from a non-Empire country. This would show that they preferred, or favoured, British goods.

This would lead to a growth in the volume of goods going from Britain to these colonies, and thus to higher employment in Britain.

But the colonial ministers did not see why their people should be asked to help Britain, unless they got something in return. So they asked that, in exchange, Britain should show a preference for food coming from the colonies. They wanted Britain to put a tariff on food imported from Denmark, Russia, or America and a lower tariff (or no tariff) on food imported from the colonies.

Chamberlain saw the sense in their argument, and in 1903 he asked his Cabinet colleagues to agree to this proposal for imperial preference which would have needed a reintroduction of a British tariff – on food in particular.

Balfour, the Prime Minister since 1902, was uncertain what to do (Fig. 26.2). This uncertainty angered some of the Cabinet. The Duke of Devonshire resigned and took with him others who believed that Free Trade had to be maintained. They thought that Balfour was going to give way to Chamberlain's demands for a change of policy. But he did not change – he could not make up his mind. So in September 1903 Chamberlain resigned. He wanted to be free to start a campaign for tariff reform.

The Tariff Reform Campaign

Chamberlain addressed mass meetings throughout Britain in the autumn and winter of 1903. He explained how a British tariff would help create employment in Britain. He also showed how a growth of trade with the Empire would lead to more employment.

He explained why the colonies would only agree to imperial preference if they made a similar gain from a British tariff which favoured their food exports to Britain. He claimed that this would mean a tariff of about 10p on 28lbs of corn or flour, a 5 per cent tariff on foreign meat and dairy produce, and about 10 per cent on manufactured goods.

The government would collect the revenue from these import taxes, and Chamberlain proposed that this money could be used to provide old-age

Fig. 26.2 'Follow Me, Leader.' The Hind Legs: 'My dear Arthur, of course you're the only conceivable head*; but we're going* my *way!' This cartoon appeared on 14 February 1906, by which time the division in the Tory Party had helped the Liberals to win the election.*

Fig. 26.3 Children of the poor in Lambeth in 1890. These were the products of a century of 'progress' and industrial growth.

pensions. He also promised that the government would be better able to tackle the problem of unemployment, low pay, and poverty (Extract 26.2 and Fig. 26.3).

The Liberals and Tariff Reform

During the election of 1900 the Liberals had been a badly divided party. The Liberal Imperialists wanted to support the war against the Boers; other Liberals, known as Little Englanders, wanted to condemn that war. In the 'khaki' election the Liberals were heavily defeated.

Chamberlain's tariff reform campaign helped to re-unite the divided party. All Liberals agreed that Free Trade was good. They could all show that Chamberlain's proposals would lead to higher prices – for manufactured goods and for food. They made a big issue out of the Free Trade 'loaf' and the tariff reform 'loaf': they claimed that Chamberlain's loaf would be either smaller or more expensive than the Free Trade loaf.

Henry Asquith, a leading Liberal Imperialist, followed Chamberlain around the country. He organized meetings to take place on the night after a Chamberlain meeting, and explained the dangers of giving up Free Trade. It was easier to understand the 'big loaf'–'little loaf' argument than to follow Chamberlain with his masses of figures.

The 1906 Election

The Conservative Party was badly split by the tariff reform argument (Fig. 26.2), and in December 1905 Balfour resigned. Sir Henry Campbell-Bannerman became Prime Minister of a Liberal government and called a general election.

During the election campaign the Liberals continued to use the 'big and little loaf' argument. They also showed how the Conservatives had helped South African mine owners to recruit labourers from China by a method that was nicknamed 'Chinese slavery'. The owners brought Chinese workers to South Africa only after they had signed a document that tied them to a particular owner for seven years. During that time they had to live in a camp provided by the owner, and repay the cost of their journey from China. This was not slavery; but the Liberal Party, a hostile Press, and Nonconformist preachers made life very difficult for the Tories. 'Is this what they died for?' was the question on cartoons showing scenes from the recent Boer War alongside scenes of Chinese coolies chained to mine owners.

After their failure in 1900 the Liberals had not dared hope that it would be easy to get back into power again. In 1903 the Liberal Chief Whip was Herbert Gladstone, son of the Grand Old Man. He went to Ramsay MacDonald, a leader of the Labour Representation Committee (later called the Labour

151

Party) and made a deal with him. Gladstone showed MacDonald that both of their parties were opposed to the Tories, and both of them hoped to find voting support from people opposed to the Tories. But if both the anti-Tory parties put up candidates in the same constituency, a Tory might win even if most of the voters were opposed to him. So Gladstone proposed an electoral pact, or agreement. Both Gladstone and MacDonald agreed that they would persuade their local associations to withdraw candidates in certain constituencies. This would allow only one anti-Tory candidate to stand. If a Liberal candidate was withdrawn, the local Liberals would vote for and work for the Labour candidate. If a Labour candidate was withdrawn, the trade unions and other Labour workers would vote for the Liberal candidate. The Labour Party agreed to this pact. So, in many constituencies the Tory candidate faced only one, well-supported candidate.

The Result

The divided Tories won only 157 seats. The Liberals won 400. The Irish Nationalists, now re-united under John Redmond, won eighty-three seats, and the new Labour Party won twenty-nine seats as well as having another twenty-four which were won by candidates put forward by the Miners' Union. We can say that there were fifty-three Labour M.P.s in the Commons in 1906.

Balfour said of these fifty-three: 'We have here something bigger than a Liberal victory'. These M.P.s had been elected by the working class, but the Liberals also depended on the working class for their victories. Was there room in British politics for two parties of the Left? Would the Liberals move further to the Left? Would they 'steal the Labour Party's clothes' by proposing radical policies? If they did this, would they lose the support of the older-type Liberals who still remembered Gladstone and the policies of self-help?

A New Era

No one knew in 1906 what the future held for the Liberal and Labour Parties. What was very clear, however, was that Britain had entered on a new stage of development. The tariff reform campaign may have failed, but it had clearly shown that Britain was no longer able to claim to be the world's industrial leader. During the election campaign Chamberlain, many Liberals, and all Labour candidates had also argued in favour of social reform – for old-age pensions, aid for the unemployed and homeless, and

for other victims of the self-help of the nineteenth century. Socialism, in one form or another, was now acceptable to an increasing number of people. One sign of this was the growth in the number of Labour M.P.s elected in 1906. The days of self-help were coming to an end.

Questions

Extract 26.1

Education and industry, 1914

We suffer in this country from want of experts. Instead of many experts, as in Switzerland, and as in the United States, we have taken too few steps to produce experts. It is no use saying to the manufacturers 'Employ more chemists'. There are no properly trained chemists to employ. At the beginning of the war I was chairman of a committee which had to go into one of the great chemical industries, and I found that we had become dependent upon Germany; even great discoveries that we had made in this country had been left to the Germans to use. I asked why it was, and I was told, 'We cannot get chemists. The Germans make the product in such a way that it is best to buy from them.'

The other day I inquired how many trained chemists there were available for the hundreds of chemical industries that there are in this country. I found that there were only 1,500 trained chemists in this country altogether. Our public schools do not prepare boys for the study of chemistry; nor do our secondary schools. Nor are our universities equipped to produce these men. We have only 1,500 trained chemists in this country. On the other hand, four large German chemical firms, which have played havoc with certain departments of our trade, employ 1,000 highly trained chemists between them. Those men were trained and produced by the great schools which exist there for that purpose.
(Speech by Lord Haldane in the House of Lords, 12 July 1916.)

1. Why did the more modern industries require more 'experts' than older industries such as coal and cotton? Does the country need more or fewer such experts today than in 1914? Explain your answer.
2. Why did this demand for 'experts' lead to a demand for more, better, and varied educational opportunity in Britain?
3. Britain had fewer experts than other countries. How far, if at all, was this the fault of the government? Give reasons for your answer.
4. How far does this extract help you to understand Germany's success in the expansion of her overseas trade? (Fig. 26.1.)

Extract 26.2

Life for the hard-working poor, 1902

The wage for a labourer in York is from 18s. to 21s.; the minimum expenditure necessary to maintain in a state of physical efficiency a family of two adults and three children is 21s. 3d., or, if there are four children, 26s.

Wages paid in York are insufficient to provide food, shelter and clothing adequate to maintain in a state of bare physical efficiency, even if the diet is less generous than that allowed in the Workhouse.

And let us understand what 'merely physical efficiency' means. A family living upon the scale allowed for in this estimate must never spend a penny on railway or omnibus; never go into the country, unless they walk; never purchase a halfpenny newspaper; never write letters to absent children. They cannot save, join sick club or Trade Union; they cannot pay the subscriptions. The children have no pocket money for dolls, marbles or sweets. The father must not smoke or drink. The mother must never buy any clothes for herself or for her children. Finally, the wage-earner must never be absent from his work for a single day. If any of these conditions are broken, the extra expenditure is met, and can only be met, by limiting the diet; or in other words by sacrificing physical efficiency.
(B. Seebohm Rowntree, *Poverty: A Study in Town Life*, 1902.)

1. What was the average wage for a labourer in York in 1902?
2. Why were the families of such workmen unable to 'maintain . . . physical efficiency'?
3. What do you think of the diet that would maintain 'physical efficiency'? Make a list of the things on which they must 'never spend a penny'.
4. How did this list affect the family's use of their free time?
5. Why did such families not take out any insurance policies?
6. Why was it unlikely that even this low wage could be guaranteed?

Fig. 26.1

1. What did 'that chap' do to win orders from foreign customers?
2. Why did John Bull feel that he did not need to do so?
3. Was John Bull right to think that his goods were better? What evidence do you have that some foreign goods were better than similar British goods?
4. How far does this cartoon explain some of the unemployment from which Britain suffered in the 1880s and 1890s? What – according to the cartoonist – was the main cause of that unemployment?

Worksheet

(A)
1. Explain the decline of British industrial power as it would have been explained by (i) Lord Salisbury (ii) an American industrialist (iii) Alfred Marshall (iv) Haldane (Extract 26.1), and (v) a Fair Trader.

2. Why was Britain able to lend so much money to foreigners? Explain how this helped (i) some British industries (ii) the countries or firms that borrowed the money. Why did some people think it was wrong to lend so much money?

3. Why did Chamberlain want to build up the trade carried on between the countries in the Empire? How did he try to do this? Why did he fail?

4. Explain: tariffs; imperial preference.

5. Explain why Chamberlain resigned and went on a tariff reform campaign.

(B)
1. Write the letters that might have been sent by:
(a) an Indian on the growth of the Indian textile industry, 1900;
(b) a British industrialist after a visit to an American factory;
(c) a Fair Trader complaining of Britain's policy of Free Trade;
(d) someone who had heard Chamberlain speaking in 1903–4;
(e) a Labour supporter after the 1906 election.

(C)
1. Write the headlines that might have appeared above reports on:
(a) the rise in imports from Germany;
(b) the Jubilee, 1897;
(c) the resignation of (i) the Duke of Devonshire (ii) Chamberlain;
(d) one of Chamberlain's speeches, 1903–4;
(e) Asquith's speech on 'big loaf, little loaf';
(f) the results of the election, 1906.

2. Make the poster that might have been used to advertise ONE of the following:
(a) the book called *Made in Germany*, 1896;
(b) a Fair Trade meeting;
(c) a Jubilee party in 1887 or 1897;
(d) a tariff reform meeting addressed by Chamberlain;
(e) ONE of the parties fighting in the 1906 election.

27 More Reforms of the Parliamentary System, 1866-1911

1832 – The Final Settlement

The first Reform Act was passed only after a long struggle (Chapter 12). There were riots in many towns, threats by William IV to create a large number of new Lords, and two elections before the Bill was passed.

Politicians who had played a part in that struggle thought that they had made a great achievement. Lord John Russell spoke of a 'final solution' to the question of the franchise and the distribution of seats. Robert Peel wrote of the Reform Act as 'a final settlement' (p. 76).

What Had 1832 Done?

In Chapter 12 we saw how the 1832 Act changed things. About 400,000 people got the vote for the first time. They were the rich people living in the large houses on the outskirts of industrial towns and villages.

The Reform Act was a sign that a new class of rich people had grown up in industrial Britain. The owners of mills and mines, factories and railways, banks and engineering shops had become very well off. They were very important in the *economic* life of the country. Their money allowed them to buy large houses and employ many servants; they had climbed up in the *social* life of the country. The 1832 Act gave them a share in the *political* life of the country.

What about the Workers?

In 1832 the vast majority of workers lived a very poor life. They had low wages, lived in crowded and poor housing, and played only a small part in the economic life of the country. They were also very low down the social scale, and they did not get a share in the country's political life.

But during the 1840s and 1850s conditions improved – for a small number of workers. By 1860 some of them had formed their own trade unions (Chapter 19), which gave them their own welfare system of social benefits. Some of them had formed the Co-

operative Society (p. 80), and about a million of them had started to save in the Post Office Savings Bank. Thousands of them saved through Building Societies and bought their own homes.

The skilled workmen had climbed the *social* ladder and were very important in the country's *economic* life. Therefore, it is not surprising that there were also demands for them to be allowed a share in the country's *political* life.

For and Against More Reform

Palmerston was easily the most important and popular politician in the 1850s. He was totally opposed to more parliamentary reform, and had played a small part in the struggles over the 1832 Act.

But other, younger politicians saw things differently. John Bright, an owner of a textile mill and M.P. for Rochdale, had become convinced that the better-off workers deserved the vote. In 1831 a Whig M.P. and historian, Macaulay, had argued in favour of the new middle class. He had said: 'A class which had been of no account, expands and becomes strong. It demands a place in the system. If this is refused, then comes the struggle between the young energy of one class and the privileges of another.' In 1865 John Bright used almost the same argument – but in favour of the working class.

Bright was a Radical M.P. and had helped lead the Anti-Corn Law League (Chapter 15). It was Bright who persuaded Gladstone to look at the question of 'votes for the workers'. He showed Gladstone how some of the workers had done what the Whig–Liberals wanted people to do – they had helped themselves. They had formed the Co-ops, and built their own libraries and Mechanics' Institutes where they went for a variety of evening classes; they had saved and bought their own homes; they had supported the war against the American slave-owning states even though this meant years of unemployment and hardship (p. 113). All this, said Gladstone in 1866, showed 'the increased fitness of the working classes for the exercise of political power'.

Gladstone's Reform Bill, 1866

Palmerston died in 1865. In 1866 Gladstone brought in a Reform Bill. He proposed to give the vote to all adult males who owned or occupied property rated at £5 a year. You will see that this was no wildly democratic move; it would have added only a small number to the voting lists. Gladstone wanted to reward the small number of workers who had begun to count in the country's economic life and who had started to climb the social ladder.

But even this modest proposal was too much for some of his Whig–Liberal colleagues, and Robert Lowe led a small group against his own Prime Minister. Lowe was afraid that the proposals would lead to mob rule (Extract 27.1). Bright nicknamed Lowe and his followers the 'Adullamites' after a Biblical group which hid away in a dark cave because it was frightened to face the world as it really was.

But Lowe had the last laugh. His group combined with Disraeli's Tories to defeat Gladstone's proposals.

Fig. 27.1 Disraeli, as Fagin, stealing the idea of Parliamentary reform from the pocket of Lord John Russell who was the Prime Minister in 1866.

Disraeli's Reform Bill

Gladstone resigned and the Queen invited Lord Derby to form a government. Disraeli became Leader of the House of Commons. However, Derby retired after a few months and Disraeli became Prime Minister for the first time.

In 1866 he had opposed Gladstone's Reform Bill, but he knew that, one day, there would be a successful Reform Act. He decided that it would be a good thing if the Tory Party brought in such an Act. Disraeli wanted people to believe that the Tories were the party of reform (Fig. 27.1).

He knew that he could depend on the support of Gladstone. He was too honest to oppose in 1867 something that he had put forward in 1866. So Disraeli proposed, at first, something very much like Gladstone's Bill. But his Cabinet questioned the £5 clause. Why not £4? or £3? or £2? they asked. Gradually they came to the point where the Bill contained no mention of money value at all. This was too much for Lord Cranborne. He was the eldest son of the Marquess of Salisbury, and in 1867 he was Secretary for India. He resigned from the Cabinet.

Disraeli's Bill proposed that, in the borough constituencies, the vote should be given to every male adult householder and to any tenant paying £12 a year in rent, and lodgers paying £10 a year for unfurnished rooms. This gave the franchise to about $1\frac{1}{2}$ million new voters. Even some of his own supporters called this a 'leap in the dark' – how would these new voters behave? Others called it 'shooting Niagara' – a dangerous business. But the Bill passed through Parliament and became the Parliamentary Reform Act 1867.

In addition to giving the vote to many working-class men, the Act also dealt with the question of the constituencies, as we shall see below.

The Ballot Act 1872

In 1872 Parliament brought in the Ballot Act. This set up the system of voting which we still use (Fig. 20.3 on p. 115). Voters drop their voting slip into a locked and sealed box, so that no one knows for whom anyone has voted. No employer could now punish workmen for not doing as they had been told.

Corrupt Practices Act 1883

During his 'Ministry of All the Troubles' (Chapter 23) Gladstone brought in a Bill aimed at putting an end to bribery and corruption at election times. This Act laid down how much money each candidate could spend during an election. This money would be spent on posters, leaflets, speakers' expenses, and so on. There would not be enough left over for the sort of vote-buying that had been common in the old days. Politicians now had to win the votes by promising better policies.

The Third Parliamentary Reform Act 1884

The 1867 Reform Act applied only to the borough seats; it said nothing about the franchise in the county constituencies. From 1883 onwards there was a campaign to give the county seats the same treatment as the borough seats. Bright and his Radical supporter, Chamberlain, were the leaders in this campaign.

In 1883 the Conservative Party was led by Salisbury. Even though the new voters had given Disraeli a huge majority in 1874, Salisbury still feared democracy. So he was opposed to any talk of a reform of the franchise in the county constituencies.

In 1884 a Reform Bill passed through the Commons but was rejected by the House of Lords. But the Bill was pushed through the Commons again, and

this time the Lords agreed to let it pass – provided that there was another Act to deal with the re-distribution of the constituencies.

The 1884 Act gave the whole country a common voting system. The franchise was given to every adult male householder and to every lodger paying £10 a year for unfurnished rooms. This added about 6 million to the voting lists. It was easily the most important of the three Reform Acts in terms of the numbers of voters.

The Constituencies, 1867 and 1885 (Fig. 27.2)

In 1867 boroughs with less than 10,000 people lost one of their M.P.s but still kept one. This meant that there were forty-five seats to be redistributed. Fifteen of these were given to new towns which now had M.P.s for the first time. Liverpool, Manchester, Birmingham, and Leeds were given an extra seat – so that they now had three M.P.s. Graduates of the University of London were allowed to return an M.P. as the older Universities of Oxford and Cambridge had always done. The remaining twenty-five seats were given to the counties where the population had increased since 1832.

Fig. 27.2 The distribution of constituencies in Cornwall, Lancashire, Yorkshire, Cheshire and Derbyshire, 1867–85.

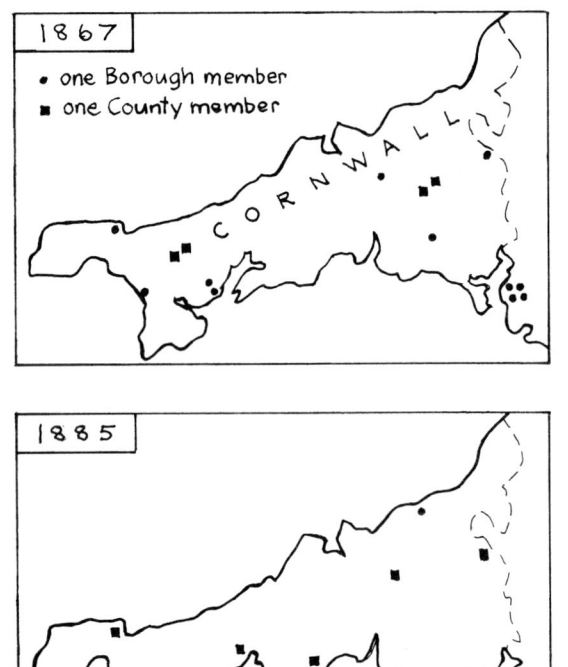

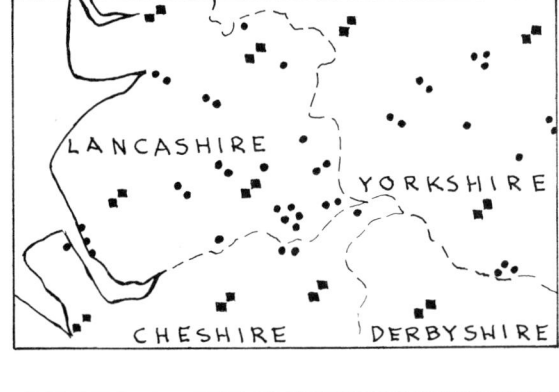

The changes made in 1885 were even greater. Seventy-nine towns that had populations of less than 15,000 lost their right to elect an M.P., and thirty-six towns with populations between 15,000 and 50,000 lost one of their M.P.s. They became single-member constituencies. Towns with populations between 50,000 and 165,000 were given two seats. The country, including the larger cities and towns, was divided into single-member constituencies. This is very much the system we have today.

Votes for Women?

After 1885 one adult in every seven had the right to vote. About half the adult men could not vote. There were the ones who shared their overcrowded houses with other families and so were not householders; and there were the over-21s who lived at home. The father alone had the vote.

But at least all men could think that, one day, they might get a vote if they became householders or lodgers of expensive rooms. What about women? In the 1860s John Stuart Mill tried to get Parliament to agree to give women the vote on the same terms as men (Fig. 27.3). He spoke during the debate on the second Reform Bill in 1867 – but he got little support.

Women played little part in the country's *economic* life; they did the lowest paid jobs when they worked in factories or mills. They had little part in the country's *social* life; very few of them went on to higher education; and until 1882 a woman lost her right to own anything when she got married (p. 133). Women were definitely second-class citizens. The wives of rich men were 'birds in a gilded cage'; their daughters were supposed to prepare themselves for marriage and for a similar 'imprisonment'. So it is not surprising that few men thought that women should have the vote.

Fig. 27.3 A Punch *cartoon entitled 'Mill's logic, or franchise for females'.*

During the last quarter of the nineteenth century there was some improvement in women's position in society. More of them went to secondary schools and took School Certificate examinations (the older form of O Level). Some went on to university and became qualified as doctors or teachers; many got well-paid jobs in some of the new large department stores; and others got jobs as telephonists, typists, clerks, and Civil Servants. Some women began to count in the country's *economic* life, and the richer women had always played a part in the country's *social* life.

So there was a rise in the demand for women to have a share in the country's *political* life. In the 1880s Mrs Millicent Fawcett founded the suffragist movement. She and her supporters hoped that argument and persuasion would be enough to get men to change their attitudes and give women the vote.

But Mrs Fawcett's campaign had no success, and in 1903 Mrs Emmeline Pankhurst formed the Women's Social and Political Union (W.S.P.U.). She decided that the campaign of 'votes for women' would have to become more outspoken and even violent; the men answered her violence with their own (Extract 27.2). We shall see in Chapter 32 that after 1906 the suffragettes were part of that violent society which led some people to think that Britain was on the point of a revolution.

The House of Lords

Today we still call the House of Lords the 'Upper House' of the two Houses of Parliament. Throughout the nineteenth century it gave plenty of evidence that it was, indeed, more important than the House of Commons. It rejected the 1831 Reform Bill – and only allowed one to pass in 1832 when the King threatened to swamp the Lords with new peers. In 1884 it rejected one Reform Bill proposed by Gladstone and imposed its own terms before allowing another to pass; and in 1893 it rejected Gladstone's Home Rule Bill.

Between 1906 and 1909 it proved to be too strong for the Liberal government (Chapter 31), but during the nineteenth century there had been a steady movement towards democracy. From 1832 through to 1884–5 there was a growth in the number of ordinary people who could vote. From 1872 onwards politicians had to depend more on policies than bribery if they wanted to get elected; and because of an increase in the number of workers who could vote, the politicians had to offer policies that would appeal to the workers.

So it is not surprising that the position of the House of Lords should be challenged in this more democratic system. In Chapter 32 we will see how this challenge was mounted by the Liberals in 1909 and how the Lords tried to resist it. But the passing of the Parliament Act 1911 (p. 183) had to be seen as a result of the growth of the more democratic system which had developed during the nineteenth century.

Questions

Extract 27.1

Robert Lowe against reform, 1866

The government are proposing to enfranchise one class of men who have been disenfranchised heretofore. What good are we to get by this extension of the franchise? The effect will be to add a large number of persons to our constituencies of the class from which, if there is anything wrong going on, we may naturally expect to find it. It will be to increase the expenses of candidates. If experience proves that corruption varies inversely as the franchise you must look for more bribery and corruption than you have hitherto had. The first result . . . will be an increase of corruption, intimidation, and disorder, all of the evils that happen usually in elections. But what will be the second? The second will be that the working men of England, finding themselves in a full majority of the whole constituency, will awake to a full sense of their power. They will say 'We can do better for ourselves. Don't let us any longer be cajoled at elections. Let us set up shop for ourselves. We have objects to serve as well as our neighbours, and let us unite to carry those objects. We have machinery, we have our trade unions, we have our leaders all ready. We have the power of combination . . . and when we have a prize to fight for we will bring it to bear with tenfold more force than ever before.'

(Robert Lowe, Speech of 13 March 1866.)

1.   Which 'class of men' were enfranchised by the Reform Act 1867? When did men living in county constituencies get the same right? When did all men over the age of 21 get the right to vote?
2.   Why was Lowe opposed to the proposal to give the vote to working men?
3.   Was there more corruption after 1867 than there had been before? Why was it more difficult, and costly, to organize bribery after 1867 than in previous elections?
4.   How and when did workers show 'a full sense of their power'?
5.   How did Lowe affect the future of the 1866 proposals?

Extract 27.2

The Suffragettes, 1905

The life of the old Parliament, dominated by the Conservative Party, was drawing to an end and the country was on the eve of a general election. The Liberals hoped to be returned to power. Liberal candidates went to the country with promises of reform in every possible direction. . . . We determined to demand whether their reforms were going to include justice to women. We began this work at a great meeting in Free Trade Hall, Manchester, with Sir Edward Grey as the principal speaker. . . . Annie Kenney and my daughter Christabel were charged with the mission of questioning Sir Edward Grey. They sat quietly through the meeting, at the close of which questions were invited. Several questions were asked by men and were courteously answered. Then Annie Kenney arose and asked: 'If the Liberal Party is returned to power, will they take steps to give votes for women?' At the same time Christabel held aloft the little banner that everyone in the hall might understand the nature of the question. Sir Edward Grey returned no answer to Annie's question, and the men sitting near her forced her rudely into her seat, while a steward pressed his hat over her face. . . .

Annie Kenney stood up in her chair and cried out over the noise of shuffling feet and murmurs of conversation: 'Will the Liberal Government give votes to women?' Then the audience became a mob. They howled, they shouted and roared, shaking their fists fiercely at the woman who dared to intrude her question into a man's meeting. . . . Flung into the streets, the two girls staggered to their feet and began to address the crowds. Within five minutes they were arrested on a charge of obstruction and, in Christabel's case, of assaulting the police. Both were summonsed to appear next morning in a police court, where, after a trial which was a mere farce, Annie Kenney was sentenced to pay a fine of five shillings, with an alternative of three days in prison, and Christabel Pankhurst was given a fine of ten shillings or a jail sentence of one week. Both girls promptly chose the prison sentence.

(Emmeline Pankhurst, *My Own Story*, 1914, pp. 47–8.)

1. Who was the Prime Minister at the time of the 1905 election?
2. Why did the Liberals expect 'to be returned'? Give three reasons for (i) the defeat of the Tories, and (ii) the victory of the Liberals.
3. What office did Grey hold after 1906?
4. Why did he ignore the question put by Annie Kenney?
5. How did the men in the crowd treat the women when they continued to put their questions?
6. Why did these women prefer to go to prison than to pay the fine?
7. When did some women gain the right to vote for the first time? How did an Act of 1928 increase the number of women voters?

Fig. 27.1

1. Which Party proposed parliamentary reform in 1866?
2. Name two of the leading supporters of the 1866

Reform Bill. Name one leading rebel against the Bill.
3. How did Disraeli 'dish the Whigs' in 1867?
4. When had he accused Sir Robert Peel of doing the same thing? How had he treated Peel at that time?
5. Who rebelled against Disraeli's proposals in 1867? How did Disraeli treat him when the Tories won the election in 1874?

Worksheet

(A)
1. Make a list of the main points in Bright's argument in favour of allowing the working class the right to vote.

2. What was the importance of the Reform Act 1867 to the working class? Give THREE examples of laws that were passed between 1868 and 1880 to help working-class people.

3. What were the main differences between the tactics of Mrs Fawcett and Mrs Pankhurst?

4. Why and when did the House of Lords come under attack from the Commons in the late nineteenth century?

5. Explain: Franchise; ballot; constituencies.

(B)
1. Write the letters that might have been sent by:
(a) one of the first girls to qualify as a doctor;
(b) a working-class voter in 1872 comparing voting before and after the Ballot Act;
(c) a suffragette after one of the demonstrations.

2. Draw a set of graphs to show growth in the number of voters during the nineteenth century.

3. Make a time chart and mark on it the main events mentioned in the text. Write a brief note on each of the events that you mark on the chart.

(C)
1. Write the headlines that might have appeared above reports on:
(a) Gladstone's Bill, 1866 – in Liberal, Whig, Tory, and working-class papers;
(b) the success of Disraeli's Bill – in papers as in (a);
(c) the passage of the 1884 Act – in papers as in (a);
(d) Mill's proposals for granting the franchise to women – in papers as in (a) and in a magazine edited by and for women;
(e) the 1905 meeting (Extract 27.2) – in papers as in (a) and in a suffragette paper.

2. Draw the poster that might have been used for ONE of the following:
(a) a meeting to hear Bright, 1865–7;
(b) a meeting addressed by Mrs Pankhurst, 1905.

28 Trade Union Development, 1867-1914

After the Royal Commission, 1869

In the 1850s and 1860s skilled workers earned a relatively good wage, and enjoyed regular employment. These men could afford the weekly fee paid to their union (Chapter 19). In return, they had their own welfare system of social benefits for the old, unemployed, and sick members of the union.

In 1868 the Gladstone government set up a Royal Commission to examine the position of trade unions, and in 1869 the Commission published its report. This argued that trade unionism ought to be encouraged: the self-help of the working man had won the admiration of the middle-class members of the Commission.

Gladstone, 1868–74

Under Gladstone two Acts were passed concerning trade unions:

1. The Trade Union Act 1871. This was passed to protect trade unions against dishonest officials (p. 110). A trade union could register with the Registrar of Friendly Societies. He would have to approve the union's rules and the way in which the leaders used the funds. After his approval, a union was then *a legal body*. As such it could take a dishonest official to court and so protect its funds.

2. The Criminal Law Amendment Act 1871. This was passed on the same day as the Act meant to help trade unions. This Act allowed trade unions to call a

Fig. 28.1 A cartoon from Punch *warning the working class that they had little to gain from strikes.*

strike (Fig. 28.1), but it forbade any picketing of factories or works.

Union leaders knew that if they were not allowed to organize any picketing, they would not be able to use the strike weapon properly. Their anger with Gladstone may help to explain why many workers voted for Conservative candidates at the 1874 election.

Disraeli, 1874–80

In 1875 Disraeli's government helped pass two Acts to aid trade unions:

1. The Conspiracy and Protection of Property Act made peaceful picketing lawful. It also said that a trade union could do anything which would be lawful if it were done by an individual.

2. The Employers' and Workmen's Act said that if an employer or workman broke their contract, they could be sued in the civil courts. Here the guilty party could be made to pay damages. Before 1875 the law said that an employer could not be sued for breaking his contract. But a workman could be sued – and in the Criminal Court where judges could impose prison sentences.

The Unskilled Workers

But we have to remember that the unions we have been reading about were only for the skilled workers. Even as late as 1885, there were only about 200,000 men enrolled in unions.

The great bulk of British workers did not have any skills. They did not get decent wages and they had no secure regular employment. We know a good deal about the lives of the unskilled workers and their families because of the writings of men such as Seebohm Rowntree (Extracts 28.1 and 26.2 on p. 153).

They lived in overcrowded and badly furnished homes because they could not afford to rent anything better. Their clothes were bought at junk shops or picked up from dustbins. They had a very poor diet and often had to rely on the hand-outs from soup kitchens organized by bodies such as the Salvation Army.

Unions for Unskilled Workers

The well-paid skilled worker, living in his own home, did not feel that he had to do anything to help the unskilled workers. Since he had got on by his own efforts, he thought that everyone else should be able to get on in the same way. It was Rowntree who showed that there was a poverty cycle (Extract 28.1). In other words, the children of the poor likewise became unskilled and poor when they grew up.

No one thought that unions could be organized for the unskilled. If they went on strike an employer could easily find other men to do their work; and since they earned very little, they would not be able to afford to pay union fees. Therefore, they would not have a strike fund to pay money during a strike.

Joseph Arch, 1872

Joseph Arch was a hedge-cutter and a preacher in Nonconformist chapels in Warwickshire. In 1872 he tried to help the agricultural work-force. These were probably the worst paid and most poorly housed workers (Fig. 28.2). He set up a National Agricul-

Fig. 28.2 'The Cottage.' Mr Punch (to Landlord): 'Your stable arrangements are excellent! Suppose you try something of the sort here! Eh?' The cartoonist felt that British farmers paid more attention to their animals than they did to their workmen. Conditions in farmworkers' cottages were often worse than those in the homes of factory workers.

tural Labourers Union in 1872, and branches were set up all over the country in 1872 and 1873. But the farmers, who employed the labourers, refused to recognize the union, and when the men threatened to go on strike, the employers locked them out (1874).

But the labourers could not hold out for very long and hunger drove them back to work. The imports of cheap food from America had, by 1874, resulted in many farmers having a falling income. This meant that they offered even lower wages in the 1870s than in the 1860s.

Arch's union collapsed after the failure of the strike of 1874.

Girls and Men, 1888–9

In 1888 Annie Besant, a left-wing journalist friend of Bradlaugh's (p. 131), helped to organize a union among the girls who worked in the match-making factory owned by Bryant & May's. Here, for less than 1p an hour, the girls dipped matches into phosphorus. This often gave them a terrible disease known as 'phossy jaw' caused by the fumes from the phosphorus. It could be fatal, but even if a girl recovered, she might lose the whole of her lower jaw.

In 1888 Besant organized them into a union. She led them into a strike and forced the employers to put up their wages – to about 1½p an hour.

In 1889 London's gas was provided from the gasworks of the London Gas Light and Coke Company. Men shovelled coal into huge furnaces which produced the gas. They worked for twelve hours at a time and for seven days a week. In August 1889 Will Thorne organized them into a Gas Workers Union. He demanded an eight-hour day without any fall in pay, and the employers gave way when the men threatened to go on strike.

Socialist Societies

During the 1880s some men had set up small societies that aimed to show that life could be better for the mass of British workers. One of these societies was the Social Democratic Federation. This had been set up by a rich man, H. Hyndman. He had read and translated some of the works of Karl Marx, and he hoped to set up a Communist Society in Britain. Very few people joined his federation – or any other of the socialist societies; most people were too tired to go to meetings or to read pamphlets. But those who did join behaved like fervent apostles of a new religion. They spoke at factory gates and at markets where people were shopping.

Will Thorne was a member of the S.D.F., so were John Burns, Ben Tillett, and Tom Mann. These men helped to organize the most famous of the strikes by unskilled workers. This took place on London Docks in 1889.

The London Dockers' Strike

There were many thousands of men employed in London's docks. Some of them were skilled men who had their own unions, but the majority were unskilled workers. They crowded around the dock gates each morning, and waited for a foreman to come out and pick the men he wanted to help load or unload a ship. Men fought like animals to attract his attention. They waited there until there was no more work for the day, then they went home, with no money. Even those who were picked out only got 2p an hour.

In August 1889 Tillett organized a Tea Workers' and General Labourers' Union at Whitechapel. He demanded that no one should be taken on for less than four hours and that wages should be 2½p an hour with more for overtime.

Tillett's union had no funds and little organization, and few people expected that he would succeed. But he managed to win the support of all the other dock workers in all the other trades, and everyone came out on strike.

John Burns organized the 100,000 men and their families on a series of marches through London's streets. This created a good deal of public sympathy for the men and their families. Money was collected to buy food for the strikers' families, and dockers in Australia sent £30,000 to help.

The strike lasted for five weeks. Finally the employers agreed to sit on a Mediation Committee set up at the Lord Mayor's Mansion House. Here, under the chairmanship of the Catholic Cardinal Manning, an agreement was reached on 15 September 1889. The dockers got their 2½p. More importantly, the Dock, Wharf, Riverside & General Labourer's Union was formed with Tillett as full-time secretary.

The Dockers' Strike and Other Workers

Other unskilled workmen saw the victory of the dockers as a signal for them to form their own unions. In 1889 and 1890 unions were formed for unskilled workers in the textile industry and bricklayers' labourers. There was even a General Labourers' Union.

Unlike the older unions for skilled workmen, these new unions had no funds – their members earned too little to pay more than 1p a month. Nor did they have much organization – the union could not afford offices, travelling expenses, and so on. But they did have great enthusiasm, and men really thought that they were going to make a great change in their working lives and living conditions.

The Older Unions

After 1889 the leaders of the older unions changed their rules so that unskilled men could join at lower fees – and for smaller benefits. They hoped to head off the growth of the new, larger unions for unskilled workers – but they had left it too late.

In the 1890s some members of the older unions began to demand that their leaders adopt some of the enthusiasm and militancy of the new unions. In the 1860s and 1870s the older unions had boasted that they very rarely had to organize a strike; they managed to get what they wanted by negotiating with employers. But in the 1890s there was an increase in unemployment among the skilled workers (Chapter 26), and this changed their attitude towards strikes, their employers, and their hopes for the future. Things would not always get better. Indeed, it seemed as if they might get much worse.

The New Unions and Politics

Tillett and the other leaders of the unskilled knew that they had won only a small victory in 1889. How much difference would it make to a family if the father earned 2½p instead of 2p an hour? They would still have too little to live on. The pawnshop (Fig. 28.3) would still have to be used to get money for food and rent.

The unskilled would never be able to save for their old age, or for periods of sickness and unemployment. Tillett and the other socialists knew that the unskilled would only get pensions, unemployment pay, and decent housing if Parliament passed Acts about these things.

There was no sign that either the Liberals or the Conservatives would do much about these issues. So Tillett, Mann, Burns, and others helped to organize their followers into a new political party (Extract 28.2). We will learn more about this in Chapter 29.

Taff Vale, 1900–2

In 1900 the Amalgamated Society of Railway Servants (now the N.U.R.) organized a strike against the Taff Vale Railway Company in South Wales. When the strike ended, the company sued the union for the losses it had suffered because of the strike. The case went from one court to another until it was finally settled by the Law Lords in the House of Lords.

They decided that the union had to pay the company £23,000 in damages. It also had to pay £19,000 in legal costs.

Many people saw this as a middle-class attack on trade unions, and union leaders realized that they would be unable to organize a strike without the danger of having to pay hefty sums in damages. This meant that they had no weapon with which to fight the employers.

In 1902 union leaders asked the Conservative

Fig. 28.3 A pawnshop.

government to introduce a Bill to give them the right to strike without fear of being prosecuted for damages. Balfour refused. Many of the union leaders then saw, for the first time, that they too needed a political party to speak for them in the House of Commons. One result of the Taff Vale judgement was a rapid growth in the membership of the Labour Party (p. 169).

Violence and unemployment

After 1902 there was a continual growth in the number of men joining trade unions. There was also a slow-down in the development of British trade and industry – which led to more unemployment. Strikes were common as men opposed employers' attempts to bring down wages, and clashes between strikers and blacklegs, police, and soldiers were frequent.

It is not surprising that many middle-class people thought that things were getting out of hand. They welcomed the Taff Vale decision; and they were also frightened by the growth of the Labour Party which relied on trade union money. Some of this was sent to the Labour Party to pay M.P.'s expenses in the days before M.P.s got a salary. It was also used to pay for elections – pamphlets, posters, leaflets, and so on.

The Trades Disputes Act 1906

In 1906 there were fifty-three Labour M.P.s in the House of Commons (p. 152). They asked the Liberal government to do something about the Taff Vale judgement, and in 1906 Parliament passed an Act which said that no union, no union leader, or member could be taken to court for damages. This put unions and their members in a very privileged position. It certainly meant that they could organize strikes without fear of being prosecuted.

The Osborne Case, 1908–9

The unions had now got back their strike weapon. They also had, in the Labour Party, a political weapon. Employers had failed to take away their strike weapon – maybe they could take away the political one.

In 1908 W. V. Osborne was secretary of the Walthamstow branch of the Amalgamated Society of Railway Servants. He was a Liberal and objected to some of his weekly fee being used to help the Labour Party. He prosecuted his union. This case was also taken from one court to another until it was settled by the Law Lords. They decided that a trade union could not use its funds for political purposes.

This was a serious blow to the Labour Party. However, the Liberals went some way to helping the party by the Parliament Act (1911). One clause of this Act said that M.P.s were to get a salary of £400 a year.

The Trade Union Act 1913

This Act stated that a union could use its funds for political purposes. However, if any union member did not want any of his money to be used in this way he could sign a form to say so and he would then pay less each week than men paying into the political fund. He could 'contract out' of paying to the political fund. Few men did so, though, and the Labour Party's funds benefited.

Trade Unions in 1914

After 1910 there was a steady growth in the number of men joining trade unions. Fear of unemployment,

the attempts of employers to bring down wages, and a rise in prices had made more people concerned about their conditions.

There was also a steady growth in the size of trade unions. These larger, national unions organized national strikes (Chapter 32). They were, in one sense, a sign of that violence which dominated British society in the period 1910–14. This rise in trade union activity was the forerunner to the General Strike of 1926 (Chapter 37).

Questions
Extract 28.1

The life of the worker from birth to death

> The life of a labourer is marked by five alternating periods of want and comparative plenty. During early childhood he probably will be in poverty until he, or some of his brothers or sisters, begin to earn money and thus augment their father's wage sufficiently to raise the family above the poverty line. Then follows the period during which he is earning money and living under his parents' roof; for some portion of this period he will be earning more money than is required for lodging, food, and clothes. This is his chance to save money. If he has saved enough to pay for furnishing a cottage, this period of comparative prosperity may continue after marriage until he has two or three children, when poverty will again overtake him. This period of poverty will last perhaps for ten years, i.e. until the first child is fourteen years old and begins to earn wages; but if there are more than three children it may last longer. While the children are earning, and before they leave home to marry, the man enjoys another period of prosperity – possibly, however, only to sink back again into poverty when his children have married and left him, and he himself is too old to work.
> (S. Rowntree, *Poverty*, 1902.)

1. Make a table to show the 'five periods' in the life of working men. You might use the ages 0–11, 12–25, 26–40, 41–64, and 65 and over as guide-lines.
2. You can make an illustration of this cycle of poverty on a piece of graph paper. On the x-axis (or horizontal) write the ages of the workmen from birth to 70 years. Mark the y-axis (or vertical) with the words 'Affluence' above the horizontal, and 'Poverty' below the horizontal. Now draw the graph which illustrates the table you have made in answer to Question 1.
3. What causes of poverty are mentioned in this extract? Are these the causes of poverty today? Give reasons for your answer.
4. Why were the children of poor families likely to become poor working men when they grew up? How might they escape from this cycle of poverty? Do you think that the cycle still operates today?

Extract 28.2

The new unionism, 1889

From the Dock Strike of 1889, the present-day organization of the wage-earners took its rise . . . and the Socialist Movement which introduced . . . the Labour Party . . . dates from this great event. Trade Unionism among the general workers was regarded as an illegitimate offspring, and treated like one by the Trade Unionism of the skilled crafts. To set our Union on its feet and to win the respect of the craft Unions, we had to demonstrate the strength of our purpose, the soundness of our strategy, and the skill of our generalship in actual warfare with the employers. The Dock Strike was a test, not only of intelligence and will on our part, but of the ability to seize opportunities as they arose, to evoke and to make use of public sympathy as one of the weapons of our warfare.

(Ben Tillett, *Memories and Reflections*, 1931.)

1. Why did the dockers go on strike in 1889? What did they want?
2. What other famous strikes took place at about this time? How do you explain the increase in labour unrest in the 1880s?
3. Who, in the working class, thought that 'the general workers' could not form trade unions? What did the 'general workers' themselves think of their chances of forming unions? (See Extract 28.2 for a clue.)
4. What had the unions for skilled workmen achieved for their members by 1889? How did the unions for the unskilled differ from the unions for the skilled workers?
5. Why did the dockers need the support of the public? How did they set out to win that support? Why did so much help come from Australia?
6. Public opinion turned against trade unions around 1900. Can you suggest reasons for this change?

Fig. 28.3

1. What is the meaning of 'pawning'?
2. Why did people go to pawnshops in the nineteenth century?
3. There are few pawnshops today. What does this tell you about the standard of living of the mass of the British people today?

Worksheet

(A)

1. Using two columns draw up lists to show the difference between Gladstone and Disraeli in their treatment of trade unions.

2. Show how and when trade unions had become recognized and privileged bodies by 1880.

3. Using two columns, show the differences between the craft unions and the general unions as regards (i) the type of workmen in each (ii) their funds (iii) the benefits paid (iv) organization (v) their political views. Add a sentence under each of the headings to explain your answers.

4. Explain the increasing militancy by working-class men at the end of the nineteenth century.

5. Explain (i) the origins, and (ii) the results of the Taff Vale dispute. How might Balfour have won working-class support for the Conservatives in 1902?

6. Explain (i) the origins, and (ii) the result of the Osborne case. Why was it an important case for the Labour Party?

(B)

1. Write the letters that might have been sent by:
(a) a worker in the London Gasworks after their success in 1889;
(b) a worker in London docks about the problem of getting work;
(c) a union leader after the House of Lords decision in the Taff Vale case.

2. Make a graph to show the cycle of poverty (Extract 28.1) with a man's age marked along the horizontal axis and with periods of poverty marked as minus signs on the vertical axis.

3. Draw a time chart to show the main events mentioned in the text. Add a sentence to explain each of the events and dates you have marked on the chart.

(C)

1. Write the headlines that might have appeared, in papers controlled by the industrialists, workers, Liberals, and Conservatives, above reports on:
(a) the Trade Union Act 1871;
(b) the Criminal Law Amendment Act 1871;
(c) Disraeli's Trade Union Acts 1875;
(d) the Match Girls' Strike 1888; also the headline that might have appeared in a paper for women readers;
(e) the London Docker's Strike 1889;
(f) one of the marches through London organized by Burns;
(g) the Taff Vale decision; also the headline that might have appeared in the magazine issued by the Amalgamated Society of Railway Servants.

29 The Rise of the Labour Party, 1867-1914

The Failure of the Other Parties

In 1885 Joseph Chamberlain fought the election on the 'unofficial programme' (p. 133). The Radical Liberal knew that there was a good deal that was wrong in Britain. He wanted to do something about the old, the unemployed, the poverty in which many children lived (Fig. 29.1), and the great problem of slum housing (Extract 29.1).

In the Conservative Party there was, at the same time, the Radical Tory, Lord Randolph Churchill. He wanted the party to follow Disraeli's example and to cure these social problems.

But, as we have seen, both Radicals were defeated,

Fig. 29.1 Chamberlain wanted to introduce policies to help relieve poverty, seen here so clearly in the ragged clothes and sad faces of these children from Snowfields School, London.

and in 1886 Chamberlain left the Liberal Party. He joined the Conservative Party and, after 1895, used his energies and influence to help the growth of the British Empire. Churchill was even less lucky. In 1886 he resigned from his post of Chancellor of the Exchequer, and died soon afterwards.

After 1886 neither the Liberals nor the Conservatives did much about the country's social problems. A new party would have to be created to tackle these difficulties.

The Second Reform Act 1867

The 1867 Reform Act gave the vote to millions of working-class men living in the industrial towns (p. 155). How would they use these votes?

In 1869 a group of workers formed the Labour Representation League. They wanted to see working men elected as M.P.s. In some constituencies – particularly in mining valleys – the majority of voters were working men. In the past the Liberals had won such seats; and some Liberals realized that working men would be bound to win an election if any of them came forward as candidates. They decided to ask working men to stand in certain constituencies, and in 1874 two of them, Alexander Macdonald and Thomas Burt, two leaders of the miners' unions, were elected. They were working men. In Parliament they sat with the Liberals and earned the nickname of 'Lib-Labs'.

Working Men and Self-help

Burt and Macdonald were former miners. They had seen how the miners and other skilled workers had improved their conditions of living and of work during the nineteenth century. One reason for this improvement was Free Trade. This had led to lower prices for food and other imports. As the cost of living fell, so the standards of the workers had improved. The craft unions had also played their part in improving living standards. Skilled men had got better wages and shorter working days. Through their unions they had their own welfare services (p. 110). It is not surprising that Burt, Macdonald, and their skilled workmen believed in the doctrine of self-help.

The Failure of Self-help

But after 1875 it was clear that self-help had failed. Some employers and some workmen had a relatively good life, but the mass of the people lived in terrible conditions (Extract 29.1 and Fig. 29.1).

Self-help – and Free Trade – failed to provide the growth in trade which Britain had enjoyed in the 1850s and 1860s. By 1895, when Chamberlain became Colonial Secretary, there was high unemployment. We have seen how Chamberlain tried to cure this by helping the growth of colonies in Africa (p. 144).

The evidence for the failure of self-help was provided by the writings of people such as Rowntree (p. 164), Booth and Mrs Reeve. In 1900 the country was provided with even more bitter evidence of the failure. Over half the men who volunteered for service in the Boer War failed the simple medical test. These men were the product of a century of industrialization and self-help.

Socialism

In the 1880s a number of societies were set up by men who wanted to show that things could be better. The founders of these societies wanted a government to tackle the country's social problems. This would mean higher taxes to provide the money for housing, pensions, unemployment benefit, and so on.

H. M. Hyndman founded the Social Democratic Federation in 1881. This was a small society, and it never had more than 700 members. But it published a great deal of propaganda that was read by some working people; and it won the support of the more active workers – such as Mann, Tillett, and Burns. We have seen how they helped to organize the London Dockers' Strike.

Mann, Tillett, and others spoke at open air meetings – sometimes holding three on a Sunday. They helped working people to see that life might be better. In 1884 William Morris, a poet and artist, left the S.D.F. to form the Socialist League. This was another small society. Morris was well known and he used his influence to show his better-off friends that things could be improved.

In 1884 a small group of lecturers and authors founded the Fabian Society. The Fabians thought that a policy of patient explanation would lead to a victory for good sense. They produced pamphlets to show how a government could help the unemployed and badly housed; they hoped that the Liberals would see the need to pass the Acts needed to improve things. In 1893 the Fabians realized that the Liberals were not going to do anything, and Bernard Shaw, a leading playwright and Fabian, then wrote a famous letter in which he advised trade union leaders and working men in general to support the new Labour Party.

Robert Blatchford

The S.D.F., the Socialist League, and the Fabians

produced very good pamphlets and propaganda, but many working people could not understand these serious works. Robert Blatchford was a journalist. In the 1890s he produced a newspaper, the *Clarion*, which was easy to read and which became very popular. Throughout the country men and women formed Clarion clubs, choirs, cycling groups, and savings clubs. Blatchford used the newspaper and the clubs to preach the need for a change in government attitudes, and in 1894 he put many of his *Clarion* articles into a book called *Merrie England*. This sold over one million copies – a sign of the number of people who read Blatchford's newspaper.

Keir Hardie

Hardie (Fig. 29.2) was a Scottish miner. In 1888 he had tried to get the Liberals in mid-Lanark to let him stand as their Lib–Lab candidate in a by-election. They refused, so Hardie stood instead as the Scottish Labour Party candidate. He came bottom of the poll.

In 1892 Hardie stood as Labour candidate in West Ham in London and John Burns was Labour candidate in Battersea. They both won. They were the first working men to be elected without support from the Liberal Party.

The Independent Labour Party 1893

In 1893 Hardie organized a conference at Bradford for representatives of the small Labour clubs and socialist societies. The conference agreed to the setting up of the Independent Labour Party. But in 1895 both Hardie and Burns lost their seats, and the I.L.P. had no M.P. in the Commons. But it continued to grow outside Parliament. Branches were set up in the industrial towns, and by 1897 there were over 380 branches – half of them in Lancashire and Yorkshire. The members of the I.L.P. gave a great deal of their free time to handing out leaflets, organizing meetings, and preaching the doctrine of socialism.

The Trade Union Movement and the I.L.P.

In 1889 the London dockers had won a great industrial victory but even with their better wages the dockers were still unable to afford decent housing, clothes, or food.

Burns, Hardie, and Bernard Shaw saw that the working men had to be organized to win a political victory. They could form a new party and send their own people into Parliament. This might force

Fig. 29.2 Keir Hardie addressing a meeting in Trafalgar Square in May 1913.

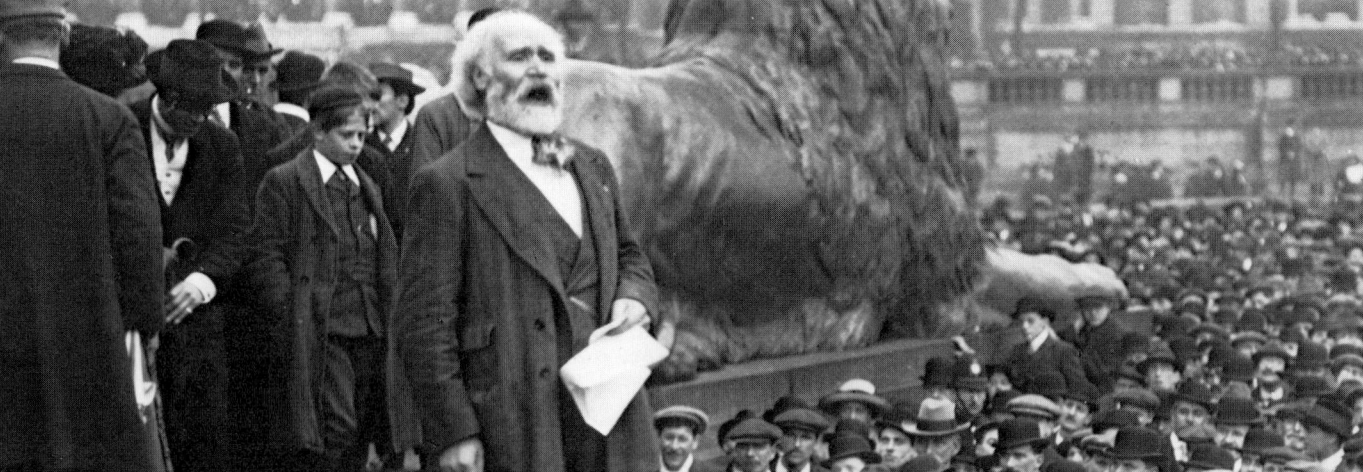

Parliament to pass Acts about pensions, housing, and so on.

The trade unions had branches throughout the country, and these could be used to recruit members to the new party. They could also form the centres from which Labour candidates could fight elections. The unions had the money that the party would need to fight elections and to support the M.P.s after they had been elected.

But the leaders of the older unions wanted nothing to do with this new, socialist party. The leaders of the craft unions were believers in self-help, and therefore did not think that they needed government help. So in the 1890s the annual conference of the trade union movement turned down Hardie's appeal for support for his I.L.P.

The 1899 Conference

By 1899 there was a change in the sort of men attending the annual conferences of the trade union movement. There were more representatives from the new, large unions for unskilled workers, and they wanted to support Hardie and his party.

Some of the older leaders of the craft unions had retired. In their places were younger men who had read Blatchford, Shaw, Morris, or Hyndman. They, too, wanted the union movement to support Hardie.

In 1899 Hardie once again proposed a resolution calling for a conference of unions and societies interested in forming a new working-class party. This was carried by 546,000 to 434,000. This tells us something about the size of the trade union movement. Today's conferences show votes totalling about 13 million. The 1899 vote also shows that the union movement was badly split over the political future.

1900 Conference

On 27 February 1900 there was a meeting at the Memorial Hall in Farringdon Street, London. Representatives were sent by the unions that had supported Hardie in 1899. There were also representatives from the various socialist societies and from the co-operative societies.

This conference decided to set up a new party. It was called the Labour Representation Committee. It did not take the name 'Labour Party' until just before the 1906 election.

The conference elected an executive to run the new party. This had seven representatives from the trade unions, two from the S.D.F., and one from the Fabian Society.

An Uncertain Start, 1900

Few of the craft unions had sent representatives to the 1900 conference, but these were the unions that had the most money and best organizations. The new party was short of money, and in 1900 it was also short of M.P.s. Thirteen candidates stood in the 1900 election; only Hardie was successful (Extract 29.2).

But the Taff Vale decision helped the new party to grow. We have seen how that decision affected the industrial power of the trade unions (p. 163), and we have also seen how the Balfour government refused to put things right (p. 163). Leaders of the craft unions joined the new Labour Party to try to get the law changed.

The Electoral Pact, 1903

By 1903 the Labour Party had won three by-elections. Hardie had been joined in Parliament by David Shackleton from the Weavers' Union who was M.P. for Clitheroe, Will Crooks of the Coopers' Union, M.P. for Woolwich, and Arthur Henderson of the Ironfounders', M.P. for Barnard Castle. They had won because the Liberal candidates had withdrawn from the fight. In other by-elections the Labour candidates had been defeated when fighting against both a Tory and a Liberal candidate.

Ramsay MacDonald was Secretary of the Labour Party. Herbert Gladstone was Chief Whip of the Liberal Party. Gladstone persuaded MacDonald that both of their parties were opposed to the Conservatives; he showed that they both depended on the same group of voters. If they split that vote, the Tories would win the general election whenever it came. So they agreed to let only one anti-Tory candidate stand. In some places the Liberal would withdraw; in other places Labour would withdraw its candidate. This would leave only one anti-Tory candidate who would get the joint support of the Labour and Liberal voters.

The 1906 Election

As a result of the pact the Labour Party did very well in the 1906 election. It put up fifty candidates, and won twenty-nine seats. In addition, there were twenty-four working men elected as Lib–Labs. By 1910 they had joined the Labour Party which now had fifty-three M.P.s.

During the next five years the Labour M.P.s persuaded the Liberal government to pass the Trades Disputes Act (1906) and the Trade Union Act (1913). These, as we have seen, affected the industrial and political powers of the trade unions (p. 164). In general, the Labour M.P.s supported the Liberal government's attempts to set up a Welfare State (Chapter 31), but many of them wanted to do more than the Liberals wished to do (Fig. 29.3). There were, by 1914, signs that the Labour M.P.s were going to become more than merely radical supporters of the Liberals. This would become clear in the 1920s (Chapters 36 and 38).

Questions

Extract 29.1

Housing conditions for the poor, 1883

The information does not refer to selected cases and there has been no exaggeration. This must be to every Christian heart a bitter cry, for the help of the Church.

You have to penetrate courts reeking with poisonous gases from the sewage and refuse scattered in all directions, courts never visited by a breath of fresh air. You ascend rotten staircases. You grope your way along dark and filthy passages swarming with vermin. Then you get to the dens in which thousands herd together. Eight feet square is the average size of very many rooms. Walls and ceilings are black with the accretions of filth which have gathered in the boards overhead; it is running down the walls; it is everywhere. A window is half stuffed with rags. You may discover a broken chair, a tottering old bedstead or the mere fragment of a table; but more commonly you find substitutes for these things in the shape of rough boards resting upon bricks, an old hamper or box turned upside down, or more frequently still, nothing but rubbish and rags.

(Rev. Andrew Mearns, *The Bitter Cry of Outcast London*, 1883.)

1. Why could the author of this extract claim that his description was one which could be applied to many areas?
2. Who, according to the author, should be appalled?
3. Why was there a danger of disease as a result of

Fig. 29.3 This cartoon entitled 'Forced Fellowship' comments on the fears of some Liberals that the Liberal Party might be forced to introduce radical policies because of the coalition with Labour.

conditions outside the houses?

4. What was the average size of a room? Compare this with the size of a room in your own home.

5. Why was there a danger of disease as a result of conditions inside the home?

6. Why were people forced to live in these conditions?

7. These slums would have to be cleared and new houses built. Why would this require (i) legislation (ii) a more active local authority (iii) increased taxation?

Extract 29.2

The birth of the Labour Party, 1900

The new movement did not begin well. At the end of the first year only 40 Trade Unions out of about 1,200 had affiliated, with a membership of 353,000. The great organizations of the miners and the textile workers looked on the new movement with suspicion and undisguised hostility. The first Annual Conference was held in Manchester in February 1901. I well remember the feeling of despondency which prevailed. . ..

During the previous year (1900) a General Election had taken place. Keir Hardie was again the solitary independent Labour member of the new Parliament. His return raised a financial problem for the National Council of the I.L.P. There was no payment of members from the National Exchequer in those days. . ..

Hardie had no private means. He was running *The Labour Leader*, but that was a burden rather than a source of income. I have a letter from him written to me at this time in which he puts his financial position frankly before me. He paid fourteen shillings a week for rooms in London, his food and other expenses he put at a pound a week, secretarial help and postage cost him fifteen shillings. In addition he had to provide for his home in Scotland, and for clothing and railway fares. To meet these necessary expenses, he was obliged to take meetings at week-ends and almost nightly during the Parliamentary recess. These were the circumstances of the first Independent Labour M.P.

(Philip, Viscount Snowden, *An Autobiography*, 1934, vol. I, pp. 93–5.)

1. When was the 'new movement' founded? What were its connections with (i) the I.L.P. (ii) the socialist societies?

2. What percentage of trade unions had affiliated to the party?

3. Explain the reluctance of other unions to join the movement.

4. When were M.P.s paid 'from the National Exchequer' for the first time? How much did they then receive? Why was this important for Labour M.P.s?

5. How did Hardie get the money he needed to live?

Fig. 29.3

1. Who was Prime Minister between 1908 and 1914?

2. Make a list of the ways in which his government helped the working class.

3. Why, according to this cartoon, had the Liberals passed laws to help the workers?

4. Was the Labour Party in a position to force the government to do as Labour wanted (i) between 1906 and 1910 (ii) after 1910? Explain your answers.

5. What did this artist think of the Labour Party? Explain your answer.

Worksheet

(A)

1. Make a list of the reasons for the rise of the Labour Party after 1867.

2. Explain the meaning of the term 'Lib–Lab'.

3. Why did George Bernard Shaw want the trade unions to help the new party?

4. Why and how did the T.U.C. change its attitude towards forming a Labour Party after 1889?

5. Why did the Labour Representation Committee grow stronger between 1901 and 1903?

6. Explain the meaning of and importance of the Electoral Pact, 1903.

(B)

1. Write the letters that might have been sent by:
(a) one of the poor on the subject of self-help (Extract 29.1 and Fig. 29.1 might help you to write this letter);
(b) a founder member of the I.L.P. on his activities;
(c) John Burns complaining of the T.U.C. refusal to support Hardie's party in the 1890s.

(C)

1. Write the headlines that might have appeared above reports on:
(a) the formation of the Labour Representation League, 1869;
(b) the election of MacDonald OR Burt in 1874;
(c) the formation of the Fabian Society, 1884;
(d) the formation of the I.L.P. in 1893;
(e) Hardie's election, 1892;
(f) the formation of the Labour Representation Committee, 1900.

2. Make a time chart and mark on it the principal events and dates noted in the text. Write a brief note explaining each of the events and dates you have chosen.

3. Draw or paint a poster that might have been used to advertise a meeting of one of the early socialist societies.

30 The Government and State Education, 1760 - 1914

Today's Schools

Today everyone has to go to school between the ages of 5 and 16. Many stay on at school after that, and a lot who leave at the age of 16 go to part-time courses at a Technical College or a College of Further Education to get extra qualifications in their craft or profession.

This was not always so, though. As we shall see in this chapter there was a time when the government played no part in the education of the country's children. Only those who could pay fees went to school. Throughout this chapter we will see why, when, and how the government became involved in the question of education.

Fee-paying Schools

These schools were, and still are, free from government control. There were the hundreds of boarding schools to which rich people sent their sons; the few boarding schools where the daughters of rich families went; and the thousands of small private day schools.

Fig. 30.1 A dame school painted in 1856.

Some were very good – Disraeli received his education at one (p. 119). But the majority were very poor schools where the children learned very little (Fig. 30.1).

Schools for the Poor

Many parents could not afford even the 1p or 2p charged by the local 'dame'. The Church of England and the other Churches provided some of these children with some schooling. In 1800 the Church of England had about 20,000 charity schools where children paid no fees. The money for these schools was given by the better-off members of the Church. They were willing to pay this because they hoped that the schools would teach the children to be good workers and servants (Extract 30.1).

The Methodists started Sunday schools, the only day on which most working children could get to any school. Robert Raikes, a factory owner in Gloucester, helped to spread the idea of Sunday schools, and by 1795 there were 295,000 such schools.

No Schooling

There was no training for teachers at the time, and so many children learned very little. But at least they had the chance to learn something: about three-quarters of the country's children never went to school at all in 1800. Their parents needed the small wage they could earn at work.

Monitorial Schools

In the 1790s two men working in different parts of the country thought of a new way of providing schools for the children of the poor. Andrew Bell was an Anglican vicar; Joseph Lancaster was a former Quaker. Both of them asked rich people to give money to build a large hall or schoolroom in which 500 or more children could sit. One teacher with the help of a few older pupils (or monitors) could teach all these children to read, write, do simple sums, and learn their scripture.

In 1811 the National Society was set up to help run the schools founded by Andrew Bell where all the pupils were taught the Anglican religion. In 1814 the British and Foreign Schools Society was set up to run the schools founded by Lancaster. In these schools religion was taught – but not the Anglican religion.

These two societies were called Voluntary Societies because the supporters of the societies provided the money freely or voluntarily.

The Government and the Schools

In 1805 and again in 1819 some M.P.s tried to get the government to give 25p a year for each child's schooling, but even this very small amount of money was too much for Parliament. Few M.P.s believed that taxpayers' money should be spent on children's schooling. Their attitude was if people would not help themselves then Parliament ought not to step in to help them.

1833–9

However, in 1833 Parliament decided to grant £20,000 to be divided between the two Voluntary Societies. When a Society could show that the people in a town had collected towards the setting up of a school, it could get some help from the government's grant. But if the people of a district were too poor to collect money, there would be no payment by the government. In 1839 the grant was increased to £30,000, and also in that year the government set up a Committee of the Privy Council to supervise the distribution of this money. The government sent out inspectors to examine the schools and to report on the education being given.

An Increasing Grant

After 1840, new Voluntary Societies were set up by Catholics, Jews, Wesleyans, and other religious groups. The two older and larger Societies set up many new schools. So the grant had to be increased: in 1846 it was £100,000, in 1857 it was over £541,000, and in 1860 it was over £2 million a year. In 1856 the government had set up an Education Department, supervised by a member of the Cabinet – a sign that education was becoming more important in the eyes of the government.

The Newcastle Commission, 1858–61

In 1858 Gladstone was the Chancellor of the Exchequer. He wanted to cut income tax which had risen because of the Crimean War, and he hoped also to cut the spending on education. Palmerston's government set up a Royal Commission on Education under the Duke of Newcastle. Commissioners were sent out to see what was happening in the schools which cost the government so much money.

The Commission published its report in 1861. It showed that many children did not go to school at all, and many others started at the age of 5, or 7, or 9 – whenever their parents could afford to let them go. Many of these left after a few months or a year or so – when a job became available; many went to school when the weather was fine but did not go when the weather was bad; and others stayed away for the whole summer – to earn money picking fruit or helping in harvesting.

It is not surprising, then, that the Commission claimed that the government was not getting value for money. However, it is perhaps surprising that the Commission should have wanted the schools to provide only a very elementary education. After all, by 1861 Britain was half-way through the second (or 'railway') stage of the Industrial Revolution, and needed a better-educated work-force.

Payment by Results, 1861

Palmerston appointed Robert Lowe to take charge of the Education Department. One of his first tasks was to set up a new way of paying the grant. The grant would now be paid only after the school had been visited by an Inspector who would examine the pupils in reading, writing, spelling, and arithmetic.

A school would get its money in two parts. There would be a grant of 20p each year for every child who was present on the day of the inspection. This meant that teachers tried to force children to attend on that day even if they were very ill. The Inspector would not accept the evidence of the register as proof that a child really existed and came to school.

That 20p was one-third of the possible grant. The other two-thirds, or 40p a year, was paid only for those pupils who passed the Inspector's examination. Since teachers' salaries depended on the size of the yearly grant, they gave most of their attention to making sure that the children were well prepared for the inspection. They did not bother about history, science, music, art, or other subjects that were not going to be examined. Lowe promised that his new system, or Revised Code, would lead to one of two things. The schools might become more efficient – and all the children would pass the examinations; in that case the grant would have to be increased. But if the schools did not teach the children properly, they would fail the examinations, and the grant would be lower. So, as Lowe said, the system would 'be either efficient . . . or cheap'.

W. E. Forster

In 1867 Parliament passed the second Reform Act (p. 155). Lowe had opposed Gladstone's proposals, but once the Act was passed, he argued that 'it will be necessary to educate our master' now that working men make up the majority of the voters. He argued that the government would have to spend more on education.

In 1870 Lowe was replaced by W. E. Forster. He realized that the country was falling behind in the industrial race, and Britain was not developing the new, science-based industries. One reason for this was that British workmen were not educated enough to work in such industries. Forster wanted to spend more on education.

The 1870 Education Act

In 1870 Forster persuaded Parliament to pass a very important Education Act. Under the terms of this Act the whole country was divided into about 2,500 school districts. A survey was to be made in each district to see whether there were enough places in Voluntary Schools for all the children between the ages of 5 and 11. If there were not enough the ratepayers of the district had to elect a School Board. This Board could collect a school rate, buy land, and build Board Schools. The religious teaching in these schools was the subject of long debate in the House of Commons. In the end Parliament accepted an amendment proposed by Mr Cowper-Temple. This stated that religious teaching in the Board Schools would not follow any particular Church's doctrine, and that the religious lesson was to be either the first in the morning or the last in the day. Parents could ask that their children be allowed not to attend these classes. School Boards were allowed to charge fees, but a Board could, if it wished, allow children to come in without paying if 'the parent is unable to pay the same'. Boards were allowed to make their own by-laws. They could, for example, make attendance compulsory from the age of 5, but few did so. Only in 1880 did the government make attendance compulsory. Fees were abolished in 1891 and the school leaving age was raised from 11 in 1893 to 12 in 1899.

After the 1870 Act

Forster's Act increased the grant paid to the Voluntary Societies which educated most of the country's children – even as late as 1890. But by 1900 the Societies found that their schools were not as well furnished as the local Board Schools. These had the school rate to provide the money needed for workshops, science laboratories, art rooms, and so on.

Some School Boards were very active. They forced unwilling children to come to school (Fig. 30.2), and they also helped the more ambitious and clever pupils, as we shall see.

County councils had been established in 1888. The government allowed these councils to provide technical schools. Money for these schools was paid by the Science and Art Department attached to the Museums in Kensington. The Board of Agriculture also gave a grant when a technical school provided agricultural science in its curriculum.

Some School Boards decided that the children in their schools ought to have a chance to do some of this higher work, and allowed children to stay on in higher-grade classes until they were 14. Some Boards even opened Higher Grade Schools. Money for these classes and schools came from the school rate and from the Science and Art Department.

Robert Morant

In 1898 Robert Morant was a junior Civil Servant in the Education Department. He had been a brilliant student at Oxford University and was one of the first men to enter the Civil Service after the reforms made by Gladstone (p. 115).

Morant was unhappy with the way in which the country's education system was organized. There were about 2,500 School Boards and 25,000 schools run by the various Voluntary Societies. The Education Department had to deal with all these Boards and schools.

There were also the county councils which were supposed to handle technical education – although some Boards did so as well. Separate from all these were the grammar schools which were still fee-paying schools over which the government had no control.

Morant wanted to abolish the School Boards, and to provide more money for the Voluntary Schools. He also wanted to make some link between the elementary schools, the technical schools, and the grammar schools.

Fig. 30.2 A London School Board truancy officer captures two boys who had stayed away from school.

The Cockerton Judgement, 1901

In 1899 the headmaster of the Camden School of Art disagreed with the way in which the London School Board was spending part of the school rate to pay for Higher Grade Schools. A government official, Cockerton, was sent to examine the Board's spending; he was advised by Morant. Cockerton claimed that the Board was acting illegally. The 1870 Act that set up the Boards stated that Boards could spend money only on elementary education.

This led to a court case. The judges decided that Cockerton was right, and that School Boards could not, legally, run higher-grade classes or Higher Grade Schools.

The 1902 Education Act

The Cockerton judgement weakened the position of the School Boards. They had, previously, opposed Morant's proposals for reform. Now they wanted an Act to put things right. The 1902 Act was piloted

through Parliament by A. J. Balfour who also became Prime Minister in 1902 (p. 145).

This Act abolished the School Boards set up in 1870. The 348 county councils and county borough councils were given responsibility for education. They became the local education authorities (L.E.A.s). The voluntary schools were to get their money from the new education authority in the counties and county boroughs and not from the Education Department.

The new L.E.A.s could, if they wished, build secondary schools. They could also, if they wanted, 'take over' any grammar schools in their area which asked to become a rate-aided school.

Nonconformists were very bitter because the Voluntary Schools – mainly Anglican and Catholic – would get help from the local rates. Some, led by a famous preacher, Dr Clifford, even refused to pay their rates. This Act helped to unite the Liberal Party which had been badly divided by the Boer War. We have already seen that it was further united by Chamberlain's tariff reform campaign in 1903 (p. 151).

The 1907 Act

The 1902 Act came too late to help a future Labour M.P., Herbert Morrison (Extract 30.2). Like millions of others he left school to find work when he was 13.

His parents could not afford the fees charged at the grammar schools and at the newly built county secondary schools. In 1907 Parliament passed an Act which said that one-quarter of all the places at county secondary schools had to be offered as free places for children from the councils' elementary schools (Fig. 30.3). This meant that there had to be an examination to choose the council school children who would be allowed to go free to the secondary school. This was the start of the 'eleven-plus'. We will see later that this system came in for a good deal of criticism, and after 1945 led to the development of the comprehensive school.

Questions

Extract 30.1

My plan of instruction is extremely simple and limited. They learn on weekdays such coarse work as may fit them for servants. I allow of no writing for the poor. My object is not to make fanatics, but to train up the lower classes in habits of industry and piety. I know of no way of teaching morals but by teaching principles; or of inculcating Christian principles without imparting a

175

good knowledge of Scripture. I own I have laboured this point diligently. The only books we use in teaching are two little tracts called 'Questions for the Mendip Schools', The Catechism, broken into short sentences, Spelling Books, Psalter, Common Prayer, Testament, Bible. The little ones repeat 'Watts' Hymns'. The collect is learned every Sunday. They generally learn the Sermon on the Mount with many other chapters and psalms.
(Hannah More, writing to the Bishop of Bath and Wells in 1801.)

1. Hannah More and other founders of charity schools were attacked as dangerous people during the French Revolutionary Wars. What word in this extract best shows that Hannah More was not a revolutionary?
2. What jobs were her pupils going to do when they left school?
3. Why did she not allow the children to learn to write?
4. What were the books she used to teach the children to read? Can you suggest why she used these books?
5. What was the main aim of Hannah More's schools?

Extract 30.2

Herbert Morrison leaves school, 1902

... My parents had a small house – the inevitable 'two down, three up' of the Victorian working-class dormitory areas of long rows of houses – in Brixton.

The Policeman's Household

It was a desirable job because the pay, by comparison with jobs open to him, was not too bad. It was also steady with one's future clearly mapped. There was a pension. In those days few of his class could expect as much.

My mother was an excellent cook. Our food was simple, but we did not really know what it was to go really hungry. In this perhaps we were more fortunate than many of our class and environment .... White bread, margarine, jam, potatoes and tea were the staple diet day in and day out of vast numbers of workers. Except for potatoes, these items were virtually worthless as sources of nutrition. Of these foods we had our share but we also had meat on some days.

Board School

My first school was the Stockwell Road Board School (now Stockwell L.C.C. Primary). This was one of the schools set up as a result of the famous Education Act of 1870 which took the exclusive responsibility of education from the Church and shared it with the School Boards. Education was not free; if parents had money they had to pay, though admittedly a quite nominal sum.

When I was about eleven I went to Lingham Street Church of England School because Stockwell Road was short of upper standards.

The time was coming, 1901, when my education was to be regarded as completed, so far as full-time schooling was concerned. Secondary education was hardly thought of by parents of my class and time ... Secondary education remained a privilege of the wealthy or aristocratic boy until after the Balfour Act of 1902 authorized local authorities to provide secondary education. This Act came into force after my fourteenth birthday some months before which avid discussion was taking place about how I should earn my living. The upshot of the discussions was that I should start to earn my living as an errand boy for my elder brother Harry, who had recently set himself up in business as a grocer. My wages were five shillings a week.
(Herbert Morrison, *An Autobiography*, 1960)

1. Why was a policeman's job 'desirable' in 1902? The policeman earned £1.50 a week. What does this tell you about the wages of many other people in the working class?
2. Why was Morrison 'more fortunate' than many of his friends?
3. Why did Morrison leave school in 1902?
4. Find out more about the career of Herbert Morrison. He became an important London county councillor and a member of Labour Cabinets. What does this tell you about the fairness of the educational system in 1902?

Fig. 30.3

1. Why was this lesson known as 'drill?' Can you say where the name came from?
2. During which lesson might you be asked to do exercises such as this? Ask your teacher why the name 'drill' was dropped in favour of the modern name.
3. Today you have to wear some special clothing for such exercises. Why did teachers not insist on this in 1900?
4. Why did class-rooms smell after lessons such as this? Look at Fig. 30.2. Why did teachers have to have lessons on (i) washing hands (ii) combing hair (iii) the dangers of spitting in public (iv) table manners? Why are such lessons not given in modern class-rooms?
5. Why did the drill-master have to insist on discipline during this lesson? Why do modern teachers allow children greater freedom?

Worksheet

(A)

1. Why did many children not go to school at all before 1870?

2. Why did many children only attend for part of the school year?

3. Write a brief note on EACH of the following: Sunday schools; Monitorial schools; the National Society; the British and Foreign Schools Society.

4. What were the Voluntary Societies? How did they get the money to build and maintain their schools?

5. Why was there an increase in government spending on elementary education between 1833 and 1860? Why did Lowe want to reform the system of paying grants?

6. Explain the system of payment by results.

7. Why did Forster bring in an Education Bill in 1870?

8. Why did Morant want a new Education Act in 1902?

9. Write a brief note on EACH of the following: the Cockerton judgement; L.E.A.s; Dr Clifford; the 1907 Education Act; the Dame School.

(B)

1. Write the letters that might have been sent by:
(a) a parent explaining a child's absence from school in (i) the summer time (ii) the winter time (iii) for a period of sickness;
(b) a teacher OR a pupil after the visit of the Inspector after 1862;
(c) a working-class child who has gone to a secondary (grammar) school in 1908.

(C)

1. Write the headlines that might have appeared above reports on:
(a) the opening of a new Voluntary School in the 1830s;
(b) Forster's Education Act;
(c) the 1902 Education Act;

2. Paint or draw the posters that might have been used:
(a) to advertise the election for a School Board;
(b) to advertise a Non-conformist protest meeting, 1902.

Fig. 30.3 A drill lesson in a Board School in London, 1906.

31 The Liberals and the Welfare State, 1906-14

The Election, 1906

In the 1906 election the Liberals won 377 seats, the Conservatives 157, the Irish Nationalists eighty-three, and the Labour Party with its allies had fifty-three.

During the election the Liberals used the issue of Chinese slavery (Fig. 31.1) to blacken the Conservative name, but they also promised to repeal the Education Act and to bring in some social reforms. Their leader, Campbell-Bannerman, appointed Henry Asquith to the post of Chancellor of the Exchequer. David Lloyd George, a young Welsh solicitor, became President of the Board of Trade. In 1908 the Prime Minister retired because of ill health, and Asquith became Prime Minister. Lloyd George became Chancellor and a former Tory M.P., Winston Churchill, went to the Board of Trade.

Helping Some Workers

In 1906 the government helped pass the *Workmen's Compensation Act*. It extended the terms of the 1897 Act to cover another 6 million workers (p. 143).

The *Trades Disputes Act* (1906) undid the damage done by the Taff Vale decision (p. 163).

In 1909 the government helped pass the *Trade Boards Act*. This set up government boards to fix the wages and working conditions for thousands of people who worked in their own homes. Tailoring, lace-making, and matchbox-making were industries that relied on the work done by women in their own homes. They did not get the protection of the Factory Acts, and most of them worked very long hours for very little pay. The 1909 Act was a major reform for these workers. In future the government boards would fix wages in these industries.

Helping the School Children

In 1906 Parliament passed the *School Meals Act*. Many parents were too poor to provide their children with a decent meal. The 1906 Act allowed L.E.A.s (p. 175) to collect a special rate to pay for a school

Fig. 31.1 A Liberal poster used during the 1906 election.

meals service to provide a meal for poor children.

In 1907 the government established the *Schools Medical Inspection Service*. Every L.E.A. had to employ doctors and nurses to inspect all school children at least once a year (Fig. 31.2). There would be a regular check on the children's health. The government hoped that this would lead to the

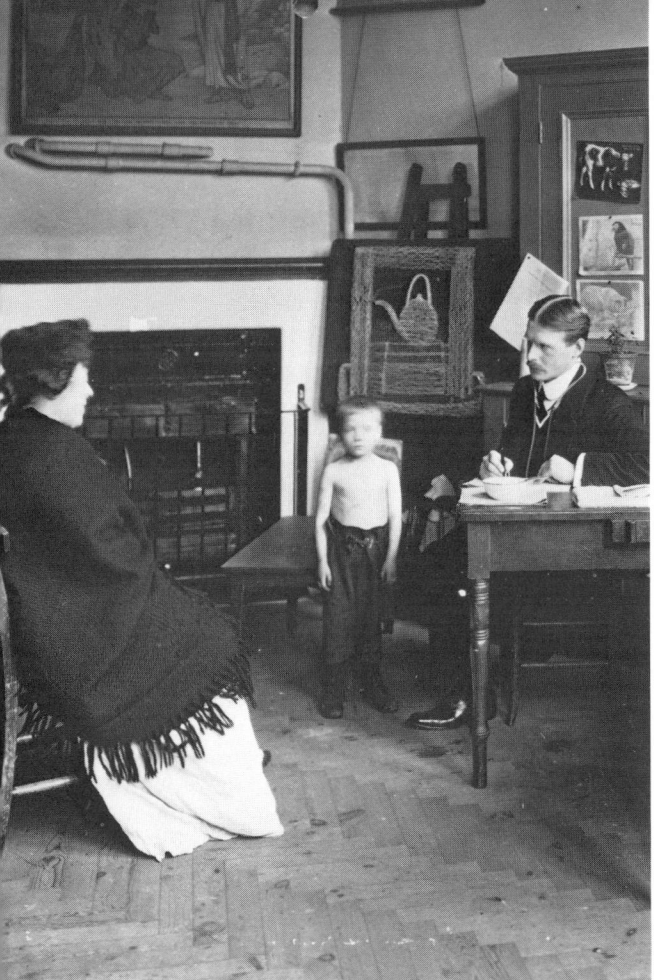

Fig. 31.2 A school medical inspection at Holland Street School, London, in 1911.

Helping Cleverer Children

The 1907 Education Act said that one-quarter of all places at county secondary schools had to be kept as free places for children who had been taught at elementary schools. This gave clever children from poor families a chance to get the sort of education that had only been available to children whose parents could afford to pay the fees charged in such schools.

Helping the Old

Old age was a major cause of poverty. Booth, Chamberlain, and others had suggested the paying of a government pension to old people (p. 151), and in the 1908 Budget, Asquith included a clause about old-age pensions. Lloyd George brought in an Old Age Pensions Bill. This provided for the government to pay a pension of 25p a week to everyone over the age of 70 unless their income was already higher than £21 a year (Extract 31.1 and Fig. 31.3).

Fig. 31.3 The first pension day, January 1909.

elimination of some of the diseases common at the time. The healthier children would then grow to become healthy workers and soldiers which the country needed.

Helping Older Children

The government supported a series of Acts aimed at helping children. One of these set up *Juvenile Courts*. In the past any child caught doing wrong was sent for trial at an ordinary court where magistrates and judges were used to dealing mainly with adults. The setting up of the Juvenile Courts allowed magistrates to take a fresh look at the way in which young offenders ought to be treated.

The government also introduced a Bill that limited the number of hours that a child could work after school hours or during a week-end. Other Acts made it illegal to sell alcohol, tobacco, and fireworks to children.

Labour Exchanges, 1909

The Balfour government had set up a Royal Commission to look into the working of the Poor Law, and in 1909 it published its report. This asked for great changes in Poor Law administration. It wanted to transfer the Poor Law relief from the Poor Law Guardians to the county councils. This did not take place until 1929 (chapter 35).

It also showed that a great deal of unemployment occurred among 'casual' workers, employed on a day-to-day basis. The report argued that the government ought to set up Labour Exchanges where employers could go and say what workers they wanted and the unemployed workers could find out what jobs were available.

In 1909 Churchill piloted a Labour Exchanges Act through Parliament. The first Exchanges were opened in 1910, and by 1914 they were filling over a million vacancies each year.

The House of Lords Versus the Liberal Majority

In 1906 Balfour said that 'the great Conservative Party should still control, either in Power or in Opposition, the destinies of this great Empire'. Even if the Liberals had a large majority in the Commons, the Conservatives would always have a majority in the Lords. The Lords would use their power to oppose Bills brought up from the Commons.

Of the 602 peers there were only 88 Liberals; the rest were Conservatives (355) or Liberal Unionists (124); and the remaining thirty-five included the bishops and royal princes. There were no Labour members of the Lords.

After the election, the House of Lords did as Balfour had promised. They threw out or greatly altered some Bills brought from the Commons, and rejected the Liberal Education Bill in 1906 and 1908. They also threw out a Licensing Bill which would have cut down the number of public houses in each town. They threw out Bills dealing with Irish town tenants, agricultural holdings, and plural voting. This last would have taken away a person's right to vote in every constituency where he owned property – something which favoured the Conservatives.

The Liberals Versus the House of Lords

In 1907 Campbell-Bannerman proposed that if a Bill passed through the Commons, it should become law within a year no matter what the Lords thought

about it. Balfour argued that this would be unfair. He claimed that the Lords was 'the watchdog of the constitution'; Lloyd George replied that it was really 'Mr Balfour's poodle' which barked when he told it to.

This resolution passed through the Commons by 432 votes to 147. But it was only a resolution and not a Bill, so it never went to the Lords. The Upper House continued to throw out Liberal Bills.

The voters began to turn against the government, and results in several by-elections showed a swing back to the Conservatives. Maybe this was due to the people's anger at the government's failure to do more? If so, then the Lords had to be challenged.

Lloyd George and New Liberalism

In 1908 Lloyd George became Chancellor. He wanted the Liberals to tackle the question of poverty, and argued that Gladstone's Liberalism, with its belief in self-help, had failed to cure the country's problems. He wanted a New Liberalism. This would need great increases in taxation and the growth of the part played by government in the social and economic life of the country.

If the Liberals did not tackle these problems then people would turn to support the Labour Party in the hope that it would do something radical.

The Budget, 1909

In 1908 Parliament passed the Old Age Pensions Act. These pensions had to be paid for out of increased taxation.

At the same time, the government ordered the building of eight new warships, and this also led to increased taxation.

So in 1909 the new Chancellor, Lloyd George, brought in a Budget which proposed to put up income tax, taxes on whisky and other drink, and to impose a new land tax.

The Budget was introduced into the Commons at the end of April 1909. Its proposals on taxation horrified the rich people of the country; their newspapers told them that they would be taxed out of existence. In the Commons the Conservatives kept the debate going until late in November – an unusually long time for a Budget to be debated.

On 30 November the Lords rejected it. It was the first time that the Lords had ever thrown out a Budget. Since the ordinary people, represented in the Commons, paid most of the taxes it had always seemed right that taxation – and the Budget – should be left to the Commons.

Election, January 1910

The government had no right to collect taxation once its Budget had been rejected, so an election had to be held. The Liberals campaigned on the issue of 'Commons versus Lords'. Was it right that a handful of men should hold the future of the country in their hands?

The result of the election pleased no one. The Liberals came back with 275 seats – they had lost about 100 of the seats they had won in 1906. The Conservatives had 273 seats – so they still could not form a government. The Labour Party had forty seats – losing a number of seats they had won in 1906. The Irish Nationalists got eighty-two seats.

The Budget Again

The Lords now allowed Lloyd George's Budget to pass, but this became a smaller issue in the much larger argument over the future of the Lords. Between 1910 and 1912 there was a long, bitter debate on this issue (Chapter 32).

The National Insurance Act 1911

Having defeated the Lords over the Budget issue, Lloyd George turned to the question of unemployment and sickness. We have seen that the older, craft unions paid their members when they were unemployed or off work because they were ill (p. 110). Other workmen took out policies with an insurance company or a Friendly Society which paid them when they were unemployed or sick.

Only the better-off workers could afford these weekly payments, but many of these had to stop paying when they were unemployed; this meant that they then lost all the money paid in over the years.

Lloyd George knew this. He proposed a National Insurance Scheme. This scheme had two parts:

Part 1 dealt with *Health Insurance*. All manual workers earning less than £160 a year had to be insured under this scheme. The workman, his employer, and the government paid into an Insurance Fund. In return for this weekly payment the workman could receive free medical attention from a doctor when ill. He would also get 10 shillings (50p) a week when off work owing to sickness for a period of not more than 26 weeks. After this he could claim a disablement pension of 5 shillings (25p) a week. The insured workman could also get free hospital treatment if he suffered from tuberculosis (or consumption) which was then a very common illness

among poorer people. His wife was entitled to claim £1.50 as a maternity benefit.

Notice that the Act did nothing for the workman's family – except for the maternity benefit. Nor did it say anything about hospital treatment – except for the tuberculosis patients. There was no mention about dentists or opticians. This Act was only a stepping stone towards the modern Welfare State.

Part 2 of the 1911 Act dealt with *Unemployment Insurance*. This only applied to workers in 'building construction, shipbuilding, mechanical engineering, ironfounding, and vehicle construction'. Every workman in these industries had to have an 'unemployment book'. Each week his employer put a 5d (about 2p) stamp in the book. Half this sum was paid by the insured workman.

The insured workman received a payment at the Labour Exchange when he was unemployed. The government intended that the Insurance Fund should always be self-financing; the benefits to the unemployed would be paid from the money paid in by the workers and employers. It was hoped that the government would never have to pay into this fund. We will see, though, that in the 1920s and 1930s this was never the case (Chapter 35).

Notice that this part of the Act covered only a small number of workmen. It also provided unemployment benefit for only a short period. What happened when the man was out of work for more than fifteen weeks? The Poor Law Guardians would then have to come to his help. Notice too that this part of the Act did not lead to more taxation. The Labour M.P.s in the Commons argued that the government ought to pay into the Insurance Fund as it was paying into the Health Fund, but Lloyd George and the Liberals would not go that far. They still had some of the old Liberal ideas of self-help, and this part of the Act was a government attempt to help men to help themselves.

The End of Reform

National Insurance was the Liberal government's last major reform. It passed the Trade Union Act in 1913 (p. 164), but after 1911 the government was heavily involved in the debate over the House of Lords and Ireland.

Questions

Extract 31.1

(A) The size of the pension

Means of Pensioner	Rate of Pension per week	
Where the yearly means of the pensioner as calculated under this Act:	s.	d.
Do not exceed £21	5.	0.
Exceed £21 but do not exceed £23.12s.6.	4.	0.
Exceed £23. 12s. 6d but do not exceed £26. 5s. 0d.	3.	0.
Exceed £26. 5s. 0d. but do not exceed £28. 7s. 6d.	2.	0.
Exceed £28. 7s. 6d. but do not exceed £31. 10s. 0d.	1.	0.
Exceed £31. 10s. 0d.	No pension	

[5p = 12d or 1s]

(B) The welcome for the pension

> There were one or two poorer couples, just holding on to their homes, but in daily fear of the workhouse. When . . . the Old Age Pensions began life was transformed for such aged cottagers. They were relieved of anxiety. They were suddenly rich. When they went to the Post Office to draw it, tears of gratitude would run down the cheeks of some, and they would say as they picked up their money 'God bless that Lord George!' (for they could not believe that one so powerful and munificent could be a plain 'Mr'), and 'God bless *you*, Miss!'
> (Flora Thompson, *Lark Rise to Candleford*, 1909.)

1. Why is this described as 'pensions on a sliding scale'?
2. On how much per week were old people expected to manage without a pension? What does this tell you about their standard of living?
3. Why were some old people 'in daily fear of the workhouse'? Why had they not saved for their old age? How do you explain their tears of gratitude?
4. Why was the payment of the pensions a break with the tradition of self-help? Make a list of Acts passed between 1906 and 1914 which also mark the break with that tradition.

Fig. 31.2

1. About half the men who volunteered for the Army during the Boer War were found to be unfit to serve. Why did this make the government take action about the health of the children? Why were the medical failures called 'the result of a century of industrial development'?
2. How would the school medical service help to improve the health of the future workmen and soldiers?
3. Why did this service lead to an increase in taxation and rates?

Worksheet

(A)
1. Make lists of the ways in which the Liberal government helped (i) children (ii) poor workers (iii) other workers (iv) the unemployed (v) trade unions.
2. Why and how did the House of Lords oppose the Liberal government (i) 1906–9 (ii) in 1909?
3. What were the major differences between Old Liberalism and New Liberalism?
4. Give TWO reasons for the increase in taxation in 1909.
5. Who gained by Part 1 of the National Insurance Act? List FOUR ways in which the modern National Health Service is an improvement on the 1911 Act.
6. Who benefited from Part 2 of the National Insurance Act?

(B)
1. Write the letters that might have been sent by:
(a) a sweated worker;
(b) a poor child after the passing of the Schools Meals Act (Fig. 29.1 on p. 166 and Fig. 30.2 on p. 175 might help you);
(c) a mother who has been to a medical inspection (Fig. 31.2);
(d) a worker who has used the Labour Exchange to find a job;
(e) a worker who has benefitted from EITHER Part 1 OR Part 2 of the National Insurance Act 1911.

(C)
1. Write the headlines that might have appeared above reports on:
(a) the serving of free school meals;
(b) the payment of the first old-age pensions;
(c) the opening of the local Labour Exchange;
(d) the rejection of the Budget by the Lords, 1909;
(e) the passing of the National Insurance Act 1911.

2. Draw or paint the posters that might have been used by ONE of the parties in the general elections of (i) 1906, OR (ii) 1910.

3. Make a time chart and mark on it the main events and dates noted in the text. Write a brief note explaining each of the events and dates you have chosen.

32 A Violent Society, 1910-14

The Danger of a Revolution?

In 1910 American newspapers told their readers of 'Revolution in England' (Extract 32.1). We know, today, that there was no such revolution. But the Americans were not the only ones who, in 1910, thought that the country was on the edge of one. Why did people think like this? What had gone wrong with Britain under the Liberals? Who were the people who were supposed to be organizing such a revolution?

The House of Lords, 1910-12

In November 1909 the House of Lords threw out Lloyd George's Budget (Chapter 31). After an election in January 1910 the Budget was passed through the Lords, but the Liberals wanted to make sure that the Lords would not be able to do this again.

In 1910 the Liberals had to rely on the votes of the eighty-two Irish M.P.s to get Bills through the Commons. The Irish Leader, John Redmond, told the Liberals that his M.P.s would only vote for the Liberals if the government promised them an Irish Home Rule Bill. The Liberals gave him this promise, but Redmond went a stage further. He knew that the Lords had thrown out Gladstone's Home Rule Bill in 1893, and therefore he wanted the government to bring in a Bill to curb the power of the Lords.

King Edward VII was unhappy at seeing the House of Lords in conflict with the Commons, and tried to get the leaders of both major parties and of both Houses to settle their differences. Unfortunately the experienced King died in May 1910, and his son became King George V. He held a series of conferences at Buckingham Palace, but these failed. The Lords and the Conservatives insisted that the Lords had to keep the power to throw out any Home Rule Bill.

The Prime Minister, Asquith, now asked for another election. He wanted British voters to show what they felt about the powers of the Lords. The election was held in December 1910 (Extract 32.1), and the result was almost the same as that in January. The Liberals lost one seat and the Conservatives gained one. The Irish M.P.s were now, if anything, even more important to the Liberals.

In 1911 the government brought in a Parliamentary Bill. This stated that the House of Lords would not be allowed to amend or reject any Bill dealing with taxation. Such Finance Bills were to be settled in the Commons alone; on other Bills, including, for example, a Home Rule Bill, the Lords would have only a delaying power. They could reject such a Bill when it came from the Commons, but if the Bill came to them in three successive sessions of Parliament then the Lords would have to allow it to pass. This, as we shall see, was very important in the case of the Irish Home Rule Bill.

Hedgers and Ditchers

The Parliament Bill was debated in the Lords in June 1911 and it seemed as if the Lords would throw it out. This is not surprising. Asquith then told Lord Lansdowne and Balfour that the King had agreed to create as many new Liberal Peers as would be needed to pass the Bill through a larger house of Lords.

The majority of the Lords did not want to see a large increase in the number of lords. This majority was prepared to do a deal with the government; they were nicknamed 'hedgers'. Lord Halsbury (Fig. 32.1) was the leader of a small number of 'ditchers' who were prepared to fight to the last ditch.

In the end the Bill passed the Lords by 131 votes to 114. Thirty-seven Conservative Lords voted with the government, and the majority of Lords did not vote at all. The Parliament Act 1911 took away some of the powers of the Lords, and the Commons was now seen to be the more important of the two Houses. This was an important step for parliamentary democracy.

The Irish Problem

In 1912 the government brought in an Irish Home Rule Bill. Although the Bill was rejected by the Lords in 1912, as a result of the Parliament Act of 1911 it would become law in 1914. The Irish had been right to insist on the Parliament Act as the price for supporting the Liberals.

But it was not going to be as simple as that. The vast majority of the Irish people were Catholics, but the majority of people in Ulster were non-Catholics. In 1912 the Protestants of Ulster did not want an Irish Parliament in Dublin, because the majority of M.P.s were bound to be Catholics. The Ulster Protestants were frightened that this Catholic Parliament would pass anti-Protestant laws.

Ulster and Civil War

In 1910 a Protestant lawyer M.P., Edward Carson, became leader of the Ulster Unionist Council.

Carson recruited 100,000 Protestants into the Ulster Volunteers. These were supplied with arms bought in Europe, and were trained by former soldiers in the British Army (Fig. 32.2). Carson also got 500,000 Ulstermen to sign the Ulster Covenant. This was a document that promised that 'under God' the Ulster Protestants would never surrender to Catholic government (Extract 32.2). If the Liberals went ahead with their plans, then Ulster would fight a war of independence.

Fig. 32.1 This cartoon was captioned: 'The Old Trojan'. Lord Lansdowne: 'Don't lug that infernal machine into the citadel. The thing's full of enemies.' Lord Halsbury: 'I know. That's where my heroism comes in.'

Fig. 32.2 Anti-Home Rule men drill in Belfast in September 1912. These men, who had signed the Covenant, were prepared to take up arms against Liberal proposals for Home Rule. ▼

The Conservatives and Ulster

It was bad enough to have the Ulster Protestants preparing to make civil war against the British government. It was even more alarming to find that the leaders of the Conservative Party came out in their support. Bonar Law made it clear that he would support the Ulstermen no matter what they did (Extract 32.2(A)).

The British Army and Ireland

Some Conservatives talked of trying to get the King to sack the Liberal government and to make himself a sort of dictator. Others used their power to get the government to make some changes in the Home Rule Bill. In March 1914 the Bill came before the Commons for the third time – having been rejected by the Lords in 1912 and 1913. Asquith agreed to try to help the Ulster Protestants, and he now included in the Bill a clause that said that the voters of any Irish county could vote to stay out of the new Ireland – but for only six years. Carson and the other leaders of Ulster did not think that this 'temporary reprieve' went far enough, but on the other hand, Redmond and the Nationalists thought that it went too far.

Then came the Army crisis. Part of the British Army was stationed in Ireland, and there was a very large Army base in the Curragh, near Dublin. If it came to a fight with Ulster, the soldiers in the Curragh could expect to be sent to fight against the Ulster Volunteers.

Many of these soldiers were Ulstermen. Most of the officers were supporters of the Conservative Party. Carson, Bonar Law and other leaders of the revolt against the Home Rule Bill met senior officers. These agreed to sign a letter saying that they would 'prefer to accept dismissal if ordered north' to fight against Ulster. Asquith sent his Secretary of State for War to see Brigadier Hough, the leader of the officers at the Curragh. Hough persuaded the minister to accept the demands of the officers – that the Army would not be used in Ulster. This meant that the government had no army to use if Ulster did rise in revolution (Extract 32.2(C)).

The 'Curragh Mutiny' was seen as a sign that the government's power had been broken. What sort of government was it when its own army refused to obey orders? Maybe it is easy to understand why Germany thought that Britain would not get involved if there was a war.

But the government went ahead with its plans for Home Rule. It had to, because it depended on Irish support in the House of Commons. The Irish Bill was passed through the Commons for the third time in September, but by then Britain was involved in the First World War. King George V suggested that the Irish Home Rule Act should not come into operation until the war had ended. So the problem was put off for the time being.

A Working-class Revolution?

From 1910 onwards the cost of living started to increase. This was a result mainly of a rise in import prices. At the same time there was also an increase in the level of unemployment. This was due mainly to the fall in world trade and a continual rise in the flow of foreign goods into the country. Even for men at work there was a decrease in wages. This, combined with the higher prices, meant a heavy drop in living standards.

This was the first such fall for about forty years. Men had become used to rising living standards, and had expected this rise to go on for ever. When standards fell, men fought hard to try to get them back to where they had been.

In 1910 there was a good deal of unrest in industry. There were many strikes, and these often led to violent clashes with the police or the Army (Fig. 32.3). An increasing number of workers joined trade unions in the hope that unions would help restore their living standards. By 1914 there were over 4 million members of trade unions.

Tillett helped to form the large nation-wide Transport Workers' Union. His union joined with the Railwaymen and the Miners in signing the document that drew the three very large unions into the Triple Alliance. As we shall see in Chapter 37, this was a working-class attempt to create a large group that might even take on and overthrow a government.

Mann, Tillett, and a miners' leader, A. J. Cook, wrote and talked about a new idea – syndicalism. This was the belief that the workers in an industry ought to be allowed to control it: miners should control mining, railwaymen should control the railways, and so on. The syndicalists would have deposed the old owners, the men who had put up the money to start off the industry. The syndicalists thought that the industries had grown because of the work done by the workers; they believed that the workers had 'earned' control of their industries.

It is not surprising that the Conservatives and many Liberals thought that the working class had grown too powerful, and some were afraid that British workers might try to take over the government of the country. This helps to explain why Churchill, once a reforming Liberal, became very critical of the working class's new attitude (Fig. 37.3 on p. 218).

Fig. 32.3 During the national transport strike of 1911 the government sent troops to protect policemen in Liverpool.

Violent Women

Unrest with the Lords, problems with national strikes (Fig. 32.3), and the fears of civil war in Ireland formed the background to this period. But perhaps the most surprising violence came from a group of women. We have seen (p. 158) that women had been trying to get Parliament to give them the vote since 1867. We also saw that Mrs Pankhurst formed the Women's Social and Political Union in 1903. The Union campaigned for 'votes for women' as did the older suffragist societies. But the campaign of the W.S.P.U. was a very violent one. Groups of women organized the smashing of windows in London's Oxford Street and Regent Street. Others chained themselves to the railings of Buckingham Palace and 10 Downing Street. One, Mrs Emily Davison, threw herself beneath the hoofs of the King's horse at the Epsom Derby in 1913.

Post-boxes were set on fire, pictures at galleries were slashed, the work of the Commons interrupted from public galleries, and political meetings interrupted by constant heckling.

The police used violent methods to try to break up demonstrations, and when some women were sent to gaol they were treated violently by the prison authorities. Many of them went on hunger strike to try to draw attention to their case. For a time the government ordered that such prisoners should be forcibly fed (Fig. 32.4). Liquid food was poured down tubes which were forced down throats or through nostrils. There was a public outcry at this, and so the government ordered that this had to stop. The authorities were afraid that there would be an even greater outcry if a hunger striker were to die, so when the prisoners became very weak they were released. Then when they had grown stronger at home they were rearrested under what became known as the Cat and Mouse Act.

While men were alarmed by the rise of trade union activity and by the nature of the Irish problem, they could argue that these were old problems. People had become used to them. But women had never behaved in this violent way before, and to many men, it seemed that such behaviour was unnatural. They refused to believe that women ought to be allowed an equal place in society, and they refused to believe that the W.S.P.U. represented the majority of women in Britain.

So, despite the efforts of the suffragettes, women did not get the vote – they had to wait until 1918 (p. 198).

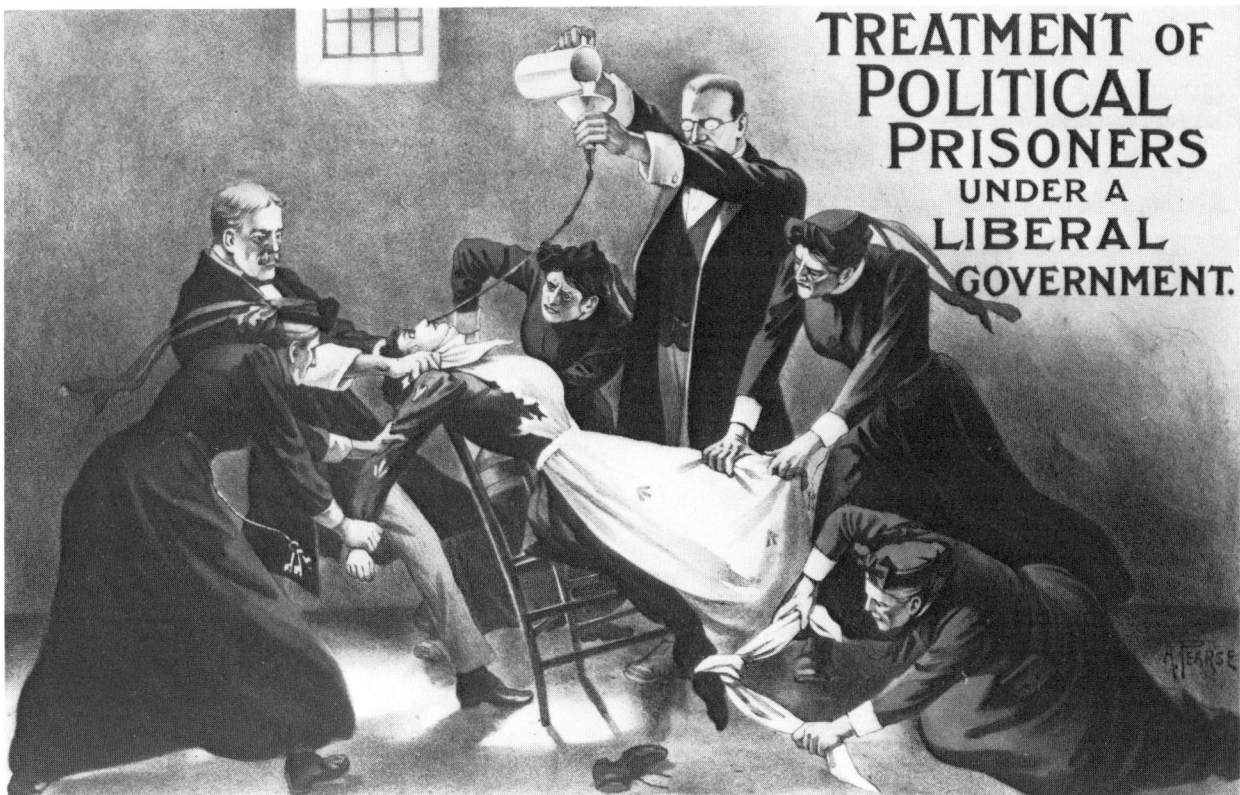

Fig. 32.4 A poster issued by the suffragettes to protest against forcible feeding of women on hunger strike in gaol.

Questions

Extract 32.1

Lords v. Commons, 1910

The Government lost no time in introducing a Parliament Bill. This Bill provided that the House of Lords would have no control at all over national finance; the House of Commons would have the last word in all matters of legislation. The maximum duration of Parliament would be reduced from seven years to five years.

In October my wife and I went to America to give a short series of lectures. We were in Pittsburg when the news came of the breakdown of the Conference and the Government's decision to dissolve Parliament. The American newspapers gave alarmist reports of the political crisis in England, and one evening newspaper in Pittsburg came out with a front-page scarehead in letters an inch deep: 'Revolution in England!'

When I emerged from the station at Blackburn the great square outside was packed by a dense crowd. . . . The route through the principal streets to the market-place was marked by scenes of unprecedented en-

thusiasm. . . . It was a great start for our election campaign, which a week later ended in a triumphant victory. This contest was fought exclusively on the House of Lords issue.

For the second time within twelve months the country had decided the issue of The Peers *versus* The People. The Liberals and Labour and the Nationalists combined had a majority of 126 over the Unionists.

(Philip Viscount Snowden, *An Autobiography*, 1934, vol. I, pp. 211–13.)

1. Make a list of the ways in which the powers of the House of Lords were to be limited by the Parliament Bill, 1910.
2. Why were the Liberals anxious that the Lords should have 'no control over national finance'?
3. Why did the Bill reduce the life of a Parliament from seven to five years?
4. Which organization had wanted each Parliament to last for only one year? Why did they want an election each year? Do you think this would be a good thing? Why?
5. Why was there a second election in 1910? What was the main issue at the second election? How did the result of that election affect the position of the Irish Nationalist Party?
6. Why did the Irish Party support the proposals in the Parliament Bill? What Act concerning the future

of Ireland was passed in 1912? Why was that Act 'safer' than Gladstone's Act in 1893?

Extract 32.2

(A) The Blenheim Pledge

Whilst I had still in the party a position of less responsibility than that which I have now, I said that if an attempt was made as part of a corrupt Parliamentary bargain, to deprive these men of their birthright, they would be justified in resisting by all means in their power including force.

I can imagine no length of resistance to which Ulster will go in which I shall not be ready to support them.
(Bonar Law, Speech at Blenheim, 27 July 1912.)

(B) The Ulster Covenant

We, men of Ulster . . . humbly relying on the God whom our fathers confidently trusted, pledge ourselves to stand by one another in defending our cherished possession of equal citizenship in the United Kingdom, and in using all means which may be found necessary to defeat the present conspiracy to set up a Home Rule Parliament in Ireland. And in the event of such a Parliament being forced upon us, we pledge ourselves to refuse to recognize its authority.
(*The Ulster Covenant*, 1912.)

(C) The Army mutiny

It may interest you to know that a very large number of officers all over Ireland resigned. I understand that a large body have consented to remain on, on condition that they are not expected to act in Ulster. I hear now that a large number of non-commissioned officers and men are saying that nothing will induce them to take sides against Ulster.
(Sir Edward Carson, Letter to Bonar Law, 23 March 1914.)

1. Who led the Tory Party before Bonar Law?
2. What did Bonar Law mean by 'a corrupt Parliamentary bargain'? Why had this 'bargain' been made?
3. Which 'men' were going to be deprived of their 'birthright'?
4. What was Bonar Law inviting these men to do? Do you think he should have made these suggestions?
5. Why did Ulstermen not want Home Rule for Ireland? How did Ulster differ from the rest of Ireland?
6. Why might the German Kaiser have welcomed the reports mentioned in Extract 32.2(C)?
7. 'Britain is ungovernable'. Why, if at all, was this true in 1914?

Fig. 32.1

1. Which group in the lords was led by (i) Lansdowne (ii) Halsbury?
2. Who wanted to bring new peers into the Lords? Why?
3. Who was King in 1911? When had he come to the throne?

Worksheet

(A)
1. Name FOUR groups of people who wanted great changes in this period. Explain briefly what each group wanted and why they became violent between 1910 and 1914.

2. Why were the Irish M.P.s in a stronger position in 1910 than they had been in 1909? How did they use that power (i) against the House of Lords (ii) to gain Home Rule for Ireland?

3. Using the following list of dates, show how the Ulster crisis developed in this period: 1910; 1911; 1912; 1914.

4. Why was there more militancy among the working class after 1910? Give TWO signs of it.

5. How did the government treat the suffragettes who (i) demonstrated (ii) were imprisoned?

(B)
1. Write the letters that might have been sent by:
(a) a Liberal explaining the 1911 Parliament Act;
(b) Lord Lansdowne, explaining why he persuaded most of the House of Lords to abstain in the vote on the 1911 Act;
(c) one of those who signed the Ulster Covenant;
(d) a Liberal protesting against Bonar Law's speech (Extract 32.2(A));
(e) a women prisoner.

(C)
1. Write the headlines that might have appeared above reports on:
(a) the passing of the Parliament Act 1911;
(b) the 'Curragh Mutiny' (Extract 32.2(C));
(c) a workman complaining of police action against strikers (see Fig. 32.3);
(d) a woman who has taken part in a demonstration.

2. Make a time chart and mark on it the principal events and dates noted in the text. Write a brief note explaining each of the events and dates.

3. Draw or paint the posters that might have been used to advertise:
(a) a meeting to be addressed by an Irish M.P., 1911;
(b) a meeting of Ulster Protestants, 1912.

33 Steps towards War, 1900-14

Britain and Europe 1800–1900

By 1900 Europe was divided into two opposing armed camps. In one were Germany, Austria, and Italy, and in the other were France and Russia. Britain was in neither camp, although she was more friendly to Germany than she was to Russia or France. But in 1914 Britain went to war alongside France and Russia and against Germany and Austria. Why did Britain become more friendly with her former enemies, France and Russia? Why did Britain become violently opposed to her former friend, Germany?

Bismarck and France, 1870–80

After he had defeated France in 1871 Bismarck wanted a long period of peace. He wanted to give German industry a chance to catch up with Britain. Bismarck had taken Alsace and Lorraine from France in the peace treaty of 1871, and this gave Germany very valuable coal and ironfields. Bismarck was afraid that France might try to get these back – by war if necessary. He was not afraid of France on her own, but he was afraid that another country might join with France in an anti-German alliance. This would have forced Germany to fight two powers at the same time. Bismarck did not want this to happen.

The Dreikaiser Bund or Three Emperors' League, 1872

In 1872 Bismarck persuaded the rulers of Russia and Austria to join the German Emperor in the Three Emperors' League. The rulers agreed that they would always be friendly towards each other; they also agreed to be on their guard against the spread of democratic and republican ideas from France.

It seemed as if Bismarck had succeeded in his aim of isolating France.

The Dual Alliance, 1879

But, as we have seen, Russia and Austria were rivals in the Balkans. They both wanted to get some gains as Turkey continued to crumble. In 1878 Bismarck supported Austria's claims – and so offended Russia (p. 127). In 1879 he went a stage further, and signed an alliance with Austria. This was an alliance that benefited Austria more than Germany.

This was a secret treaty. Russia did not know about it. This helps to explain why she was willing to sign a Reinsurance Treaty with Germany and Austria. This confirmed the agreement reached in the Three Emperors' League and was signed every three years – 1881, 1884 and 1887.

In 1882 Bismarck persuaded Italy to join Germany and Austria in the Triple Alliance. This made it even more certain that France would not be able to find an ally in Europe.

Russia and France, 1894

In 1888 a new, young and ambitious Kaiser came to the throne of Germany – Kaiser William II. He did not want to allow Bismarck to run things. The Kaiser wanted to be his own master. In 1890 he refused to sign the Reinsurance Treaty with Austria and Russia, and Bismarck resigned from office.

Now Russia felt that she was on her own, and on the other side of Europe, France was on her own.

The French government knew that Russia wanted to become an industrialized country, but Russia did not have the money to pay for the machinery and other goods she needed to build up her industry. So the French government made huge loans to the Russians (Fig. 33.1), and by 1894 politicians in both countries had become friendly enough to sign an alliance. They agreed to help each other if either was attacked by Germany or Austria. Europe was now divided into two armed camps.

Britain and the Alliances

Britain was more friendly to the Triple Alliance than

"WHAT WILL HE DO WITH IT?"

STARVING RUSSIAN PEASANT. "IS NONE OF THAT FOR *ME*, 'LITTLE FATHER'?"

Fig. 33.1 Look at the questions on this cartoon on page 194.

to the Dual Alliance of Russia and France. Russia was Britain's traditional enemy.

Britain's relations with France were no better. Indeed in 1898 the two countries almost came to war over the Sudan (p. 144).

Britain and Japan, 1902

In 1896 the German Kaiser had sent his congratulations to the Boers for having defeated the Jameson raiders (Extract 33.1 and p. 145). This annoyed British politicians, but it did not change British attitudes too much. Indeed in 1900 Chamberlain went to Germany to ask that both countries sign an alliance. He wanted to get German help against Russian expansion into Manchuria.

But the Germans were not interested, so the British turned to the Japanese. In 1902 the Anglo-Japanese Alliance was signed. This stated that if either country

was involved in a war with only one country, the other would remain neutral. But if either was involved in a war with two countries, then the ally would come into the war. In 1904 Russia and Japan went to war. France should have gone to the help of her ally, Russia, but she was afraid that if she did Britain would then come to the help of her ally, Japan. So France stayed out, and Japan defeated Russia.

Britain and Germany, 1900–4

The German Kaiser was driving Britain into the arms of France and Russia. He had annoyed people with his 'Kruger telegram' (Extract 33.1). Much more importantly he decided that his country should have a navy as large and powerful as the British Navy.

In 1897 he appointed Admiral Von Tirpitz as Minister of Marine. Between 1898 and 1908 Tirpitz persuaded the German Parliament to pass a series of Navy Bills. He and the Kaiser wanted to build a 'fleet so strong that Britain would be unable to challenge it without risk of losses that would threaten her position as the world's largest naval power'.

The British could see that Germany needed a large army. But what did Germany want with a large navy? To the British politicians the answer seemed very clear: Germany was going to attack Britain. She was already taking part of Britain's trade, now she was going to take her Empire.

The Naval Race, 1906–9

In 1906 Britain began to modernize her Navy, and a new type of battleship, the *Dreadnought*, was completed in 1907. This could outgun any ship afloat. The Germans announced that they were going to build their own *Dreadnoughts*. So there began a naval race. Both countries spent millions of pounds trying to keep ahead of the other; this of course increased the tension between them.

Britain and France, 1903–4

Lord Lansdowne was British Foreign Secretary in 1903. The French Foreign Minister was Delcassé. Both men realized that there was a good deal of anti-German feeling in their countries, and they both wanted to bring their two countries closer together.

In 1903 King Edward VII paid a state visit to France. This started off badly but ended in a great triumph, so the politicians took advantage of the sudden friendship to sign the *Entente Cordiale* in

1904. This was not an alliance; it said nothing about Germany. It was an attempt to make the two countries more friendly. France agreed that Britain should have a free hand to develop Egypt, and in return France had a free hand to take over Morocco.

A Crisis, 1905

The German Kaiser was annoyed at the signing of the *Entente*. In March 1905 he visited the Moroccan port of Tangier, and announced that Germany had a growing interest in Morocco. This was seen as a threat to French interests. Many people thought that the British would not support their friend if there was any danger of a clash with Germany over Morocco.

In January 1906 an international conference met at Algeciras to settle this Moroccan question. The Liberals were now in power. The Kaiser must have hoped that the new government would not back the *Entente* that had been signed by the Conservatives. But he was wrong. In Algeciras in North Africa France got what she wanted – control of the Moroccan police force and of the banking system. Germany got nothing.

In fact things took an even worse turn as far as Germany was concerned. Sir Edward Grey was the British Foreign Secretary. He agreed that army chiefs should have talks about the ways in which both countries would use their armies if a war broke out. These military talks did not make the *Entente* into an alliance, but they did change it from a mere settling of past differences over Egypt and Morocco (Extract 33.2).

Britain and Russia, 1907

In 1904 Russia had been defeated by Japan. Britain now realized that she did not have much to fear from Russia. On the other hand, the Kaiser seemed to go out of his way to rouse British fears about the future of the Balkans and the Middle East.

When he was visiting Damascus the Kaiser invited Muslim people everywhere to look to Germany as their friend and ally if they rose in revolt against their colonial masters. The British ruled over many Muslims in India, the French ruled millions in North Africa. This Damascus speech was seen as an anti-*Entente* move by the ambitious Kaiser.

Germany proposed the building of a railway from Berlin to Baghdad. Germany claimed that this was merely an attempt to help develop German trade, but Britain knew that such trade links often led to the growth of an Empire. The railway was seen as a German attempt to develop her own Empire in the

Fig. 33.2 The ageing Emperor of Austria seizing Bosnia and Herzegovina in 1908.

Middle East and threaten British power in India.

So Germany replaced Russia as Britain's 'bogey-man' in the Middle East, and in 1907 this was made clear. Sir Edward Grey signed an *Entente* with Russia. Russia agreed to keep out of Afghanistan and Tibet; and both countries divided Persia into two spheres of influence, agreeing to respect each other's rights in that country. This agreement made no mention of Germany or Austria.

Crisis No. 2, 1908

In 1908 the Austrians announced that they were going to annex Bosnia and Herzegovina which they had occupied since 1878. Serbia objected and appealed to the Russians. Germany announced that she would support Austria's move. Neither Britain nor France were willing to support Russia and Serbia, so Russia was unable to act. Austria had succeeded. On the other hand, Serbian anger grew, and this was to prove fatal in July 1914 (Fig. 33.2).

191

Haldane and the British Army

Lord Haldane was the British War Minister. He had agreed to the military talks between the French and British military staffs after 1906; he also reformed the British Army. He created a General Staff to take command of the Army, and set up an Expeditionary Force of six infantry divisions and one cavalry division. This was kept in a state of readiness to be sent to the Continent within a few days of the outbreak of war.

He also established the Territorial Army. This was made up of volunteers who met regularly to get some military training. They would be used as a defence for the home country when the regular Army was sent to fight abroad.

Haldane also encouraged British public schools to set up Officers' Training Corps, so that older pupils would get some military training while still at school. If war came they would be better prepared to become officers.

Crisis No. 3, 1911

In 1911 there were a number of uprisings in Morocco against the inefficient Sultan, so France sent an army to the capital, Fez, to restore order.

Germany thought that this showed that France was going to annex Morocco. The Kaiser claimed that German business interests in Morocco would be defended by German power, so he sent a small warship, the *Panther*, to the Moroccan port of Agadir.

This move alarmed Grey who thought that the Kaiser might try to develop a naval base on the African coast. As we have seen, the Liberal government was busy pushing through the National Insurance Bill (p. 181). The Chancellor, Lloyd George, wanted to spend money on social reform, and many people wondered what he would say about the Agadir crisis. Would he support Grey who wanted to stand up to Germany? Would he want to back down so that there would be no danger of war?

In July 1911 Lloyd George spoke at a dinner in the Mansion House, London, and made it clear that he backed Grey. The powers once again met in conference to settle this problem. The result was that France got a free hand in Morocco, and Germany withdrew the *Panther* and got some worthless strips of land in the Congo basin.

Anglo-French Naval Talks, 1912

Following this crisis the British War Minister and Foreign Secretary agreed to allow the naval chiefs of both countries to hold talks. In 1912 it was agreed that the British would take most of their warships out of the Mediterranean and increase the number of ships in the Atlantic and in the English Channel. The French took their ships from their northern ports and assumed responsibility for patrolling the Mediterranean. Here again the *Entente* became something more than an understanding; it came close to being an alliance (Extract 33.2).

Fig. 33.3a The Balkans in 1900.

Fig. 33.3b The Balkans in 1914.

The Balkans, 1912–13 (Fig. 33.3)

In 1912–13 there were two wars in the Balkans. One result of these wars was that Turkey was almost driven out of Europe; another was that Serbia grew much larger. This frightened Austria. On the other hand Serbia, having won two wars, wanted to challenge Austria – over Bosnia and Herzegovina.

June–July 1914

On 28 June 1914 the heir to the Austrian throne, Archduke Franz Ferdinand, was murdered in Sarajevo, the capital of Bosnia.

The Austrians claimed that the murder had been planned by secret societies based in Serbia, and so decided to punish the Serbs. The Kaiser promised to support Austria; his generals were willing to risk a war over this. They knew that in 1914 they could defeat both France and Russia. However, they were afraid that as time went on these two powers would get stronger and Germany would not be able to defeat them.

On 23 July Austria sent a series of demands to the Serb government. If the Serbs had accepted these demands, Serbia would have become an Austrian protectorate – as Morocco was a French protectorate after 1904. To make matters worse, the Austrians only gave the Serbs two days in which to give their answer.

On 24 July Serbia accepted most of the demands but asked for time to consider others. Austria refused, and on 25 July Russia announced that she would have to mobilize her forces in case they had to be sent to help Serbia.

On 28 July Austria declared war on Serbia, and Russia then ordered partial mobilization (30 July). Germany demanded that Russia should call off this mobilization, but Russia refused to do so. Germany declared war on Russia (1 August), and also on France.

Britain and the War

So far, Britain was not involved. Most of the ministers in the Liberal government wanted to stay out of the war, and most of them did not know about the military and naval talks. Grey told them about these talks and showed that the naval talks made it morally necessary for Britain to help France. However, no decision was taken on the 1st, 2nd or 3rd of August.

Germany's plans for the speedy defeat of France had been drawn up in 1900 by an army leader,

Schlieffen. He wanted a massive drive through Belgium, across northern France, around Paris, and back towards the German border.

On 2 August Germany asked the Belgian government to allow their troops to go through Belgium. Belgium refused, so on 3 August the Germans invaded Belgium. Since 1839 the British had insisted on the neutrality of Belgium, but this had now been broken by the invasion. On 3 August the King of Belgium appealed for British help and on 4 August Britain declared war on Germany. Huge cheering crowds surrounded Buckingham Palace, and there was a welcome for the war which people hoped would be over by Christmas. The poet, Rupert Brooke, wrote, 'Now God be thanked who has matched us with this hour'. Few people understood Grey who said: 'The lamps are going out all over Europe; we shall not see them lit again in our lifetime.'

Questions

Extract 33.1

The Kruger telegram, 1896

> I express my sincere congratulations that . . . without appealing for the help of friendly powers you have succeeded by your own energetic action against armed bands which invaded your country . . . and have thus been enabled to . . . safeguard the independence of the country against attacks from the outside.
> (Kaiser William II to President Kruger.)

1.   Which 'armed bands' had invaded 'your country' in 1895?
2.   What evidence is there in this extract that Germany might have sent an army to help the Boers?
3.   Why was Germany better fitted to send such an army in 1905 than in 1895?
5.   Why did this telegram increase British hostility to Germany?
5.   Who was Colonial Secretary in Britain in 1896? What had he hoped to arrange with Germany before 1895?

Extract 33.2

Anglo-French naval talks, 1911–12

> My dear Ambassador,
>   From time to time in recent years the French and British naval and military experts have consulted together. It has always been understood that such consultation does not restrict the freedom of either Government to decide at any future time whether or not

to assist the other by armed force. We have agreed that consultation between experts is not, and ought not to be regarded as an engagement that commits either Government to action in a contingency that has not arisen and may never arise. The disposition, for instance, of the French and British fleets respectively at the present moment is not based upon an engagement to co-operate in war.

I agree that, if either Government had grave reason to expect an unprovoked attack by a third Power, or something that threatened the general peace, it should immediately discuss with the other whether both Governments should act together to prevent aggression and to preserve peace, and, if so, what measures they would be prepared to take in common. If these measures involved action, the plan of the General Staffs would at once be taken into consideration, and the Governments would then decide what effect should be given to them.

Yours, etc.,
22 November 1912.   E. Grey.

1. When had Army 'experts' had their first con-sultations? Which crisis led to the holding of such consultations?
2. When had 'naval' 'experts' held similar con-sultations? Which crisis had led to the holding of such consultations?
3. Say briefly what were the results of these 'naval and military' consultations for (i) the British Army, and (ii) the British Navy.
4. How did these consultations change the nature of the *Entente Cordiale*?
5. What was the meaning of the 'disposition . . . of the French and British fleets. . . .'?
6. Why did Britain have a moral obligation to side with France in July 1914? Why did she not enter the war at the same time as France?

Fig. 33.1

1. Which country had (i) given these loans (ii) taken the loans?
2. Why did the second country want the money?
3. How does this compare with the loans given by Britain to foreign countries?
4. What does the cartoonist suggest he might 'do with it'? Why did this increase British fears of both the countries involved in this deal?

Worksheet

(A)
1. Why did Austria want an alliance in 1879? Why did she gain more from the alliance than Germany?

2. Why and where was Britain opposed to (i) France in Africa (ii) Russia in the Far East in 1900?

3. Make a small time chart and mark on it the steps by which the enmity between Britain and Germany grew between 1896 and 1914.

4. What did (i) Britain, and (ii) Japan gain from the 1902 Alliance?

5. What were the differences between an alliance and an *Entente*? Show how and why the nature of the Anglo-French *Entente* changed after 1904.

6. Explain the crisis in Morocco in (i) 1905, and (ii) 1911. Which of these was the more serious? Why?

7. Write a brief note on EACH of the following: the British Expeditionary Force; the Territorial Army; the *Dreadnought*.

8. Make a diary-type list to show how the world drifted into war after the murder of the Archduke at Sarajevo.

(B)
1. Write the letters that might have been sent by:
(a) a German complaining of the failure to sign the Reinsurance Treaty, 1890;
(b) a British merchant trading in China after the signing of the 1902 Alliance;
(c) a British M.P. complaining of the building of a German navy;
(d) a British M.P. explaining the significance of the talks between the French and British military and naval chiefs (Extract 33.2).

(C)
1. Write the headlines that might have appeared above reports on:
(a) the signing of the Franco–Russian Alliance;
(b) the arrival of the Kruger telegram (Extract 33.1);
(c) the signing of the Anglo–Japanese Alliance;
(d) the publication of the German Navy Bills;
(e) the signing of the 1904 *Entente*;
(f) the signing of the Anglo–Russian *Entente*;
(g) the crisis of 1911;
(h) the murder at Sarajevo;
(i) the invasion of Belgium;
(j) the declaration of war by Britain.

2. Make a time chart and mark on it the principal events and dates noted in the text. Write a brief note explaining each of the events and dates you have chosen.

3. Draw or paint a poster that might have been used by British recruiting offices in 1914.

34 The First World War, 1914-18

Mons, August 1914

The Germans hoped to knock France out in a quick campaign. Under the Schlieffen plan seven German armies drove through Belgium and into northern France. On Schlieffen's timetable they were to link up with German armies at Strasbourg within forty-four days.

But within days of the declaration of war the British Expeditionary Force was in Belgium. It was commanded by Sir John French. About 100,000 British soldiers had their first taste of battle at Mons. Their rifle fire was so rapid that the Germans believed that each battalion had about twenty-eight machine-guns – whereas in fact they had only two. The German advance was delayed, but at a high price. The Cheshire Regiment for example went into Mons with twenty-seven officers and 1,007 men. When the Battle of Mons ended in September only six officers and twenty-nine men were left alive.

Ypres, September 1914

The Germans drove the British from Mons, but there was another stand at Ypres. Here the commander was Sir Douglas Haig. Once again the British kept the much larger German army at bay. French roused the men by telling them that the Kaiser had referred to his 'contemptible little army'.

The Battle of the Marne

The German timetable had been interrupted. Meanwhile the Russians had mobilized quickly, and so the German commander, Von Moltke, took men from France to reinforce the troops facing the Russians.

The German commander in France, Von Kluck, gave up the Schlieffen plan. He cut across northern France, and hoped to reach the River Marne which was only a few miles from Paris. The British Commander, Sir John French, and the French Commander, Marshall Joffre, led their armies into the Battle of the Marne.

Troops were rushed back from Alsace and Lorraine. An army was raised in Paris itself and taken to the front in taxis and omnibuses. The Germans were driven across the River Aisne. Paris had been saved. There now began that long period of trench warfare.

Trench War 1914–18

We know a good deal about life in the trenches from the writings of former soldiers (Extract 34.1). These trenches were strengthened by wide barriers of barbed wire and sandbags. The defenders always had the advantage in trench warfare; the attackers were weighed down with heavy packs on their backs, trenching tools at the sides, ammunition bandoleers, and a few Mills bombs. Having slithered through the mud of the 'No-Man's Land' between the two lines of trenches the attackers then had to clamber through the barbed wire and make their way over the last few yards to the enemy trench.

All the time the defenders were riddling the advancing lines with machine-gun fire. The few who got through the wire were picked off by rifle fire or were killed in hand to hand battle in the trenches (Fig. 34.1).

Still the commanders on both sides insisted that their men were to attack. There were large-scale attacks on the Somme (1916) and Loos (1916), at Messines, Vimy Ridge, and Cambrai in 1917, and at St Quentin in 1918.

On the first day of the Battle of the Somme (1 July 1916) over 60,000 men were killed out of a British force of 100,000. Many others were seriously wounded and yet more simply drowned in the mud.

By the time Haig called off the offensive the British had suffered 400,000 casualties. This was, in Churchill's words, 'the graveyard of Kitchener's army' of volunteers. German and French losses were equally great before the Battle ended in heavy snow on 17 November 1916.

Weapons

The machine-gun was a great advance on the rifle,

and gave the defenders a great advantage over the attackers. The Germans used poison gas in 1915: modern science made warfare even more terrible than it had been. The British developed a new weapon – tanks that travelled at about 3 miles (5 kilometres) an hour. They were first used at the Somme in 1916, but most of them got bogged down in the mud while others were destroyed by enemy artillery. Only four did any real damage, but even these were captured by the Germans when they got too far ahead of the rest of the Army. However, by late 1917 and 1918 the tank proved to be a very effective weapon.

Both sides also used aircraft. At first the aircraft had open cockpits and were made of canvas stretched over wooden frames. Their engines were small – managing to get the planes to a speed of only about 50 miles (80 kilometres) an hour. They had very limited range and no weapons. Pilots carried a few bombs on the floor of the cockpit, and tossed these over the sides when they saw enemy troops or convoys (Fig. 34.2).

By the end of the war there had been a great development in aircraft building. Some planes had four engines, and had a much longer range. The Germans had been the first to work out how to fire a machine-gun through the revolving propeller when they fitted a Fokker E1 with interrupter gear in 1915, but by 1916 the British and French had also learned how to do this. Despite these advances, the aeroplane played a very small part in the First World War.

War on Other Fronts

In October 1914 Turkey came into the war on Germany's side. This closed the route through which the British and French might have sent help to the Russians. In March 1915 a fleet of old battleships was sent to try to get through the Dardanelles. Several of the ships were sunk by mines, and the plan to capture Constantinople was abandoned.

Plans were now drawn up for an attack on Gallipoli to take Constantinople from the rear. But this was a disaster. Too few men were sent, and the Army Commander, Sir Ian Hamilton, delayed his attack. The Turks had plenty of time to prepare their defences. The British, Australian, and New Zealand forces landed in April 1915, but the Turks, led by Mustapha Kemal, a German-trained officer, had the advantage of being up on the hills. The Allied troops did not get far from the beaches.

Fig. 34.1 (top) British soldiers off duty in a front-line trench, 1916.

Fig. 34.2 (below) Captain Hawker won a V.C. for shooting down two German aeroplanes and driving off a third on 25 July 1915.

Winston Churchill had argued strongly for this attack, and when it failed he was sacked from the Cabinet. In December 1915 and January 1916 the remaining Allied forces were brought off the beaches; Turkey had kept the Allies out. In November Bulgaria joined the war on Germany's side, and this led to the defeat of Serbia. The Allies kept 600,000 men at Salonika in northern Greece as a sign that they had not abandoned the Eastern Front, but this force suffered from shortages of food and other supplies. Many men died from malaria.

British forces were also involved in desert campaigns against Turkey. The Palestine campaign was aimed at preventing Turkey from invading Egypt, and the advance into Mesopotamia from the Persian Gulf was meant to protect Britain's oil supplies. In 1916 the Turks defeated the British at Kut-el-Amara. But in 1917 the British captured Baghdad. In Palestine General Allenby captured Jerusalem in December 1917 and in September 1918 made a triumphal entry into Damascus.

The War at Sea

There were very few naval battles during this war. The two fleets did meet in the Battle of Jutland in May 1916, but after a day's fighting the Germans withdrew. They claimed the victory because they had lost fewer men and ships. However, the British also claimed victory because the German fleet withdrew through the Kiel Canal and never sailed again.

The Germans used submarines (or U-boats) to attack British merchant shipping, and in February 1917 the Germans announced a campaign of unrestricted submarine warfare (Extract 34.2). Two hundred and sixty-six British ships were sunk in February, 338 in March, and 430 in April. Supplies ran low – there was only six weeks' supply of corn left in Britain at the end of April 1917.

The government then forced the unwilling naval chiefs to agree to a system of convoys. Naval ships were to protect merchant ships by sailing in groups. This led to fewer losses. By May 1918 the German U-boats were suffering heavy losses as the armed naval vessels attacked them (Extract 34.2).

The End of the War

In April 1917 the Americans entered the war, and this brought fresh troops into the fighting.

The submarine campaign had failed to starve out Britain, but the British naval blockade had led to great shortages of food and other supplies in Germany. The German Commander, Ludendorff, knew in the winter of 1917–18 that Germany would crumble if he did not win a quick victory.

In March 1918 he ordered a series of thrusts. First these were aimed at British forces who fought a number of battles around Arras and Amiens. Then in April the German attack switched to the north. Once again the Flanders fields around Ypres were the scene of great slaughter. By the end of April this attack had been halted. The Germans then switched to the Aisne Valley, and here they defeated the French. As in 1914, they made their way to the Marne and the roads to Paris. The fresh American troops were thrown into battle to defend Paris.

Then on 18 July Foch, the Supreme Commander of Allied forces, ordered a counter attack. Tanks rolled, artillery blasted, and aircraft bombed German lines. The Germans broke – for the first time. In August the British defeated the Germans at Amiens – 'the blackest day in the history of the German army,' said Ludendorff. By the end of September the whole of the Allied line was advancing, and on 4th October the German commanders asked for a truce. The Allied reply was the Fourteen Points on which the American President hoped to reshape the world.

The Germans refused to accept these terms, and Ludendorff resigned. The Allies pressed on, and on 9 November the Kaiser gave up his throne. German politicians declared their country a republic. These politicians accepted the terms of the Armistice which ended the fighting at 11 a.m. on 11 November 1918.

The Workers at Home and the War

The war was an important period for the development of the trade union movement. Trade union leaders and workers gave their support to winning the war, and many unions gave up their right to strike. Others agreed to allow unskilled workers, including women, to do work previously only done by skilled men. This 'dilution' was essential if the country was to produce enough munitions.

Trade unionists were also called in to help the government. John Hodge, the Secretary of the Smelters' Union, became Minister for Labour in 1916. G. N. Barnes, Secretary of the Engineers' Union, became Minister for Pensions. Thousands of union members were involved in the 2,000 or so national and local committees set up to help the war effort. This experience was important. It developed trade unions' own self-respect. It also showed other people that unions and their members were as loyal as anyone else.

Standards of Living

During the war millions of homes had higher incomes

than they had had in 1913. High wages were paid to workers and millions of women found well-paid jobs in factories and workshops (Fig. 34.3). There was no unemployment. Many families ate more nutritious and more varied food; they were able to afford better clothes. Reports from school medical inspections speak of an improvement in the condition of the nation's children between 1914 and 1918.

The Government and Industry

In 1916 and 1917 the submarine campaign led to food shortages in Britain, and so the government passed the Corn Production Act (1917) which guaranteed farmers a price for their crops. Farmers ploughed up land that had been left unworked since the 1870s, and by 1918 there was a rise of 50 per cent in British food production.

The government wanted British factories to produce millions of guns, bullets, and shells, so it bought new machinery from America. This was installed in some old factories and in hundreds of new ones. For the first time British workers learned to use mass production methods – and Britain entered another stage of her industrial development.

The government wanted to make sure that the country's mines produced enough coal and that the country's railways could carry all the goods needed to further the war effort. So during the war the government took control of the railways and coal industry. This was a far cry from the Old Liberalism of the Gladstone period.

The War and the Labour Party

In August 1914 Hardie had addressed an anti-war rally in Trafalgar Square (Fig. 29.2 on p. 168), but once Belgium had been invaded the mood of the party changed. Hardie was shouted down in his own constituency when he spoke against the war effort, and MacDonald, another anti-war leader, resigned from the post of Chairman of the party. Arthur Henderson became leader. In May 1915 he was invited into the Cabinet where he was joined in 1916 by Hodge and Barnes.

There was a growth in the number of members in trade unions – and the Labour Party grew richer. In 1918 the Representation of the People Act gave the vote to all men over the age of 21 and all women over the age of 30. This gave the vote to millions of men and women from the working class. The Labour Party could hope to get their support in future elections.

The War and the Liberals

When the government declared war on Germany, John Morley resigned from the Cabinet. He and several other Liberals believed that war was wrong. Other members of the party did not go that far, but many of them did not agree that the government had to take control of coal and railway industries; they did not want the government to interfere with the industrialists running the engineering industry; they did not think that the government ought to guarantee prices to farmers.

So there were great strains in the Liberal Party in 1914 and 1915. These strains were revealed by the long debate over recruitment for the Army. At first Kitchener had relied on volunteers, but the slaughters of 1914 and 1915 soon proved too much for this voluntary system.

Generals wanted even more men to throw into battle. Where were they to come from? Between June 1915 and May 1916 Parliament debated this issue. At the end it was agreed that every man between the ages of 18 and 40 had to register for service; millions of men were conscripted into the services. Twenty-seven Liberal M.P.s voted against this interference with a man's freedom.

There was an equally long and bitter debate over munitions. The generals called for more shells and guns, but industry was not producing them in 1914 and 1915. In August 1914 Lloyd George became Minister of Munitions, and he was responsible for the Munitions of War Act 1915.

This gave the government the right to limit the profits made by industrialists; many factories were taken over and new government-owned factories were built. The results were good – the guns and shells were delivered. But many Liberals disagreed with this industrial policy.

Asquith's Fall

In May 1915 Asquith asked the Conservatives to join the Liberals in a Coalition government. By December 1916 many of these Conservatives were not satisfied with the way in which Asquith was running the war. Lloyd George asked Asquith to set up a small War Cabinet of four members to run the war, but Asquith refused, and Lloyd George resigned. On 5 December Asquith also resigned and suggested to the King that he should ask Bonar Law to form a government. Law refused to do so, and the King then sent for Lloyd George who became Prime Minister in December 1916.

The Maurice Debate, April 1918

In April 1918 there was a debate on whether Lloyd George's government was doing enough to help the soldiers fighting on the Western Front. Some generals wanted even more men and material. General Sir Frederick Maurice wrote a letter to the *Morning Post* in which he accused Lloyd George of 'starving the Front of the men and material needed'. Lloyd George defended himself by quoting figures supplied to the government by Sir Frederick Maurice himself. Many Liberals voted against Lloyd George – because of the way he had overthrown Asquith. But the Conservatives voted for Lloyd George who won the debate.

The Coupon Election

As soon as the war ended in November Lloyd George decided to call an immediate election. He sent out a letter to every candidate he supported. Asquith called this a 'coupon'. It is because of this that the Election has become known as the Coupon Election. Not one of those who had voted against him in the Maurice Debate got this support. In the feverish mood of the time most candidates supported by Lloyd George won and Asquith's followers were heavily defeated. After the election there were 338 Conservatives and 140 Lloyd George Liberals on the Coalition side. On the other side, there were fifty-nine Labour M.P.s and twenty-seven Asquithian Liberals. For the first time Labour was the official Opposition. For the last time a Liberal was Prime Minister.

How to Use the Government's Power

During the war the government had got new powers over industrialists and farmers, and over coal, railways, and munitions industries. In 1918 the government brought in a system of food rationing – so that it controlled the amount of some foods that people might buy.

In the period 1914–18 the government had spent about £7 million every day on fighting the war. This had led to a large increase in taxation – and without any of the fuss that had surrounded the 1909 Budget.

How would governments behave after the war? How would politicians use the powers they had enjoyed during the war years? Would they agree with the Labour Party and 'make a war on poverty'? Or would they give up their powers, sack their Civil Servants, and bring taxation levels back to their pre-war levels?

What about the people? What would they want? Having enjoyed a rise in living standards between

1914 and 1918 would they go back to the lower standards of 1913? Would women give up their newly won freedom?

In 1917 and 1918 Lloyd George had asked for working-class support so that the country could be saved. In return he had promised to build a country 'fit for heroes to live in'. Would he be able to produce such a country? Was this only a wartime promise, to be forgotten once the war ended? These were some of the questions that faced the country in 1919.

Questions

Extract 34.1

In the trenches 1916

A good trench was about six foot deep, so that a man could walk in safety from rifle-fire. In each bay of the trench we constructed fire-steps about two feet higher than the bottom of the trench, which enabled us to stand head and shoulders above the parapet. During the day we would snatch an hour's sleep, on a wet and muddy fire-step, wet through to the skin ourselves.

If anyone had to go to the company on our right he had to walk through thirty yards of waterlogged trench which was chest-deep in water in some places . . . .

The duckboard track was constantly shelled, and in places a hundred yards of it had been blown to smithereens. It was better to keep off the track when walking back and forth, but then a man had to make his way sometimes through very heavy mud.

(Frank Richards, *Old Soldiers Never Die* (Faber, 1964), pp. 58–60, 269.)

1. Why was the trench six foot deep? Why did the men make a fire-step?
2. Why, even during the summer, might it be 'wet and muddy'?
3. Why did artillery-shelling make 'a bog of mud'? How did this affect the chances of the attackers? How did it affect the comfort of the defenders?

Extract 34.2

Submarine warfare, 1916–18

At first they relied on cruisers and mines and other established methods of attack on our Mercantile Marine . . . . When the last roving cruiser had been beached, the German Admiralty put more faith in the little swordfish which had already destroyed more enemy ships in a month than the cruisers had succeeded in sinking during the whole of their glorious but short-lived career. When they realised the power of this invention they set about building submarines on a greater scale and constructing much larger types . . . .

By the end of 1916 British shipping destroyed by enemy action – mainly by submarines – amounted to 738 vessels, with a tonnage of over 2,300,000 tons, nearly one-fifth of the total British tonnage existing at the outbreak of the War . . . . No wonder we thought we could not continue the war much longer. And in spite of these persistent and heavy losses no counter measures had been prepared to exercise any restraining effect . . . .

As soon as the new Administration was formed in December 1916 the submarine problem was one of the first we took in hand . . . . We considered several suggestions for coping with the situation: (1) the institution of a regular system of convoys for all the merchant shipping from the moment it reached the danger zones . . . (7) a considerable increase in home supplies of food, timber and ore – coupled with a reduction in consumption.

(David Lloyd George, *War Memoirs* (Ivor Nicolson and Watson, 1933).)

1. Why did the Germans attack 'our Mercantile Marine'? What did they hope to achieve by these attacks? How far were they successful?
2. List three ways in which they made their attacks. Which was the most successful? Can you suggest why?
3. What was meant by 'convoys'? Why did the Admiralty oppose this system?
4. Why did the U-boat campaign lead to a shortage of food in Britain?
5. Why was there an expansion of British agriculture?
6. Why did the government bring in a system of food rationing? Do you think this is a fair system? Why? Why did many working people have a better diet during the war than they had in peacetime?

Fig. 34.3

1. Why did the government welcome the entry of women into industry during the war? Why were there not enough men to do the work that had to be done?
2. How did the increase in the number of women workers affect the incomes of some families? Why did many families have a higher standard of living during the war than they had had in peacetime?
3. How did having a job affect the pride and self-confidence of many single girls? Why was the idea of going to work a great change for middle-class girls but not for girls from working-class families?

Worksheet

(A)
1. Write a brief note on EACH of the following: Mons; the Schlieffen plan; the Marne 1914.

2. Why were few attacks successful between 1915 and 1918?

3. Write a brief note on EACH of the following: The Somme; the tank; the convoy system.

4. Explain how and why aeroplanes became stronger and more powerful between 1914 and 1918. What was the achievement of Alcock and Whitten-Brown in 1919?

5. Why did the British attack at Gallipoli? Why did the attack fail?

6. How do you account for Germany's initial success and her defeat in 1918?

7. Why was there an expansion of food production in Britain during the war? Why did the government introduce a system of food rationing?

8. Make a list of the ways in which the war put a strain on the Liberal Party.

9. Why was there an improvement in children's health during the war? In what ways could this improvement be shown?

(B)
1. Write the letters that might have been sent by:
(a) a soldier fighting at (i) Mons, 1914 (ii) the Somme, 1916 (iii) the Front in September 1918;
(b) a woman who has gone to work EITHER in a munitions factory OR on a farm;
(c) a Liberal M.P. who was angry at Asquith's fall from power in 1916;
(d) a mother whose son is in the Navy when she hears about the end of the war.

(C)
1. Make a time chart and mark on it the principal events and dates noted in the text. Write a brief note explaining each of the events and dates you have chosen.

2. Draw or paint a poster that might have been used to advertise an election meeting, November 1918, at which Lloyd George was to speak.

3. Paint your own idea of 'Life in the Trenches, 1916'.

Fig. 34.3 Women at work in a munitions factory.

35 The State of Industry and Trade, 1919-39

Lost Markets

During the war British industrialists were unable to export as much as they had, so some of their former customers made things for themselves. Countries that had once bought their textile goods from Britain found that it was fairly easy to make these. The Lancashire cotton industry had been among the first to grow in the first stage of the Industrial Revolution; it was also among the first to suffer as other countries became industrialized.

New Industrial Giants

During the war American and Japanese industrialists had been free to make and sell goods. They sold these in countries that had bought British goods before 1914. When the war ended, their customers kept on buying Japanese or American goods, so more markets had been lost to Britain. Many firms could not sell their goods; more factories closed; and more people were thrown out of work.

New Industrial Countries

A number of small countries saw the beginning of their Industrial Revolutions after 1919. Rumania, Poland, Hungary, and Czechoslovakia were among these. They were never going to be industrial giants like Japan and America, but they did produce some goods that they once bought from Britain. This meant a further fall in the demand for British goods.

Tariffs

After 1919 more countries became industrialized. All of them put tariffs on imports, and this cut down the demand for imports. Britain depended on other countries buying her goods, but tariffs made it more difficult to sell them. There was a fall in the demand for British products.

Primary Prices

Britain had always sold a large percentage of her goods to non-industrialized countries. During the war there had been a rise in the prices which the warring countries paid for wool for uniforms, rubber for tyres, and food for their people.

This increase in prices meant a higher income for the owners of farms and mines. This encouraged them to spend money on expanding their farms and developing more mines.

Once the war ended all this changed. The Europeans produced food on land that had been battlefields, and therefore did not need as much foreign food. Governments stopped buying wool and copper; the war was over and so they did not need uniforms and munitions. The mine owners and farmers found that just when they had more to sell, there were fewer people who wanted to buy their goods. There was a very sharp fall in the prices they could get for their produce.

People now had smaller incomes. This meant that they could buy even less than they had bought in 1913, and since they bought less, there was less work available in Britain.

Coal – a Special Case

In 1913 British miners had dug out almost 300 million tonnes of coal; about 100 million tonnes of this was sold abroad. Coal was used to drive ships and railway engines; to drive the steam-engines in factories; and it was burned on the large, open fires in homes in cold countries.

In the 1920s and 1930s the industry declined. Oil and electricity were used to drive ships and factory machinery. House builders put smaller, more efficient grates in new houses, and industrialists learned to lag their boilers and pipes so that they used less coal in their factories.

There were also more countries producing coal. In Poland, Germany, and America mine owners spent a lot of money on machinery. Their miners produced more coal per hour than did the British miner using the old-fashioned pick and shovel. German, American, and Polish coal was cheaper than hand-produced British coal. Therefore, less British coal was sold.

Shipbuilding, another Special Case

In 1913 British shipyards built about two-thirds of the world's ships. These yards were concentrated around the Tyne and Wear and the Clyde.

During the war the shipyards had been busy turning out new ships to replace those that were sunk by the Germans. New yards were opened, and old yards were expanded to meet the government's demand for more shipping.

But in the 1920s and 1930s there was a sharp drop in the demand for ships. Japan and America had become shipbuilding countries, and even Greece and Poland built some of their own ships. British yard owners found it impossible to sell ships, and many yards were closed. This led to a rise in unemployment. It also led to a fall in the demand for iron, steel, and coal so that there was a further increase in unemployment (Fig. 35.1).

The most tragic example of the effects of the closing of a yard was seen at Jarrow. The town depended almost entirely on the one shipyard where most of the men in the town worked. When this was closed in 1931 about two-thirds of the men in Jarrow lost their jobs.

Summary

In the following table the levels of trade and British exports in 1913 are taken and each is given the figure of 100. The figures for 1929 and 1937 have been translated into percentages of the 1913 figure:

	World Trade	Level of British exports	British share of world trade (%)
1913	100	100	14
1929	133	87	11
1937	128	72	10

Depressed Areas

The sharp fall in the level of British exports led to a corresponding decrease in the level of employment in those industries that had once sold their goods abroad. In particular, there was a drop in the demand for coal, cotton, shipbuilding, and in the iron and steel industries that supplied the shipbuilding industry.

Now these industries were concentrated in certain regions of the country. The decline of the demand for textiles meant very heavy unemployment in Lancashire. The effects of the decline in the coal industry were most clearly seen in South Wales and Scotland. In Merthyr and Dowlais, Maryport and Abertillery

Fig. 35.1a Unemployment in Britain, 1928–36.

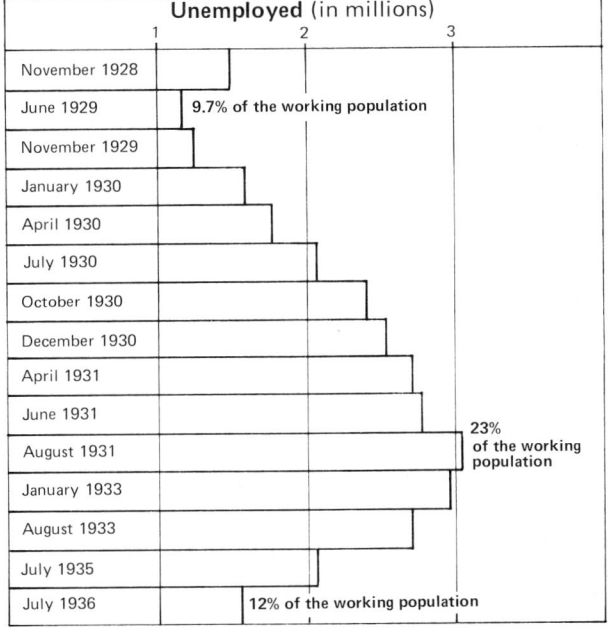

Fig. 35.1b Unemployment in 1934 in various towns throughout Britain.

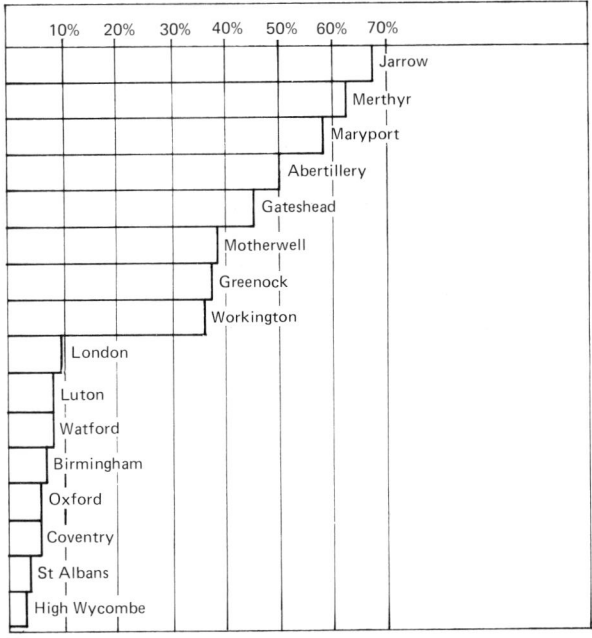

over half the men were out of work in 1934 (Fig. 35.1).

Scotland, South Wales, Lancashire, and the North-East became known as the Depressed Areas. Here there were high levels of unemployment, and thousands of people went after every job advertised in the local Press or at the Labour Exchange. Here thousands of men crowded into the reading rooms of local libraries; many went to look at the 'Jobs Vacant' columns, some went into the libraries merely to keep warm.

New Industries

But elsewhere in the country new industries grew at a very rapid rate. There were industries linked with electricity; Hoover and other firms produced vacuum cleaners, radios, toasters, irons and other goods. The motor vehicle industry also grew; Morris, Austin, and other manufacturers produced thousands of cars, lorries, and buses every year. There was a growth in the petro-chemical industry, in which firms such as B.P., Esso, and I.C.I. were leaders.

What Was New About These Industries?

These industries were unlike the older industries – coal, cotton, iron and steel, and shipbuilding. Most of the machinery in these new industries was driven by oil or electricity and not by coal. This made them cleaner and more pleasant to work in.

In the nineteenth century an industrialist had been forced to build his mills or factories on or near a coalfield. The new industrialists needed oil or electricity to drive their machinery, and in the 1920s the National Grid made electricity readily available anywhere in the country. This allowed the new industrialists to choose where they would build their factories.

The new industries sold most of their products on the home market and did not export much of their output. These new industrialists therefore tried to build their factories as near London as they could. London, after all, had about one-sixth of the people in Britain. The new industrialists knew that they would sell about one-sixth of their output in or near London.

New, Prosperous Areas

The new industries provided employment for millions of people. Some of these were already living in the areas where the factories were built, but millions more emigrated from Wales, Scotland, and Lancashire in search of work in these new industries.

Older people with families, with mortgages, or council houses were less free to move from the Depressed Areas into the new booming areas. In contrast, the young, the unmarried and the childless couples were more free to move. So there was a migration of these people from the Depressed Areas, and this meant these areas became, if anything, even more depressing since the populations tended to be older.

In some areas, though, there was a very low level of unemployment, even in the worse days of the depression (Fig. 35.1).

The Government and the Unemployed

Every government between 1919 and 1939 had to deal with the problem of finding money to pay to the unemployed.

1911

On p. 181 we saw that the government had brought in a system of Unemployment Insurance for the builders, engineers, and shipbuilders. The workers and their employers each paid 2½d (about 1p) into an Insurance Fund. An unemployed and insured worker could draw 7 shillings (35p) for no more than fifteen weeks in a year.

1914–18

During the war the government widened the Insurance Scheme, and workers in the munitions industry were brought into it. Since few of these were out of work, the Insurance Fund had a large surplus each year.

1919–20

The government allowed former soldiers to claim unemployment payment while looking for a job, even though most of these had never paid into the Insurance Fund. They received what was called an *uncovenanted* payment. It was a hand-out or a *dole*. The same privilege was given to industrial workers who lost their jobs because of the change-over from making war goods to making peacetime goods.

1920

In 1919 and 1920 there was a high level of employment, because firms expanded to provide the goods needed to rebuild Europe. Lloyd George's government brought in a new Unemployment Insurance Act. This said that all workers (except domestic servants, farm-workers, and Civil Servants) earning less than £250 a year had to be insured. As in 1911 the workers and employers paid into the Insurance Fund, and after paying twelve weeks' contributions, a worker was entitled to receive unemployment benefit for fifteen weeks in a year. He would be given 15 shillings (75p) a week while out of work.

The dole, 1921

In 1920 there were less than a million out of work. Lloyd George hoped that the post-war boom would last, but it came to a sudden end in 1921. By the end of the year over 2 million men were out of work, and they could draw their unemployment benefit for fifteen weeks only. The government then had to bring in a new scheme. Once the men had got through their fifteen weeks of insured benefit they would continue to receive the same payment as an *uncovenanted* benefit. This could not come from the Insurance Fund. It had to be paid directly by the government. This increased the amount of taxation that the government had to collect each year.

1927

Neville Chamberlain was Minister of Health in the Baldwin government, 1925–9, and in 1927 he brought in a new Unemployment Insurance Bill. By this time the payments out of the Insurance Fund were much greater than the payments into it. Chamberlain reduced both the benefits paid to the unemployed and the payments that had to be made by workers and employers. He also extended the time for which an unemployed man could claim benefit. Instead of the original fifteen weeks, Chamberlain allowed a payment for an indefinite period. This ended the dole. Unemployed men would now continue to get their payment from the Insurance Fund. This Fund could not possibly meet all the demands made on it, so the government had to put money into it each year. In 1930 this came to about £50 million.

The End of the Poor Law Guardians, 1929

In 1929 Chamberlain made a major reform of local government. As part of that reform Chamberlain abolished the Poor Law Guardians who had run the Poor Law system since 1834 (Chapter 37). In future the Poor Law would be handled by the Public Assistance Committees of the county boroughs and county councils.

The Insurance Fund and the Political Crisis, 1930–1

In 1930 Parliament passed a new Unemployment Insurance Act. This made it easier for a man to claim unemployment benefit. He no longer had to prove that he was 'genuinely seeking work'; men in Jarrow, Merthyr, and other centres of massive unemployment had long ago given up a search for a job.

The Act also dealt with the problem of men who had never worked and so had never paid into the Insurance Fund. In the past they had been allowed to claim 'transitional' benefits until they found a job. In future, they too would be allowed to claim benefit alongside men who had paid into the Fund.

This increased the amount that the government had to put into the Fund. At the same time there was a rapid rise in the number out of work from 1,200,000 in October to 1,600,000 in March 1930. In 1931 this figure rose to 3,000,000 (Fig. 35.1), and the government had to pay even more into the Fund.

At the same time the government was getting less in taxation – because there were fewer people earning enough to pay income tax. This meant that the government was not collecting as much as it was spending. This is known as a *deficit*. In the 1970s governments had deficits each year of about £10 thousand million. In 1930 governments and bankers thought that a deficit of £50 million was a sign that the country was going bankrupt.

The Labour Chancellor of the Exchequer was Philip Snowden. He wanted to wipe out the deficit. He proposed to cut the amount paid in unemployment benefit so that the government would not have to pay so much into the Insurance Fund. Some members of the Cabinet did not agree and the Prime Minister, Ramsay MacDonald, had to resign in August 1931 (Chapter 38).

The National Government, 1931, and the Means Test

A new government came into office in August 1931. It cut the unemployment benefit, so that a married man with two children now received £1.36 a week instead of £1.50.

At the same time the government brought in the *Means Test*. This meant that when a man applied for benefit he had now to declare all the family's sources of income. He had to declare earnings made by his wife or children, any pension coming into the house, and any savings he might have made. Officials at the Labour Exchange examined these figures. If they said that the family income was high enough, the man might get no benefit. If the income was not high

Fig. 35.2 Unemployed Londoners look through the 'situations vacant' columns in a hopeless search for jobs.

enough, a man would get a certain amount of benefit.

There were fights at Labour Exchanges when clerks refused to give men the benefit they had got before the Means Test.

Life on the Dole

We know a good deal about life in the 1930s, for many writers have left us their memories of the period. They all tell of the patched clothes and poor housing; they show how the unemployed (Fig. 35.2) tried to forget their misery in cinemas and at football games (Extract 35.1); and they all write about the poor diet and low standard of living (Extract 35.2). There are still people alive who lived through these hard times. For them 'the thirties' were indeed the years of depression.

Questions

Extract 35.1

Life on the 'dole' 1937

The average income of a family on the dole averages around about thirty shillings a week. At least a third of the whole population of the industrial areas are living at this level. The Means Test is very strictly enforced . . . .

But they don't necessarily lower their standards by cutting out luxuries and concentrating on necessities; more often it is the other way around . . . .. Two things have probably made the greatest difference: the movies and the production of cheap clothes. The youth who leaves school at fourteen and gets a blind-alley job is out of work at twenty, probably for life; but for two pounds ten on the hire purchase system he can buy himself a suit

which, for a while and at a little distance, looks as though it had been tailored in Savile Row. The girl can look like a fashion plate at an even lower price. You may have three halfpence in your pocket and not a prospect in the world, and only the corner of a leaky bedroom to go home to, but in your new clothes you can stand on the street corner, indulging in a private daydream of yourself as Clark Gable or Greta Garbo, which compensates you for a great deal . . . .

You can't get much meat for threepence, but you can get a lot of fish and chips . . . .. It is quite likely that fish and chips, art-silk stockings, tinned salmon, cut-price chocolate (five ounce bars for sixpence), the movies, the radio, strong tea and the football pools have between them averted revolution.

(George Orwell, *The Road to Wigan Pier* (Gollancz, 1937/Penguin, 1970.)

[5p = 1s = 12d, 1 ounce = 28.3 g]

1. Explain this reference to the Means Test. Show how it worked and explain why people hated it.
2. What 'luxuries' were bought by the unemployed? Why? What might they have bought instead of fish and chips?
3. What was meant by 'movies'?
4. Explain the reference to 'Clark Gable and Greta Garbo'.
5. What, according to Orwell, had 'averted a revolution'?

Extract 35.2

Food for the unemployed

The end of this month will make it two years since I worked last. Myself, wife and three children lived first on 32s. a week and since on 29s. 3d. a week.

The family budget works out like this:

	p	s. d.
Rent	55	11. 0.
Coal (1½ cwt. [76.2 kg])	14	2. 9.
Gas (cooking and washing)	6	1. 2.
Light (electric)	5	1. 0.
Club subscription, (boots, clothing, crockery, bedclothing, etc.)	15	3. 0.
Burial insurance	3	0. 9.
Groceries	32	6. 6.
	130	26. 2.
Balance:	16	3. 1.
	146	29. 3.

The balance has to buy everything that goes towards making a meal outside of bread, margarine and a cup of tea, for a family of five for all the week.

Just work it out. 105 individual meals to be provided out of 16 pence! That is less than a halfpenny a meal. This means that we live mostly on tea and toast.

This diet has resulted in recurrent illness. The youngest child has had pneumonia three times since February of last year. She is now suffering from bronchitis, and, according to the doctor, is probably developing TB.

The oldest child was in hospital last month with pneumonia. It was out one week and has now gone back again. I myself have only been signed off 'fit' today after an illness lasting a month.

The rent has been missed to meet the extra expenses that always crop up during sickness. And now a registered letter has come from the corporation with one week's notice to quit!

(Fenner Brockway, *Hungry England* (Gollancz, 1932.)

1. Why was this family's income only 146p week? What would happen to this income if the mother or one of the children went to work?
2. Why did the budget include a sum for 'burial insurance'?
3. Why did Brockway mention 105 individual meals? Explain how he arrived at that figure.
4. Why was there little meat, fresh fruit, or vegetables in this family's diet?
5. How does this extract help to explain the high rate of sickness among the families of the unemployed?

Fig. 35.1

1. What was the total of unemployment in April 1930? In April 1931? When did the level of unemployment start to go down? Why was it lower still in 1940?

2. Mark on a map the towns with high levels of unemployment in 1934. What were the main industries of these towns?
3. Mark on a map the towns that had low levels of unemployment in 1934. How do these figures help to explain why so many men left South Wales to look for work?
4. Why did some people write about 'Two Nations' in the 1930s?

Worksheet

(A)
1. Why and to which countries did Britain lose some of her exports market during the war?

2. Why was there an increase in the number of countries imposing tariffs after 1918? What effect did this have on British exports?

3. Why did primary producers get higher prices for their products in 1918 than in 1913? Why did they get much lower prices in 1922? What effect did that have on British exports to those countries?

4. Why was there a fall in world demand for coal in general, and British coal in particular?

5. Why was there heavy unemployment in areas that had specialized in shipbuilding?

6. Why were some areas described as Depressed Areas? Name FOUR such areas.

7. Why were the owners of new industries able to build their factories away from the coalfields? Why did they prefer to do so?

8. Make a diary-like list of the changes in the payments of Unemployment Benefit between 1911 and 1931.

9. Write a brief note on EACH of the following: The dole; primary prices; the Public Assistance Committees.

10. Why was the Insurance Fund in debt in 1931? Why did that lead to a political crisis?

11. Why did men organize hunger marches in the 1920s and 1930s? What did they hope to achieve?

(B)
1. Write the letters that might have been sent by:
(a) someone living in one of the Depressed Areas;
(b) one of the men looking for a job;
(c) after the visit of the Means Test Officer;
(d) a family living on the dole (Extracts 35.1 and 35.2).

36 Three Prime Ministers, 1918-24

Lloyd George, Bonar Law, Balfour, and the rest of the Coalition Cabinet wanted the wartime government to remain in power. Having 'won the war' (Fig. 36.1) they wanted to enjoy peacetime office.

The Russian Revolution, 1917

In February 1917 the Tsarist government had been overthrown by a Russian revolution, but in October 1917 the democratic government was overthrown by a Bolshevik revolution led by Lenin and Trotsky.

In Britain many people were frightened by this Bolshevik revolution. Was it the start of a world-wide revolution by working-class people everywhere? Lloyd George thought it was, as did many other ministers and politicians. The Americans, French, and British sent troops and supplies to help the anti-Bolsheviks during the civil war that followed the Bolshevik revolution.

'Homes fit for heroes'?

Lloyd George had promised to build 'Homes fit for heroes' to replace the Victorian slums, and in 1919 Dr Christopher Addison, Minister of Health, piloted a Housing Act through Parliament. Local authorities were given the power to build houses. The government promised to pay councils £260 for every house that was built. This subsidy meant that the councils had to pay less out of their rates, and councils could charge lower rents for these subsidized houses.

The Act was not a success. In the post-war boom 1919–20, there was a sharp rise in the prices of such items as timber, glass, bricks, and rubber.

A council house cost £1,200 to build. Councils had to charge very high rents which only the better-off workers could afford.

The Trade Unions

Trade unions welcomed Lloyd George's Unemployment Insurance Act (p. 204). They were also pleased

Fig. 36.1 The world's leaders at the Versailles Peace Conference, 1919. From left to right: Lloyd George; the Prime Minister of Italy, Orlando; the Prime Minister of France, Clemenceau; and President Wilson of the U.S.A.

with the boom in industry in 1919 and 1920. Most of their members had jobs, and many unions won important wage increases. In September 1919 the government still controlled the railways. It tried to cut the minimum wages paid on the railways from 51 shillings (£2.55) to 40 shillings (£2) per week, but the railwaymen, led by J. H. Thomas, threatened to go on strike. On 5 October 1919 the government climbed down, and said that it would postpone the cuts for at least a year.

In March 1920 the miners, led by Robert Smillie, won a wage increase from the government, which still controlled the country's mines. This was followed by a victory for the transport workers, led by Ernest Bevin. He won the title of the Dockers' K.C. (King's Counsel or lawyer) for the wage increase he won for his members at a Commission of Inquiry.

Fig. 36.2 A poster issued by coal-mine owners to explain their position during the 1921 coal strike.

The End of the Boom, 1920–1

The post-war boom came to an end in the autumn of 1920. By early 1921 about 2 million men were out of work – over one-fifth of the men insured in the Unemployment Insurance scheme. The government controlled the coal industry in 1919 and 1920 while coal was selling at £6 a tonne, and the industry was making a profit. But when the boom ended and coal prices fell to about £1 a tonne, the government handed the mines back to their private owners. On 31 March 1921 they announced that they would cut wages to bring the cost of production down from £2 a tonne. The miners refused to accept these cuts, and on 1 April there began a coal strike (Fig. 36.2).

The Triple Alliance

The miners now called on the railwaymen and transport workers to come out on a sympathetic strike. This is what the three unions had agreed to in their Triple Alliance (p. 185). J. H. Thomas and Bevin agreed to bring their members out on strike on 15 April 1921.

Lloyd George met the leaders of all three unions. The miners' leader, Frank Hodge, was trapped into agreeing that he would accept a government promise to keep miners' wages at their old level while discussions were held with the owners on other matters. His members were angry at this. They did not want to appear to be offering any concessions to owners. But Thomas and Bevin claimed that the threat of the strike by the three unions had forced the government to make a good offer to the miners. The threatened strike was called off. The miners were left on their own. Their strike went on until 1 July, when they were driven back to work by hunger. They got worse terms from their owners than they were offered in April, so it is not surprising that 15 April 1921 – the day when Thomas and Bevin called off their support – has become known as 'Black Friday' in trade union history.

The Geddes Axe, 1922

The miners were only the first to suffer. In 1922 Lloyd George appointed Sir Eric Geddes to bring in a series of cuts in government spending. He had seen how

209

unemployment payments had gone up (p. 205), and he wanted to cut down on spending by other government departments.

Geddes cut the money spent on the Army and Navy. He closed the few Day Continuation Schools that had been opened because of the 1918 Education Act. It had been hoped that all children would be given at least one day a week off work so that they could go back to school for one day a week between the ages of 14 and 18; it was thought that this would allow them to gain extra qualifications. Geddes also cut the amount of money going to health and welfare services and the payments made to councils for building houses.

In one sense Geddes succeeded. There was a drop in the amount of government spending, but because of the cuts there was an immediate rise in unemployment. And because of cuts in the salaries of Civil Servants, teachers, and others, there was less spending, and a drop in the demand for goods. This led to yet more unemployment.

Wages

Employers found that they could not sell all they produced, so they sacked some people. They also tried to bring down the prices they were charging in the hope that this would help improve the chances of selling their products. So there were cuts in the wages paid in shipyards and docks, cotton and woollen industries, in printing, and on the railways. The miners had only been the first to suffer. During 1922 all workers learned that the boom was over.

Ireland

In 1914 the Liberals had set aside the Home Rule Act until the war had ended (p. 185). On Easter Monday, 1916, some Irish extremists, the members of Sinn Fein ('Ourselves alone') had staged an unsuccessful rebellion.

In the 1918 election seventy-three Sinn Feiners were elected as M.P.s for Irish constituencies. But they refused to go to Westminster. Instead, they went to Dublin and made themselves into an Irish Parliament; they announced that Ireland was now a republic.

The British government arrested most of the Irish M.P.s. But one, Eamonn de Valera, escaped from Lincoln Gaol, and went to America where he collected about £200,000 from Irish-Americans. Another Sinn Feiner, Michael Collins, led an Irish Republican Army (I.R.A.) in attacks on police stations, Army barracks, and houses owned by English landowners. 'Burn everything British, except

coal' was a slogan of the time.

The government sent over troops recruited from ex-servicemen (the Black and Tans) to put down the I.R.A. There was a good deal of savagery on both sides. Lloyd George's solution to this problem was to persuade Parliament to pass the Government of Ireland Act 1920. This set up separate Parliaments in Dublin and in Belfast. The Protestants of Ulster were delighted, but the Sinn Fein refused to accept this division of their island.

The Civil War went on until June 1921 when Lloyd George invited leaders from Dublin and Ulster to come to talks in London. Collins led the Sinn Fein delegates. They reluctantly agreed to accept the terms of the treaty that gave Ulster its independence and which named the rest of Ireland the Irish Free State. The Irish Parliament voted by sixty-four votes to fifty-seven to accept this treaty. De Valera was among the fifty-seven, and he led one side in the Irish Civil War which lasted until 1925. Collins led the 'Free Staters' who wanted to accept the treaty. He was only one of the hundreds who were killed during this savage struggle which did not end until de Valera called off his campaign in 1925.

Chanak 1922

In 1919 Lloyd George seemed to be the most powerful politician in Britain. But by 1922 his position had weakened. Many people opposed his Irish policy; some hated the terrorism practised by the Black and Tans; others disliked the treaty that had given the Irish Free State its independence. Workers were opposed to the Geddes Axe and the rise in unemployment. Ex-servicemen remembered the promise he had made – and his failure to provide them with homes or jobs (Fig. 36.3). There was a scandal about the way in which he collected about £2 million from the sale of titles and other honours (Extract 36.1).

In addition to all this, he had little to show for his work abroad. India was seething with revolution; and Europe was still not enjoying the fruits of peace. Germany had not been made to pay for the war but was discontented with the peace treaty of 1919, while France had been angered by the way in which Lloyd George tried to make things easier for Germany. Greece and Turkey were involved in a war for the control of Constantinople and Aanatolia, and in August 1922 their armies were facing each other in Asia Minor. Lloyd George spoke in the House of Commons in favour of a Greek victory, and seemed to suggest that Britain would support Greece. The Turks were led by Mustapha Kemal, the hero of Gallipoli (p. 197). He was afraid that Britain might

Fig. 36.3 A queue of unemployed men waiting outside a labour exchange in 1924.

act, so he struck first. He swept the Greeks out of Asia Minor and advanced to the area around the Dardanelles where the Allies had stationed troops at Chanak.

The French and Italian governments withdrew their troops. The British had only six battalions with which to fight the Turks. Fortunately the Turks did not attack, and war did not break out. But there had been a grave danger, and most Conservatives blamed Lloyd George for exposing Britain to that danger.

The Conservatives, 1922

Bonar Law had led the Conservatives into the Coalition with Lloyd George in December 1916. He admired Lloyd George.

After the war he had persuaded the Conservatives not to use their voting strength against the 'Welsh Wizard'. But in 1921 Bonar Law retired because of ill-health, and the new leader of the Coalition Conservatives was Austen Chamberlain, eldest son of Joseph Chamberlain. Conservative M.P.s were less willing to listen to his advice to support Lloyd George.

The Carlton Club, 19 October 1922

Chamberlain called a meeting of all Conservative M.P.s on 19 October 1922. He told them that he and the other Conservative ministers in the Coalition government supported Lloyd George. He argued that the party ought to be fighting socialism and Bolshevism and not Lloyd George. Chamberlain

hoped that he would be able to put an end to the grumbling against the Prime Minister. But Baldwin, a junior minister, argued that the party ought to break from Lloyd George and fight the next election as a separate party. Bonar Law came back from his sick bed to support Baldwin, and by 187 votes to 87 the M.P.s agreed with Bonar Law and Baldwin. At five o'clock that afternoon Lloyd George had resigned, and a few days later the Conservatives elected Bonar Law as their leader and he became the new Prime Minister.

The 1922 Election

Bonar Law called a general election. The Conservatives won 347 seats, Labour won 142, and the divided Liberals won 117 (sixty-five going to Asquith's supporters and fifty-two to Lloyd George's). The Conservatives had an over-all majority, but Labour got 4½ million votes – about a third of all the votes cast at the election. Among the Labour M.P.s was Ramsay MacDonald who had been defeated in the 1918 election. He was chosen as the leader of the Parliamentary Labour Party by sixty-one votes to fifty-eight cast for J. R. Clynes who had led the party since 1918.

Baldwin in Power

Bonar Law was a very sick man, and he retired in May 1923 and Baldwin became Prime Minister. Those Conservatives who had served in the Coalition

211

– Chamberlain, F. E. Smith, and others – refused to serve under him.

Baldwin knew that the most serious problem facing the country was rising unemployment (Fig. 36.3). He also knew that his party had to try to bring back Chamberlain and the other former Coalition ministers. He tried to tackle both difficulties by announcing his belief in the need for a British tariff system. This would attract the support of Austen Chamberlain. It would also give British industry some protection against the foreign goods that were pouring into the home market.

On 25 October 1923 he addressed the Conservative Party's Conference at Plymouth, and spoke of the need for a tariff. But in 1922 Bonar Law had promised that there would be 'no fundamental change' in the British trading system. Baldwin argued that he could not bring in a tariff without having first put this to the voters.

The 1923 Election

As in 1903 the demand for a British tariff united the Liberals. The Labour Party also campaigned against a tariff. The results showed that the British people did not support the ending of Free Trade. The Conservatives won 257 seats, Labour 192, and the united Liberals 158.

Baldwin could have formed a government with the support of the Liberals, but he had a great dislike and distrust of Lloyd George. This fear was greater than his fear of the Labour 'bogeymen' of whom most of his Tory colleagues were afraid.

So Baldwin resigned and advised the King to send for MacDonald. Baldwin knew that MacDonald would not be able to do anything radical – because the Liberals and Tories could combine to vote his party down.

The First Labour Government, January 1924

On 22 January 1924 MacDonald, Clynes, Henderson, Thomas, and the other Labour ministers went to Buckingham Palace to meet the King. George V noted in his diary: 'Today 23 years ago dear Grandmama [Victoria] died. I wonder what she would have thought of a Labour government!'

MacDonald was both Prime Minister and Foreign Minister. He was very successful. He persuaded the French to take their troops out of the Ruhr region. This allowed the Germans to begin working their coal and iron industry again and helped restore their economy. He supported an American plan for reducing the amount that Germany was to pay in reparation for the cost of the war. He supported the League of Nations and persuaded eight other countries to sign the Geneva Protocol. They agreed to use their armies and navies to enforce the decisions of the League of Nations. If countries had honoured this agreement, maybe the world would not have had to fight the Second World War in 1939–45.

Domestic Policies

Philip Snowden was the Chancellor of the Exchequer. He and the majority of his colleagues were old-fashioned in their economic views. They believed in Free Trade – as Gladstone had done; they thought that governments should not spend more than they collected in taxes; they believed that taxation should be kept as low as possible.

So there was little done to help the unemployed. Snowden would have nothing to do with men who thought that the government ought to spend millions of pounds on road building as a way of providing work.

Unemployment benefit was raised by a few shillings. The main reform was a Housing Act that was pushed through by John Wheatley. This gave bigger subsidies to councils for building working-class homes. As a result of this Act about half a million new homes were built by 1939.

Politics and the Fall of the Government

MacDonald officially recognized the Russian government, and made a trade treaty with Russia. This annoyed all the Conservatives and many Liberals. MacDonald knew that he had to depend on the continued support of the Liberals (Fig. 36.4). He resented their attacks on him as a 'Russian-lover'.

In the summer of 1924 the government was planning to bring a court case against J. R. Campbell, the editor of a communist paper. He had written articles appealing to British soldiers not to fight against the working class in Britain or abroad. This was an incitement to mutiny.

But after a long consideration of the affair, Sir Patrick Hastings, the Attorney-General, decided not to bring the case. This decision was attacked by the Liberals and Conservatives; they claimed that the government was 'soft' on communism.

There was a vote of censure on the government in October, and the Conservatives and Liberals combined to defeat the government. MacDonald resigned and called for a general election.

THE LABOUR BIRD AND THE LIBERAL WORM.

WORM. "IF YOU KEEP ON SWALLOWING ME LIKE THIS I SHALL TURN."
BIRD. "WELL, AND THEN?"
WORM. "I SHALL DISAGREE WITH YOU." [*The Bird carries on.*

Fig. 36.4 One view of the relationship between the Labour government and the Liberal Party in 1924.

The 1924 Election

This was the first election in which politicians used the 'wireless'. It is best remembered, though, for the Zinoviev letter. This was supposed to have been sent to the British Communist Party by a Russian Bolshevik leader. It told them how to get control of the Labour Party and the trade union movement and how to bring about a workers' revolution. The Foreign Office published the letter and sent a note of protest to Russia. MacDonald was busy campaigning in Wales and at first ignored the letter. The Conservative newspapers reprinted the letter and argued that it showed the danger of allowing Labour to hold power again.

Today it is certain that the letter was a forgery. The Labour Party claimed that the letter had lost them many votes, although there is little evidence to support this. In fact the party gained half a million more votes in 1924 than in 1923, but most of these votes were gained in safe Labour seats. The results showed that the Conservatives had 415 seats while

Labour only had 152. The Liberals had fared even worse; they only won forty seats. They had paid the price for bringing down the first Labour government.

Questions

Extract 36.1

Selling titles, 1922

> I am authorized to offer you a knighthood or a baronetcy.... A knighthood will cost you £12,000 and a baronetcy £35,000.... You will be asked to meet someone in Downing Street and three or four days before the List is announced, you will be asked to pay £10,000 or £30,000 as the case may be – and I am permitted to take the balance, which represents the fees. There are only five knighthoods left for the June list – if you should decide on a baronetcy you may have to wait for the Retiring List which a retiring Prime Minster is allowed to recommend on a change of government.
> (Interview with an agent and someone looking for a title, 1922.)

1. What titles are used by a man with (i) a knighthood, and (ii) a baronetcy?
2. Why would someone pay more for a baronetcy than for a knighthood?
3. Which Prime Minister lived at No. 10 Downing Street in 1921–2?
4. How much money did the 'salesman' get for selling these honours?
5. We have a 'June List' today. Why? Which people receive honours in today's Lists?
6. What was a 'Retiring List'? When was the most recent one issued in Britain?
7. How did the Prime Minister use the money he received from selling these honours?

Extract 36.2

The end of Coalition, 1922

> *Mr Austen Chamberlain:* I have asked you and my friends in the Cabinet to meet me because it was you who elected me as your leader in the House of Commons. For months past the strain placed upon your leaders has been increased by the failure of support from the party behind them....
> The real issue (at the next election) is not between Liberals and Conservatives. It is between those who stand for individual freedom and those who are for the socialization of the State. This is not a moment to break with old friends.

Mr Stanley Baldwin: The Prime Minister ... is a dynamic force. A dynamic force is a very terrible thing. It is owing to that dynamic force that the Liberal Party has been smashed to pieces, in time the same thing will happen to our party. ...

Mr Bonar Law: The feeling against the continuation of the Coalition is so strong that if we follow Austen Chamberlain's advice our party will be broken, and a new party will be formed. ... It will be a repetition of what happened after Peel passed the Corn Bill.
(Report of Meeting of Conservative M.P.s, 19 October 1922.)

1.   What was the position of Austen Chamberlain in the Conservative Party? Who had been head of that party before him? Why had he retired by 1922?

2.   Why were many Conservatives opposed to the policies of the Coalition government?

3.   What were, according to Chamberlain, 'the real issues'? How far was this view a result of the Bolshevik victory in Russia?

4.   Why would Chamberlain's advice lead to a break-up in the Conservative Party? Who hoped to lead the new anti-socialist party?

5.   What position did Baldwin have in the Coalition government? Why was he afraid of Lloyd George? When had Lloyd George 'smashed' the Liberal Party?

6.   Why was Bonar Law's presence at this meeting (i) unexpected (ii) important for Baldwin and his supporters?

7.   Who became Prime Minister after Lloyd George? Why did he retire within a few months? Who then became Prime Minister?

Fig. 36.2

1.   What fraction of the total cost was taken by wages? How might the owners have got out the same amount of coal with fewer workers?

2.   How did some landowners benefit from 'royalties'? Find out when they lost these payments.

3.   Coal exports were falling because British prices were too high. How did the owners propose to cut their costs? Why did the miners refuse to accept their proposals?

Worksheet

(A)

1.   Why did the government pass a Housing Act in 1919? Why was it of little benefit to most workers?

2.   Write a brief note on the coal industry 1918–21. Why was Black Friday so important to the miners?

3.   Why did the government cut the level of government spending after 1921? Why did that lead to more unemployment?

4.   Write a brief note on the history of Ireland 1916–21. Why was there a civil war in that country after 1922?

5.   Make a list of the reasons why Lloyd George was so unpopular in 1922.

6.   Write a brief note on EACH of the following: Dail Eireann; Chanak; the meeting at the Carlton Club 1922.

7.   Why did Baldwin want a British system of tariffs in 1923?

8.   Write a brief note on EACH of the following: (i) the success of the Labour government, 1924 (ii) the major failures of that government (iii) the reasons for its defeat in the elections, 1924.

9.   Write a brief note on EACH of the following: the Campbell case; the Zinoviev letter; the Russian trade treaty.

(B)

1.   Write the letters that might have been sent by:
(a) a Labour M.P. explaining the party's success in the 1918 election;
(b) a union leader outlining the success of the unions in 1919–20;
(c) a miner on strike in July 1921;
(d) one of the M.P.s who had been at the Carlton Club meeting, 1922;
(e) one of Lloyd George's friends explaining why he had been so popular in 1918 but so unpopular in 1922.

37 Baldwin's Second Government and the General Strike, 1924-9

Baldwin's Ministers

Baldwin 'made up' with the former Coalition ministers with whom he had quarrelled in 1922. Austen Chamberlain became Foreign Secretary and his half-brother, Neville Chamberlain, became Minister of Health.

Churchill had rejoined the Conservative Party over the tariff issue in 1923, but Baldwin thought he might still team up with Lloyd George to try to form a Centre Party. So, in 1924, Baldwin gave Churchill the position of Chancellor of the Exchequer.

Neville Chamberlain

Neville was much less well known than his half-brother Austen, but between 1924 and 1929 he proved to be a very able Minister of Health. His ministry pushed twenty-five Acts through Parliament. There were reforms of the Poor Law (p. 205), National Insurance, and the rating systems. A Widows', Orphans' and Old Age Pensioners' Act (1925) gave pensions of ten shillings (50p) a week to all people over 65 and to all widows, who also received an allowance for dependent children. There was a very important Local Government Act (1929). County and county borough councils had to appoint Public Assistance Committees to deal with the unemployed (p. 205), and they were also given greater powers to deal with public health, hospitals, child welfare, roads, and town and country planning. All this work has earned Chamberlain the right to be called a founder of the modern Welfare State.

But the Baldwin government is best remembered for the General Strike of May 1926. We cannot understand this unless we first look at the question of Britain's trade and her lending of money to foreign governments and industrialists.

British Money Going Abroad

Before 1914 the British loaned a good deal of money to foreigners (p. 149). British firms sold their goods in foreign countries and received gold in return. Other British firms bought goods from foreign countries and paid for them with gold. But Britain sold more than it bought; more gold was earned than spent. It was this surplus that was loaned to foreigners.

A Changed Society after 1920

After 1920 British firms exported less than they had done previously (p. 202), but Britain continued to import food, raw materials, and goods for sale in shops. Britain no longer earned enough to lend overseas, and this displeased the bankers of the City of London.

Foreigners continued to come to Britain to ask for money for their industrial development, so British bankers went to other foreign countries to borrow gold. They then loaned this abroad.

How did they make any profit? British bankers only paid 2 per cent interest on their borrowings from France, but when they loaned this to Japan they charged 8 per cent interest.

Montagu Norman

The work of bankers in the City of London was supervised by the Governor of the Bank of England, Montagu Norman. He did not seem to have understood that the war had changed things; people had been forced to sell their large houses because they could not afford to run them, and many rich people could not now afford to pay maids and butlers. But Montagu Norman did not seem to have noticed any of this, nor did he seem to have noticed that Britain was not selling as much abroad as she had done in 1913.

The Gold Standard

If you look at a banknote you will see the words: 'I promise to pay the bearer on demand the sum of. . . .' Before 1914 you could exchange notes for real gold, but when the war started the government ordered that this had to stop. It needed the country's gold to buy goods in America. The government also issued its own Treasury Notes to pay the firms making guns and other weapons.

By 1918 vast amounts of Treasury Notes were being used in Britain, and everyone seemed to have plenty of money. One result of this was a rise in prices; another was that foreigners paid less for British pounds when they bought them in the foreign banks. In 1913 £1 was worth 4.86 American dollars, but by 1918 £1 was worth only 4.20 dollars.

This fall in the value of the pound led to a fall in export prices. In 1913 a shipment of coal worth £1,000 would have cost 4,860 American dollars; in 1919 it would only have cost 4,200 American dollars.

Montagu Norman knew that British bankers had done well when the pound was worth 4.86 dollars. So, in the 1920s he tried to turn the clock back, and make the pound worth more than it really was. Winston Churchill, the Chancellor of the Exchequer, agreed with Norman's arguments, and in his 1925 budget he announced that in future the pound would be worth 4.86 dollars.

Effects of this Revaluation

Most people welcomed the news that the 'pound would be able to look the dollar in the face'. Few listened to John Maynard Keynes – a famous economist – who said that Britain would now find it even harder to sell goods abroad. That shipment of coal valued at £1,000 now went up from 4,200 dollars to 4,860 dollars. The same was true of all other British exports; they all became about 14 per cent dearer.

The Coal Industry Again, 1925

British coal owners could not export much coal even when the pound was worth only 4.20 dollars (Chapter 35). When its price went up after 1925, they sold even less. They wanted to bring down prices by cutting miners' wages; they also proposed a longer day for the reduced pay. A. J. Cook, the Secretary of the Miners' Union, coined the slogan: 'Not a penny off the pay, not a minute on the day!'. The miners once more asked for the help of other trade unionists. The railwaymen and the transport workers agreed to call a sympathetic strike.

Baldwin did not yet want to face the Triple Alliance (Fig. 37.1), so on Friday, 31 July 1925 he agreed to pay a subsidy to the mine owners so that wages could be kept at the existing level – while a Royal Commission examined the state of the coal industry. This is known as 'Red Friday' in trade union history.

Commissions on Coal

In August 1925 a commission was set up under Sir Herbert Samuel, a Liberal politician. This was the sixth commission to examine the coal industry since 1918. The first, under Judge Sankey, had reported in 1919. It had told Lloyd George that the mines ought to be nationalized, but the government had ignored this demand. Miners felt that commissions brought them no benefit – governments paid no attention to reports that they did not like.

The Report of the Samuel Commission came out in March 1926. It argued that the industry ought to be reorganized, and that the government stop paying the subsidy to the owners. It proposed wage cuts and a working day of eight hours instead of seven.

The Miners and the Report

The government agreed to end the subsidy on 30 April 1926. The owners announced a new scale of wages – lower than those put forward by Samuel. The miners declared a coal strike to start on 1 May 1926.

Once again the miners asked for the support of other unions, and on 1 May there was a meeting of representatives from a large number of unions. They gave the General Council of the TUC powers to handle the dispute and to call on other unions to come out on strike in support of the miners.

Fig. 37.1 How a Punch *cartoonist saw the power and threat of the Triple Alliance.*

THE PROBLEM-PICTURE OF 1921.

HOW TO MAKE THE TAIL WAG.

The T.U.C. and the Government

On 1 May the miners were on strike, and the T.U.C. was involved in talks with the government to try to solve the problem. Late in the evening of 3 May printers at the *Daily Mail* refused to print an article that criticized the workers. This had not been done on the orders of the T.U.C., but Baldwin used it as an excuse to break off talks with them (Extract 37.1). The General Strike started on the next day, 4 May.

The T.U.C. sent out strike notices to workers involved in transport, railways, docks, printing, electricity generating stations, and in the steel, chemical, and building trades. This has earned it the title of the General Strike. But the majority of workers were not called out on strike.

What Was the Strike about?

The Strike had started over a dispute in the coal industry. Were the miners going to have to take cuts in wages? If they did, would other workers also have to take cuts later on as happened in 1921 (p. 210)?

Baldwin argued that the T.U.C. was trying to make the government do what it did not want to do – continue to pay the subsidy to the mine owners. Baldwin argued that this was a fight between Parliament and the Trade Union Congress, but the T.U.C. denied this.

The Events of the Strike

The government had been defeated on Red Friday, 1925, but Baldwin had learned a lesson from that failure. He had set up the Organization for the Maintenance of Supplies (O.M.S.). This meant that the country was divided into regions, each controlled by a Civil Commissioner. He had the power to call out the Army, to enrol special constables, and to recruit volunteers to act as drivers, porters, and dockers. When the Strike started on 4 May 1926 the O.M.S. went into action. Sailors were sent in to run the generating stations; volunteers drove buses, lorries and trains; and troops guarded convoys of lorries carrying food and other supplies (Fig. 37.2).

At first there was little violence between strikers and police or Army, and in Plymouth there was even a football match between strikers and police. But after two or three days there was a change. Stones were thrown at buses and lorries, and trams and buses were overturned. A leading Liberal lawyer and M.P., Sir John Simon, declared that the Strike was illegal; the Catholic Cardinal Bourne condemned it as a 'mortal sin'; and the BBC put out only reports favourable to the government. MacDonald, the Labour leader, was not allowed to broadcast to put the miners' case.

The leaders of the T.U.C. became increasingly worried. Should they call out workers in other

Fig. 37.2 Armoured cars escort a convoy of lorries carrying food along the East India Dock Road. Striking dockers line the street.

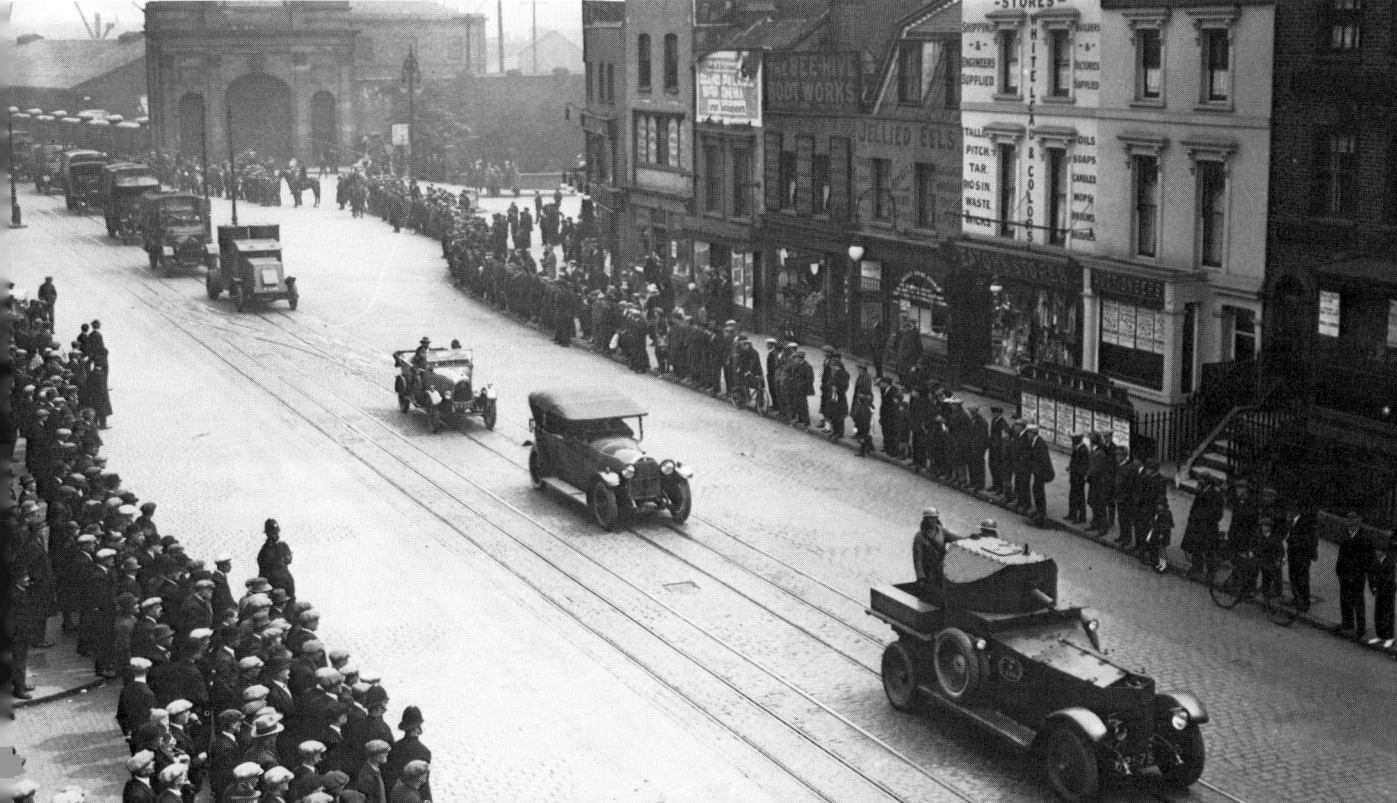

industries? Were they right to force the government to continue the subsidy? Was it illegal? Would they go to gaol when it was over? Where would it end, and how?

Thomas and other leaders met Sir Herbert Samuel, and he agreed to act as a link between the T.U.C. and Baldwin. Baldwin demanded an end to the Strike before he would agree to talk about the miners' problems. The T.U.C. did not call any of the miners' leaders to their talks, but instead they sent a small group to tell Baldwin that they were willing to call off the Strike. The Strike ended on 12 May 1926. Most leaders of the local strike committees found it very hard to understand why they had to call off a strike which their members wanted to continue. When they went back to work many workers found their employers in a very harsh mood. Some offered lower wages than they had been paying before the Strike, and many men who had been known to be strike leaders did not get their jobs back.

But the miners did not go back. They described the T.U.C.'s action as a 'betrayal'. They stayed out until December when once again they were driven back by hunger. They had to accept even lower wages in December than they had been offered in April 1926, and for many miners there was no return to work. Many owners found that they could not sell their coal and their mines did not reopen.

The Trades Disputes Act 1927

Baldwin had promised the T.U.C. leaders that there would be no victimization once they called off the Strike. In reality, many employers made the return to work as hard as they could. Some refused to allow trade unions to be organized in their factories, wages were cut, and some men not taken on again.

The government itself showed that it meant to put the unions in their place (Fig. 37.3). In 1927 the Trades Disputes Act made a sympathetic strike illegal. Civil Servants could not belong to a union connected with the T.U.C. The Act altered the law about the unions and their political funds. Members had to write a letter asking to be allowed to pay the political levy; they had to *contract in*. Under the 1913 Act every union member paid the levy unless he *contracted out*. This was intended to limit the political power of the unions and the Labour Party.

A Reforming Government, 1925–9

In 1926 Parliament passed the Electricity Act. This set up the Central Electricity Board to distribute electrical power along the National Grid. This was a sign that even the right-wing government was forced to

nationalize some industries or organizations. The government also gave the BBC a charter making it a public corporation.

In 1928 the government supported the Equal Franchise Act which gave women the vote on the same terms as men. Women had taken another step along the road to equality with men.

The Economy

Between 1925 and 1929 there was some improvement in the state of trade – except in the older industries such as coal, cotton, shipbuilding, iron, and steel. Unemployment remained well above 1 million – but in the new booming areas around London and the Midlands things seemed to be picking up.

There was a similar improvement in foreign affairs. The League of Nations was the centre of long discussions about disarmament. Churchill ordered a reduction in the size of the Army and Navy and almost succeeded in scrapping the Air Force. Sixty nations signed a Pact named after the French Foreign Minister (Briand) and the American Secretary of State (Kellogg). The Kellogg–Briand Pact said that nations would renounce war as an instrument of government policy. This was welcome news to the

Fig. 37.3 How the unions saw Churchill's hostility towards them in 1926.

people who still remembered the horrors of 1914–18, but the Pact did not say how differences between nations were to be settled. It was, in fact, an expression of hope rather than a solution to the world's problems.

The General Election 1929 (Extract 37.2)

By May 1929 Baldwin hoped that people would have forgotten the bitterness of the Strike and the Trades Disputes Act. He also hoped that the 7 million women who had got the vote in 1928 would support him. He campaigned on the slogan of 'Safety First'. The Liberals under Lloyd George argued that the government ought to spend money on road building, housing, new generating stations, and on railway modernization. This would create more employment.

Labour claimed that it alone had the cure for unemployment, and the results showed that many people believed this. Labour won 287 seats, the Conservatives 261, and the Liberals only 59. Labour was now the largest party in the Commons, but as in 1924, it had to rely on Liberal support. MacDonald became Prime Minister for the second time in May 1929, and Snowden, Thomas, Henderson, and Clynes became his most important ministers. Margaret Bondfield became the first women Cabinet minister when she became Minister for Labour, and Thomas was given the job of finding a cure for unemployment.

Questions

Extract 37.1

The beginning of the General Strike (1926)

> It was now Monday, May 3rd. We were approaching the most fateful decision of the whole dispute. We knew that any attempt to impose a decision on the miners would be resisted. They would say that they had been badly let down. . . . It would be even worse than Black Friday of 1921. . . . Herbert Smith (the miners' leader) was sitting at the table immediately opposite Pugh (the chairman of the Negotiating Committee of the T.U.C.). He pointed out that the miners were now actually locked out. While we were talking a message came to say that Baldwin wanted to see us. . . .

> Baldwin looked very troubled, and before we sat down he said that the printers had refused to print an article in one of the London papers. That was a challenge to the Government and no Government could go on negotiating in these circumstances. . . . This was a bombshell to us, as we had no knowledge whatever of the incident to which he referred. We concluded that the incident had deliberately been used as a means of terminating the negotiations. . . . We made for the door somewhat perplexed, and with a feeling that we had not been treated fairly.
> (Lord Citrine, *Men and Work* (Hutchinson, 1964).)

1. Why were the miners 'locked out' on 3 May?
2. What had happened on Black Friday, 1921?
3. In which of the 'London papers' had the workers refused to print an article? Why had they done so? How far, if at all, was the T.U.C. to blame for this refusal?
4. Why did Citrine believe that 'we had not been treated fairly'?
5. How had (i) the government, and (ii) the T.U.C. prepared for a General Strike since October 1925?

Extract 37.2

The general election of 1929

> The election of 30 May, 1929, was historic because for the first time women were placed on equality with men . . . and not unnaturally the so-called 'flapper vote' occupied attention among all party organizers.
> The Tories relied on the face of 'Honest Stan' to see them through. The lugubrious portrait stared down from tens of thousands of posters. Underneath was the negative slogan of 'Safety First'. . . . Equally unfortunate for the Tories was the idea of an election theme-song. Talking pictures were the sensation of the time, and everyone knew 'Sonny Boy' sung by Al Jolson. . . . An expert re-wrote this song with the title of 'Stanley Boy'. Parodies of the parody enlivened meetings considerably.
> The Liberals were quite a formidable opposition. Lloyd George was making a final attempt to rehabilitate his party with a national campaign which promised to conquer unemployment within twelve months.
> Labour wanted no theme songs or miracle cures. It went to the country with a well-considered document, *Labour and the Nation*.
> (Lord Morrison of Lambeth, *An Autobiography* (Odhams, 1960).)

1. When were women 'placed on equality with men'? What was meant by the 'flapper vote'?
2. What was the slogan used by the Conservatives during the 1929 election? Why was this not a sufficiently strong appeal for many working-class families?

3. Why were 'talking pictures the sensation of the time'? Who was Al Jolson? What was particularly notable about his song, 'Sonny Boy'?

4. Were the Conservatives wise to have made up a song on 'Stanley Boy'? Why?

5. Which famous economist supported Lloyd George's claim that unemployment could be conquered? When, in fact, was there full employment for all British workers?

6. Why was the result of this election particularly important for (i) the growth of the Labour Party, and (ii) the decline of the Liberal Party?

Fig. 37.3

1. To which government had Churchill belonged between 1906 and 1914? What had that government done to help trade unions in (i) 1906, and (ii) 1913?

2. What office did Churchill have in the government of 1925–9? Which of his actions had made it more difficult for the coal owners to sell coal overseas?

3. Make a short list of the ways in which unions were 'punished' in 1927.

4. What was the significance of the words on the victim's arms? Why did the artist show these words on separate arms? (See Fig. 37.1 for a clue, but also check on your answer to Question 3 in this picture.)

Worksheet

(A)

1. Why does Neville Chamberlain deserve the title 'a founder of the Welfare State'? Name TWO other politicians who have a claim to a similar title.

2. Make a list of the major reforms carried out by the Baldwin government, 1925–9.

3. Why was Britain able to lend a great deal of money abroad in 1913? Why was she less able to do so in 1923? Why did the bankers want to do so? How did they manage it?

4. Why did Britain return to the gold standard? What was the effect of that return on (i) export prices in general (ii) coal prices in particular (iii) the level of unemployment?

5. Explain the causes of the General Strike as seen by (i) the miners' union (ii) the T.U.C. (iii) the government.

6. Why did the T.U.C. call the Strike off?

7. Write a brief note on EACH of the following: O.M.S.; Montagu Norman; the Trades Disputes Act; the Kellogg–Briand Pact.

(B)

1. Write the letters which might have been sent by:
(a) a Conservative M.P. explaining why Baldwin brought Austen Chamberlain and Winston Churchill into the Cabinet in 1925;
(b) one of those who was forced to sell his large London home;
(c) one of the union leaders who supported the miners in 1926.

(C)

1. Write the headlines which might have appeared above reports on:
(a) the return to the gold standard, 1925;
(b) Red Friday, 1925;
(c) the miner owners' decision on wages, April 1926;
(d) the start of the General Strike, 3 May 1926;
(e) the end of the Strike;
(f) the granting of the BBC charter, 1926.

2. Draw or paint the posters which might have been used by EACH of the parties during the 1929 election campaign.

38 The Second Labour Government, 1929-31

1929 Election

After 1925 Germany and other countries in Europe had recovered from the effects of the post-war slump. This recovery was due almost entirely to the huge loans which American banks gave to various European countries and companies. These used the money to build factories, buy machinery, and generally make their industries get back to work.

This meant that the British exporter could sell more goods in a booming Europe, and that meant more jobs for people in Britain. So Prime Minister Baldwin expected to win the election which he called for June 1929.

But there were still over 1 million men out of work – about 11 per cent of the working population (Extract 38.1), and the voters seemed to think that the Labour Party would do something to bring down that figure. The results of the election gave Labour 285 seats, the Conservatives 260, and the Liberals 59.

The Work of the Labour Government, 1929-31

As we shall see, the government became involved in the greatest depression the world had ever seen in 1930–1, but in June 1929 no one knew that this was going to happen. So there was a good deal of interest in the appointment of Margaret Bondfield to the post of Minister of Labour. She was the first woman to sit in a Cabinet, and this seemed to be a sign that this would be a 'modern' government.

In 1930 the government pushed through a Coal Mines Act. This reduced the miners' working day to $7\frac{1}{2}$ hours. It also set up a commission to reorganize the coal industry. Maybe, it was thought, there would be an end to the violence of the 1920s.

A Housing Act (1930) was Labour's attempt to revive the Wheatley Act of 1924. The government also announced plans for clearing away the slums which disfigured the majority of Britain's industrial towns.

In Chapter 40 we will see that MacDonald, the Prime Minister, and Arthur Henderson, his Foreign Secretary, worked hard to try to get the countries of the world to accept a policy of disarmament.

Labour and Plans for Unemployment

J. H. Thomas was given the post of Lord Privy Seal. This gave him a seat in the Cabinet without having to look after a ministry. His job was to provide plans to bring down the level of unemployment, and to help him in this he had two junior ministers – the more important of whom was Sir Oswald Mosley.

Thomas persuaded the Chancellor, Philip Snowden (Fig. 38.1), to allow him to spend £42 million on what were called 'public works'. Roads, bridges, houses, hospitals and schools could be built with the help of this money.

This money would be paid to the various companies doing the various works. They would use it to buy machinery and materials, and pay labour and staff.

Fig. 38.1 Philip Snowden, Chancellor of the Exchequer, in 1930.

This would mean an increase in employment at the firms making the machinery and supplying the various materials – bricks, glass, and so on.

The Mosley Plan, 1930

Snowden was not willing to allow Thomas to spend more than £42 million. He thought that government spending (including the £42 million) had to be equalled by government income (or taxation), but he did not want to put up taxation to provide more money for Thomas to spend. He thought that if taxes went up, people would have less money to spend. This, he said, would mean a drop in their buying power and so a rise in unemployment among people whose goods might have been bought by the taxpayers.

Mosley, the Chancellor of the Duchy of Lancaster, wanted the government to spend much more. He wanted to spend hundreds of millions of pounds to tackle unemployment. He wanted a system of tariffs to stop the flood of foreign goods into Britain, and he wanted the government to provide good pensions for older workers so that they would retire and make way for younger unemployed people.

The government rejected this plan, and so Mosley resigned. He put his case to the 1930 Labour Party Conference, but this too rejected his plan. Mosley then left the Labour Party and formed the Fascist Party. He saw himself as the leader who would save Britain from depression.

Profit-making and Wealth

During the 1920s the American economy had grown at a very rapid rate. In the presidential election of 1928 President Hoover had said that America would soon be the country where there would be a 'chicken in every pot and two cars in every garage'. In 1929 an American businessman told Americans that they were 'only at the beginning of a period which will go down in history as a golden age'.

Many companies made vast profits during this period. Companies making cars, household gadgets and films, as well as companies owning stores and shops became very profitable. People who owned shares in such companies received a large profit each year. This made their shares very valuable, and so other people wanted to buy them. This buying and selling of shares took place at the American Stock Exchange in Wall Street, New York (Fig. 38.2).

People were able to buy large numbers of shares because of what was known as 'buying on the margin'. They only had to put down ten cents for each dollar's worth of shares they wanted to buy. The rest of the money had to be paid after a month or so. By that time they hoped that the price of their shares would have gone up, and that this would enable them to sell at a higher price. They could then pay what they owed and have money left over. This was how millions of ordinary Americans made huge profits during the 1920s. Shop assistants, lift-boys and hotel porters, barbers, clerks, and lorry drivers took part in this gambling on company shares. Many of them borrowed money from local banks to provide themselves with the money needed to 'buy on the margin'. Banks also used their customers' money to gamble on the Stock Exchange and so make high profits – for the bank.

Less Profitable America

In the scramble to buy shares, few people thought about the real value of the shares they were buying. They only saw that the demand for shares kept pushing up their prices.

Fig. 38.2 Wall Street, New York.

In fact in 1928 and 1929 the profits of the majority of American firms had been falling. Car firms found that while they could produce millions of cars, not all of them were being sold. This over-production led to a fall-off in trade. Men were laid off and unemployment queues grew longer.

American farmers had provided the chicken that Hoover wanted to see in every pot. They had also produced the wheat, cotton, and other products – but in too great a quantity. In 1929 wheat was cheaper than it had been for over 400 years. There were similar falls in the prices of coffee, cotton, meat, potatoes, and other foodstuffs. This drastic fall in prices brought down the cost of living. But it meant ruin for farmers whose income fell. They had too little money – so they bought less from their local stores. This meant a drop in orders from millions of such stores – and unemployment in the factories supplying those stores.

The Crash, October 1929

The bankers were the first people to realize that they were lending money to buy shares which were not really worth the money being paid for them. They began to ask people to repay the loans taken out to buy shares. People then had to sell their shares to get that money. Almost everyone was forced to do this. Millions of Americans were trying to sell shares which few Americans wanted to buy, and this led to a rapid fall in share prices. Newspaper headlines reported 'Panic', 'Record Selling of Stocks', 'Heavy Falls in Prices'.

As the value of the shares fell, many companies were ruined. Factories closed down and shops were shut because owners had no money to pay wages. Banks that had loaned money could not get it back from ruined customers, and so hundreds of banks closed down; millions of people lost the savings they had left in the banks.

The Effect Overseas

There was a fall in the demand made by American firms for raw materials, and this drove down prices even further.

American banks had loaned a great deal of money to European banks during the prosperous 1920s. Now, in 1929, they tried to get that money back. This meant that many of these banks had to get money back from customers who had used it to build up a business. Many of these businesses and industries had to be closed down, and this increased the level of unemployment throughout Europe. In 1931 in Germany there were 5 million men out of work – one in every three.

Effect in Britain

The fall in primary prices – food and raw materials – led to a fall in British living costs, but it also meant a drop in British sales to the primary-producing countries. This in turn led to a rise in the level of the unemployment (Extract 38.1).

And as the number of the unemployed went up so too did the amount of money that the government had to pay into the Unemployment Insurance Fund. If there were 940,000 out of work, the money coming into the Fund exactly equalled the money being paid out to the unemployed. But in 1929, 1930, and 1931 the number of unemployed continued to rise until it reached the startling figure of 3 million. This meant that the Fund was spending more than it took in, and the difference had to be made up by the government – which had to get that money from taxation.

In 1928 the Conservative government had put almost £12 million into the Fund. In 1930 this went up to nearly £37 million and in 1931 to about £55 million. We might be tempted to think that these were not large sums of money, because we have become used to governments spending thousands of millions of pounds. But we ought to remember that the spending in 1931 was almost five times as great as the spending in 1929. This was obviously a very serious problem.

The Budget Deficit, 1930–1

The huge increase in the amount being poured into the Insurance Fund meant that the government was spending more than it received in taxes. In February 1931 the Chancellor warned the country about this. He also set up an Economy Committee under Sir George May to look into this problem. This Committee was to report to the Chancellor in August 1931.

The Banking Problem, 1930–1

We have seen in Chapter 37 that the London bankers made high profits from borrowing money from French and other European banks to lend to overseas investors.

In 1931 European banks began to fear that the British government was not going to tackle the problem of its budget deficit. They thought that the government would cover the deficit simply by printing more money. This would push down the value of the pound – something which we have seen happen in the 1970s. If this happened the pound would be worth fewer francs, lira, marks, and so on. This frightened the European bankers. They thought they might get back much less than they had loaned to the British.

This fear was increased in the summer of 1931 by a series of collapses in the European banking system. On 7 July 1931, the headlines told of 'German banks on verge of collapse' – largely as a result of the recall of the American loans. On 15 July the headlines claimed that 'Financial Crisis involves all Central Europe'.

On 16 July 1931 foreign bankers started to take their money out of London. By 31 July the Bank of England had to go to banks in America and France and ask for a loan of £50 million in gold. If this had not been given, the Bank of England would not have been able to repay the loans which were now being 'called in' by frightened bankers on the Continent.

The May Committee Reports

On 31 July Parliament went into summer recess. On 1 August the Report of the May Committee was published. This showed that the government was spending £120 million more than it was getting in taxation. The Committee called for a slight increase in taxation and a large cut in government spending. In particular it called for a cut in the money paid to the unemployed.

The Prime Minister sent his Cabinet colleagues off for their summer holidays with instructions 'to study the Report'. But the European bankers would not wait that long, and by the middle of August the Bank of England had used up the loan of £50 million. It now went back to the French and American banks to ask for another £80 million. They refused to give this extra loan. Montagu Norman, Governor of the Bank of England, had collapsed under the strain, so it was his Deputy and another Director of the Bank who went to see MacDonald on 11 August 1931. They explained that the loans would not be given unless the government cut its spending and balanced its budget.

The Government Debates the May Committee's Report

MacDonald called his ministers back from their holidays to discuss the crisis facing the Bank and the country. He argued that the government would have to make the economies suggested in the Report. This was the policy supported by Montagu Norman from his sickbed, by the May Committee, by the Civil Servants advising the government, and by the Chancellor, Snowden.

A small number of ministers were unwilling to agree to this harsh policy. Henderson and others took the advice of the General Council of the T.U.C., and argued that the Bank should give up its attempts to keep the pound at its 1925 level. It certainly ought not to ask the unemployed to take a cut in their benefits.

The Government Splits, 23 August 1931

On 23 August the Cabinet voted to accept a watered-down version of the *May Report*, but the leaders of the Liberal and Conservative Parties would not agree to support such a motion if it was brought before the House of Commons. MacDonald then went to see the King, George V. He told him that the Opposition (which had more seats in the Commons than did Labour) was asking for even more cuts. He warned the King that Henderson and other Labour ministers would resign if he tried to put these demands before the Commons. He therefore offered his resignation to the King.

The King consulted Baldwin and Herbert Samuel (of the Liberals). Both agreed to serve under MacDonald in a National government in an effort to save the pound and to overcome the crisis. MacDonald agreed to form such an All-Party government. This came as a surprise to most of his colleagues. On 24 August they had gone to Number 10 Downing Street to hear about the fall of the government (Extract 38.2). When MacDonald came back from Buckingham Palace he told them about the formation of the National government. Many Labour ministers thought that MacDonald had deserted the party which, in 1903, he had done so much to help.

The National Government

MacDonald formed a Cabinet in which there were two Liberal ministers, four Conservative ministers, and three other Labour ministers (Snowden, Thomas, and Sankey) in addition to MacDonald himself (Fig. 38.3).

This government accepted the cuts that Snowden proposed. There were cuts in the salaries of the Civil Servants, teachers, police, and members of the armed forces. There was a 10 per cent cut in the unemployment benefit and an increase in income tax.

These all helped to balance the budget. The European bankers then gave the £80 million loan.

Fig. 38.3 The National Government, 1931. Standing from left to right: Sir Cunliffe Lister (Conservative); J. H. Thomas (National Labour); Lord Reading (National Liberal); Neville Chamberlain (Conservative); Sir Samuel Hoare (Conservative). Sitting from left to right: Philip Snowden (National Labour); Stanley Baldwin (Conservative); Ramsay MacDonald (National Labour); Sir Herbert Samuel (Liberal); Lord Sankey (National Labour).

But all this was of little help. There was a mutiny at the naval base at Invergordon in Scotland where the sailors refused to obey orders to sail after hearing about the cuts in their pay. Europeans thought that this was the beginning of 'the English Revolution'. More bankers took their money out of London and the £80 million was quickly spent.

On 21 September the government announced that it was no longer going to hold the pound to its 1925 level. It quickly fell to 3.40 dollars. This was a devaluation of the pound. This helped to lower the price of British exports and helped make them easier to sell.

The 1931 Election

The government had come into existence to save the pound – which it did not manage to do. MacDonald had promised that once the crisis had been overcome, there would be an election on the traditional party lines. He failed to keep that promise. In October 1931 he called a general election. He asked for a 'doctor's mandate' to cure the nation's sickness. The National government won 554 seats (Conservatives 473, National Labour 68, and National Liberals 13). Labour won 52; Lloyd George's Liberals won 4. It was this Parliament that set about trying to deal with the domestic and foreign problems facing Britain in the 1930s.

Questions

Extract 38.1

Unemployment levels, 1929–31

1. Look at the table below. What percentage of workers were unemployed in (i) 1929 (ii) 1931? If there were 3 million people out of work in 1931, how many were at work in that year?

	1929	1930	1931
			Percentages
Coal-mining	19.0	20.6	28.4
Cotton textiles	12.9	32.4	43.2
Woollen textiles	15.5	23.3	33.8
Shipbuilding	25.3	27.6	51.9
General engineering	9.9	14.2	27.0
Building	14.3	16.2	22.7
Boot and shoe manufacture	15.5	15.2	22.2
Motors, cycles and aircraft manufacture	7.1	12.1	19.3
Total insured workers aged 16+	11.0	14.6	21.5

2. In 1979 there were 1.5 million unemployed, but there were 23 million people at work. How far does this help to explain why unemployment is not as serious a problem as it was in 1931?

3. In which industries was unemployment above (i) 50 per cent (ii) 40 per cent (iii) 30 per cent (iv) 22 per cent?

4. Which areas were most affected by high unemployment in coal-mining, cotton textiles, woollen textiles, shipbuilding?

Extract 38.2

Hugh Dalton and the fall of the Labour Government, 24 August 1931

> ... At 2.30 the Cabinet Room is crowded. ... J.R.M. sits alone on the other side of the long table. He had originally summoned us, he says, to tell us that our salaries were to be cut. ... But now he has to tell us that the Government is at an end. He is very sorry. We shall be told it is a bankers' ramp. But that is quite untrue. He has received most valuable help from the bankers. It was quite essential to get a loan quickly. Otherwise sterling would have collapsed. There would have been a run on the banks. ... He thinks the crisis could have been avoided if the Cabinet hadn't changed its mind at a critical point. A plan had been drawn up and agreed which would have sufficed to secure a loan. But then the Cabinet went back on it. This made necessary a Government of Persons, not of Parties. He is going through with this. He has not called us here to ask us to join him. Most of us are young men, with our political careers before us. He realises he is committing political suicide. He is not going to ask any of us to do the same. ...
>
> (Hugh Dalton, *The Fateful Years* (Mullen, 1957).)

1. Who was 'J.R.M.'?
2. Which members of the Cabinet thought that the crisis was a 'bankers' ramp'?
3. Over what had 'the Cabinet changed its mind'?
4. Did 'sterling' collapse after Britain came off the gold standard? What does that tell you about the accusation that it was a 'bankers' ramp'?

Worksheet

(A)
1. Why were banks in America (i) able to, and (ii) willing to lend money to European banks and firms? How did that benefit Britain in the 1920s?

2. Why did the American banks recall their European loans in 1929? What effect did that have in Germany? How did this affect the loans that foreign bankers had made to Britain?

3. Why were share prices in America (i) rising during the 1920s (ii) rising too quickly in 1928–9?

4. Write a brief note on EACH of the following: Wall Street; buying on the margin; the Unemployment Insurance Fund.

5. Why was there a depression in the agricultural areas of America in the late 1920s? How did this affect the level of employment in American industry?

6. Name TWO countries that relied on agriculture for their employment. How were they affected by the fall in food prices? What effect did this have on (i) British exports and employment (ii) British living standards in the 1930s?

7. What is the meaning of a budget deficit? Why was there a fall in the government's income from taxation in 1930–1? Why was there a rise in some government spending in that year?

8. How did the May Committee propose to meet the budget deficit?

9. Why did the news of the *May Report* frighten European bankers?

10. Why was the Labour Cabinet split over the *May Report*?

11. Why was the government formed in August 1931 called a National government? Why did it fail to keep its promises?

(B)
1. Write the letters that might have been sent by:
(a) Mosley or Keynes on a remedy for unemployment;
(b) Snowden arguing against Mosley (or Keynes);
(c) a farmer complaining of the fall in prices in 1929;
(d) the owner of a shop in a country town explaining why he is going out of business;
(e) a union leader who was opposed to the cuts proposed in the *May Report*;
(f) a former Labour voter explaining why he voted for the National government in 1931.

2. Write extracts that might have appeared in the diaries of ONE of the following in 1931: Snowden; MacDonald; a French banker; a member of the T.U.C.

(C)
1. Write the headlines that might have appeared above reports on:
(a) the appointment of Margaret Bondfield;
(b) the appointment and task of J. H. Thomas;
(c) the Wall Street Crash;
(d) the *May Report*;
(e) the split in the Labour Cabinet;
(f) the formation of the National government;
(g) the decision to abandon the gold standard;
(h) the result of the election, 1931.

39 The Government at Home, 1931-9

In Chapter 38 we saw the way in which the Labour government's plans for dealing with unemployment were overtaken by the Great Depression following the Wall Street Crash (Fig. 39.1). In Chapter 35 we saw that this depression was one that most severely affected the old industries – coal, iron, and steel, shipbuilding, cotton, and woollen textiles. We also saw that there were, in Britain, 'two nations'. In the Depressed Areas there were millions of unemployed without hope of getting a job. In other parts of the country there were the workers in the new industries. These had a rising standard of living during the 1930s.

Fig. 39.1 The hopelessness of an unemployed man in Wigan in November 1939. He was still out of work two months after war had begun. Ten of the town's fifteen mills were shut and seventeen out of the forty pits remained closed.

In this chapter we will see how the National government tried to deal with the high unemployment that affected the Depressed Areas. We will also see how there was a fall in the high level of unemployment – for reasons that had little to do with government policy.

The End of Free Trade

After the 1931 election, Snowden became Viscount Snowden and a member of the House of Lords. The new Chancellor of the Exchequer was Neville Chamberlain, son of Joseph Chamberlain. In Chapter 26 we saw how Joseph Chamberlain had tried to get the country to accept a policy of tariff reform as one way of curing the rising unemployment of the end of the nineteenth century. He failed, but in February 1932 his son brought in an Import Duties Bill. This allowed most food and some raw materials to come into the country without having to pay any tariff. About one-quarter of imports would have to pay between 10 per cent and 20 per cent as import duties while about half of Britain's imports would have to pay even higher rates.

This was intended to make foreign manufactured goods more expensive, so that it would be easier for British manufacturers to sell their goods at home. This would lead to more jobs and a fall in unemployment. The car industry was one that benefited from this policy of protection. William Morris, Herbert Austin, and other manufacturers produced the millions of British cars bought by prosperous Britishers in the 1930s (Extract 39.1).

Empire Free Trade – a Failure

Chamberlain hoped to be able to follow the other part of his father's policies, to reduce the tariffs on goods bought and sold between the countries of the Empire. In the summer of 1932 there was an Imperial Conference in Ottawa, Canada, but the Commonwealth countries wanted to protect their own industries against competition from British imports. Canada wanted to try to develop her trade with

America. She did not want to hinder that growth by putting tariffs on American goods.

So the Ottawa Conference failed to agree on Chamberlain's policy of imperial preference. Instead, there were a number of trade treaties between Britain and some of the Commonwealth countries. Britain also signed such treaties with other countries – Argentina, Russia, Finland, and others. Britain agreed to buy an agreed amount of their goods in return for their putting lower tariffs on British goods, or for agreeing to buy a certain quantity of British goods – notably coal.

Resignations from the Government

Snowden resigned from the government over the end of the traditional policy of Free Trade. The Liberals in the government were split over the issue. Some, led by Samuel, resigned. Others, led by Sir John Simon, opposed the end of Free Trade but stayed on in the government. Gradually these Simonite National Liberals became Conservatives in all but name.

The Government's Money Policy

Chamberlain took over Snowden's policy of trying to balance the budget. By 1934 he had managed to do even better than that; he collected more in taxation than he spent. This allowed him to increase unemployment benefit to its former level. He also raised the salaries of teachers and others whose wages had been cut in 1931. In 1935 he went further and restored these salaries to their former level.

One way of getting the budget to balance was by cutting the amount of money spent by the government on such things as roads, bridges, and houses. This was a short-sighted policy. It meant that there was a lower demand for machinery and for raw materials than there would have been if the government had built more roads and more houses. In Germany and America the governments tackled the question of unemployment by spending even more on these 'public works'. Germany was covered with a network of high quality motorways – and millions of people were employed as a result. Britain had to wait until the 1960s for her motorways – when they cost even more to build and when there was almost no unemployment.

Another way of cutting government spending was by reducing the amount paid in interest on the National Debt. In February 1932 the Bank of England reduced the interest rate from 6 per cent and by June 1932 it had fallen to only 2 per cent. The government then announced that instead of paying 5 per cent on its borrowing from lenders it would in future pay only $3\frac{1}{2}$ per cent. This saved the government about £3 million each year.

The low rate of interest charged by the Bank ought to have tempted industrialists to borrow 'cheap' money to build new factories and put new machinery in their existing factories. This would have helped to reduce the level of unemployment. But the industrialists followed the examples of the government. The Government spent less on roads, bridges, and houses; the industrialists spent less on building and machinery. They missed a chance to re-equip British industry and also to provide work for millions of people.

The Government and Industry

The government seemed willing to retreat into a sort of shell. Industry was to be protected from foreign competition by a wall (or shell) of tariffs. Behind this wall, the government and industry spent less than they had spent before 1931. Instead of trying to create work by new industry or building, the government and industry cut down the amount of work. They accepted the fact that there was a world depression and that fewer goods could be sold.

The government helped to set up the British Iron and Steel Federation – run by the owners of the iron and steel companies. These were helped by a high tariff on imported iron and steel. This helped to make British iron and steel appear cheaper to the domestic consumer. There was a rise in output from 5 million tons (of steel) in 1931 to 13 million tons in 1937. At the same time the Federation reorganized the industry. Many old works were closed down – which led to a rise in unemployment in certain areas. Some new ones were opened in other areas but the Federation refused to allow the construction of a new works planned for Jarrow. The Federation wanted to avoid the problem of over-production and Jarrow had to continue to have about 70 per cent of its men unemployed.

There was a similar history of cutting down in shipbuilding. A company called National Shipbuilders Security was formed in February 1930. This got money from the Bankers' Industrial Development Corporation to buy up shipyards which it then closed down until the number of yards equalled the amount of work that was thought to be available. It was this company that bought up and closed Palmers' of Jarrow in 1934.

Help to Industry

In 1934 the government agreed to provide loans up to £$9\frac{1}{2}$ million for the building of ships for the North Atlantic service. This money helped to pay for the building of the *Queen Mary* on Clydeside (Fig. 39.2).

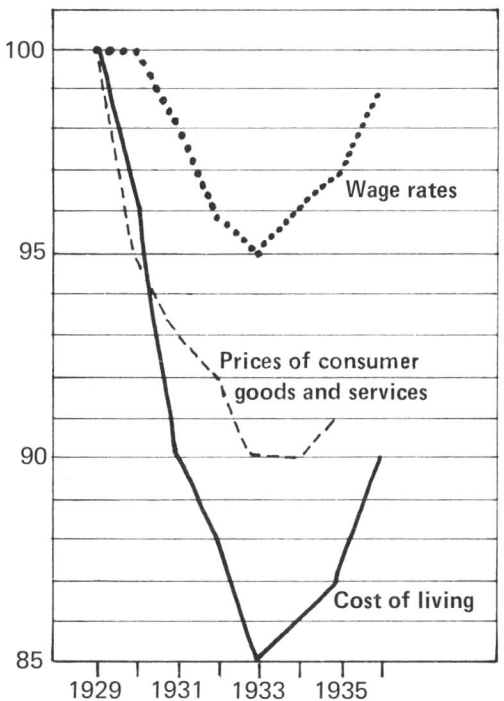

Fig. 39.2 The launching of the Queen Mary *on Clydeside, 1934 – and the end of a job for many thousands of workers.*

In 1934 the government passed the Special Areas Act. This appointed two commissioners who were given £2 million to try to attract industry to build new factories in the Depressed Areas. But Hoover, Morris, and other industrialists did not have to rely on coal power to drive the machinery in their new factories. Nor did they need the brawn of the workmen in the older industries on their new assembly lines. So there was no reason why they should go to the old, Depressed Areas. They preferred the green fields around London and Oxford to the squalid towns of industrial Britain. They wanted their new industries to be different from the old ones, with their history of battles between labour and the bosses. So the commissioners had very little success in attracting industry to the old, decaying, areas. Some industrial estates were built – but the small factories that were developed tended to employ mainly women and unskilled machine minders. It was rearmament and the fear of war that brought life and work to the old industrial areas. Under the threat of war the government found the money to pay for armaments, for tanks, and for the iron and steel needed for these war goods. Jarrow went back to work again as did South Wales, Scotland, and the North-East.

The Better-off 'Second' Nation

Many millions of people had a higher standard of living in 1938 than they had in 1934. But little, if any, of this rise was a result of government policy. Certainly the tariff system helped to provide some work for people, in firms which otherwise might have had to face a flood of cheap foreign goods; and certainly the lowering of the Bank Rate and the adoption of a 'cheap' money policy helped. But the recovery of the 1930s was a result of much more than these two government policies.

Much more important was the fall in the cost of living (Fig. 39.3). At the same time there was only a

Fig. 39.3 The evidence for rising living standards in the 1930s.

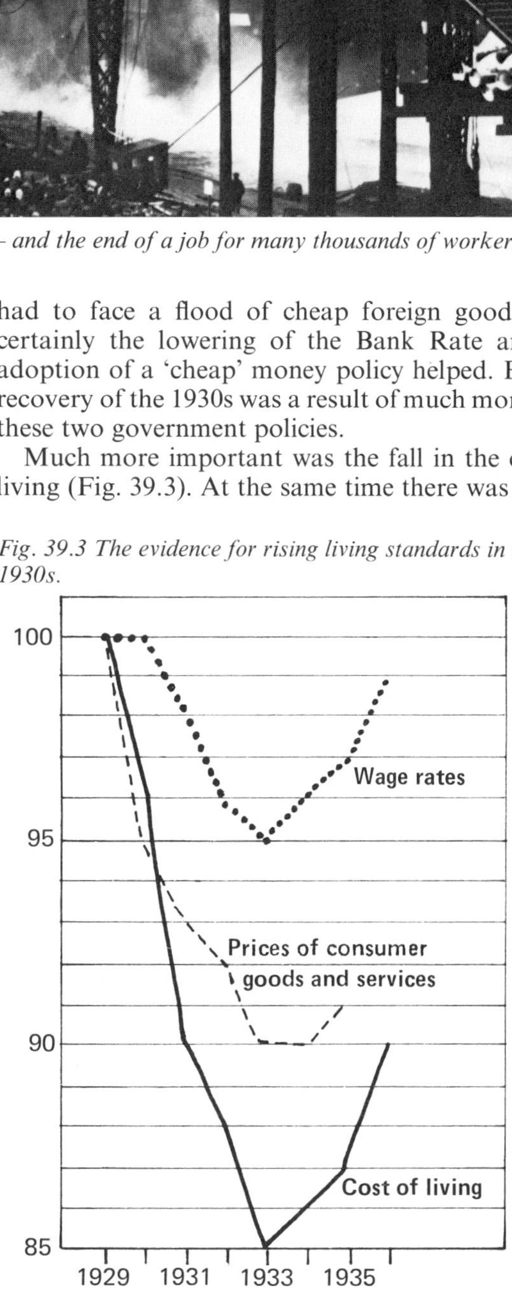

slight fall in wage rates. People had to pay less for their food and clothing because of the fall in world prices, so they had money to spare to spend on motor cars, wireless sets, telephones, and other household goods. This provided employment in the industries making these goods.

People also had money to spend on what are called 'services'. During the 1930s there was a rise in the number of people employed in laundries and dry cleaning works, hotels and restaurants, entertainment and sport; there were more people employed in the supplying of gas, water and electricity, in building, the Civil Service, shops, banking and insurance.

The Signs of this Prosperity

In the 1930s there was an almost continual increase in the number and size of shops such as Woolworth, Marks & Spencer, and other chain stores. These shops were one sign of the fact that people had money to spend. During the 1930s, for the first time, most families bought at least one daily newspaper – another sign that they had money to spare. By 1939 the *Daily Express* sold 2.3 million copies every day; the *Daily Herald* sold just over 2 million, while the *Daily Mail* sold 1.5 million.

In the 1920s over 2 million wireless sets were sold, and by 1939 there were over 11 million wireless sets in British homes. The wireless had become part of normal life. So, too, had going to the cinema. In 1928 Al Jolson starred in the first of the 'talking pictures', and by 1934 there were over 4,000 cinemas in Britain. Even the poor could escape from the harsh reality of their grim lives in the cheap, warm cinema with its exciting or romantic films.

The Housing Boom

But the most lasting sign of the prosperity of the 1930s are the millions of new homes that were built and bought by the prosperous workers. The following table tells us a good deal:

	Council houses (millions)	% of all housing (millions)	For sale (millions)	%
1920–9	1.0	66	.5	33
1930–9	.7	25	2.0	75

The sharp drop in the number of houses built by local councils is not surprising. The government wanted to cut its spending – and one way of doing this was by cutting the number of houses built with government help.

It is the sharp rise in 'houses for sale' which is worth some study. The figures show that about 2 million people were sufficiently well-off to buy their own homes during the depressed 1930s. There were a number of reasons for this.

1. There was a drop in the cost of house building. Prices of materials, such as timber, fell along with the prices of food and other primary products. In 1921 it had cost £1,200 to build a small three-bedroomed house. In 1925 this price had fallen to £440; in 1931 the cost was £350, and in 1935 only £320.

2. Building Societies changed their policies about lending. These Societies had been started by working men in the nineteenth century. The Societies made a loan to a house buyer, charging him interest each year on the amount he owed. Until 1930 they wanted the loan to be repaid in ten years – so that they could lend the money to another house purchaser.

In the 1930s these Societies grew much bigger. People who had money to save might have invested it in an industrial company – but in the 1930s there were not many companies looking for such investment. The Building Societies became a favourite form of saving by the prosperous British. This allowed the Societies to lend money to many people – and to put off the date of repayment for twenty years instead of ten.

The Societies gained from the fall in the Bank Rate. When the government had been paying $5\frac{1}{2}$ per cent on the National Debt, the Societies had to pay 6 per cent or more to attract savers. This meant that they had to charge borrowers 7 per cent or more. After 1931 the government only paid $3\frac{1}{2}$ per cent on their Debt, which meant that the Societies could now cut the rate they paid to the savers – and the rate they had to charge the borrowers. These various changes are summarized in the following imaginary examples:

Example 1: Buying a house in 1921

Cost of house	£1,200
Interest at 6 per cent	72
Total cost of interest over ten years	720
Total cost of house over ten years	£1,920
Annual repayment over ten years	192
Weekly repayment:	£3.69

Example 2: Buying a house in 1935

Cost of house	£325
Interest at 4 per cent	13
Total cost of interest over twenty years	260
Total cost of house over twenty years	£585
Annual repayment over twenty years	29
Weekly repayment:	0.55p

It is obvious that more people could afford a repayment of 55p a week than could afford one of £3.69 a week. One result of this boom in house building was a large increase in the number of people employed in the building and construction industry. Another was an increase in the numbers employed to provide water, gas and electricity to these new homes. There was also a rise in employment in firms providing the furniture, floor covering, curtains and other things bought by the new house owners – helped by the development of the hire-purchase system.

The Election, 1935

In Chapter 38 we saw that the National government brought in the 'Means Test' in 1931. We also saw that it set up the Unemployment Assistance Board in 1934 after the passing of the Unemployment Act 1934.

There were protests against the way in which the Means Test and the Assistance Board did their work. Hunger marches were organized by the Union of Unemployed Workers and by other bodies throughout the country. The very small Communist Party of Great Britain claimed the credit for organizing these demonstrations. Mosley's British Union of Fascists also tried to win support from the unemployed. During the 1930s there were many clashes between the fascists and communists. But neither of these extremist parties had any political strength. In May 1935 MacDonald resigned as Prime Minister once the people had celebrated the Silver Jubilee of King George V's accession to the throne in 1910. The new Prime Minister was Stanley Baldwin. In September, the Labour Party had its Annual Conference, and the party leader, George Lansbury, asked the Conference not to vote for a policy of rearmament. The Conference did not listen; over 2 million votes were cast for a policy of rearmament against the threat of Germany. Lansbury resigned, to be succeeded by Clement Attlee.

In October 1936 Baldwin called a general election to be held on 14 November. The Conservatives won 387 seats (compared with 454 in 1931); there were thirty-three National Liberals; and eight National Labour M.P.s. Labour won 154 seats (compared with only fifty-two in 1931).

MacDonald was defeated by Emmanuel Shinwell in the constituency of Seaham. Another seat was found for him and he remained a member of the government until May 1937 when Chamberlain succeeded Baldwin. By that time Baldwin had steered the country through the problem of the abdication of King Edward VIII who wanted to marry a divorced American, Mrs Simpson. The accession of King George VI in 1936 meant that this was the year in which the country had had three Kings.

There was little, if any, change in the government's domestic policy under Baldwin and Chamberlain. The main change in policy was in foreign affairs.

Questions

Extract 39.1

The motor car in the 1920s

By 1923 British manufacturers were using mass-production methods and the car was becoming reasonably trustworthy; one seldom saw a car drawn up at the side of the road with the driver underneath as he tinkered away. In 1923 cord fabric was first used for tyres, prolonging their lives by five thousand miles. By 1924 the increasing use of cars by week-enders brought the Baby Car into the market. The 'Austin Seven' cost £165. Then came the solid-tyred Trojan four-seater at £125, and the Morris Minor.

It was not only the lower price of the mass-produced car that recommended it, but the readiness with which spare parts could be supplied.

Buses began to run on new routes; as cities spread out, so the local buses extended their itineraries. The long-distance charabanc challenged the railway for speed and comfort, and made night journeys from the north and west of England to London. The charabanc opened up rural districts which were still almost inaccessible by rail.
(Robert Graves and Alan Hodge, *The Long Weekend* (Faber, 1950).)

1. Why were car prices falling 'by 1923'?
2. Why do 'trustworthy' and 'prolonging' help to explain the increase in the number of car owners?

3. How did the development of bus services affect the growth of suburbs? Who had been able to live there before? Why?

4. What effect did the ownership of a car have on family life?

5. Why did the division between town and country break down in this period?

Extract 39.2

Improved living standards, 1920–39

Most remarkable was the looks of women. The prematurely aged wife was coming to be the exception. Children were fewer, healthier and gave less trouble; labour-saving devices were introduced, especially for washing, cleaning and cooking – the introduction of stainless cutlery saved an appreciable amount of time; this was only one of a hundred such innovations.

Advertising of branded goods was simplifying shopping. Housewives came to count on certain brands of goods; food was sold in the nearest possible stage to table-readiness; the complicated processes of making custard and other puddings were reduced by the use of prepared powders. Cereals, eaten with milk, began to challenge bacon and eggs in prosperous homes, and the bread and margarine of the poor.

Bottled and tinned goods grew more plentiful. The only choice (had been) soup, salmon, corned beef, Californian fruits and potted meat; by the thirties almost every kind of domestic and foreign fruit, meat, game, fish, vegetable could be bought. Foodstuffs were also gradually standardized: eggs, milk and butter were graded and guaranteed.

(Robert Graves and Alan Hodge, *The Long Weekend* (Faber, 1950).)

1. 'The prematurely aged wife was … the exception'. How did (i) the children (ii) household inventions contribute to this improvement?

2. Name three inventions which made (i) washing (ii) cleaning (iii) cooking easier. Why did this reduce the need for domestic servants?

3. How did (i) advertising (ii) branded goods simplify shopping?

4. In what ways (i) was it easier to prepare a meal (ii) were similar breakfasts being eaten in the homes of 'the prosperous' and 'the poor'?

5. What bottled and tinned goods became available? How does this (i) help the housewife (ii) indicate a rising standard of living for many?

Fig. 39.3

1. Why did the cost of living fall between 1929 and 1933?

2. Why was the cost of living lower in 1936 than in 1929?

3. Which fell most – wage rates or the cost of living? What does this tell you about the living standards of people who had a job in the 1930s?

4. How does this graph help to explain the rise in the demand for (i) newspapers (ii) cinema seats (iii) consumer goods (iv) new houses (v) holidays away from home? Why did this rise in demand lead to more employment for some people?

Worksheet

(A)

1. Why did the government introduce import duties in 1932? Why were there no duties on food?

2. Why were import duties more beneficial to (i) the car industry, and (ii) the steel industry than to the coal industry?

3. Why did the government cut its spending in 1932? What effect did that have on the level of employment? Why would it have been sensible to have spent more on building (i) council houses (ii) roads?

4. Why did the government want a cut in interest rates? Why did that make it easier for people to buy houses and the goods to go in them? Why did most industrialists not build new factories or machinery?

5. Why were 2 million families able to buy new homes in the depressed 1930s?

(B)

1. Write the letters that might have been sent by:
(a) one of the special commissioners appointed in 1934 explaining his failure to get industrialists to move into the Depressed (or Special) Areas;
(b) Morris or Hoover explaining why they would not build their factories in South Wales or in the north-east of England;
(c) one of the unemployed (Fig. 39.1) who moved into one of the more prosperous areas in search of work;
(d) one of the 2 million families moving into their new home.

2. Draw or paint the advertisement that might have appeared for:
(a) the 1932 Morris – which cost only £100;
(b) one of the new electrical gadgets – vacuum cleaner, toaster, washing-machine, wireless;
(c) vacancies for work in a car factory.

40 British Foreign Policy, 1919-39

The Hope for Peace

During the 1920s and the early 1930s there was a widespread hope and belief that the world had 'finished with war'. There were several reasons for this optimism:

1. The League of Nations had been set up as part of the peace settlement after the First World War. The League consisted of (a) an Assembly that met at least once each year. Every member state sent representatives to this Assembly; (b) a council that met at least three times a year. At first the council consisted of representatives from the great powers (Britain, France, Italy, and Japan) and four others chosen from among the smaller nations.

The Council was supposed to take action to avoid future wars. It had the power to order action to be taken against any nation found guilty of warlike behaviour. In the 1920s there were some signs that the League was not going to be able to work as its supporters hoped. In 1923, for example, Italy (a permanent member of the Council) invaded and seized the island of Corfu which belonged to Greece. The League asked Italy to hand back the island, but she refused. The League then decided that Italy could hold on to the island. Might, it seemed, was right.

But there was still a widespread hope that the League would prevent nations going to war.

2. Few people believed that the nations of the world would ever again want to go to war. The memories of the slaughter of the First World War were still fresh in people's memories. There was also the belief that any future war would be even more costly in life and damage. People thought that the new aeroplanes would be able to destroy cities and their inhabitants.

This explains why, in 1928, sixty-five nations signed a document put forward by the American Secretary of State, Kellogg. In the Kellogg–Briand Pact the nations agreed never to use war as an instrument of policy; this amounted to the 'outlawing of war'.

The Cost of a War

There was another reason for the belief that there was not going to be another war. We have already seen that in the 1920s and early 1930s the world went through a trade depression, and there was large-scale unemployment in most countries. Most politicians thought that one cure for unemployment was for governments to spend less money – and so be forced to collect less taxes. They thought that if people paid less taxes, they would have more of their own money to spend. This would lead to a higher demand for goods – and so for more workers to produce the goods.

But if a country was to prepare for a war it had to spend vast sums on armaments. This would lead to an increase in taxes.

Churchill (1925–9), Snowden (1929–31), and Chamberlain (1931–7) were British Chancellors of the Exchequer during this period. They all agreed that the country could not afford to prepare for war. Churchill persuaded his Cabinet colleagues to work on the assumption that there would be no war for at least ten years, and each year after 1925 he pushed the threat of war forward by another year. It was Churchill who was responsible for the Royal Air Force being starved of money for new aeroplanes throughout the years 1925–9. After 1931 it was Chancellor Chamberlain who insisted until 1935 that Britain could not afford to rearm. Even after 1935 the government was only willing to rearm slowly until 1938.

People and Politicians

But it would be very unfair to think that it was only the politicians who were against war and rearming. There was a great war-weariness throughout the country – not surprising after the slaughters of 1914–18. This mood was illustrated by the results of a debate at the University of Oxford Union in February 1933. The students at the University voted by 275 to 153 'that this House will in no circumstances fight for its King and Country'. The students were only saying what most of their countrymen believed. In 1934 the League of Nations Union organized a Peace Ballot in Britain. This showed that the vast majority of Britons were in favour of the League of Nations and of disarmament by all countries.

Labour's Foreign Policy, 1929–31

When he became Prime Minister in 1929 MacDonald chose Arthur Henderson as his Foreign Secretary, although he himself continued to play a large part in foreign affairs as he had done in 1924.

In October 1929 the Labour government opened diplomatic relations with Russia. They had done so in 1924, but the Conservative government had broken off relations in 1927.

In 1930 there was the London Naval Conference. Britain, America, and Japan agreed to limit the size of their navies; Britain cut down the size of her cruiser fleet from seventy to fifty. The three nations agreed that Britain and America should have navies of the same size while Japan should be allowed to have three ships for every five in the British or American fleets. This was known as the 5:5:3 ratio.

In 1930 all Allied occupation forces were removed from the Rhineland – a sign that the nations believed that Germany was not going to be a warlike nation, and that she and France would live together in peace.

In 1930 and 1931 MacDonald and Henderson helped the preparations for a Disarmament Conference which finally met at Geneva in 1932. It was hoped that the nations would agree to cut down their spending on arms, but as soon as the Conference met it became clear that there was little hope of success. Germany asked that she be allowed to have an army, a navy and an air force as large as those of France. France, on the other hand, argued that she ought to be guaranteed against the danger of a future German attack. In January 1933 Hitler became Chancellor (or Prime Minister) of Germany. By October 1933 he had taken Germany out of the Disarmament Conference and the League of Nations (Fig. 40.1).

Japan and Manchuria

Ever since 1911 China had been involved in a series of civil wars as Sun Yat Sen and his democratic followers tried to set up a people's government. Japan had taken advantage of China's weakness to develop economic links with the Chinese province of Manchuria, and in 1931 the Japanese army in Manchuria attacked the Chinese city of Mukden and claimed Manchuria for the Japanese people.

China appealed to the League of Nations in January 1932. Japan was a great power and a

Fig. 40.1 Hitler at a party rally in 1934.

member of the League Council. What would the League do? It sent a Commission of Inquiry to examine the state of affairs in Manchuria. The Commission condemned the Japanese invasion. Japan resigned from the League and invaded China itself. The League had failed to stop a war. It was becoming increasingly obvious that the League was powerless to do the job it had been set up to do.

The National Government's Policy, 1931–5

The National government came to power in September 1931. It was this government that sent representatives to the Disarmament Conference. It was also this government's Foreign Secretary who agreed that the League had failed in Manchuria; and which saw the danger of Hitler who came to power in January 1933.

In 1935 the government began to spend more money on armaments – against the opposition of the Liberal and Labour Parties which claimed that the League had the key to a peaceful future.

A major argument in the 1920s and 1930s had been about the rights and wrongs of the way in which Germany had been treated by the peacemakers in 1919. Many people, including the Germans themselves, thought that she had been treated too harshly. Even as early as 1925 there were signs that both France and Britain were willing to see some changes in the terms of the Versailles Treaty. In 1925 they signed the Locarno Pact with Germany. This stated that Germany's western frontier (with France and Belgium) was to stay as it was. But this led many people to think that Germany's eastern border (with Poland and other countries) could be redrawn.

When Hitler came to power he boasted that he would build a large army, a huge navy, and a powerful air force. This frightened the other powers. So in 1935 Britain, France, and Italy held a conference at Stresa. Here they agreed to resist any illegal attempt to revise the Versailles Treaty.

But the British politicians then undid the good done at Stresa. They signed a naval agreement which agreed that Hitler's Germany could have a navy that would be equal to 35 per cent of the British Navy. This frightened the French. So in May 1935 France made a separate defensive alliance with Russia.

The Abyssinian Crisis, 1934–6

In October 1922 Mussolini had become the dictator of Italy. In 1925 his government had proposed that Abyssinia be allowed to join the League of Nations, and in 1935 he signed the Stresa Agreement with Britain and France. Italy was, at that time, opposed to German ambition to seize Austria.

In October 1934 Mussolini ordered the invasion of Abyssinia. During the winter of 1934 and throughout 1935 there were clashes on the border between Abyssinia and the Italian colony of Eritrea.

On 7 October 1934 the League condemned Italy's invasion. All League members agreed to stop trading with Italy – to make it difficult or even impossible for her to continue her illegal attack. No one was to supply her with the steel, rubber, and so on that she needed. However, there was a major loophole in this decision. The League itself said that Italy could be supplied with oil – the most important commodity for a warring nation. The League was shown to be too weak to stop the invasion.

In the summer of 1935 Mussolini appealed to Britain and France to allow him a free hand in Africa. He argued that they had seized colonies in the nineteenth century, and that he was simply continuing their old policy. Britain and France were uncertain of what they should do; they needed Mussolini's support in the Stresa Front againt Hitler.

In December 1935 the British Foreign Secretary, Sir Samuel Hoare, went to Paris to meet the French Foreign Secretary, Pierre Laval. They drew up a plan by which Italy would be allowed to take two-thirds of Abyssinia. When this agreement was reported in the newspapers there was an outcry against it, and Hoare resigned. He was succeeded by Anthony Eden. But there was no change of policy. By May 1936 Mussolini had conquered the whole of Abyssinia – and had also become less than friendly to his allies in the Stresa Front (Fig. 40.2).

Fig. 40.2 Hitler with his fellow-dictator, Mussolini, in Munich, 1937. Here they signed the Pact of Steel which linked the future of Germany and Italy.

Hitler and the Rhineland, March 1936

The Treaty of Versailles had said that the Rhineland area should be kept free from armed forces. This was to be a 'buffer zone' between France and Germany.

On 7 March 1936 Hitler ordered his troops into the Rhineland. This 'invasion' was contrary to both the Treaty of Versailles and the Locarno Pact of 1925. At first the British government seemed to be willing to act. Certainly Hitler was frightened that the British and French might send troops (Extract 40.1). On 9 March Eden went to consult the French, and on 12 March the French Foreign Minister came to London. Chamberlain, the Chancellor of the Exchequer, told him that public opinion would not support action of 'any kind'. The French thought that a firm stand by them and the British would have stopped Hitler, but the British government did not agree, and so Hitler remained in the Rhineland. Once again the League, the British, and French had failed to stop an aggressor.

The Spanish Civil War, 1936–9

In February 1936 there were elections in Spain. The new government was made up of socialists and communists. It did nothing to stop attacks on the property of the Catholic Church. Priests and nuns were killed. At the same time there was an anti-government movement in the Basque region where the people wanted their own government.

In July 1936 part of the Spanish army stationed in Spanish Morocco invaded mainland Spain under the leadership of General Franco. His forces were welcomed by the landowners and by the leaders of the Catholic Church. There was then a savage civil war in which the Franco forces at first controlled the countryside while the government forces controlled most of the towns.

Germany and Italy sent troops, aeroplanes, and munitions to help Franco, and Russia sent supplies and men to help the government side. Here it seemed was the battleground for that struggle between the extreme left and the extreme right which divided Europe in this inter-war period.

Britain and France tried to get the nations of the world to keep out of the war, and proposed a policy of non-intervention. This really helped Franco who received far more help from Germany and Italy than the government got from Russia.

By 1939 the whole of Spain was under Franco's control. The extreme right had won another victory.

Eden's Resignation, 1938

In 1937 Baldwin retired and Chamberlain became Prime Minister. Like the majority of the British people he had a hatred of war; he hoped that the League would keep the world free from war. Like most observers he thought that a major war would be both very costly and totally destructive.

As with most people in Britain he had a deep hatred of Russian communism. He realized that to defeat Hitler would require an alliance of the major powers – including Russia. But Chamberlain distrusted Russia where Stalin was busily involving in killing the majority of the leaders of his army. Could Stalin's Russia provide a strong ally in the event of war? Most British people thought that the answer was 'no'.

So Chamberlain thought that the only way to deal with Hitler and Mussolini was to negotiate with them over their grievances. In 1938 he tried to reopen relations with Mussolini which had been broken off during the Abyssinian crisis. He hoped to bring Mussolini back into the Anglo–French alliance. His Foreign Minister, Anthony Eden, disagreed. He wanted Italian troops to be taken out of Spain. Chamberlain was willing to 'give up' Spain in the hope of getting Italy on his side against Hitler. Eden resigned – the new Foreign Secretary was Lord Halifax.

Hitler and Austria, 1938

In January 1938 Austrian Nazis tried to overthrow the socialist government in Austria. The Chancellor, Schuschnigg blocked this attempt.

He was then called to a meeting with Hitler who bullied him into accepting the Austrian Nazi leader, Seyss–Inquart, as Chief of Police. Schuschnigg proposed to hold a referendum to ask the Austrian people whether they wanted to unite with Germany. Hitler was afraid that the Austrians might vote against such a union, so he rushed troops to the Austrian border while again he called Schuschnigg to another meeting. Here he forced him to resign and to make way for Seyss–Inquart. He then invited Germany to march into Austria on 12 March. Chamberlain sent a note of protest but took no action against this further breach of the Treaty of Versailles.

Czechoslovakia, 1938

In 1937 Hitler had drawn up his plans for the conquest of Central and Eastern Europe (Extract 40.2). This involved the conquest of Czechoslovakia, one of the new states created by the Treaty of Versailles. There were Germans living in the north of the country who did not like being under Czech rule. They were attracted by the German propaganda in favour of a 'greater' Germany.

In 1938 the Germans in Czechoslovakia were led by Henlein. He demanded the creation of a separate Sudeten–German state. The Czechs refused, so Hitler threatened to invade the country on behalf of 'the downtrodden Germans there'. In September 1938 Chamberlain was afraid that there was going to be a major war, so he sent Lord Runciman on a mission to Czechoslovakia to see whether there were grounds for Britain trying to make an agreement between Germany and the Czechs. This was already agreeing that the Germans had some right to some share in Czech territory. It was almost a promise that Britain would help to break up a state which she herself had helped to create at Versailles.

On 15 September 1938 Chamberlain flew to Berchtesgaden to see Hitler. He and the French Prime Minister, Daladier, met Czech representatives and told them that they would have to make some sacrifice. At first they refused, so on 22 September Chamberlain flew again to meet Hitler. He persuaded him not to take any action until Britain had finished arguing with the Czechs.

Meanwhile the Czechs mobilized their army; the French called up their reserve army; and the British fleet prepared for war. Children were evacuated. Trenches were dug in London's parks as a defence against air raids.

Munich, 1938

On 28 September 1938 Chamberlain was explaining the position to the House of Commons when a note was passed to him inviting him to a third meeting with Hitler. Chamberlain flew to Munich where he met Hitler, Mussolini, and Daladier. The Czechs were not invited, nor were their allies, the Russians. On 29 October Britain and France signed a document which gave Hitler all that he wanted. The Czech Prime Minister, Beneš, resigned, and Hitler claimed that he would make no further demands in Europe. Chamberlain flew back to tell the cheering crowds that he had brought 'Peace for our Time' (Fig. 40.3).

After Munich

But the German appetite had not been satisfied – it had only been whetted. Her enemies had been weakened. Russia was convinced that Britain and France would not fight.

On 13 March 1939 Hitler invited the Czech Prime Minister to Berlin, and forced him to agree to Germany's taking over the rest of his defenceless country. On 15 March Chamberlain complained of this fresh attack which tore the 'whole policy of appeasement into ruins'.

But the Prime Minister had been aware of this in September 1938. He had come back from Munich to order that the R.A.F. be built up by the development of six squadrons of new Spitfires and Hurricanes. By September 1939 the R.A.F. had twenty-six such squadrons. The radar system was extended to provide an early warning system along the coast from the Orkneys to the Isle of Wight.

In April 1939, after Hitler's take-over of Czecho-slovakia, peacetime conscription was brought in: everyone between the ages of 18 and 42 had to register for service in one of the armed forces. French and British military staffs held conversations about the distribution of forces in the event of war.

Preparations were made to defend the civilian population against attack from the air. An Emergency Fire Service was set up; 400,000 air raid shelters were ordered for distribution among the people in Britain's towns; plans for evacuating women and children were completed.

Poland

Having conquered Austria and Czechoslovakia Hitler then turned his attention to Poland. He demanded that the former German port of Danzig should be given back to Germany. He also proposed to take over the territory that linked Poland with this port. This 'Polish corridor' ran through what had once been Prussia.

In April 1939 the British government gave a guarantee that she would help Poland if she were attacked. On 27 April 1939 the students at the University of Oxford Union voted by 423 votes to 326 that 'In view of this country's commitments and the gravity of the general situation in Europe, this house welcomes conscription'. This vote reflects not only the change in the opinion of students. It also shows how the British people had been forced to see

Fig. 40.3 Neville Chamberlain and Hitler during the crisis over Czechoslovakia in September 1938.

that war was the only way in which Hitler could be stopped.

In May 1937 Hitler signed a Pact of Steel with Mussolini. This was not a surprise. But in August 1939 Hitler signed an agreement with Stalin's Russia. The British had been having talks with the Russians, and hoped to draw them into an anti-German alliance. Hitler amazed the world by this agreement with Russia. War was now almost inevitable.

On the 1 September 1939 German forces invaded Poland. Two days later Britain and France declared war on Germany. The policy of appeasement had failed.

Questions

Extract 40.1

Hitler's fear over the Rhineland, 1936

> . . . The special train in which we rode to Munich . . . was charged . . . with the tense atmosphere . . . from the Fuhrer's section . . . . Even later, . . . he always termed the remilitarisation of the Rhineland the most daring of all his undertakings. 'We had no army worth mentioning; at that time it would not even have had the fighting strength to maintain itself against the Poles. If the French had taken any action, we would have been easily defeated; our resistance would have been over in a few days.'
>
> (Albert Speer, *Inside the Third Reich*, 1970.)

1. Which countries might have stopped this occupation of the Rhineland? Explain why neither of them was willing to do so.
2. Show why this occupation broke the terms of the Treaty of Versailles. Which country was most threatened by this occupation?
3. Why was Hitler very anxious on the day of the occupation? What, do you think, might have happened inside Germany if this move had been halted?

Extract 40.2

Hitler and living space

> The Fuhrer then stated: The question for Germany is where the greatest possible conquest can be made at lowest cost . . . . If the Fuhrer is still living, then it will be his irrevocable decision to solve the German space problem no later than 1943–5 . . .. It must be our first aim, in every case of entanglement by war, to conquer Czechoslovakia and Austria simultaneously . . . . The Fuhrer believes that England and perhaps also France have already silently written off Czechoslovakia . . . Feldmarschall von Blomberg and

> Generaloberst von Fritsch . . . repeatedly pointed out that we should not run the risk that England and France become our enemies . . . .
>
> (*The Hossbach Document*, 1937.)

1. In which year did Hitler gain control of (i) Austria (ii) the Sudeten districts of Czechoslovakia, and (iii) the Bohemian districts of Czechoslovakia?
2. What evidence is there that the army leaders were reluctant to agree to the occupation of Czechoslovakia?
3. What evidence is there in this document that Hitler was thinking of a war with Russia? Why did this please the leaders of Britain and France?

Worksheet

(A)
1. Write a brief note on (i) the Assembly, and (ii) the Council of the League of Nations.

2. Why did most people (i) hope for, and (ii) expect a long period of peace after 1918?

3. Why did the government make cuts in its military spending in the 1920s?

4. Give TWO pieces of evidence that show that in the 1930s the British were opposed to a more militant foreign policy. Write a brief note on EACH of the pieces you have chosen.

5. Why did the Disarmament Conference fail?

6. Give THREE examples of the League's failure to act as it should have done. Explain the major weaknesses of the League.

7. Why did Britain begin to rearm in the 1930s? Why did the government only allow a modest programme of rearmament?

8. Write a brief note on EACH of the following: The Stresa Front; the 5:5:3 ratio in battleships; Manchuria; the Rhineland.

9. Why did Anthony Eden resign in 1938?

(B)
1. Write the extracts that might have appeared in the diary of a Czech during the crisis of 1938. Write the extract he might have written in March 1939.

(C)
1. Make a time chart and mark on it the main dates and events noted in the text. Write a brief explanation of each of the dates and events you have chosen.

2. Draw the posters that might have been used to advertise: (a) the debate in the Oxford Union (i) 1933 (ii) 1939; (b) the Peace Ballot 1934.

41 The Second World War and British Society, 1939-45

The Fighting War, 1939–45

In this chapter we will be looking at the way in which the war led to changes in the social and political life of Britain. The Second World War fell into three parts. Between 1939 and the summer of 1942 Germany and Italy swept everything before them. As you can see from Fig. 41.1, they conquered most of Europe, including a large part of Russia. They had defeated the British in North Africa and were ready to capture Egypt and the Suez Canal. In December 1941 the Japanese launched their attack on Pearl Harbor and by the middle of 1942 they had captured the colonies belonging to Britain, France, and Holland in southeast Asia.

Fig. 41.1 The defeat of the Axis powers, 1943–5.

In 1942 the second stage of the war began, which Churchill called 'the turning point'. The Russians halted the German advance at Stalingrad in September 1942. The severe Russian winter came to the help of the defenders. In February 1943 the Germans were forced to surrender to the Russians – the first major set-back for the Axis powers in Europe. By then the British had won the Battle of El Alamein (October–November 1942) and were driving the Germans and Italians across North Africa. And even before that the Americans had defeated the Japanese at the Battle of Midway Islands (May–June 1942) and so prevented the invasion of Australia.

The third stage of the war, covering the years 1943, 1944, and 1945 saw the Allies victorious everywhere. Hitler committed suicide on 30 April 1945 and the Germans surrendered on 7 May. 8 May 1945 was celebrated as V(ictory in) E(urope) Day. On 6 and 8 August 1945 the Americans dropped atomic bombs on Hiroshima and Nagasaki in Japan and on 14 August the Japanese surrendered and the Second World War was over.

The Government and the Country's Manpower

The Chamberlain government had started the conscription of men into the armed forces in the summer of 1939 – before the war started. As soon as the war began Parliament passed a National Services Act. This stated that all men between the ages of 18 and 41 had to register for service. By the spring of 1940 over $1\frac{1}{2}$ million men had joined the forces.

In the middle of 1940 France had surrendered and it seemed that the Germans would invade Britain. The government organized the Local Defence Volunteer force from men aged between 17 and 65 who were not already in the armed forces. This force was later renamed the Home Guard. Its job was supposed to have been to defend the country against German invaders. In fact, the Home Guard had too few weapons and too few men to have done much good, but it was a sign of the nation's determination that it would 'never surrender'.

Not every man of military age was taken into the forces. Workers in key jobs were not called up – munitions workers, coal-miners, and so on. In May 1940 Chamberlain was forced to resign, and Churchill became Prime Minister. He invited leading members of the Labour Party to join his government. Attlee, the party leader, became Deputy Prime Minister. Ernest Bevin, leader of the Transport and General Workers' Union, became Minister of Labour. It was Bevin who was responsible for the direction of labour. Workers were forced to leave jobs in non-essential industries and compelled to work in industries producing war goods; and it was Bevin who introduced a second Conscription Act in the autumn of 1941. This forced unmarried women to join one of the women's services or to go to work in one of the essential industries. The whole country was actively drawn into the war.

The Government and the Country's Industries

Churchill's government quickly brought the whole of industry under direct or indirect government control. Government officials were appointed to control Britain's transport system; they also ran the country's railway system and the docks. A Ministry of Fuel and Power was set up in 1942 to direct the country's coal industry, although the mines remained in private ownership. When too many miners left the mines to volunteer for the services, Bevin organized a scheme whereby some young men were sent to work in the mines instead of joining one of the services.

In 1940 Churchill appointed his friend, Lord Beaverbrook, to the post of Minister of Aircraft

Fig. 41.2 Oxford Street, London, after a night of bombing.

Production. Beaverbrook (the owner of the *Daily Express*) and Bevin had to make sure that the services were provided with enough weapons and supplies. Beaverbrook was responsible for the production of enough aircraft. In September 1940 the Germans launched their massive attacks on Britain (Fig. 41.2), but they were defeated in this Battle of Britain by the much smaller R.A.F. Beaverbrook's success can be judged by the fact that at the end of the Battle of Britain, the R.A.F. had more machines than it had had at the start – in spite of very heavy losses.

Beaverbrook and Bevin persuaded trade unions to give up some of their privileges. Unskilled people did work previously only done by skilled men. Unions agreed to give up their 'normal' working day and to work longer hours so that munitions could be produced in sufficient quantity. The nation's industry was almost totally involved in the war effort.

The Government and the Nation's Supplies

An increasing number of firms were forced to produce wartime goods. This meant that there was a shortage of peacetime goods – clothes, toys, building materials, and houses. German submarine attacks on British shipping meant that there was a drop in British imports – of food, petrol, and raw materials.

Petrol was rationed as soon as war started; only people who could prove that they needed their cars received a ration. In January 1940 the government introduced food rationing. Everyone was entitled to a small supply of meat, sugar, butter and other fats, and so on. There was also a system of clothes rationing; everyone was allowed so many 'points' in a clothing rations book. The government then fixed the 'points' value of different sorts of clothes; a pair of socks cost two points while an overcoat cost twenty.

Lord Woolton was appointed to the post of Minister of Food. He controlled the system of rationing, announcing an increase when supplies rose, and a decrease when supplies became scarcer. It was Woolton and the Ministry of Agriculture that encouraged the British to 'grow more food'. Farmers cultivated land that had never been dug before; and families were encouraged to dig up their own gardens to produce vegetables.

The Government and Its Powers

In the 1930s some economists had asked the government to spend £100 million on roads, bridges, houses, and other 'public works'. But, as we have seen,

Snowden, Chamberlain, and other ministers argued that the country could not afford to 'buy its way out of unemployment'. Once the war started, however, economists and ministers changed their policy. The war cost about £15 million a day – or about £105 million each week and this money was found. There was a large increase in income tax. It rose from its peacetime level of 22½p in the pound to 37½p in 1939 and to 50p in 1942. The government imposed a purchase tax on luxury goods – jewellery for example – which meant that the richer people paid even more tax if they bought such goods.

In 1939 and 1940 the government pushed through Emergency Powers Acts. These allowed the arrest and imprisonment of people without trial; all German nationals and many British fascists were interned. The Acts also allowed the government to impose restrictions on newspapers and other publications. For a time the *Daily Worker*, the communist paper, was closed down. A Ministry of Information was set up to control the newspapers and to decide what could and could not be printed.

This was, in every sense, a 'total war'. The nation's industry and manpower was totally involved; the government controlled almost every part of everyone's life. Few people complained, for they realized that this was part of the price that had to be paid if Britain was to win the war. Indeed some people almost welcomed this growth of government power – being used for a very good purpose. Some wanted that same power to be used after the war – to defeat other enemies such as poverty and unemployment.

A Destructive War

In the 1920s and 1930s politicians and ordinary people had thought that air raids would quickly destroy a country, its towns, and industries. Wartime experience proved that this was only partly true. The country was not destroyed. Bombing from the air did not bring the war to a speedy end, but it did do a great deal of damage. Thirty thousand people were killed in air raids; about 3 million homes were damaged or destroyed; many ports were severely damaged as were bridges, railways, and roads (Fig. 41.2).

Since there was a shortage of materials few of these houses, bridges, and so on could be rebuilt during the war. The British would have to pay for that rebuilding after the war.

The war had another 'cost'. For about six years there was little if any new machinery built for British industry. The railway system did not get any new equipment. The country did not build the million or

Fig. 41.3 Evacuee schoolchildren wave goodbye to their parents.

so houses that it would have built if the war had not taken place. It is impossible to work out how much modernization, building, and development would have taken place if there had not been a war. But we can say that there would have been a great deal of such building, and this would have to be done after the war.

There was a third 'cost'. Britain was forced to sell off about £2,000 million of those investments she had made in overseas countries. She needed money to pay for essential imports. Some of these materials were paid for by exports, but exports were much smaller during the war than they had been in peacetime. Many of those essential imports had to be paid for by the money got from selling our investments. In peacetime the interest on those investments had been about £200 million a year, but the country would not have that income after the war. In future, British exports would have to pay for more of Britain's imports.

Nor was this the end. For during the war Britain borrowed vast sums of money – from America, Canada, India, Egypt, and other countries. By 1945 Britain owed about £4,000 million. After the war she would have to pay interest on that money and also have to start to repay the loans. Britain would have to export goods to get the money to pay that interest.

Evacuation and Social Change

In 1939 the government organized a system of evacuation. Mothers and children were taken from London and other cities and sent to live in the smaller towns in the countryside where the danger of air raids was much less. After the air raids had begun in 1940 there was more evacuation and by the end of the war millions of women and children had learned a new way of life in the countryside (Fig. 41.3).

The evacuees came, mainly, from the overcrowded cities and towns. Many of them were children and women from poor homes. In the countryside they were sent to live with better-off families. At first they shocked their hosts by their lack of cleanliness, their poor clothing, their ignorance of habits of hygiene, and so on. But as the time went on their better-off hosts came to see that the poverty and ignorance of the evacuees was a result of the conditions in which they had been forced to live. This led to the demand for a better deal for these people. Evacuation helped to create new attitudes on the part of the hosts – who argued in favour of paying higher taxes so that the evacuees might have better housing, better schools, more jobs, and so on when the war was over. The evacuees learned that the poor conditions in which they had lived could be improved. They, too, demanded a change after the war.

The War and People's Expectations

During 1942 and 1943 the government set up a number of committees and commissions to make plans for the future. These committees produced reports and the government published its own idea of what might be done to make sure that the committees' plans were put into operation – after the war. So there was a plan for full employment; the government showed how it would be able to make sure that everyone who wanted a job could have one. There would be no slump after this war as there had been in 1921. There was a plan for reconstruction; the government showed how a new Britain could be built from the ruins of the war. There would be new industries, new roads, new houses, and schools – and a chance for a new life for many millions who had suffered in the depressed years of the 1930s. There was a report on the location of industry; the government would force industry to build its new factories in the old industrial areas. Wales, Scotland, the North-East, and the other Distressed Areas would get a new life from the inflow of the new industries and new jobs (Extract 41.1).

In 1944 Parliament passed an Education Act. This said that the school leaving age would be increased from 14 to 15 and, as soon as possible, to 16. It said that every child would have a secondary school education – free of fees. No one would be able to buy a place at a grammar school. All places would be open to children who passed the selection examination.

In 1945 Parliament also passed the Family Allowances Act. This gave help to the 2,500,000 families in which there was more than one child. A mother was given an allowance of 25p a week for each child after the first. We may think that 25p is a small sum of money, but in 1945 it was about 5 per cent of the skilled worker's wage.

Beveridge, 1942

So during the dark days 1939–45 the people were taught by the government to look forward to a better life after the war. This was particularly true of the report produced by Sir William Beveridge. In 1942 the government asked him to examine the way in which the existing system of Social Insurance worked. Beveridge went much further than the government intended. He did examine the way in which the system of Health and Unemployment Insurance worked, but he also showed that there were 'five Giant Evils; Want, Disease, Ignorance, Squalor and Idleness'. He showed how a government could defeat these Evils by policies on employment, pensions, unemployment and sickness benefit, housing, education, and a health service (Extract 41.2).

His report appeared in December 1942, and it became a best-seller with millions of people buying copies of this large book. They read of the way in which life could be better for everyone – if only the government would pass the laws needed, collect the taxes to pay for the reforms, and set up the ministries and departments needed to organize the reforms.

Churchill and his government (including the Labour ministers) argued that the country would not be able to afford to do all this in the years after the war. Industry would have to be rebuilt and the country put back on its feet before these schemes could be brought in.

The Army and Beveridge

During the war, millions of men were conscripted into the forces. Men from all social classes mixed with one another in barracks, on air fields, and on ships. One result was that men from different classes learned to respect one another. Better-off men learned about unemployment, poverty, and ill health from men from industrial towns and cities. This led to a demand, by the better-off, for a change after the war.

During the war most men spent a great deal of time away from actual fighting. To help fill in their time the government organized a system of education for people in the services. The Army Bureau of Current Affairs produced leaflets for discussion in small classes. Young officers were sent out to lead discussions – on Beveridge and other reports. In this way men learned of what might be done – if only governments were willing to act. When they heard that Churchill was opposed to some of these changes, they voted against him.

The End of the War and of the Coalition

In May 1945 the Germans surrendered. Churchill asked the Labour ministers in the Coalition to agree to fight the next election as a Coalition government. He wanted to 'win the peace' before starting party warfare again. The Labour ministers agreed, and reported this to the party's Annual Conference at Brighton in June 1945. However, the Conference defeated their proposals, so Attlee had to tell Churchill that the next election would have to be fought on the old party lines.

On 15 June Parliament was dissolved. The polling day was 5 July, but the results were not announced until 26 July so that the votes of the men in the services could be collected and sent back to their home constituencies. Most people thought that Churchill, the war hero, would win the election for the Conservatives. But when the results were announced the Labour Party had won 393 seats to 189 for the Conservatives, and had got a bigger majority than the Liberals had won in the famous election of 1906. The British people had voted for a better future.

Questions

Extract 41.1

The government and the location of industry, 1940–5

In January 1940 the Royal Commission on the Distribution of the Industrial Population reported that the best distribution of industry and population would not come about without continual guidance by the Government: that it was not in the national interest that a quarter of the population should live and work within 25 miles [40 kilometres] of Charing Cross. Between 1932 and 1937 five-sixths of the new factories built in Britain had been built in Greater London.

The Commission urged that Greater London should be 'put out of bounds' for new industrial development. I was in favour of it and of treating Greater Birmingham similarly.

By 1943 the Ministry of Town and Country Planning had been set up. Discussions began which led to the State Paper on Employment Policy published in May 1944.

To secure full employment in the Distressed Areas I regarded some national control of industrial location as vital; by giving information to employers who were in doubt where to locate new factories; and by the use of building licences which, for new industrial buildings, the Board of Trade controlled.

In August 1943 Sam Courtauld came to see me. He wished to act in conformity with the Government's plans for post-war employment; I suggested that he should put some of the new factories which his firm were going to build in Distressed Areas. I sent him particulars of a number of suitable sites and he adopted several of my suggestions.

Lord McGowan of I.C.I. told me he regarded it as a duty to help by location of new enterprises to prevent unemployment. And I.C.I. played up very well by building big new plants at Wilton on the Lower Tees. I gave them all the help I could through building licences.
(Hugh Dalton, *The Fateful Years* (Muller, 1957).)

1. Where did 'a quarter of the population' live in 1940? Why had many manufacturers built their factories near London in the 1920s and 1930s?

2. Why did wartime experience show that it was not good for so many people to live in and around London? Who would have to give 'continual guidance' on the distribution of industry? Why is there a link between the distribution of industry and the distribution of the population?

3. Why was Greater London 'put out of bounds' for new industrial development?

4. Which two government departments are mentioned in the extract? Which was the newest of these in 1944?

5. Name three areas of the country which were known as 'Distressed Areas'. How would a better distribution of industry help to provide employment in these areas?

6. Which government department controlled building licences? How could this system of licences be used to prevent industrialists expanding in Greater London?

7. Which two firms are mentioned in this extract? How did their development help to provide employment in the Distressed Areas?

Extract 41.2

Before the National Health Service

The national health insurance system provides a general-practitioner service for 21 million of the population, the rest have to pay whenever they desire the services of a doctor. A person ought not to be financially deterred from seeking medical assistance at the earliest possible stage by the financial anxiety of doctor's bills.

In the second place, the national health insurance scheme does not provide for the self-employed, nor for the families of dependants. It depends on insurance qualifications; if you cease to be insured, you cease to have free doctoring. Furthermore, it gives no backing services; in an overwhelming number of cases the services of a specialist are not available to poor people.

Our hospital organisation has grown up with no plan; it is unevenly distributed over the country and very often the best hospital facilities are available where they are least needed. In the older industrial districts of Great Britain hospital facilities are inadequate. Many of the hospitals are very much too small to provide general hospital treatment.

In addition, the health of the people is not properly looked after in one or two other respects. As a consequence of dental treatment having to be bought, it has not been demanded on a scale to stimulate the creation of sufficient dentists and there is a shortage of dentists. About 25 per cent of the people can obtain their spectacles and get their eyes tested by means of the assistance given by the approved societies, but the general mass of the people have no such facilities.

Another of the evils is that sufficient attention has not been given to deafness and hardly any attention has been given so far to the provision of cheap hearing-aids. (Aneurin Bevan, Minister of Health, in a speech on the Second Reading of the National Health Service Bill, House of Commons, 30 April 1946.)

1. When had the 'national health insurance scheme' been started? Who were provided with 'general practitioner' service under this system? Who had to 'pay whenever they required the services of a doctor'?
2. Why did millions of people not seek medical advice when they were ill?
3. Why did people who had paid insurance sometimes have to pay when they required a doctor's services?
4. Why did many people not receive the attention of specialists when they needed them?
5. Where were hospital facilities inadequate? How had this been shown to be important during the war?
6. Why was there a shortage of dentists in 1945? Why did the majority of people not get their eyes tested before 1948?

Fig. 41.1

1. Write two sentences to show the importance of each of the following: Stalingrad 1942; El Alamein 1942.
2. Which countries were conquered by Germany in 1939–42?
3. Which army landed at Casablanca in 1942? Why did this invasion anger some French people?
4. Which countries were freed by the Russians 1943–5? How did this affect the future for these countries and for relationships between Russia and the Western powers (America, Britain, and France).
5. Why did Churchill argue in favour of an invasion of southern and south-east Europe? Which of Britain's allies was most opposed to these plans? Why?

Worksheet

(A)
1. Why did Churchill invite Labour leaders to join his government? What part was played in the war by (i) Attlee (ii) Bevin, and (iii) Morrison?

2. Make a list of the ways in which the government increased its control over EACH of the following: Industry; manpower; supplies; taxation. Why did some people believe that those powers should be used after the war?

3. How and why was there an increase in food production during the war?

4. Why did the government introduce a system of rationing by coupon instead of allowing prices to rise so that there would have been rationing by price? How did this policy affect people's attitudes towards the belief in 'fair shares'?

5. Show how the war affected EACH of the following: Housing; industrial development; Britain's ability to pay her way in the post-war world.

6. Make a list of the reports produced by the wartime government that dealt with the post-war world. How did such reports affect people's expectations for the future?

7. Why was the *Beveridge Report* the most important of the wartime reports? Why was it welcomed by the majority of the nation?

8. Show how (i) evacuation, and (ii) conscription brought different classes of people closer together. How did this affect people's voting behaviour in 1945?

9. How did the government propose to deal with the Depressed Areas? Why did this involve using the powers of several ministries? (Extract 41.1).

10. Make a list of the reasons why Labour won the election in 1945.

(B)
1. Write the letters that might have been sent by:
(a) someone living in a bombed town in wartime Britain (see Fig. 41.2);
(b) one of the children evacuated from a poor home AND one of the 'foster' mothers who took the child into her comfortable home;
(c) a mother who has just drawn her first Family Allowance in 1945;
(d) a soldier writing about his hopes for the post-war world.

2. Draw or paint the poster that might have been used to:
(a) invite recruits for the Home Guard;
(b) advertise a meeting to be addressed by Beveridge.

42 The Labour Government, 1945-51

What Did It Want to Do?

On 26 July 1945 Clement Attlee went to Buckingham Palace; King George VI appointed him as his Prime Minister. Attlee then chose his government. Ernest Bevin became Foreign Secretary; Hugh Dalton, an economist, became Chancellor of the Exchequer (Extract 41.1 on p. 244); and Herbert Morrison (Extract 30.2 on p. 176) became Lord President of the Council with the job of looking after the development of the economy.

Attlee, Morrison, and Dalton wanted to do four things:
1. To keep the promises made in the Report on Full Employment. There was to be no return to the depressed days of the 1930s. There was to be no post-war slump as in 1921;
2. To create the welfare system outlined in the *Beveridge Report*;
3. To rebuild war-damaged Britain and help in that modernization of industry which had not been done between 1939 and 1945;
4. To try to get British exports flowing again. This would mean that industry had to be helped to turn from making war goods to making peacetime goods (Extract 42.1).

The Difficulties They Faced

During the war Britain had been forced to sell about £2,000 million of her overseas investments. After 1945 Britain had a smaller income from overseas than she used to have. At the same time, Britain had run up debts to overseas countries, and so money had to be earned to pay the interest on this debt.

Between 1939–45 Britain had lost most of her export market, and so after 1945 British exporters had to try to build her contacts again. Industry had to produce the goods needed in the export market, and, as Attlee realized, this meant that the British people had to do without some of the goods they would have liked to have (Extract 42.1).

The government had to repair the damage done by bombing raids. They had to replace the 3 million or so houses that had been destroyed; they had to build new ships to take the place of the 16 million tonnes of shipping sunk by submarines. They also had to help build up new industries – modern steelworks, new oil refineries, larger chemical works, and so on. This took a great deal of material – timber, glass, steel, and so on. A great deal of this had to be imported – and Britain did not have the money to pay for all these imports. This forced the government to put restrictions on what the British people could buy

Restrictions

The British people had suffered a great deal of hardship during the war. They had been promised that life would be better after it, but few of them understood that Britain was not as rich in 1945 as she had been in 1939. The politicians did; they knew that the country could not import as much as the people might have wanted.

So after 1945 the British people had to suffer almost the same restrictions as they had suffered during the war. Food rationing continued – so that there would not be an increase in the imports bill. Clothes, petrol, and sweets continued to be rationed. No one could repair or even paint his house without getting a licence from a government official. The country could not afford to import too much timber – so that only essential things were permitted.

The government kept taxation at a high level – to make sure that the people did not have too much money to spend. If they had had that money they would have wanted to buy all sorts of products – and the country could not yet afford them.

Loans and More Restrictions

A large part of the world had been affected by war damage. This meant that most of the things Britain needed for her rebuilding had to come from America or Canada. In 1945 the economist, Keynes, went to America and persuaded the United States and Canadian governments to lend Britain £1,000 million to buy raw materials, machinery, and food.

"Now don't forget—anyone hanging around with a wistful look in their eye—let 'em have it—bing, bang!"

Fig. 42.1 Giles, the cartoonist, comments on the introduction of bread rationing.

Keynes had hoped that this loan would last until about 1950, and that by then the country would have recovered and exports would be paying for imports. But Keynes failed to realize that there was a great shortage of timber, machinery, iron and steel, and so on; he also forgot that France, Belgium, Holland, and all the other bomb-damaged countries would need these goods for their own recovery. Therefore, the price of these imports rose very sharply after 1945, and by 1947 import prices were almost twice as high as they had been in 1939. This meant that Britain's £1,000 million did not last as long as Keynes had hoped, and it did not buy as much as he had hoped. By the time the loan ran out in 1947–8 Britain was only half-way through her rebuilding.

Things were made worse by severe droughts in 1945 and 1946 in food-producing areas of the world. This meant that there was less food available, which pushed up prices. The British government had to force the people to eat even less in 1946 than they had eaten in wartime. Bread was rationed because of high prices and a grain shortage (Fig. 42.1); in 1947 potatoes were rationed; in 1948 rations of fats, meat, and other things were lower than they had been during the war. The weekly ration list was:

Milk	2 pints a week
Bread	2 loaves a week
Meat	$7\frac{1}{2}$p – but this went down to 3p in 1949.
Cheese	$1\frac{1}{2}$ ozs
Butter and margarine	6 oz
Cooking fat	1 oz
Sugar	8 oz

1 oz = 25.34 g   1 pint = 0.568 litre

The Export Drive

Britain had to double the exports she used to sell in 1939, but this could not be done quickly. Factories had to be rebuilt; new industries had to be developed; contacts had to be made with buyers in the importing countries. All this took time.

By 1947 exports were beginning to rise and the government could look forward with some confidence to the future. But by then the country was almost bankrupt; the loans from America and Canada had been spent. Where was Britain going to get the money it needed to pay for essential imports? Were the British people to be asked to cut their thin rations even further?

Marshall Aid

In 1947 the American Secretary of State was a former general, George Marshall. He knew that the British and other Europeans were still suffering from the effect of the war; he saw that it would take many years for these countries to get back to normal, so he proposed a scheme to help them. He offered this help to all European countries – but Stalin did not allow any of the Eastern European countries to take this help. Britain received £2,400,000,000 between 1948 and 1951. This money helped to buy the imports Britain needed without having to cut down on the imports of food (Extract 42.2).

Devaluation 1949

In 1947 the Chancellor, Dalton, was forced to resign because he had told a journalist what he was going to do in his November 1947 Budget. His successor was Sir Stafford Cripps. He had been President of the Board of Trade and had been responsible for the export drive, the rationing system, and had become known as Mr Austerity (or Hardship).

Cripps continued to ask the people for greater efforts. Rations were cut in 1948 and 1949; exports were almost doubled by 1949. But Cripps saw that things were not going as quickly as he wanted, and so in September 1949 he announced that in future the British pound would be worth only 2.80 dollars instead of the 4.03 it had been worth before that. This devaluation of the pound pushed down its value, and this made British exports cheaper – as you can see from this example:

	4.03 dollars to £	2.80 dollars to £
£400 car:	1,612 dollars	1,120 dollars

Cripps hoped that this would make it easier to sell British exports. However, this devaluation pushed up the prices of imports, as you can see from this example:

	4.03 dollars to £	2.80 dollars to £
Wheat costing 1,000 dollars:	£248	£357

This rise in prices of goods that Britain imported led to a demand for higher wages. This helped to create the problem of inflation from which the country has suffered ever since.

Signs of Success

By 1950 the economy seemed to be on the right course. Exports were now at twice their 1938 level while imports had hardly gone up at all. Britain was earning enough money to pay for the produce she imported. Bread, petrol, clothes, and potatoes were gradually taken off rations, and people could buy as much as they wanted. It was clear that within the next couple of years there would be no more rationing.

Housing

Also by 1950 Britain was building about 200,000 houses a year. Bevan (Fig. 42.2) wanted to build more; the British people wanted more houses. But there was still a shortage of timber and the country could not yet afford to import as much as it would have wished. But by 1950 the country had built almost 1 million new homes – many more than had been built in the six years after 1918 and many more than were built in any other European country between 1945 and 1950.

Nationalization

One of the things for which the Attlee government will be remembered is the nationalization of some parts of British industry. Pre-war governments had already nationalized the Central Electricity Generating Board (1926) and the British Overseas Airways Corporation (1939). Between 1945 and 1949 the Labour government nationalized the Bank of England (1946), the coal industry (1947), electricity supply (1947), civil aviation (1947), the gas supply industry (1948), the transport system – railways and road transport (1949), and the steel industry (1949).

The Labour government intended to use these industries to help the economy to develop. Coal and transport prices were held down between 1947 and 1950, and this meant that other industries did not have to pay high prices for coal or for having their goods carried by road and rail. This kept down the prices of these goods; exports were cheaper as a result and the cost of living within the country was held down.

However, since the coal and transport industries did not get paid as much as they should have, this meant that these industries ran at a loss. The government had to make up those losses out of taxation. People began to think that nationalized industries were inefficient, and that they cost the taxpayer a good deal of money.

Fig. 42.2 Aneurin Bevan, Minister of Health and Housing, visits a housing exhibition in July 1947.

In 1946 Parliament passed the National Health Service Act. Everyone who needed it was entitled to medical treatment without payment. They were allowed the services of dentists, opticians, surgeons in hospital, and nurses at home or in hospital. Aneurin Bevan was responsible for piloting this Act through Parliament. He and the rest of the Cabinet thought that the Health Service would cost about £140 million a year. By 1950 it was costing £350 million a year and as costs and wages have risen since then so the cost of the Service has gone up.

But few people disagreed with a leading Conservative, R. A. (later Lord) Butler. In 1950 he claimed: 'I think that we should take pride that the British race has been able, shortly after the terrible period (1939–45) through which we have passed together, to show the world that we are able to produce a social insurance scheme of this character.' Another leading Conservative, Robert (Lord) Boothby, told the Young Conservative Conference in 1949 that the country had gone through 'the greatest social revolution in its history'.

Social Reforms

The Attlee government will also be remembered for the way it put into practice the ideas proposed in the *Beveridge Report*.

In 1946 a new National Insurance Act was passed. All adults except married women had to pay weekly contributions to cover themselves against sickness, unemployment, and their retirement. Everyone would be entitled to insurance benefit if away from work owing to illness or unemployment; everyone would get a retirement pension. The government would also pay other benefits – maternity grants, death grants, and widows' pensions.

James Griffiths, a former Welsh miner, was in charge of this insurance system, and it was Griffiths who brought in the Industrial Injuries Bill. This was a state insurance scheme that replaced the Workmen's Compensation Acts of the past. Men injured at work would now be entitled to a state benefit.

In 1948 the government set up the National Assistance Board to provide for people who were not entitled to benefits from the Insurance Act – the blind, deaf or crippled; deserted and unmarried mothers; and the wives of criminals. The Board provided homes for the homeless and the old, and gave weekly grants to people with incomes too small to give them a minimum standard of living.

In 1966 this Board and the Ministry of Pensions and National Insurance were combined in the Ministry of Social Security – as Beveridge had proposed in 1942.

Education

In 1947 the government carried out one of the clauses of the 1944 Act. The school leaving age was raised from 14 to 15. This meant that thousands of young people who would have gone to work had to stay on at school for another year. This increased the labour shortage from which Britain was suffering at the time.

New Towns

In 1946 Parliament passed the New Towns Act. Sixteen new towns were to be built in England, Wales, and Scotland. Eight of these were to take people out of overcrowded London, and the rest were to take people from other overcrowded cities – Cardiff, Liverpool, Glasgow, and so on. This was the Labour government's attempt to put into practice the recommendation made by Beveridge in his attack on squalor.

These new towns were not merely large housing estates on the outskirts of cities and towns. Each of the new towns had its Development Corporation which used government money to buy the land needed for a town of between 50,000 and 100,000 people. Architects were appointed to build the new towns – with their industries, cinemas, shopping areas, schools, offices, halls, and so on. In the new towns people would not only have a house, they would also find work and make their lives in a New Britain.

Fig. 42.3 The rebel left-wingers at the 1951 Labour Party Conference. From left to right: Harold Wilson; Aneurin Bevan; Ian Mikardo; Tom Driberg; and Barbara Castle.

Other Laws

In 1946 the Labour government introduced the Trade Disputes Act which undid the damage done to the union movement by the 1927 Act (p. 218). In 1949 the government pushed through a Parliament Act, which amended the 1911 Act (p. 183), and stated that the House of Lords could only hold up legislation for one year. The Commons was to be even more important than it had been before the war.

The Election, 1950

Between 1945 and 1950 the Labour Party had not lost a single by-election – a record not equalled by any other postwar government. Many people seemed to approve of the social revolution even though this meant high taxation, rationing, licensing, and so on. In February 1950 Attlee called a general election, and the Labour Party won 13¼ million votes – the highest number ever recorded to that date.

But most of these votes came from 'safe' Labour areas. The middle classes had turned against the Labour government – because of the high taxes they had to pay and because they were unable to enjoy the standard of living that their parents had enjoyed in the 1930s. They had few, if any, servants; they went on shorter, if any, holidays. So the Labour Party lost the support of the middle class which had voted for Labour in 1945.

The result of the election was Labour 315, Conservatives 298, Liberals nine and Irish Nationalists two. This gave the Labour government a majority of six.

The Second Attlee Government, 1950–1

The government elected in 1945 had carried out most of its programme by 1950. After the 1950 election it did not seem to have much idea of what it intended to do. In October 1950 Cripps had to resign.

The new Chancellor was a young economist, Hugh Gaitskell. He accepted Attlee's policy for spending £1,500,000,000 a year on rearmament. To get this money Gaitskell had to cut down the money spent on welfare. One of his policies was to make people pay some of the money charged by dentists and to pay a fee when they handed a prescription in at the chemist. Aneurin Bevan was already annoyed that a younger man should have become Chancellor; he was even more angry at this attack on 'his' free Health Service. He resigned from the Cabinet, and other ministers followed him into resignation – Harold Wilson and John Freeman (Fig. 42.3).

The Korean War

In June 1950 the communist government of North Korea invaded the South which was under American control. The Korean War was part of the Cold War between East and West (Chapter 44). Many people thought that it would lead to a major clash between Russia and the Western powers.

The Attlee government announced that every young man would have to spend two years in one or other of the armed forces. This was part of the programme of rearmament. Britain was going to spend £4,700 million over three years to try once again to become a first-class military power.

This meant that materials that might have been used to make peacetime goods had, once again, to be used to make weapons and munitions. Many people resented this cut in their living standards. The Korean War also led to a massive rise in import prices. America and other countries wanted to buy up vast quantities of copper, zinc, tin, lead, wool, and other raw materials which would be needed during the coming war. Therefore British importers had to pay more for the raw materials they wanted. This increase in import prices led to an immediate increase in the cost of living in Britain. In 1949 the trade unions had agreed to help the country's economic recovery by not asking for wage increases, but by the middle of 1950 the combination of rising prices and stable wages led to a fall in living standards. The unions then told the Chancellor, Cripps, that the wage freeze would have to come to an end.

Other Problems for the Government, 1950–1

The Labour government had to deal with the Iranian Prime Minister, Dr Mossadeq, who nationalized the country's oil industry. This meant the end of the power of the Anglo-Iranian Oil Company. Many people felt that the government ought to have used military force to invade Persia and seize the oilfields. However, the Labour Foreign Minister, Morrison, realized that this would be opposed by the Russians and the Americans. He also knew that Britain could not afford to wage a war. Many people condemned this attitude which led to the humiliation of Britain.

An ageing Prime Minister – who had been in hospital during the quarrel over the health charges – led a divided Party into the election of October 1951. Once again the Labour Party increased its total vote, although the Tories also increased their total poll. This gave the Tories a majority of seventeen over all the other parties in the Commons. Churchill and his colleagues entered upon the task of governing a modern, more prosperous, and healthier Britain. In Chapter 43 we shall see how they helped to develop the country after 1951.

Questions

Extract 42.1

Economic problems, 1945

Williams: What about the non-nationalised industry, the private sector?

Attlee: Well, there had to be control there too. We have to have an allocation of building labour, for example, and materials and so on. I don't think people realised the extent to which this sort of planning was essential. A great deal of industry had been practically destroyed, knocked down; it had to be started again. Other industries had to switch back to civilian output. Their labour had been dispersed. They had to collect their old teams. It was a tremendous mess.
Williams: One criticism made at the time was that the pace was altogether too fast.
Attlee: We had to work fast. We had to rebuild the export trade and you can't build an export trade in a vacuum. You've got to have the fuel and power, transport, finance and all the rest to do it. And of course, because of the export situation, there had to be control of masses of things that were forbidden to our own people at home. Shops would have lovely china, for export only. Very frustrating, but you couldn't avoid it. It was often easier to sell in the home market than the foreign market. To get back into export markets that were essential for our survival we had to insist that what would sell abroad went abroad, and we had to think not only of our economic situation, which was bad enough, but of our international markets.
(Lord Atlee and Lord Francis-Williams, *A Prime Minister Remembers* (William Heinemann, 1961).)

1. What had happened to 'a great deal of industry'? How had this happened?
2. '. . . switch back to civilian output'. On what sort of output had these industries been concentrating? How had this affected the level of exports from 1939 to 1945?
3. Why was an expansion of the coal and transport industries essential if Britain were to have a successful export trade?
4. '. . . lovely china, for export only'. Why did the government forbid the sale of many things on the home market?
5. Why is it easier for a manufacturer to sell in the home market than in the foreign markets?
6. Why were 'exports essential for our survival'?

Extract 42.2

Marshall Aid, 1947

The best statement of what the Marshall Plan meant was in the *Board of Trade Journal* for 16th October 1948: 'Rations of butter, sugar, cheese and bacon would all have had to be cut by over a third and there would have been less meat and eggs. Cotton goods would have disappeared from the home market, supplies of footwear would have been reduced and tobacco consumption would have been cut by three-quarters. It would have meant even less petrol for private motoring and fewer films, newspapers, and books. Shortage of timber would have meant a further reduction in house-building, perhaps to 50,000 a year. Most serious of all, our supplies of raw materials for industry would have been affected, and might have brought unemployment figures up to 1,500,000.'

(Herbert and Nancie Matthews, *The Britain We Saw* (Gollancz, 1950).)

1. When was Marshall Aid introduced? Why was it so called?
2. Why did Britain have to import machinery and food from America? Make a list of some of the imports mentioned in this extract.
3. Why could Britain not pay for these imports in 1947 as easily as she could have done in 1937?
4. How did Marshall Aid prevent a fall in the British standard of living? What cuts would have had to be made?

Fig. 42.2

1. For which major social reform was Aneurin Bevan responsible?
2. Why did Bevan resign from the Labour government in 1951?
3. Bevan was also responsible for housing. How did he propose to deal with the problem of overcrowded cities and towns?
4. Why was there a greater shortage of houses in 1945 than there had been in 1938?
5. Why was it not possible to build a large number of new houses between 1945 and 1950?

Worksheet

(A)
1. What were the main aims of the Attlee government in 1945?

2. Why was Britain poorer in 1945 than in 1939?

3. Why did the government have to impose (i) restrictions on building (ii) rationing, and (iii) higher taxes?

4. Why did the American loan 'run out' more quickly than Keynes had hoped?

5. Explain the need for more exports after 1945. How did that help the government's policy on full employment?

6. Why is a successful export drive a cause of inflation? List FOUR other reasons for inflation in this period.

7. Explain devaluation. How does it affect the prices of (i) exports, and (ii) imports? Is it a cause of inflation? Why?

8. Why could the government claim in 1950 that its policies had succeeded?

9. Make a list of the industries that were nationalized by the Attlee government.

10. Explain the connection between the *Beveridge Report* (Chapter 41) and the National Insurance Act 1946.

11. Explain why the National Health Service was regarded as a major change in social policy.

12. How do you account for the result of the 1951 election? (You might want to draw up two lists – one explaining the Labour defeat and the second explaining the Conservative victory.)

(B)
1. Write the letters that might have been written by:
(a) a Labour minister (i) in 1945 explaining the government's aims and problems (ii) in 1947 explaining why things seemed to have gone wrong, and (iii) in 1950 claiming success for the government;
(b) one of Cripps's friends explaining the decision to devalue in 1949;
(c) a Labour minister explaining why coal prices were held down and what problems this caused for the industry;
(d) someone who has gone to live in a new town;
(e) one of the ministers who resigned in 1951 (see Fig. 42. 3).

(C)
1. Write the headlines that might have appeared above reports on:
(a) the formation of the Labour government, 26 July 1945;
(b) the signing of the American loan, 1947;
(c) the rise in world prices, 1945–7;
(d) bread rationing (see Fig. 42.1);
(e) the signing of Marshall Aid;
(f) the devaluation of the pound, 1949;
(g) the first day of the National Health Service, 5 April 1948;
(h) the outbreak of the Korean War;
(i) the nationalization of Persian oil;
(j) the resignation of Bevan (see Fig. 42.3);
(k) the results of the election, 1951.

2. Draw or paint the posters that might have been used to:
(a) ask for an export drive;
(b) show that the coal industry had been nationalized;
(c) advertise the election campaign of (i) Labour (ii) Conservatives, in 1950 and 1951.

43 Conservative Governments, 1951-64

What Was and Is Important?

In Chapter 16 we examined the long period during which Palmerston was the most important politician in the country. During the Palmerston period, foreign affairs were more important than home affairs.

The Conservatives came to power in 1951 – a hundred years after Palmerston's dismissal in 1851. But during their long rule (1951–64) it was home affairs that were more important, and this has remained true since 1964. The British people and their politicians are more interested in jobs, prices, wages, and standards of living than they are in foreign affairs (Chapter 44). In this chapter we will examine the way in which the Conservative governments dealt with home affairs.

An Improving Situation

By 1951 the country had made a great recovery.

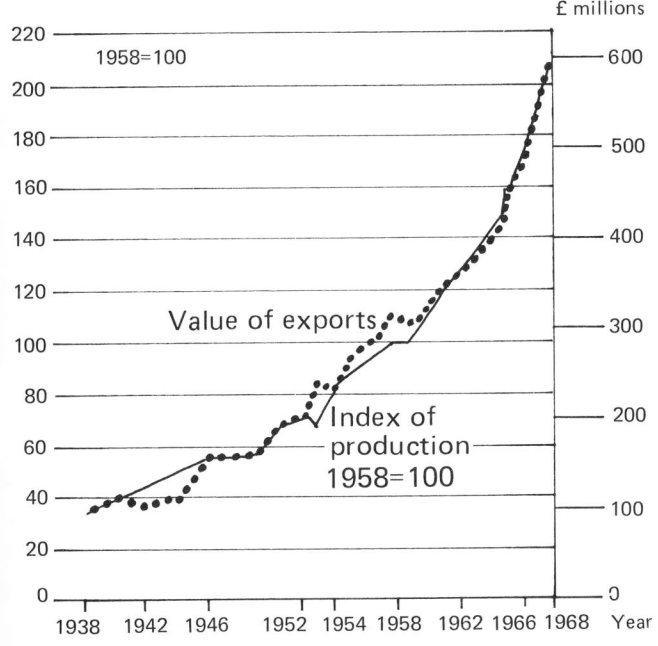

Fig. 43.1 Figures for the production and export of chemicals.

Exports were rising and were paying for most of Britain's imports. Since 1945 there had been a great deal of industrial building. The new steelworks, oil refineries, and other factories were now beginning to produce the steel, chemicals, and other goods (Fig. 43.1).

The Korean War pushed up world prices, but the two sides started peace talks in June 1951 and signed a peace treaty in 1953. This meant that the world powers did not now need to buy all the wool, oil, cotton, and other goods they had started buying in 1950. The end of the war and of that buying led to a great fall in world prices. This helped Britain; her imports now cost much less after 1953 than they had cost in 1950.

A Chance of a Better Life

There were more goods coming from Britain's factories. Because of the fall in world prices, the government needed fewer of these goods to pay for Britain's imports. So there were more goods available on the home market. The British people could now buy goods which Attlee's government had been forced to sell abroad (Extract 42.1 on p. 251).

The fall in world prices allowed the government to increase the quantity of imports. This meant that the country could import more timber – and so build more houses. Harold Macmillan became famous as the Minister of Housing who rightly boasted that the government had helped build 300,000 houses a year; this was about 50 per cent more than the Attlee government had been able to build. People welcomed the chance to get a house – and the furniture, curtains, and other things they needed.

The people had more money to spend. They earned high wages, and more and more married women went to work. In the 1930s many families had no wage earner, but since 1950 many have had two or more wage earners in the home.

The Conservative government cut the level of taxation. They could do this because they did not spend as much on rearmament as Attlee had planned.

They were helped also by the fact that as people earned more money so there were more people paying income tax.

Butskellism

In 1950–1 the Chancellor of the Exchequer had been Hugh Gaitskell. Between 1951 and 1955 the Conservative Chancellor was R. A. Butler. Many people had thought that a Conservative government might undo the work of the Labour government. It might have abolished the Health Service, the Insurance Acts, the Assistance Board, and so on. In fact it did no such thing. The Conservative government followed much the same policies as the Labour government had done. This led some people to coin a new word – 'Butskellism' – formed from the names of the two Chancellors. There was little, if any, difference between the policies of the two Chancellors.

The New Elizabethans

In 1952 King George VI died, and his daughter became Queen Elizabeth II.

Many writers thought that Britain was now about to become as great as she had been under the first Elizabeth. There was a new young Queen, a new government under Churchill, an economy that had recovered from the war, and a rising standard of living for the people.

In 1954 the government pushed through the Television Act which set up the Independent Television Authority. The I.T.A. gave contracts to various companies who were allowed to present television programmes and to charge for advertising. This was another sign of the 'new' Britain which was rich enough to buy the goods that were advertised.

In 1955 Churchill retired, and his successor was Sir Anthony Eden. He called for a general election. The Conservatives presented their record to the people; food rationing had been abolished, taxes were lower, more houses were being built, and the majority of people enjoyed a rising standard of living. The Labour Opposition under Attlee, seemed to have no new ideas to offer the people – except more nationalization. The Conservatives won 344 seats, Labour 277, and the Liberals six. Within a few months Attlee retired, and was succeeded by Hugh Gaitskell. Some people argued that the Labour Party would have to think up new ideas if it was going to win another election (Fig. 43.2).

Foreign Clouds on the Horizon

But even as the Eden government was settling in to

Fig. 43.2 A cartoon by Vicky entitled 'The Death of Socialism'. Why did he call it this?

govern the country there were signs that everything was not as rosy as it seemed. By 1955 Germany had recovered from the war, so too had Japan. Both countries had received a great deal of help from America; they had modern industries, new machinery – and a determination to win back the place they had once held in the world. By 1955 their industries were beginning to produce goods for sale abroad, and British industry was finding out that the Germans and Japanese produced better goods at a lower price than did Britain. British firms might not be able to sell their goods as easily as they had done before 1955.

Inflation

The Korean War pushed up the prices of British imports. This led to an increase in the prices of things made from these imports. The rise in prices (or inflation) was caused by a rise in costs and was known as cost-push inflation.

Workers asked for wage increases to meet the rise in the cost of living caused by the Korean War. Employers gave the increases – and pushed up their prices to the consumer. This raised living costs – so that workers asked for wage increases – and got them. You will see that this is something like a spiral; up go prices, then up go wages, so up go prices again – and so on up the spiral staircase, step by inflationary step.

Stop–Go

Almost as soon as the 1955 election was over Butler and Eden had to try to do something to stop this inflation. Butler announced changes in the hire-purchase regulations and an increase in the rates of interest people would have to pay to borrow money from the banks. The following examples show how this would work:

1. *1955*: A car cost £400. A hire-purchase company charges 3 per cent on the money borrowed and allows the repayments over thirty-six months (three years). The total interest to be paid is £12 each year, or £36 altogether. The total repayment has to be £436 – or £12.11 each month.

2. *1956*: A car costs £400. The hire-purchase company now has to charge 6 per cent (because of the increase in interest rates). The government says that repayments have to be made in twenty-four months (or two years). The total interest to be paid is now £24 a year, or £48 altogether. The total repayment has to be £448 – or £18.66 each month.

The government hoped that fewer goods would be bought at £18.66 a month than at £12.11 a month. This would force manufacturers to try to sell their goods abroad – and so send up the level of exports and help the balance of payments.

Macmillan

In 1956 Sir Anthony Eden's government became involved in the Suez Crisis (p. 262). Eden retired and Macmillan became Prime Minister. He had to try to deal with a number of problems at the same time. He had to attempt to heal the divisions in the Conservative Party; some Conservatives had wanted Eden to invade Egypt and risk the danger of a major war; others had seen that the Russians and Americans would not allow Britain to do this and had wanted the withdrawal from the Suez. Macmillan had to try to bring both sides together again. He also had to show the country that the Conservatives were not going to be a warring party – but at the same time that they would somehow make Britain count in the world. The government also had to deal with the economic effects of the Suez affair which had pushed up oil prices and so made British goods more expensive.

At first Macmillan repeated the 'stop' part of Butler's 1955 policy, and things became more difficult at home. But as soon as he could, he developed a 'go' policy. Rates of interest came down; hire-purchase companies were allowed to collect repayments over three, four or five years – which meant that the monthly payments fell. More people could afford to buy goods, and more would be employed to make these goods.

The Nature of Freedom

Macmillan boasted that 'Tory Freedom Works' – and argued that the country did not want a return to the Labour government's policies of controls, rationing, licensing, and so on. There was no doubt that, in many ways, he was right. Certainly the people enjoyed a rising standard of living. In 1957 Macmillan claimed that they had 'never had it so good' (Extract 43.1).

In the 1959 election the people showed that they preferred the Conservatives to the Labour Party. The Conservatives won 365 seats, Labour 258, and the Liberals six. This was the third successive victory for the Conservatives, (1951 and 1955 being the first two wins). It was the first time since 1832 that a party had won three successive victories, and many people began to wonder if the Labour Party would ever win again.

But there was at least one weakness in the argument about freedom. Frank Cousins was the General Secretary of the Transport and General Workers' Union in the 1950s. He argued that if Macmillan wanted freedom for all, then the unions were part of that 'all'. He used his union's power to win large wage increases for this members, and other unions did the same. Employers paid the higher wages – and pushed up the prices of their goods. Inflation became even more of a problem in 1961 than it had ever been in 1955 or 1957.

The rise in living standards led to a rise in the volume of imports. The British people could afford more furniture, cars, clothing, and so on. Some of these were made by British manufacturers, using imported raw materials; some were made by foreign manufacturers and there was a rise in the level of imports of Japanese cars, Italian footwear, etc.

This raising of living standards also led to a slow-down in the expansion of British exports. British manufacturers could sell their goods to the prosperous British. Why should they bother to try to sell them to customers overseas?

A rise in imports and a slow-down in exports led to a balance of payments crisis. Britain was trying to spend more abroad than she was earning.

1961 – A New Conservatism

Macmillan realized that if Britain continued to move in this direction the country would soon become bankrupt. Even before that, its money would become worthless as prices continued to rise. So, in 1961, he took three major steps away from the Conservative tradition.

Fig. 43.3 Vicky's cartoon of 15 July 1961 shows a confident Harold Wilson passing a depressed Selwyn Lord on the road to a planned economy.

1. He asked that Britain should be allowed to become a member of the Common Market (Chapter 44).

2. He set up the National Economic Development Council (nicknamed 'Neddy'). In this Council representatives from unions and government sit with manufacturers to work out plans for future economic development (Fig. 43.3). In 1963 little 'Neddies' were set up to examine the economic performance of various industries.

On each of these Neddies the unions had their representatives. This was a sign that the government realised that unions were now very important. They were, in one sense, almost a part of the system of government.

3. Macmillan also set up a National Incomes Commission (or 'Nicky'). The government hoped to use this Commission to regulate the pattern of wage demands and increases. Nicky was much less successful than Neddy. In July 1961 the Chancellor, Selwyn Lloyd, announced a pay pause. The government would not allow any wage or salary increases; the government could impose this restriction on people working for the government or for the nationalized industries, and so teachers, nurses, and others had no

increase in pay. But electricians working for the government-controlled Central Electricity Board threatened to go on strike if they did not get their pay increase in 1961, and the government gave in. This led to growing discontent with the Macmillan government which was seen to be incapable of dealing fairly with wages and salaries.

Immigration

During the 1950s Britain became more prosperous. Employers wanted an ever-increasing number of workers to produce goods – for sale at home and for export. At first they attracted married women back to work. By 1960 about 8 million married women were working in industry or commerce, but still there were not enough workers.

Employers and government combined to attract workers from Commonwealth countries. Between 1955 and 1961 about 400,000 immigrants came from India, Pakistan, the West Indies, and parts of Africa. They found work in London, the Midlands, and in parts of Yorkshire and Lancashire where there was a shortage of labour. They staffed the Health Service and the transport system, and did many of those unskilled and lowly paid jobs that British workers had left in order to find work in factories.

By 1961 some people had begun to use the coloured immigrants as the excuse for Britain's failures. The immigrants wanted housing – so they were blamed for Britain's housing shortage. They were willing to work – so were blamed for the unemployment caused by Selwyn Lloyd's 'stop' policy. They had to get medical help when ill – and so were blamed for the failure of the government to develop the Health Service in the prosperous 1950s.

In 1962 Parliament passed the Commonwealth Immigrants Act. This said that the only immigrants who would be allowed to come to Britain in the future would be (i) those who had jobs waiting for them (ii) people having one of a list of skills, and (iii) dependants coming to join a wage earner already here.

Macmillan, 1962–3

The close link between politics and the economy was shown clearly in the winter of 1962–3. As unemployment rose so the government became more unpopular. In 1959 the government had won a 'famous victory', but in 1962–3 it lost a series of by-elections as the people turned either to the Liberals or to Labour in the hope that they would help restore the economy (Extract 43.2).

But there was no recovery and in the autumn of 1963 Macmillan retired. His successor was the former Lord Home, who had been Foreign Minister under Macmillan.

Maudling's Boom, 1963–4

The new Chancellor of the Exchequer was Reginald Maudling. He tried to restore the government's popularity by 'buying our way to prosperity'. He lowered interest rates, cut taxes, and so helped to get more people back to work. He hoped that this would encourage industrialists to invest in new machinery so that Britain would be better able to compete with the Germans, Japanese, and other foreign competitors.

He succeeded in making the government more popular – but did not do quite enough. In the general election of 1964 Labour won 317 seats, the Conservatives 304, and the Liberals nine. The 'thirteen years of Conservative rule' had come to an end.

Wilson and a 'New' Labour Party

In 1963 Hugh Gaitskell died, and Harold Wilson became leader of the Labour Party. He attacked the Conservatives for not having done more to modernize British industry. He argued that Tory freedom had failed to work properly (Fig. 43.3); he claimed that if there were to be Neddies and Nickies they would be better run by a party which really believed in controls and planning. This, he said, was the Labour Party.

Wilson also attacked the Maudling 'boom'. This, he argued, had led to a rise in imports – of raw materials and manufactured goods, as in 1955–9. The boom had made inflation a worse problem than it had been; it had also made the balance of payments deteriorate. Indeed, when the Labour government came to power it found that the government had to borrow £800 million from overseas bankers to make up the difference between what Britain was spending and what she was earning. This was a much larger sum than Britain had borrowed in 1957 and in 1961. Britain was on the road to bankruptcy as a result of the 'thirteen years' of what Labour called 'Tory misrule'. In Chapter 45 we will see how far, if at all, future governments managed to cope with the economic problems that had become clear by 1964.

Questions

Extract 43.1

'Never had it so good', 1957

I find it a strange experience to sit here day after day and listen to the arguments presented by high prices and over-full employment. When I first stood for the House of Commons in 1923 and for the next fifteen years, one problem only held the political field. The problem of rapidly falling prices and massive unemployment. We put forward all kinds of rival views as to how it should be solved.

Today, it has solved itself, but this new trouble has come. Having solved one problem we now have the one we are discussing, that of rising prices. Every Hon. Member knows that for the mass of the people there has never been such a good time or such a high standard of living. I repeat what I said at Bedford, they have 'never had it so good'.

(Harold Macmillan, Prime Minister, speaking in the House of Commons, 25 July 1957.)

1. When did the speaker first enter the House of Commons? What major problem held the political field then?
2. What was the problem dominating the political field in 1957?
3. What did the speaker mean by 'they have 'never had it so good'?

Extract 43.2

Political effects of economic causes: 1964

The Government's electoral battering early in 1962 gave rise to rumours that Mr Macmillan intended to reshuffle his Cabinet. On 21 July at Leicester North-West the Conservative candidate finished an ignominious third, 10 per cent behind the Liberal. The next day the Chancellor of the Exchequer was sacked along with the Lord Chancellor and five other Cabinet Ministers. Many believed Macmillan was mainly acting in desperation because of the Government's recent by-election defeats.

Meanwhile Britain was enduring its worst winter since 1881. The economy had been slack throughout 1962. Now bad weather led to mounting unemployment. The number of unemployed rose to 2.5 per cent of the labour force in December 1962 (compared with 1.7 per cent a year earlier); in February 1963 the total reached 3.9 per cent, the highest figure since the fuel crisis of 1947. The number who feared unemployment was even higher; in December 19 per cent of a Gallup sample believed that they or a member of their family would be affected. The regions farthest from London were particularly hard hit; in February 7 per cent of the labour force were out of work in the North-East, 6 per cent in Scotland, and 6 per cent in Wales. During the late winter Conservative murmurings against Mr Macmillan's leadership could be heard.

(D. E. Butler and Anthony King, *The British General Election of 1964* (Macmillan, 1965).)

1. Who was Prime Minister in 1962?
2. Why did he reshuffle his Cabinet? How does this show the power of the Prime Minister?
3. What 'led to mounting unemployment'?
4. Draw a graph, or make histograms, to show unemployment figures in December 1961, December 1962, and February 1963.
5. Does the pattern of your graph, or histogram, help to explain why 19 per cent believed that they would be affected?
6. Which parts of the country were particularly hard hit?
7. How did Conservatives behave towards Mr Macmillan late in the winter of 1963?

Fig. 43.1

1. The output in 1958 is shown as being 100. What was the output in (i) 1952 (ii) 1962? What was the percentage increase (i) between 1952 and 1958 (ii) between 1958 and 1962?
2. What products of the chemical industry do we (i) wear (ii) use in the kitchen at home (iii) buy for our cars? Why should this industry have grown so rapidly since 1952 while the cotton industry declined?

3. What does this graph tell you about (i) employment in the chemical industry, and (ii) the standard of living of the British people in the post-war period?

Worksheet

(A)

1. Why was life better in 1953 than it had been in (i) 1947, and (ii) 1951?

2. Make a list of the reasons why prices continued to rise during this period.

3. Why did Britain have to borrow money from foreign bankers in 1957, 1961, and 1964? Give FOUR reasons for the continuing balance of payments problem.

4. Explain 'stop–go' and show how a credit squeeze was supposed to (i) cut down the level of imports (ii) help to increase the level of exports.

5. Why could Macmillan claim that the British people had 'never had it so good' in 1957?

6. Why did trade unions become more militant in the 1950s and 1960s? How did this affect the level of wage demands? What effect did that have on (i) inflation, and (ii) the balance of payments?

7. Why were so many coloured immigrants (i) anxious to come to Britain (ii) welcomed by many employers? Why did Parliament pass the Commonwealth Immigration Act 1962?

(B)

1. Write the headlines that might have appeared above reports on:
(a) the building of the 300,000th house in 1953;
(b) the death of King George VI;
(c) the Coronation of Elizabeth II;
(d) the Television Act;
(e) Churchill's retirement;
(f) the result of the 1955 election;
(g) the result of the 1959 election;
(h) the first meeting of 'Neddy' and 'Nicky';
(i) the appointment of Lord Home as Prime Minister.

2. Draw or paint the posters that might have been used by:
(a) the Conservative Party during the 1955 and 1959 elections;
(b) the Labour Party during the 1964 election.

44 Britain and the World, 1945-80

In earlier chapters of this book we have seen Britain gaining a world-wide Empire (Chapters 18, 25, and 26). In this chapter we shall see how and why Britain gave up its Empire and why it no longer has the same world-wide influence in international relations.

India, 1947

After 1918 there was an increasingly strong demand for Indian independence. The British made some concessions; most Indians were given the vote in 1919 as the British allowed the election of a national Parliament – which, however, had little real power. The Hindu majority controlled the Congress Party which demanded full independence. Gandhi, the leader of the Congress Party, promised that the Muslims would receive equal and fair treatment in an independent India, but the British were afraid that there would be religious riots if they granted such independence.

The Japanese victory over the British in Burma and Malaya in 1941 increased the demand for Indian Independence. It also destroyed the idea that the British could not be defeated. The Labour government that came to power in 1945 faced too many other difficulties at home and abroad to be able to cope with India.

In 1946 Attlee sent Lord Mountbatten to India as Viceroy; he had instructions to give India its Independence by 15 August 1947. He hoped to persuade the Hindu Leader, Nehru, and the Muslim leader, Jinnah, to agree to a united and independent India. Mountbatten failed. Jinnah demanded a separate state for the Muslims, and this was how Pakistan was formed. Mountbatten was honoured by being chosen to be the first Governor-General of Independent India of which Nehru was the first Prime Minister.

In 1948 Ceylon and Burma were also given their independence, and Burma decided to leave the Commonwealth. Ceylon, India, and Pakistan remained members of that Commonwealth.

Palestine, 1947

When the Turkish Empire was split up in 1920 Britain was given control over Palestine. In 1917 the government had promised to set up a National Home for Jews in this area when the war ended. It was thought that a few thousand refugees from Russia might want to make a new life in a Jewish land in Palestine.

During the 1920s and 1930s the Jews and Arabs lived in uneasy peace under British rule. There were many riots, especially when the numbers of Jewish immigrants increased because of Hitler's persecutions. Illegal armies and gangs were formed on both sides, and both fought the British as well as each other. By 1938 the British government was already tired of the problem of Palestine. When the Arabs rejected the idea of a division of the country between Arabs and Jews, the British decided that a National Home for the Jews was impossible. Jewish immigration was restricted in spite of the horrors being suffered in Hitler's Germany.

In 1945 the Attlee government inherited this problem. Britain was now a tired country without the will or means to impose peace in Palestine. In 1946 the American President, Truman, demanded that 100,000 more Jews should be admitted to relieve the problem of refugees in Europe. The British refused, but Jews entered the country illegally. Both the British and the Arab gangs fought against the Jewish terrorist gangs which helped bring in the new immigrants (Fig. 44.1).

In May 1948 the British government finally decided that it was unable to deal with the situation, and it handed the problem to the United Nations organization. This voted to recognize the new State of Israel, and Britain withdrew from Palestine.

The Berlin Airlift

During the war against Hitler's Germany the Russians had been allies to America and Britain. At various wartime conferences they had agreed to the postwar division of Europe. Russia gained control of Eastern Europe while Western Europe remained

Fig. 44.1 One of the many painful scenes in Haifa during 1946–7.

free and independent (Extract 44.1). As part of the settlement Germany was divided into four zones, each to be governed by one of the Big Four – Russia, America, Britain, and France. Berlin was a 100 miles (160 kilometres) inside the Russian zone, but it was agreed that this former capital city should also be divided into four zones. The Russians allowed the Americans, British, and French to use certain roads, canals, and railways across a 100 miles of their zone to reach their area of Berlin. Along these the Allies sent supplies, reinforcements, officials, and so on.

In 1948 the Western Allies decided that the time had come to help the Germans to rebuild their country. They allowed free elections; and they set out a programme of economic reform including the printing of a new money supply. Stalin in Russia saw a German recovery as a threat to Russia, so when the Allies issued their new money in their zones of Berlin the Russians cut the city off from the West. Berlin was to be isolated.

General Lucius Clay, then in charge of the American zone of Berlin, said, 'When Berlin falls, Western Germany will be next.' So began the Berlin airlift. Day by day the job of supplying 2 million Berliners with coal, food, and other necessities went on. At first there were only a hundred transport planes available, but soon the operation built up until an airplane was landing every five minutes of the day and night.

This airlift ended in September 1949 when the Russians agreed to reopen the roads, canals, and railways. The Allies had won an important victory; in particular, the Americans had shown that they intended to play a major role in world affairs. They had already shown this by the Marshall Plan (p. 248). Truman had said that they would do so (Extract 44.2(i)). But the Berlin airlift showed that they meant what they said (Extract 44.2(ii)).

NATO

Russia had conquered Eastern Europe (Extract 44.1 and Fig. 44.2), and the Western powers were afraid that she might try to conquer the West. No single power would be strong enough to stand up to Russia, so in April 1949 the North Atlantic Treaty Organization (NATO) was formed. It consisted of America, Britain, France, Belgium, Luxembourg, Holland, Canada, Denmark, Iceland, Norway, Italy, and Portugal.

Korea

Soon after NATO was formed, Mao Tse Tung became the Chairman of the People's Republic of China. The communists had gained an important victory in world affairs, and they used that victory to try to gain another one in Korea.

Korea had been part of the Japanese Empire. In 1945 the Russians and Americans had divided the country between themselves along the 38th parallel of latitude. The Americans wanted free elections and the formation of a government for the whole country, but the Russians refused. So in 1950 there were separate governments in North and South Korea.

In June 1950 the North Koreans invaded the South. This was Russia's answer to the American policy of 'containment' in Europe. America brought the matter of the invasion before the Security Council at the United Nations organization. The Russian delegate was not present because Russia had temporarily withdrawn as a protest against the exclusion of communist China from the U.N. The Security Council decided that North Korea was an aggressor. It also authorized the sending of a U.N. army to help the South Koreans.

The bulk of this army was provided by America. Britain, Turkey, and other countries sent small forces. At first the invaders swept everything before them. By September 1950 the U.N. forces commanded by the American, General MacArthur, were pinned down in a narrow coastal strip around Pusan. MacArthur organized a sea-borne invasion around Inchon, and the success of this led to the capture of Seoul, the

Fig. 44.2 A cartoonist's view of the division of Europe. Churchill is peeping under the curtain.

PEEP UNDER THE IRON CURTAIN

capital of South Korea. This cut the invaders off from their supply lines to North Korea. The U.N. army advanced to the 38th parallel, the border between the two halves of Korea. MacArthur planned to invade the North, and this brought the Chinese to the help of the North Koreans. Three hundred thousand Chinese troops drove the U.N. armies back beyond the 38th parallel, and once again the U.N. armies seemed to be heading for defeat.

MacArthur wanted to bomb railway lines and harbours in China. He also asked to be allowed to use the atomic bomb against the Chinese; President Truman agreed that 'the use of the atomic bomb was under active consideration'. The British Prime Minister Attlee flew to Washington to persuade Truman not to use 'the' bomb. Truman agreed, and MacArthur was sacked in April 1951. Negotiations between the two sides had begun earlier in 1950, but were unsuccessful until July 1953 when an armistice was signed. For the time being the danger of the Third World War was over. However, negotiations for a final peace continued to drag on at Panmunjon some thirty years later.

Iran, 1951

In 1951 Britain faced a new crisis in the Middle East. Britain bought most of her oil from Iran. The Anglo–Iranian Oil Company had been established for many years. It paid only a small part of its profits to the Iranian government.

When oil was discovered in Saudi Arabia the oil companies offered the Saudi government 50 per cent of their profits. The Iranian government asked the Anglo–Iranian Oil Company for similar terms. It also asked for compensation for the company's failure to pay enough during the past. The company refused, so in April 1951 the Iranian Prime Minister, Mr Mossadeq, brought in a Bill to nationalize the company's property. In August the company appealed to the Labour government to stand by it. Warships were sent to the Persian Gulf, and it seemed as if Britain might go to war with Iran.

In September the government decided that the company's case was not a strong one. Certainly it was not strong enough to deserve a war in its support. On 3 October 1951 the 350 remaining members of the staff were evacuated. They left behind a great refinery and rich oilfields.

Most British newspapers attacked the Labour government for not using force to keep British possession of these riches. During the election campaign the government was criticized for its weakness. Churchill's victory in this 1951 election was due, in part, to the hope that a Conservative government would stand up for British rights.

The Withdrawal from Suez, 1954

In November 1951 the Egyptian government cancelled the treaty that allowed Britain to station troops along the Suez Canal. Once again British women and children were evacuated from territory which many people thought was a part of the British Empire, and again the fleet was mobilized. British troops in their Canal bases were attacked by terrorist gangs, and British-owned property in Cairo and other cities was attacked and burned.

In the middle of 1952 there was an Egyptian revolt against the corrupt government of King Farouk, and he was forced to leave the country. Colonel Nasser became ruler of Egypt. In 1954 he negotiated with Britain's Foreign Minister, Anthony Eden, and the British troops were withdrawn peacefully. Britain had given up one more base in the world.

Suez, 1956

Nasser was anxious to build up Egyptian industry. One of his main ambitions was to build a High Dam on the River Nile at Aswan. This was to provide hydroelectric power for the development of industry as well as water to irrigate parts of the desert. Egypt had to ask foreign countries to help to build this dam; America, Britain, and Russia were the main contributors to this scheme.

In 1955 Egypt was at war with Israel. She bought weapons from Czechoslovakia, one of the communist states of Europe. The American Secretary of State, John Foster Dulles, thought that this showed that Egypt was moving towards communism.

On 19 July 1956 Dulles announced that America was cutting off its aid to Egypt, and Britain followed her example on the following day. On 26 July Nasser announced that he was going to nationalize the Suez Canal Company. He would use the income from the Company to provide the funds needed for the High Dam. The Canal Company was owned by French and British shareholders (p. 122), but it was registered in Egypt and was therefore an Egyptian company – and the Canal ran through Egyptian territory. Nasser certainly had as much right to nationalize the Canal Company as the British government had to nationalize any railway or coal company. He promised to pay the shareholders a compensation based on the value of their shares before nationalization.

Eden, now Prime Minister, claimed that the Canal was vital to British interests; he also argued that Nasser was behaving as Mussolini and Hitler had behaved. Eden was supported by the bulk of the British Press which asked for firm action.

During October 1956 Eden and his Foreign Minister, Selwyn Lloyd, met the leaders of the French and Israeli governments. They secretly agreed to make a joint attack on Egypt, and on 29 October Israel attacked. Within six days they had defeated the Egyptian army and had reached the Gulf of Aqaba. On 30 October British and French troops landed at Port Said after an air and sea bombardment (Fig. 44.3).

Fig. 44.3 British troops stationed along the Suez Canal. Guerrilla attacks by Egyptian nationalist groups, the climate, tents, and the sand all combined to make life here very uncomfortable.

The majority of newspapers approved of the 'British lion's roar'. The *Sunday Express* called it the 'proudest week we have known for years'. But only one day after the troops had landed, the government had to call a halt to their march along the Canal banks. The Russians threatened to use rockets to attack the invaders. American President Eisenhower was involved in an election campaign. He cut off American aid to Britain and even refused to talk to the Prime Minister over the telephone. At the U.N. the attack was condemned almost unanimously.

Britain had to withdraw her troops in a shameful humiliation which ended that 'proudest week'. The Egyptians had sunk several ships in the Canal to make sure that even if it was recaptured, it was unusable. The Canal remained closed until 1958, and by then the British had learned to pay higher prices for their oil which had to be brought around the Cape of Good Hope to Britain. Eden had realized that Britain could not act along lines which Palmerston had once followed. He retired to make way for Macmillan.

Africa

In the early 1950s there were the beginnings of demands for Independence in some African countries, but Churchill had said: 'I have not become the King's First Minister to preside over the liquidation of the British Empire.' But it was Churchill's government that negotiated the withdrawal from the Suez bases in 1954, and it was Churchill's successor, Eden, who learned that Britain could not attack and conquer Egypt in 1956; and it was Macmillan, Eden's successor, who first realized that 'a wind of change' was blowing through Africa. His government granted Independence to the Gold Coast (which became known as Ghana in 1957). Malaya, the Sudan, Cyprus, Nigeria, Tanganyika and Zanzibar, Sierra Leone, and Kenya had all gained their Independence by the time Macmillan retired in 1963

Britain and the Common Market

In 1950 six countries of West Europe pooled their coal and steel resources. France, West Germany, Italy, Belgium, Holland, and Luxembourg set up the European Coal and Steel Community to run the coal and steel industries of all six countries.

In 1955–6 they held discussions at Messina that led to the signing of the Treaty of Rome on 25 March 1957. This treaty set up the European Economic Community, or the Common Market. In the Treaty the six countries agreed:

1. to abolish import duties on goods passing from one Community country to another;
2. to impose a common Community tariff against goods coming from countries outside the Community;
3. to work towards a common system of taxation and social security;
4. to strengthen the European Parliament elected by the peoples of the six countries.

Britain had been invited to be a member of the Coal and Steel Community – but had refused. In 1955 Britain was invited to take part in the negotiations that led to the Treaty of Rome. Again, she said she could not be a member of a Common Market. She wanted a Free Trade Association with no tariffs on goods passing between the member states, but she was unwilling to have a tariff on food imports from the Commonwealth.

Britain managed to form a European Free Trade Association (E.F.T.A.) from seven of the states not in the Common Market, but these were the smaller, poorer states of Europe. By 1961 the countries of the Common Market had grown even richer. Germany and France were now richer than Britain: Macmillan's government was suffering from the effects of the slow-down in the British economy (p. 257). So in 1961 Britain applied to become a member of the E.E.C. and Macmillan appointed Edward Heath to lead the British negotiating team. But in January 1963 President de Gaulle of France announced that he would not agree to British membership.

In 1966 Prime Minister Wilson asked that Britain be allowed to join; once again, de Gaulle refused. In April 1969 he resigned as President, and in 1970 the Heath government started fresh negotiations for British membership. This time the Six agreed and in 1971 Britain became a member of the Community. The Labour Opposition argued that this was a betrayal of British interests, but when Labour came to power in 1974 the government did not try to take Britain out of the Market. They renegotiated the terms on which Britain had gained entry under Heath, and in the country's first ever referendum there was an overwhelming majority in favour of British membership of the Common Market.

But membership of the Market has not brought with it that economic revival which many people had hoped for. Since joining the Community Britain has become relatively less rich than other members of the Market (Fig. 45.1 on p. 266). Membership has not proved to be a remedy for Britain's problems.

In June 1979 the people of the nine countries in the E.E.C. voted in the first-ever international election. The European Parliament had consisted of members chosen by the governments of the various countries.

Since 7 June 1979 the M.E.P.s (Members of the European Parliament) have been those who were elected by the electors of the various countries. Britain has eighty-one M.E.P.s, including three representing the people of Ulster. But the British voters did not show much enthusiasm for this historic election. Only about one-third of them turned out to vote – and in some places only 15 per cent of the electorate voted. This compared very badly with the turn-out in most of the other countries. Britain does not seem to be as keenly 'European' as most other member countries.

Rhodesia, 1964–79

In 1961 Macmillan set up a Central African Federation of Rhodesia, Nyasaland, and Zambia, but in 1963 this broke up. Zambia and Nyasaland (now Malawi) became independent countries ruled by African politicians.

Southern Rhodesia, ruled by white politicians elected by the white minority of the population, asked for Independence, but the Conservative government refused this request until the African majority was properly represented in the Rhodesian Parliament.

In 1964 when Labour came to power in Britain, Ian Smith, leader of the United Front Party in Southern Rhodesia, declared that the country was going to take its independence with or without Britain's consent. Throughout 1965 and 1966 negotiations went on between the leaders of the two countries – but did not succeed.

Britain persuaded the U.N. organization to impose economic sanctions on the rebellious Rhodesians. No one was supposed to trade with the rebel government, but most countries continued to do so – using the ports of South Africa, Angola, or Mozambique to get their goods to Rhodesia.

As economic sanctions failed to topple the rebels, black African leaders organized a guerrilla war against the Smith government. The Russians and Chinese sent help to the rebels led by Robert Mugabe and Josuah Nkomo. By 1979 the Smith government realized that it was unable to defeat the rebels, who controlled large areas of the country, so Smith announced that there would be free elections for a Parliament in which Africans would have a majority. In April 1979 Bishop Abel Muzorewa led his party to victory in these first elections, and he became the first black Prime Minister of a renamed Zimbabwe–Rhodesia. Britain played no part in these developments. However in October/November 1979 Lord Carrington, the Foreign Secretary, played a major part in attempts to reach a lasting settlement in the affairs of Zimbabwe–Rhodesia. Representatives of the Bishop's government sat with leaders of the rebel armies and of the British government to hammer out the agreement which gave Zimbabwe–Rhodesia a new constitution, one more favourable to the black majority of that country.

The Nuclear Weapon

Macmillan became Prime Minister in 1957. In an attempt to prove that Britain was still a major power he announced that Britain would make its own hydrogen bomb.

Britain then had to find some means of delivering the bomb to its target. The government spent vast sums on Blue Streak, Black Knight, and other colourfully named rockets – all of which failed. Finally, in 1962, Macmillan decided to accept the American Polaris missile and to build nuclear-powered submarines from which the Polaris could be delivered. This special relationship between Britain and America angered de Gaulle of France. It led him to say 'No' to British entry into the Common Market in 1963.

In spite of the campaigns by the Campaign for Nuclear Disarmament and votes at Labour Party Conferences. Britain has remained a nuclear power. But this has only masked the reality of her position. During the 1970s Britain gave up most of the military and naval bases she had retained east of Suez. The British governments – Labour and Conservative – know that Britain can no longer even share the job of policing the world, a job which she did on her own in Palmerston's days.

Questions

Extract 44.1

The iron curtain

. . . From Stettin in the Baltic to Trieste in the Adriatic, an iron curtain has descended across the Continent. Behind that line lie all the capitals of the ancient states of Central and Eastern Europe. Warsaw, Berlin, Prague, Vienna, Budapest, Belgrade, Bucharest and Sofia, all these famous cities and the populations around them lie in what I must call the Soviet sphere. Police governments are prevailing in nearly every case, and so far, except in Czechoslovakia, there is no true democracy. . . .

(Extract from a speech by Winston Churchill at Westminster College, Fulton, Mo., U.S.A., March 1946.)

1. Make a list of the countries which were 'behind that line' in 1946.
2. Explain how and why the Russians controlled these countries in 1946.
3. When did the communists seize power in Czechoslovakia?
4. How did Truman react to the Russians' attempt to take power in Greece in 1947?
5. How did the Western powers react to the Russian attempt to take control of Berlin in 1947–8?
6. Which alliance was formed by the Western Powers in 1949? Explain why it was formed and what its main aim was.

Extract 44.2

(i) The Truman doctrine, 1947

> I believe that it must be the policy of the United States to support free people who are resisting attempted subjugation by armed minorities or by outside pressures.
>
> The free people of the world look to us for support in maintaining their freedom.
>
> If we falter from our leadership, we may endanger the peace of the world – and we shall surely endanger the welfare of our own nation.

(ii) The Berlin airlift, 1947–8

> . . . We (had) made the Americans face up to the facts in the Eastern Mediterranean. As a result we got the Truman doctrine, a big step. (But) it wasn't, I think, until the Berlin airlift that American public opinion really wakened up to the facts of life. Their own troops were involved in that, you see. Before that there'd been a lot of wishful thinking. In spite of everything, I don't think they really appreciated communist tactics until Berlin.
> (Lord Attlee to Lord Francis-Williams, *A Prime Minister Remembers* (William Heinemann, 1961).)

1. In which country in 'the Eastern Mediterranean' was there a civil war between 1945 and 1947? Why was Britain involved in trying to put an end to that war?
2. Why was Britain unable and unwilling to continue to try to maintain law and order in that country after 1947?
3. Why was Russia helping one side in that civil war?
4. How did the Truman doctrine differ from the foreign policies of American Presidents in the 1920s and 1930s?

5. Why were American 'troops . . . involved' in Berlin in 1948–9?

Worksheet

(A)

1. Why did Britain agree to give India its Independence in 1947? Why was Churchill opposed to this?

2. Why was there a civil war in Palestine from 1943 to 1948? Why did Britain hand the Palestine problem over to U.N. organization?

3. Explain why the Allies undertook the Berlin airlift. Why did it come to an end in 1949?

4. Why did the U.N. send an army to fight in Korea? What effect did that war have on (i) British tax levels (ii) world prices (iii) the unity of the Labour government?

5. Explain the reasons for and effects of the British withdrawal from (i) Iran in 1951, and (ii) the Suez Canal bases in 1954.

6. Why did Nasser nationalize the Suez Canal in 1956? Explain the reasons for the invasion of Suez in 1956 as seen by (i) Eden (ii) Gaitskell (iii) an Egyptian (iv) an Israeli. Why did Britain agree to withdraw from Suez in 1956?

7. Explain Britain's refusal to join the Messina discussions, 1955–7. Why did Britain want to join the Common Market in 1961? Why did de Gaulle say 'Non'?

8. How did the policy of Ian Smith change between 1964 and 1979? How do you account for this change?

(B)

1. Write the letters that might have been sent by:
(a) a Jewish immigrant in 1946 (Fig. 44.1);
(b) an Englishman working in Iran in 1950–1;
(c) a soldier stationed in Egypt in (i) 1952, and (ii) 1956.
(d) a European discussing Britain's attitude towards the Common Market in (i) 1956 (ii) 1969 (iii) 1971, and (iv) 1979.
(e) a member of the C.N.D. Movement (Fig. 44.4).

(C)

1. Make a time chart for the period 1945–79 marking on it the main dates and events noted in the text. Add a brief note of explanation for each of the dates and events you have chosen.

2. Draw or paint the poster that might have been used to advertise a C.N.D. demonstration.

45 The Last of the Swinging Sixties under the Wilson Governments, 1964-70

Foreigners and the Pound

When the Labour government came to power in 1964 it made the mistake of drawing attention to the fact that the Conservatives had left a debt of £800 million. Britain had spent that much more on imports than she had earned by her exports. This frightened many foreigners who kept large amounts of their cash in the Bank of England. They normally used that cash for trading purposes – for buying British goods or for paying other countries for goods. In 1964 they feared that the Labour government would devalue as it had done in 1949. So they took their money from Britain and bought German marks, French francs, or American dollars.

Other foreigners were frightened because British prices were rising by about 13 per cent a year in 1964. This *inflation* meant that money in the Bank would lose its value year after year (Fig. 45.1). This also drove many foreigners to take their money out of Britain.

The Wilson government had to go to the International Monetary Fund to ask for £1,000 million to help balance Britain's trading books. The government announced that it was going to bring down the rate of inflation, push up the level of exports, pay off the country's overseas debts, and build up the British economy so that the country could become wealthier.

Planning

In 1964 George Brown was put in charge of a new ministry, the Department of Economic Affairs. Within a few weeks he had produced a National Plan. The government, employers, and trade unions were going to co-operate so that the country's industries could be modernized, expanded, and made more profitable.

Brown realized that trade unions could wreck this Plan. Strikes could bring industry to a halt – and there would be too little progress. Wage demands could push up prices – and ruin the government's Plan. So in 1964 Brown persuaded the employers and the Trade Union Congress to sign a Declaration of Intent. They agreed to hold down both prices and wages. When employers and unions could not agree on a wages claim they agreed to accept the decision of a new Prices and Incomes Board set up by the government.

The government also set up the Industrial Re-organization Commission. This had the money and power to help firms that wanted to merge to form a larger body. It was the I.R.C. that helped Leyland Motors to link with the British Motor Corporation to create a motor giant organization better able to compete with the large car-producing firms of Europe.

Small Reforms

The government had only a small majority, and as it was busy trying to solve the country's economic problems there was little time for bringing in major reforms. Health prescription charges were abolished; there was a scheme of rate rebates to help less well-off house owners; the Education Minister asked local education authorities to submit plans for their areas 'going comprehensive'.

Fig. 45.1 The falling value of the British pound sterling.

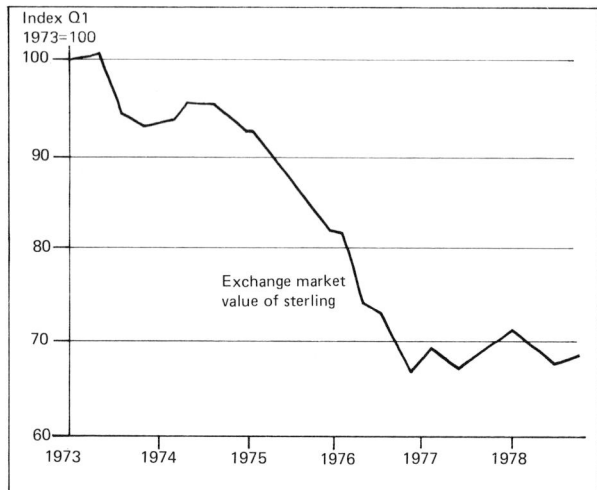

The 1966 Election

The government appeared to have some idea of how to put the country right. The Conservative Opposition found it hard to attack the government. After all, many people argued, it was the 'thirteen years of Tory government' which had caused Britain's problems. These were simply inherited by the Wilson government. The Opposition was further weakened by the way in which it replaced its leader, Sir Alec Douglas Home, with a new, young leader, Edward Heath. Meanwhile workers continued to demand and get higher wages. This gave them a chance to have a higher standard of living. The government won short-term popularity because of this improvement – but the pound became even less popular with foreigners worried about Britain's inflation.

Wilson took advantage of the government's popularity to call an election early in 1966. He campaigned on the slogan 'You Know Labour Government Works', and the electorate seemed to agree. Labour won 363 seats, the Conservatives 253, and the Liberals twelve.

Economic Reality

Within a few weeks the government's boasts were shown to be false. The leaders of the T.U.C. might sign agreements; they might sit on Planning Boards with employers and representatives of government. But the members of their unions, the men on the shop floor, were unwilling to accept their leaders' decisions. There were many, small, but damaging strikes, especially in the car industry. Wage demands continued to be too high – so that inflation continued to rise (Fig. 45.2). This meant that the balance of payments remained in deficit – Britain was spending more than she earned.

The government introduced a prices and incomes freeze; no increases were to be allowed. In the Budget the Chancellor, James Callaghan, announced cuts in government spending and the start of a credit squeeze. He also introduced a Selective Employment Tax. Employers had to pay a tax for every worker they employed. The credit squeeze and the restriction on wages was going to make it harder for manufacturers to sell their goods at home; the S.E.T. would make it more expensive for them to hold on to workers – unless they also sold their products overseas. S.E.T. was intended to help the growth of export industries.

But, unfortunately for the government, during the autumn there was a long strike by British seamen, and this halted the flow of exports from Britain's docks. On the other hand, foreign countries used their own, or other people's ships, to bring imports into Britain. Once again, Britain was spending on imports more than she earned by exports.

In 1967 the government had to take very firm action. The National Plan had to be abandoned and the I.M.F. was asked for a larger loan to help balance the trading books. The government had to announce a massive credit squeeze, cutting the amount of money spent on housing, schools, hospitals, and other public works.

The Common Market

Wilson had opposed the Macmillan application to join the Common Market, but by 1966 he had realized that Britain was now too weak to bring about its own cure. She needed the help she might find in a larger, stronger, prosperous Europe, so in 1966 he began the negotiations for British entry. De Gaulle pointed out, in 1967, that the massive credit squeeze proved that Britain was too weak a country to add anything of value to the Common Market. And in 1968, when the application went in, de Gaulle said 'No' once again.

Getting It Right

In 1967 the government announced the long-expected devaluation of the pound; it would now be worth only 2.40 American dollars. This cut the prices of British exports – but pushed up the cost of British imports.

Fig. 45.2 This cartoon is entitled: 'Down, dammit, down'. George Brown seemed more intent on holding down incomes, but failed. Prices continued to rise throughout 1964–5.

In 1968 the government had to take further action, and the new Chancellor, Roy Jenkins, announced the most severe of all the postwar credit squeezes. Then, in November, he had to announce a sharp increase in the rates of taxation. This was the price that had to be paid for a massive loan from the I.M.F.

The country suffered from this squeeze through 1969. By 1970 there were signs that things were coming right. Exports had risen and Britain was earning about £800 million a year more than she was spending on imports. This was a great turn-around from the situation inherited in 1964.

On the other hand prices were still rising – and very sharply. In 1970 prices rose by about 18 per cent – much more than had been the case in 1964. With the knowledge that the government would call an election some time in 1970 the Chancellor announced the end of the wages freeze. Unions were now free to get what they could from their employers – some demanded wage increases of 15 per cent while others got 20 per cent and a few even got 25 per cent more in wages. This helped buy more of the expensive goods. It also increased the pressure on the pound – and unlike 1966 it did not win the government much popularity.

The Unpopularity of Getting It Right

The government won few friends by its policies. Many of its supporters were angry at the cuts in spending; others were cross because of the wages freeze which had held down their incomes while the cost of gas, electricity, and other necessities went up.

Some workers showed their anger by going on strike to try to get better wages than their leaders negotiated for them. These 'unofficial' strikes brought many industries to a halt. In 1969 the Minister of Employment, Barbara Castle, produced a White Paper, *In Place of Strife*. This was supposed to be a document for discussion with employers and unions before the government brought in a Bill to deal with trade unions. The Paper proposed that unions would not be allowed to come out on strike until ninety days after first warning employers that they meant to do so. In this 'cooling off' period the government hoped that the dispute could be settled. The Paper also proposed that anyone who refused to obey this regulation would be fined or sent to prison. It is not surprising that this White Paper annoyed the union movement – which traditionally supported the Labour Party. The T.U.C. threatened that if the government went ahead with its proposed Bill, it would not provide the Labour Party with the money which it would need to fight a general election in

1970. The government then withdrew the proposals – and lost the respect of millions of people who wanted some action taken to curb the powers of the unions.

Immigration and Race Relations

The Labour Party had opposed the Conservatives' Immigration Act (p. 257), but once it was in power it found that here, as in the economy, reality had to be faced. In 1965 the government brought in the Race Relations Bill (which was reinforced by another Act in 1968). These Acts made it illegal for anyone to discriminate against a person in housing, employment, or in any public place such as a public house, a club, or a shop (Extract 45.1).

But in 1967–8 the government found itself faced with a major problem over the question of the Asian families expelled from Kenya. All these people had British passports, so in theory they were entitled to live in Britain. The government felt that the country could not absorb the millions involved, so in 1968 Parliament passed the Commonwealth Immigrants Act which said that no Asian could settle here unless he already had some family connection in the country. However, there was an outcry against the Act, and the government was forced to climb down and offer entry permits to any Asian who could prove that he had been expelled from Kenya. This change in policy angered the Conservative M.P., Enoch Powell, who began to make controversial speeches about the future effects of this continued immigration.

Ulster, 1968–70

In its 1968 Race Relations Act the Labour government tried to protect the interests of the coloured minority in the country. In Ulster the Catholics had formed a minority ever since Northern Ireland was set up as a separate province in 1921. The Protestant majority discriminated against Catholics – who had the poorest housing, less chances of getting a job, fewer M.P.s than their numbers justified, and little representation on the local councils – even of towns that had Catholic majorities.

The Protestant government had set up an armed police – the B-Specials – whose main job was to stop Catholic terrorists from coming across the border from Southern Ireland. But the B-Specials used their powers to terrorize the Catholic minority in Ulster. Houses were raided, people arrested and imprisoned without trial, Catholic business attacked – all in the name of 'hunting the terrorist'.

In 1968 the Civil Rights Movement was founded to demand equal treatment for the Catholic minority.

There were clashes with the B-Specials and with Protestant gangs, and in 1969 this flared up into civil war. The government sent in the British Army to protect the Catholic areas, and by 1970 there were 11,000 soldiers guarding the trouble spots. However, the Home Secretary, James Callaghan, seemed to have little idea of how to bring the troubles to an end.

Regional Aid

One of the problems facing Ulster was that of very high unemployment. This problem was shared by people living in other regions of Great Britain. Since 1945 there has been a continued decline in employment opportunities in the country's older industries – coal, shipbuilding, textiles, iron and steel. This has led to heavy unemployment in parts of Scotland, the North-East, the North-West and South Wales. Many younger people have left these decaying areas to find work in the more affluent south.

The Wilson government announced plans to deal with these older areas. They were described as Development Areas. Firms were offered grants, cheap loans, tax concessions, and other aids to try to persuade them to build their new factories in these less favoured areas. This policy had some success, but in spite of the new factories in these Development Areas life there remained less glamorous than it was in London or the Midlands.

Regional Politics

Many people in these outlying regions began to feel that the British government and the traditional parties were not interested in their future. In Scotland the Nationalist movement grew rapidly; in Wales the Nationalist Party, Plaid Cymru, saw its leader, Gwynfor Evans, win a Parliamentary seat at the by-election in Carmarthen, and in 1967 Winnie Ewing of the Scottish Nationalist Party (S.N.P.) won a by-election at Hamilton.

The success of these fringe parties frightened the leaders of the two major parties. Heath, on behalf of the Conservatives, promised the Scottish people that they would have their own Assembly, or Parliament, if the Conservatives won the election.

Labour and the Election, 1970

In June 1970 Prime Minister Wilson called a general election. All the opinion polls agreed that Labour would win this election and so give it a third victory in a row. The balance of payments had been put right; Britain was paying its way in the world. Under Wilson the Labour government had shown itself to be successful and very able. People were impressed with the new Chancellor, Roy Jenkins; the Defence Minister, Denis Healey; the Minister for Education, Anthony Crosland, and many other ministers who had gained the experience which only office can bring.

The government also won some benefit from the discovery in 1965 of large gasfields in the North Sea. By 1970 large quantities of natural gas were arriving through two terminals at Bacton and Easington. Gas Boards were busy converting people's gas appliances from coal-produced 'town gas' to natural gas. Gas prices were held down and some people thought that the new discoveries might lead to a new Industrial Revolution.

But the polls were wrong. The government was unpopular with many of its traditional supporters because of the wages freeze and the proposals on trade union reform. It was unpopular with other people because of its immigration policy and the way it had backed down in the proposed law on trade unions.

In the 1930s and 1940s the Labour Party had normally won the support of students and other young people. They thought that the Labour Party would bring about those changes in society which they hoped for, but by 1968 it had become clear that they had lost their faith in the Labour Party. Many of them voted for the Liberals who seemed to be a more radical party than Labour; some supported the extremist policies of the variety of Maoist, Trotskyist, and other ultra-left parties; others took part in demonstrations in support of the Vietnamese communists and against the American government; some joined the Anti-Apartheid Movement. Led by Peter Hain, a Young Liberal, they threatened to attack cricket grounds if the South African cricketers were allowed to tour Britain in 1970. The government persuaded the M.C.C. to cancel the tour. This seemed to show the young people that it was possible to achieve more by direct action than by working through the traditional political system.

But above all, the government was blamed for the continuing rise in inflation – prices were rising by about 18 per cent in 1970. If this were to be brought down there would have to be further doses of credit squeeze and controls, the policies which the Conservatives had used in the 1950s and which Labour itself had used under Wilson. But, many people thought, if the country needed Conservative policies these would be best operated by a Conservative government.

Fig. 45.3 Peter Walker (left) and Geoffrey Rippon, who negotiated Britain's entry into the Common Market, at the 1973 Conservative Party Conference.

The Conservatives and the Election, 1970

After the loss of the 1966 election Edward Heath had set up a number of committees to find out why the party had lost and what policies it ought to follow when it won power again. Heath asked younger people to take charge of these committees, people like Peter Walker (Fig. 45.3).

In 1969–70 the party leaders held a series of conferences at the Selsdon Park Hotel near Croydon to consider the findings of their committees. These were later published in simpler form in leaflets and pamphlets on the Welfare State, taxation, education, nationalized industries, trade unions and so on, and were used by party leaders and candidates to outline party policy to the voters.

The theme that ran through these documents was that Britain was a highly taxed nation which did not allow managers, workers, and others to keep enough of the money they earned. The Conservatives would cut taxation. They would also cut government spending on the Welfare State; people would have to pay more for medicine and dental treatment, parents would have to pay more for their children's school meals. The government would not spend money to help industries that could not pay their own way. Just as the individual had to stand on his own feet (and not get free milk or meals) so industry would have to stand on its own feet. This was a new look for the party of Baldwin and Macmillan.

The Election

During the election campaign Mr Wilson tried to behave like the experienced statesman. He did not rush around the country making speeches – he tried to show that he was too busy governing Britain. Mr Heath made a series of speeches up and down the country inviting the voters to try a new way to get Britain back on its feet, and when challenged about the effect of his proposed policies on prices, he boasted that he would 'cut prices at a stroke'.

To the pollsters' dismay, the Conservatives won 330 seats, Labour 287, and the Liberals six. Britain was now set on a new path – or so it seemed.

Questions

Extract 45.1

Coloured Children, 1966

> Robert Blake, 18, has just spent a fortnight looking for a job. He qualified at a London grammar school for university entrance. The companies he approached wanted staff, but he is black, and almost none of them was interested. Two white friends tried for the same jobs. The employment agency that rejected Robert inside a minute gave them a 45-minute interview, called them 'excellent material' and started phoning employers.

The Campaign Against Racial Discrimination (C.A.R.D.) has 20 cases of coloured teenagers who failed to get jobs in Manchester. In each case a white youngster who went in afterwards was offered the job. The alarming thing is that Britain's black Roberts are collecting their snubs when conditions couldn't be more favourable. There are fewer school-leavers than since 1960; employers are desperate for labour. The years ahead are less promising; the second post-war birthrate bulge starts to leave school in 1971; unemployment has started to rise. What happens then to coloured youngsters – most born and educated in Britain – could set the pattern for a generation.

(Colin McGlashan, 'Unwritten Colour Policy' in the *Observer*, 25 September 1966.)

1. How was 'Robert' discriminated against? Why would it be difficult to prove discrimination?
2. Why is the problem for black teenagers greater in the 1980s than it was in the 1960s?
3. Why might second-generation black Britishers have different attitudes to those of the original immigrants?
4. How did the Labour government deal with (i) immigration (ii) Kenyan Asians (iii) racial discrimination?

Fig. 45.1

1. Imagine that someone had saved £100 in 1970. How much would it have been worth in (i) 1973 (ii) 1975 (iii) 1978?
2. In 1970 a pound note would have bought 100p worth of goods. How much would the 1970 pound have bought in (i) 1975 (ii) 1978?
3. How does this graph explain (i) the rise in house prices since 1970 (ii) the demand for wage increases in the 1970s?

Worksheet

(A)

1. Give TWO reasons why many foreigners took their money out of Britain in 1964–5.

2. Explain why and when the Labour government had to ask the I.M.F. for help. What policies did the I.M.F. insist on?

3. Explain why and how the standard of living rose even in a time of high inflation.

4. Why did the government bring in credit squeezes in 1967 and 1968? How did these squeezes work?

5. Give FOUR reasons why the Labour government was unpopular in 1970. Write a brief note on each of the reasons you offer as part of your answer.

(B)

1. Write the letters that might have been written by:
(a) a foreigner explaining why he was taking his money out of Britain 1964–5;
(b) an M.P. explaining the National Plan;
(c) a Labour supporter complaining of government policy, 1967–8;
(d) an unemployed worker welcoming the arrival of a new factory in a Depressed Area;
(e) a Conservative supporter explaining the difference between Heath's policies and those of Macmillan;
(f) a soldier on duty in Ulster 1969–70.

(C)

1. Write the headlines that might have appeared above reports on:
(a) the 'flight from the pound' 1964–5;
(b) the announcement of the National Plan;
(c) the signing of the Declaration of Intent;
(d) the formation of British Leyland;
(e) de Gaulle's 'No', 1963;
(f) the devaluation of 1967;
(g) the withdrawal of *In Place of Strife*, 1969;
(h) the passing of the Race Relations Act;
(i) the arrival of the first Kenyan Asians;
(j) the outbreak of violence in Ulster;
(k) the electoral victory of either Gwynfor Evans or Winnie Ewing;
(l) the discovery of North Sea gas;
(m) the result of the 1970 election.

(D)

1. Draw or paint the posters that might have been used as part of ONE of the following:
(a) the 1966 election;
(b) the 1970 election;
(c) Plaid Cymru;
(d) the S.N.P.

46 The 1970s, 1970-79

Heath's New Men

In June 1970 Edward Heath formed a Conservative government (Fig. 46.1). He gave important posts to many of his bright young men. Peter Walker, for example, became Minister for the Environment. This was one of the 'Super-Ministries'. It took in the former Ministries of Transport, Local Government, Housing, and several others.

He gave important positions to several successful businessmen. One was John Davies. He had been the Chairman of Shell, the oil giant, and Secretary of the Confederation of British Industry – a sort of trade union of industrialists. He won the largest applause from the Party Conference held just after the election when he said that the government would not help loss-making industries. He described such firms as 'lame ducks', saying that industries as well as the declining industrial areas had to learn to stand on their own feet – or fall.

New Policies

Within a few months of taking office Heath's ministers had set about changing things. Margaret Thatcher, Minister for Education, announced that children over 7 years of age would no longer get free school milk; Sir Keith Joseph, in charge of the Health Service, increased the charges paid by patients for medicine and other treatment; John Davies abolished the aid to the Development Areas.

These cuts in government spending allowed the Chancellor, Anthony Barber, to announce cuts in taxation. Heath's argument had been that British managers and workers were over-taxed. Cuts in taxation allowed people to keep more of their earnings. Heath believed that this would persuade people to work that much harder.

Heath also believed that many taxpayers would spend their increased income on goods in the shops. This would provide more work for British factories, and this ought, in turn, to persuade industrialists to invest in more and better machinery. Britain would then be better able to compete with the successful nations such as Germany and Japan.

Fig. 46.1 A victory smile from Edward Heath, the new Prime Minister, on arriving at 10 Downing Street.

Disappointment

However, the history of 1970–2 proved that Heath was wrong. He went on several tours to tell industrialists and managers what he hoped would happen; he showed them that his government was providing them with the opportunity to get Britain moving again. But he found that managers and workers did not feel inspired by an extra few pence in their pay packets each week. Indeed, surveys done at the time showed that even the best-paid industrialists wanted to work less hard and to have more leisure.

The First Turn-around

Rolls-Royce was, and is, one of Britain's most famous firms, producing most of the world's aero engines. In 1971 it had a very large contract to produce a new engine for Lockheed – an American firm. However, it found that it could not produce the engine on time, and Lockheed threatened to make the company pay huge penalties for non-delivery. Rolls-Royce also showed that it could not produce the engine at the agreed price.

So, having failed to carry out its contract, Rolls-Royce announced that it was going to go out of business. It could not meet its debts to Lockheed, and it would not have the money to pay the many firms which had supplied it with materials and components.

At this point economic reality forced the government to step in. It could not allow thousands of men to be thrown out of work. So John Davies – who had once spoken scornfully of 'lame ducks' – stepped in. Rolls-Royce was nationalized; the government agreed to pay the money owing to the many smaller firms and to meet the cost of producing the engine for Lockheed who agreed to wait a little longer.

The Most Humiliating Turn-around

Ever since 1950 the Upper Clyde Shipbuilders had been receiving government help to keep their four shipyards open in the Glasgow area where unemployment was already at a high level. However, John Davies decided to cut the amount of money going to this firm, so it then announced that it could not stay in business. Four shipyards were to be closed and about 20,000 men told that they were to be unemployed.

The management of the company accepted the government's decision. But the men, led by their shop stewards, refused to do so. They occupied the yards, continued to build the ships that were there, and started a campaign to tell the public about their position. In June 1971 some of their leaders went to Downing Street to see the Prime Minister.

The government then changed its policies. In 1971 it had been unwilling to give £6 million to keep the yards open, but in 1972 it gave £40 million to help modernize them. Later the yards were taken over by an American firm and they are still in business today.

Unemployment and Political Popularity

During the election campaign Heath had promised to 'cut prices at a stroke'. But during 1970, 1971, and 1972 prices continued to rise. The Brazilian coffee crop was ruined by frost in 1971–2 and that put up the price of coffee by 400 per cent. The world's sugar crops suffered at about the same time – and sugar became four times as expensive as it had been. Indeed, for a time there was little if any sugar in British shops. The American government agreed to sell a large part of their wheat and maize crop to Russia, which meant that the world price of wheat, maize, and other food shot up.

The government was blamed for this failure to halt inflation. Maybe that was unfair. But the government was fairly blamed for some of the results of its policies. When governments spend less – on housing, hospitals, and schools – some firms have less work. Therefore, there was a rise in the number of men out of work in 1971–2. Although the government had changed its mind over Rolls-Royce it had cut help to many industries and several areas. The result was an increase in the number of firms that were unable to stay in business – and more men were out of work.

By the middle of 1971 opinion polls showed that the government was very unpopular. In a by-election at Bromsgrove, Labour won what had always been a safe Tory seat. In October 1971 the Tories held the seat at Macclesfield – but only with a majority of 1,100 compared with the majority of 11,000 with which they had won the seat in June 1970.

Major Policy Changes

Heath's government then changed most of its policies. Development Areas were told that they could get help; declining industries were given money to help them stay in business; and the government announced that it would spend about £4,000 million more than it had meant to – on housing, schools, roads, and so on.

In 1970 Heath had spoken only of 'Reward for effort'. By June 1972 he was talking of 'Fair shares for all'. This annoyed most of those who had really believed in the Selsdon Park policies. As one of them said, 'The government has stood on its head so often that there are now no heads left to stand on'.

But the increase in government spending acted as a major spur to inflation. More money went into more pay packets – but there were no more goods in the shops. This meant that prices were pushed even higher, and this forced the government to make yet another U-turn about its attitudes to wage policies.

Heath and the Trade Unions

During the election campaign in 1970 the Tories had insisted that if elected they would bring in laws to limit the powers of trade unions. In 1971 they brought in the Industrial Relations Bill. Trade Unions were supposed to register with the Registrar of Friendly Societies. His office would have the power to examine the rules of the union and the ways in which it spent its money. Most unions refused to register – and so lost their right to certain tax concessions.

The Act set up a National Industrial Relations

Court. This had the power to forbid a union to call a strike without a 'cooling off' period. It could also insist that unions held secret ballots of their members before calling a strike. Unions refused to appear before the Court, and six leaders of striking London dockers were put into prison for refusing to obey a Court ruling. But the government ordered their release – fearing a massive, and perhaps general, strike.

Wages Policies

During the election campaign the Tories had insisted that they would never have a wages freeze or any government-fixed limits on wage increases. Everything was to be left to employers and unions to sort out for themselves.

In 1970–1 unions took advantage of this freedom to win massive wage increases. This added to the inflationary spiral, and the government was forced to make yet another U-turn.

Heath had hoped that people would spend their extra money on British products, but British firms did not produce enough goods. So people bought Japanese TV's and record-players, German and Japanese cars, Danish furniture, and so on. This pushed up the level of imports, and once again Britain was spending more on imports than she was earning from her exports.

So in 1972 Heath announced the setting up of a Prices and Incomes Board. This would consider every claim for wage rises. It would also have the power to decide what the level of increase was to be.

In January 1972 the miners put in for a large wage increase, and the government ordered the National Coal Board to refuse it. The miners then went on strike, and within a few days the government realized that there would not be enough coal to drive the electricity generating stations. Therefore, the government climbed down and the miners were given their pay award – and the Conservatives were made to look very weak.

Oil prices, 1973

By the end of 1972 the British had begun to realize that they had at least one piece of luck. Oil had been found in large quantities in the North Sea. This would, one day, give Britain her own oil. It would cut the level of imports by about £4,000 million a year. It would also provide Britain with the chance of building many new industries based on its own oil supplies (Extract 46.1).

But that oil would not come 'on stream' for some time yet. In 1972–3 Britain still bought its oil from the Oil Producing and Exporting Countries (OPEC), most of which are in the Middle East.

In 1973 the OPEC governments announced massive increases in the price of their oil. Petrol prices shot up from about 35p a gallon to about 70p a gallon; this shocked the motorist. The industrialist gave the British a further shock. He had to pay more for the oil used in his business – to drive his machinery, fuel his lorries, or provide the raw materials for his plastic and other oil-based products. So he had to put up his prices, and inflation went on another spiralling upturn. The British balance of payments went further into trouble as the prices of oil imports rose.

Domestic Reforms

The government carried out some very important reforms at home. Peter Walker was responsible for the reorganization of local government. This abolished most of the old county names – Yorkshire, for example, ceased to exist. It also set up a number of new councils at parish, urban, county, and metropolitan level. All this cost a great deal of money as people were appointed to new jobs in the new councils. Few people believed that this Act provided the country with better local government. Nearly everyone agreed that it was a more expensive – and inflationary – system.

Sir Keith Joseph was responsible for a reorganization of the National Health Service. He altered the way in which the Service was administered by bringing in even more people to run it. There was no increase in the number of doctors, nurses, or hospitals, but there was a huge increase in the number of clerks and other administrators. This cost a great deal of money – and led to a good deal of unhappiness in the Service itself.

William Whitelaw, the Home Secretary, had to deal with the problem of Ulster. In 1972 he announced that the Ulster Parliament was to be abolished, and in future the Province would be governed from Britain itself – as was Wales and Scotland. He also tried to get the Catholics and Protestants to agree on a form of government-by-committee in which both sides would have representatives. The Catholics liked this, but the Protestants did not and the civil war went on with more people being killed, more soldiers being sent to maintain law and order – and the government becoming increasingly unpopular as it failed to solve the Ulster problem.

The Three-Day week

In January 1974 the miners called for another pay increase. Once again the government told the

National Coal Board to refuse it while the Prices and Incomes Board examined the claim – and once again the miners came out on strike.

This time the government seemed determined to stand firm. Mines produced no coal; generating stations produced less electricity; and shops, offices, factories and other businesses were ordered to use less power. The street lights were turned off, and floodlighting forbidden at football games and greyhound tracks. The country's industry went on to a three-day week.

The strike went on with neither side willing to climb down. The government was unable to force the men back, and unwilling to use the powers of its own Industrial Relations Act to send the leaders to gaol.

Election, February 1974

Edward Heath declared that the country was 'ungovernable' and that the problem of inflation was 'insoluble'. He called for a general election – although he had a large majority in the Commons. It was not clear what he would do if he won an even larger majority.

Harold Wilson led the Opposition into the election campaign. He promised that a Labour government would get Britain back to work, and said that there would be no wages boards to come between unions and employers during their negotiating.

Labour won 301 seats, the Conservatives 297, and the Liberals fourteen. Wilson had not done as well as he had hoped, but Heath had fared very badly. For a few days he refused to resign, and tried to persuade Jeremy Thorpe, the Liberal Party leader, to enter into an agreement by which the Liberals would have voted for the Conservatives and so given Heath a chance to continue as Prime Minister. But the negotiations broke down, Heath resigned, and Wilson became Prime Minister.

A Wages Free-For-All

The government inherited a number of major problems. There was the continuing problem of Ulster, and Rhodesia was still in rebellion. But the two main problems involved the failure of British exports to pay for imports and the continuing rise in the level of inflation now running at about 20 per cent a year.

The Wilson government allowed unions and employers to negotiate wages, and unions took advantage of this to win increases of up to 30 per cent. This led to even further price increases and higher inflation. Few people realized that prices would double every three years or so if inflation went on rising. They seemed to enjoy the rise in living standards that was the result of there being two or more wage earners in many households.

Election, October 1974

The government gave the miners the wage increases they were seeking. Coal was sent to the generating stations and within a few weeks the country was back to normal; the government claimed the credit for this. In October Wilson called an election. Labour won 319 seats, the Conservatives 277, and the Liberals thirteen. A number of seats were won by the S.N.P. in Scotland and by Plaid Cymru in Wales.

One result of this election was that the Conservatives chose a new leader, Margaret Thatcher, in place of the discredited Heath. She was the first woman to lead a major political party in Western Europe.

The Government and Industry

Wilson claimed that the Conservative policy of encouraging private enterprise had failed, so he set up the National Enterprise Board (the N.E.B.). This government Board had money to spend on helping British industry, and it was the N.E.B. that saved British Leyland from bankruptcy – at a cost of about £2,800 million. It also saved Chrysler from going out of business – at a cost of about £200 million. It saved Ferranti, the electronics firm, and provided the money needed to start off the British micro-processor industry.

The government also gave taxpayers' money to workers in firms whose private owners declared that the businesses had failed and ought to be closed down. Workers were encouraged to set up workers' co-operatives; they would choose their own board of directors and run the business themselves. But by 1979 all these ventures had failed – and the taxpayer had lost a good deal of money.

The government gave the steel industry about £400 million each year to help it keep open loss-making works and so provide employment.

Economic Reality, 1976–7

During 1975 and part of 1976 foreigners watched while the Wilson government spent thousands of millions of pounds trying to get things right in industry. They saw the rate of inflation creep up to about 28 per cent with every sign that it would continue to rise.

It is not surprising that those who had money in Britain decided to withdraw it. There was an even bigger 'flight from the pound' than there had been in 1964 – and this time the government did not try to maintain the value of the pound. This fell from about 2.20 American dollars to about 1.60. Many people feared that it would continue to fall – maybe to the point where the dollar was worth the same as the pound.

This fall in the value of the pound helped the exporters, because they could sell their goods at low prices. But it pushed up the prices paid by importers – and so increased prices in British shops. This led unions to ask for even higher wage increases.

In 1976 the government had to ask the I.M.F. for £3,000 million to help balance Britain's trading books. The I.M.F. agreed but insisted that the government make a start on putting Britain into better shape. The Chancellor, Denis Healey, was forced to announce cuts in government spending. In 1976 he cut spending by £1,000 million – so there was less house building, less money for schools, hospitals, and so on. In 1977 he had to cut back spending by £2,500 million in another effort to bring down the level of inflation and help restore the balance of payments to a healthy position.

Unemployment

If the government spends less then some firms have to sack some of their workers, and so in 1978 the level of unemployment rose to 1,500,000. In 1963 Macmillan had become unpopular because unemployment rose to about 600,000; in 1972 Heath had been frightened by reports that unemployment might rise to about 800,000. But in 1978–9 the British learned to accept a much higher level of unemployment, and school-leavers in particular found it increasingly difficult to get jobs.

Wages Policies

In 1976 the government announced that its main battle would be against inflation, even if this meant that unemployment had to rise. It invited the co-operation of trade unions in this battle.

The government and unions agreed in 1976 that no one would be allowed a wage increase of more than £6 per week. For the low-paid earning about £30 a week this meant an increase of about 20 per cent, but for the skilled men earning about £60 a week it amounted to an increase of only 10 per cent. This was much less than the rate of inflation, and meant that some people were able to buy less than they had bought the year before. Their standard of living fell.

In 1977 the Callaghan government and unions agreed that wage increases should be limited to 4 per cent, but in the next year the unions refused to accept the government's decision that wage increases should be kept to below 10 per cent for 1978. The result was that workers in government-controlled industries and in the Civil Service, Health Service and local government got about 10 per cent increases. But some workers in private industry were able to force employers to pay more than this. This meant that the average wage increases for 1978 were about 14 per cent – this was higher than the government had hoped for. But it was much lower than the unreal increases of 30 per cent that were won in 1975 and 1976.

Inflation

The cuts in government spending and the lower wage awards helped to bring down the rate of inflation. By the beginning of 1978 it was down to 15 per cent and by the start of 1979 it was down to 8 per cent. Even at that lower rate, prices would double every ten years or so – but this was much better than had seemed possible in 1973 or 1976.

The government then asked that for 1979 wage increases should be kept to 5 per cent so that inflation could be brought down to below 8 per cent. The unions refused to accept this, so the Prime Minister appealed to both the T.U.C. and the Labour Party Conference – but was rejected by both (Fig. 46.2).

The Winter of 1979

The government insisted that it would only offer 5 per cent increases to those workers whose pay it could control. Private employers paid more than this; Ford paid 15 per cent, lorry drivers won 20 per cent, and drivers of the petrol tankers got even more.

This angered the workers in the public services when they were asked to accept only 5 per cent. So between January and March 1979 the country suffered a series of strikes by ambulance drivers, hospital workers, teachers, local government workers and others whose pay was controlled by the government.

Because of this, the Callaghan government was forced to give bigger awards than it wanted. In general, people were given about 9 per cent with the promise that their claims would be examined by a Comparability Board. This could suggest even higher wage awards, and the government promised to pay such increases.

One result of these higher wages was that inflation began to creep up again. By May 1979 it was above 10 per cent with every sign that it would go higher.

Fig. 46.2 James Callaghan failed to get the TUC to accept a wages policy in September 1978.

The Election, 1979

In March 1979 the people of Wales and Scotland voted in a referendum on the question of whether their two countries should have separate Parliaments. The Welsh voted 'No' overwhelmingly. Some 32.9 per cent of the Scots voted 'yes', but this did not come up to the 40 per cent that the government had laid down as the figure needed to show that the Scots really wanted their own Parliament.

The government then refused the demands of S.N.P. to bring in the Act for a Scottish Parliament, so the S.N.P. M.P.s joined with the Tories and the Liberals to bring down the government in a vote of confidence on 28 March.

Mr Callaghan resigned and called an election. During the campaign he claimed that only wage restrictions and other Labour policies would bring inflation down and help raise the country's trading position.

Mrs Thatcher led the Tory campaign. She repeated the arguments used by Heath in 1970. She wanted cuts in taxation, cuts in government spending, and called for the 'government to get off our backs'. She promised to curb the powers of the unions – without promising to bring back the ill-fated Industrial Relations Act.

Once again, as in 1970, the Labour Party suffered because its traditional supporters decided that 'enough is enough'. The Labour government seemed to have little idea of what was to be done – except that wages should be kept down. Mrs Thatcher, on the other hand, seemed to have a new 'gospel' of freedom.

In May 1979 the Tories won 339 seats, Labour 268, and the Liberals eleven. Mrs Thatcher became the first woman Prime Minister in Western Europe (Fig. 46.3).

Questions

Extract 46.1

Aberdeen and oil

In Aberdeen and District there are now over 200 companies directly involved in the offshore oil industry and well over 300 supplying it.

It is difficult to measure the number of jobs that have been created as a spin off from the growing oil industry. It is certainly considerable. Aberdeen Airport has passenger traffic increasing at an annual rate of over 35 per cent.

The oil companies have moved into a variety of premises and there are many new offices, warehouses and factories. The cost runs into many millions of pounds. In addition new hotels are being built. At Peterhead major developments are in hand for the Harbour of Refuge, a square mile of deep water enclosed by two massive granite breakwaters. A particularly significant development is the decision by two major manufacturers of oilfield equipment to set up factories near Aberdeen. B.P. have ordered four production platforms. The biggest, being built at Nigg Bay, will be the largest ever, costing £40m. and weighing 57,000 tons. It will be pile-driven into the sea bed in 400 feet of water. The full height when complete is about 700 feet. North East Scotland's indigenous industries are expanding with considerable investment in food and

Fig. 46.3 Britain's first woman Prime Minister greeting Helmut Schmidt, the Chancellor of West Germany.

fish processing plant, cold storage and distilleries. Several oil industry training centres are proposed. Aberdeen University has established a Master of Science course in Petroleum Technology.

An active Petroleum Wives' Club has also been formed.

(North East Scotland Development Authority, 1973.)

[1 ton = 1016.05 kilogrammes 1 foot = 0.3 metres]

1. What were the immediate benefits to Aberdeen of the discovery of North Sea oil?
2. What will be the longer term benefits to the city?
3. Why has there been a change in the courses at the University of Aberdeen?
4. Why will North Sea oil lead to (i) a fall in the imports bill (ii) a rise in British exports?
5. Why will the taxation from the oil companies help the government to plan the reconstruction of British industry? Why do some people fear that we might waste the money away? (See in the chapter examples of aid to declining industries.)

Worksheet

(A)
1. Write a brief summary of the main policies of the Heath government, 1970–1, using the following words as guide-lines: (i) cuts in spending – education, trade, Development Areas (ii) cuts in taxation (iii) trade unions (iv) local government (v) the National Health Service.

2. Why was there an increase in the level of unemployment in 1971–2?

3. Show how the Heath government changed some of its policies after 1972. Explain why it did so.

4. Why did the Heath government set up a Prices and Incomes Board? What was its job? Why did it fail?

5. Give an account of the causes of and effects of the miners' strike, 1974.

6. Why was there a rise in the rate of inflation, 1972–6? How much of this inflation was due to (i) prices of imports, and (ii) wages?

7. How did the Wilson government help industrial development, 1974–6?

8. Why did the pound lose in value after 1972? How did this affect (i) the British tourists when they went abroad (ii) foreign tourists visiting Britain (iii) import prices (iv) the cost of living in Britain?

9. Why did the government have to make cuts in government spending in 1976 and 1977? Why has the Thatcher government made cuts in spending in 1979–80? What is the effect of such cuts on employment?

10. How did the government get the rate of inflation down in 1977–9? Why did it rise again?

(B)
1. Write the letters that might have been sent by:
(a) a worker at Rolls-Royce when he heard about (i) the threat of bankruptcy (ii) the government take-over;
(b) a worker at Clyde Shipbuilders when he heard about (i) the notice of closure (ii) the march to Downing Street, and (iii) the additional help from the Heath government;
(c) a housewife complaining of the rises in prices in the shops in 1973, 1976, 1979;
(d) one of the people who watched Mrs Thatcher go into Number 10 Downing Street for the first time.

2. Arrange a debate on the subject 'The government spends too much of our money'. One side should represent those who want more spending (and taxation) while the other side should represent those who want less government spending and lower taxes.

(C)
1. Write the headlines that might have appeared above reports on:
(a) the bankruptcy of Rolls-Royce;
(b) the government help to the Clyde Shipbuilders;
(c) the rise in coffee prices, 1973;
(d) the establishment of the Prices and Incomes Board;
(e) the rise in oil prices, 1973–4;
(f) the reorganization of local government;
(g) the abolition of the Ulster Parliament;
(h) the announcement of the three-day week, 1974;
(i) the results of the elections in (i) February, and (ii) October 1974;
(j) the cuts in spending, 1976 and 1977;
(k) the strikes of January–March 1979;
(l) the results of the election, 1979.

2. Draw or paint the posters that might have been used:
(a) by Labour during the 1974 elections;
(b) by the Conservatives during the 1979 election;
(c) to show the fall in the value of the pound.

47 Epilogue: May 1979 - December 1980

A Declining Economy

The first eighteen months of Conservative government were dominated by a severe decline in the economy. The rate of inflation, which was about 8 per cent a year when the government came to office, began to rise again. Unemployment also continued to rise. Like its predecessors Mrs Thatcher's government suffered from the decision by OPEC to raise oil prices in both 1979 and 1980. These increases pushed up the costs of British industry, and led to higher prices and a further twist in the inflationary spiral. As people and firms spent more money on oil and petrol they had less money to spend on other things. This led to a fall in the demand for other goods and higher unemployment. Since every country suffered from the increase in oil prices in the same way, there was a world-wide drop in the demand for goods so that some British exporters were forced to dismiss a number of their workers.

The Government Attempts to Solve the Economic Problems

In his first Budget in June 1979 Sir Geoffrey Howe, the Chancellor of the Exchequer, made some reductions in income tax. He hoped that the taxpayers, with more money in their pockets, would spend some of it on British-made goods – and so help create more jobs in British factories. He also hoped that some of the tax rebates might be used to invest in new factories and more modern machinery. In fact most of this money was spent on buying foreign goods.

The reductions in income tax meant that the government was forced to borrow more money to cover its spending. This Public Sector Borrowing Requirement (PSBR) is the main cause of the constant rise in the rate of inflation. The Chancellor, therefore, made massive cuts in government spending. But attempts to cut the PSBR were handicapped by the knowledge that each cut would lead to rises in prices, for example, of electricity, gas or rail fares, or a rise in the level of unemployment, since there would be fewer teachers, nurses employed or houses built,

and so on. Indeed, by September 1980, there was evidence that despite 'savage' cuts the government was still borrowing more than the previous Labour government.

To try to force industry and individuals to borrow less the government raised interest rates to record levels. The Minimum Lending Rate (MLR) charged by the Bank of England in July 1980 was 16 per cent. High Street banks charged 20 per cent or more. The idea of this policy was to cut the amount of money in circulation, and so make it more difficult for inflation to rise. This in fact happened. Inflation reached a peak of 21 per cent in June 1980 before beginning to fall. In September 1980 it was around 16 per cent.

A more harmful effect of this policy, however, rapidly appeared. Industrialists found it very difficult to borrow money for new machinery and factories. This meant that British industry could not expand sufficiently to create new jobs and so reduce unemployment.

Another result of high interest rates was that foreign investors began to buy British currency. This forced up the value of the pound against the American dollar, the French franc, and so on. A strong pound made it very difficult for British goods to sell successfully abroad – they became too expensive to be able to compete with similar cheaper products. On the other hand the strong pound led to a flood of cheap imports.

The decision of the Conservative government to drop the previous government's attempts at wages policies led to a further decline in the economy. One result of allowing unions and employers to negotiate freely on wages was that wages and salaries rose in the first year (ending April 1980) by about 20 per cent. Since not all employers were able to pass on these wage increases to the consumer in the form of higher prices, many businesses were forced to close down.

Although inflation continued to fall, the number of unemployed had risen to over 2 million by the end of 1980. Because bank interest rates were so high, more and more businesses found it difficult to continue trading – so the number of unemployed increased. There was strong pressure on the government from many directions, including the traditionally Conservative Confederation of British Industry (CBI), to cut the MLR to 12 per cent. At the end of November 1980 the government decided to allow the Bank of England to cut the MLR by 2 per cent to 14 per cent. This pleased few people.

The government considered that it was still spending too much money and that more cuts were necessary. Pressure was put on local councils to spend less. Wage settlements of the winter of 1980 also reflected the results of recession. They were much lower than in the previous year.

In its attempts to solve Britain's problems the government did have one advantage – North Sea oil. By 1980 Britain had become a net exporter of oil. This had a significant impact on the Balance of Payments since money was earned from the sale of oil rather than being spent on importing it as had previously been the case. This helped disguise the fact that other exporters found it difficult to sell their goods.

The Trade Unions

Mrs Thatcher's government's policy towards the trade unions was to limit their powers. This came within the responsibility of the Minister of Employment, James Prior. By September 1980 he had failed to satisfy many people. Conservative hardliners wanted him to abolish the closed shop, while his moderate proposals (to limit the activities of pickets and to pay for secret ballots in trade union elections) aroused the anger of many trade union leaders.

The Labour Party

Although the policies of the government proved to be unpopular, the Opposition failed to reap the benefit, as proved when the Gallup polls showed that Labour did not become massively more popular. One reason for this was the conduct of the Labour Party, which seemed more intent on tearing itself apart than offering the British people sensible suggestions of how the nation's problems might be overcome. It conducted a very public debate on how the party leader should be chosen, who should write the Manifesto and whether Labour M.P.s should be forced to become mere delegates of a small number of Labour Party constituency members who would have the power to dismiss an M.P. A split appeared in the party between the extreme Left, led by Tony Wedgwood Benn, and the Right. When James Callaghan resigned in the autumn, the election of Michael Foot as the new leader of the Parliamentary Labour Party seemed potentially to strengthen the position of the Left.

Zimbabwe

Despite its preoccupation with economic affairs the government was able to claim a major success in the final settlement of the problem of Zimbabwe. The British government was persuaded by President Carter and by the leaders of independent countries in Africa not to recognize the Muzorewa government elected in April 1979. Lord Carrington, the British Foreign Secretary, organized a conference in London where representatives of the rebel armies, the Muzorewa government and white political parties came together to work out the settlement which finally led to the holding of new elections. In these the Patriotic Front won a large majority and Robert Mugabe became the Prime Minister of Zimbabwe.

Index